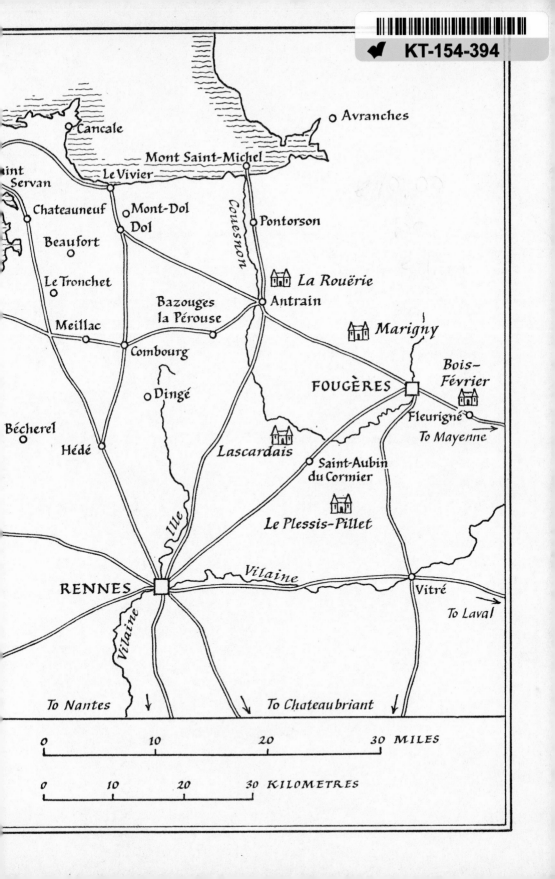

Avranches

Cancale

Mont Saint-Michel

Saint Servan

Le Vivier

Chateauneuf

Mont-Dol
Dol

Pontorson

Couesnon

Beaufort

La Rouërie

Le Tronchet

Antrain

Bazouges
la Pérouse

Marigny

Meillac

Combourg

Bois-
Février

FOUGÈRES

Dingé

Fleurigné

To Mayenne

Bécherel

Hédé

Lascardais

Saint-Aubin
du Cormier

Ille

Le Plessis-Pillet

Vilaine

RENNES

Vilaine

Vitré

To Laval

Vilaine

To Nantes

To Chateaubriant

0	10	20	30 MILES

0	10	20	30 KILOMETRES

CHATEAUBRIAND

Volume I   The Longed-for Tempests

CHATEAUBRIAND

A BIOGRAPHY

Volume One (1768-93)
The Longed-for Tempests

—⁘—

GEORGE D. PAINTER

"Levez-vous vite, orages désirés qui devez emporter
Réne dans les espaces d'une autre vie!"

1977
CHATTO & WINDUS
LONDON

Published by
Chatto & Windus Ltd
40 William IV Street
London WC2N 4DF

*

Clarke, Irwin & Co Ltd
Toronto

British Library Cataloguing in Publication Data
Painter, George Duncan
  Chateaubriand.
  Vol. 1: 1768–93.
  1. Chateaubriand, François René de, *Vicomte*
  2. Authors, French – Biography
  848'.6'09   PQ2205.Z5
  ISBN 0-7011-2184-X

Printed in Great Britain by
Ebenezer Baylis and Son Ltd
The Trinity Press, Worcester, and London

To my wife
JOAN
and to
SYLVIA TOWNSEND WARNER
and the late
MARTHE BIBESCO

Contents

List of Plates

PART ONE

The Flowers of Brittany

I

THIS PITILESS STORM

ON SUNDAY 4 September 1768 at Saint-Malo in Brittany, after seven unsuccessful attempts in eight years, the wife of René-Auguste de Chateaubriand, Comte de Combourg, produced a second son. By a convenient chance the Count's lease of their apartment at the Hôtel de la Plesse in the Rue de la Victoire had expired only four days before. There was time to hurry into their new lodging, M. Magon de Boisgarein's Hôtel de la Gicquelais in the nearby Rue des Juifs, but not to install Mme. de Chateaubriand in the parents' grand front bedroom on the second floor. The child was born instead in the next room to the rear, the future nursery of their four little daughters, oakbeamed and high, facing northeast over the grim ramparts and the infinite sea.

The summer had been stormy, and all over Brittany the ruined harvest rotted in the fields or sprouted in the granaries. A final gale rose on the eve of the Chateaubriands' removal, and raged for twenty-four days. The holy bones of St. Malo himself were led in procession round the ramparts on 18 September by the clergy and citizens headed by their bishop, Monseigneur des Laurents, a last resort which calmed the winds six days later. But the storm had reached its height on the 4th; the sandy isthmus of the Sillon was breached at high tide, and the granite peninsula of Saint-Malo became a temporary island. Rain and spray lashed the nursery window, the baby's wailing was drowned by thundering sea and bellowing wind. From the tempestuous birthroom, to the extreme left and northwest, could be seen the seaward promontory of an islet, the Grand-Bé, where now the visitor notices a low railing and squat black cross in silhouette. The child was born within sight of his grave, as he began the long roundabout journey that brings men home again.

François-René de Chateaubriand, son of the 'high and puissant' René-Auguste de Chateaubriand and his 'high and puissant' wife Apolline de Bédée, was baptised next day by M. Nouail, the bishop's grand-vicar. His godfather was his equally 'high and puissant' little elder brother, Jean-Baptiste, aged nine, his godmother was Mme de Chateaubriand's intimate friend Françoise de Contades, Comtesse de Plouër,[1] and the act of baptism was signed also by his aunt Marie Brignon de Chateaubriand, wife of the Count's brother Pierre. François-René, as he later believed, was 'nearly dead when I came to life'. His parents were ageing, his father not quite fifty, his mother forty-two; of their previous ten

children the first two and last two had died in early infancy, and another
had miscarried; the Count and his wife had each been alarmingly ill in
the spring. Perhaps his birth was difficult and he may, like the hero of
his story *René*, have been 'torn by an iron tool from my mother's womb';
even his baptism may have been hastened to save his soul from limbo.
François-René heard again and again in childhood the details of his
stormy birth. 'Their sadness has never been erased from my memory.
A day never passes without my seeing in thought the rock where I was
born, the room where my mother inflicted life upon me, the tempest
that was my first lullaby, the illfated brother who gave me a name which
I have almost always dragged through disaster. Heaven itself, it seemed,
had combined these various circumstances to lay in my cradle an
emblem of my destinies.' But on the 22nd the Count wrote staidly to
Pierre: 'Mme de Chateaubriand sends you a kiss from her bed . . . She
and the boy are both doing well', and on the 30th reported: 'Fine
weather returned six days ago.' The sun shone again on an innocent
and opalescent sea.

Brittany is a land of flowers, of golden gorse in spring and broom in
summer, of amethyst heather in autumn. The high hedge-banks are
early starred with violets and primroses, the ramparted pastures of
tethered cows are white with moondaisies, purple with vetch, red with
sorrel and campion. From every slope the sea is visible, or seems all but
visible; there is brine in the coastal air and inland rain. In the east the
highroad from Saint-Malo runs level through the marshlands of Dol
and the lost forest of Broceliande, past the castle of Combourg to
Rennes, Chateaubriant and Nantes. In the vast untravelled interior the
Black Mountains and Mountains of Arrée rise from a plateau of oak
and holly, where Merlin sleeps, gnarled little churches have bone-
heaped ossuaries and tumultuous calvaries, and the souls of the newly
dead wait at the wayside for the coach of Ankou, Death. In the west, at
the edge of the world, are sandy heaths where the stone-men raised
their granite avenues, their menhir-pillars and capstoned dolmen graves,
'bearded with lichen, scrawl'd and grey', between the low splintered
promontories of the ocean. Here the breeze from the southwest carries
a faint scent which seems to come from a magnolia or hibiscus beyond
the Atlantic, rather than from the nearby gorse-flowers. America
beckons to Armorica.

'On the land of granite walks the primitive race, itself as fine as flint,'
said Michelet. These men, said Renan, were 'the kind and virtuous
Cimmerians, who dwell on the shore of a sombre sea, bristling with
rocks, always lashed by storms', in a country where 'the clouds seem
colourless, and even joy is a little sad'. 'From a distance the landscape
looks like a forest and reminds one of England,' wrote Chateaubriand.
The Bretons are Britons, who fled from Cornwall and Wales before the

invading English and Saxons in the fifth and sixth centuries, bringing and leaving behind them their saints and language, their place-names in Tre, Lan and Pen, even the name of Brittany or Britain. These are Celts, the distant cousins of modern Englishmen, our own first blood, not reinforced as we are by the solid, boring and indispensable Anglosaxon, though later mixed a little, like ourselves, with the ambitious and feudal Norman. Their soul appears, even to themselves, to be made of contradictions: they are melancholy and gay, timid and brave, solitary and gregarious, humble and proud, careless and cunning, loyal and rebellious, visonary and practical, poets who love their home and seek exile to find themselves. They follow ideas rather than men, and if they sometimes seem faithless to a leader, it is because the leader has first betrayed their cause. They are small, thickset, dark-haired men, with broad shoulders, large crouched heads, and formidable blue-black eyes. Chateaubriand was a Breton.

The noblemen of Brittany grew ever more numerous and more impoverished. By the custom of the country the eldest son took two-thirds of the father's heritage, together with the family seat and its appurtenances; the remaining third was divided equally among the other children, and the process continued with each new generation. Soon the younger sons of younger sons shared the rich legacy of 'a pigeon, a rabbit, a fowling-piece and a hunting-dog', though each was still 'the chevalier, high and puissant lord of a dovecote, a toad-swamp and a warren'. They increased and dispersed; some remade their fortunes by marriage or war, some died celibate in the clergy, some descended to the plough, and vanished among the peasantry.

The first Chateaubriand, twenty-three generations before François-René, was the baron Brien, descendant of a nameless dynasty of thierns or local chieftains in Brittany. He rode beside William of Normandy at Hastings in 1066, and built in the strategic gap that leads from Brittany into Anjou, on the bank of the river Chère halfway between Rennes and Nantes, the square-towered keep of Chateaubriant, Brien's castle, which gave its name to the family and exists to this day. So began the line of the Barons of Chateaubriand, whose eldest sons were frequently named Geoffroy. Geoffroy I fought in the First Crusade, Geoffroy III at Bouvines in 1214, Geoffroy IV, eleventh baron, in the Seventh Crusade at Mansoura in 1250, when the Saracens took him prisoner with the King. The grateful St. Louis changed the Chateaubriand arms from peacock plumes, with the device: *I scatter gold*, to the royal fleurs-de-lis with the device: *My blood dyes the banner of France*—and either motto was to prove equally appropriate to his descendant François-René. Geoffroy IV's unexpected return from paynim captivity caused the instant death, it is said from joy, of his wife Sybille. The line of the Barons of Chateaubriand ended, after marriages with the royal blood of England, France,

Aragon and Cyprus, in Geoffroy VIII, killed at the siege of La Roche Derrien in 1347.[2]

Meanwhile, however, the family had produced two further branches. The Chateaubriands of Les Roches Baritaut sprang towards 1260 from Jean de Chateaubriand, second son of Geoffroy V, and migrated to Anjou and Poitou, taking seniority on the extinction of the baronage in 1347, and expiring in 1671. A still earlier but junior branch, the Chateaubriands of Beaufort, began with the marriage in 1251 of Briand, younger son of Geoffroy IV and the faithful Sybille, to Jeanne de Beaufort, who brought him the title and castle of Beaufort in the marsh-lands of Dol. Three centuries later, after an illustrious career in the service of the Kings of France and Dukes of Brittany, and intermarriages with the houses of Du Guesclin, Rohan and Croï, the gradual decline of the Chateaubriands of Beaufort was speeded by an appalling scandal. In 1565 the last Briand de Chateaubriand fell in love with Jacquemine de Boysrioult, wife of his own cousin, the drunken and adulterous Guy de Guitté, who promised to marry him if he would first murder her hus-band. Briand did so, with the help of his Protestant brother Christophe. He married Jacquemine a few months later, produced a son named Gilles in 1570, took to the forests when his crime came to light, and was beheaded with Christophe at Rennes. 'It will be seen,' remarked François-René with evident satisfaction in his Memoirs, 'that my brother was not the first Chateaubriand to lose his head on the scaffold.' The resourceful Jacquemine fled to Normandy and was condemned in absence to be burned at the stake; but she took sanctuary at Rouen, was pardoned in 1579, married again, became a widow for the third and last time in 1591, and lived until 1602. Little Gilles was dispossessed by his uncle Georges, whose grandson Gabriel died without offspring in 1654, 'slain through his own fault' in a quarrel. Gabriel's sister Renée, after four childless marriages, sold the castle and lordship of Beaufort in 1666, and so ended the main line of the Chateaubriands of Beaufort.

Gilles, however, had founded a new but humbler branch of his own, the Chateaubriands of La Guérande, by marrying the heiress of the manor of La Guérande, in the parish of Hénanbihen, fifteen miles north-west of Dinan. His son Christophe, born in 1597, was confirmed at the age of seventy-two in his fleurs-de-lis arms and descent from the Chateaubriands of Beaufort, and permitted to take the quality of chevalier, by the commission installed to reform the Breton nobility by Louis XIV in 1669. Christophe's son Jean, born in 1631, was the father of Michel (through whose son Alexis the La Guérande branch was con-tinued until 1818), and of René-Amaury, born in 1653, seigneur of La Villandré, who married in 1677 his distant cousin, Marie-Jeanne du Rocher du Quengo, daughter of Marguerite de Chateaubriand, a grand-daughter of the usurper Georges. René-Amaury's third son Jacques-

François, lord of the manors of Villeneuve and Les Touches, was born on 22 February 1683, and married Perronnelle Lamour de Lanjégu on 27 August 1713.

These were the grandparents of our subject, François-René, and with them we seem for the first time to enter the land of the living. The dim ancestors of seven centuries, lieges and kinsmen of kings, had scattered gold and dyed the banner of France with their blood, had seen in their time the sea and flowers of Brittany, but in silence, a lineage of ghosts. To François-René a hundred years later they seemed no more than a bundle of 'ancient rubbish', a parcel of spectral documents of baptisms, marriages, divisions of property, and deaths—'the original of 1669 with 23 other pieces on vellum and 21 on paper'—which he relegated to the appendix of his Memoirs, remarking: 'If it was my duty to produce the genealogy of my family, no one is obliged to read it'. 'What a quantity of toil has gone to certify that ashes once lived!' In fact both ghosts and documents were still powerfully alive. The underground river of the blood of the Chateaubriands was rising anew in a family of obscure country squires; the dusty parchments waited to be read again, as an intolerable written reproach, in a moment of despair and revolt, by a proud and humiliated younger son.

Jacques-François resided at his manor of Les Touches, near Guitté, in the valley of the upper Rance some fifteen miles south of Dinan. At Lattay, three miles northwest of Guitté, he acquired a minor post as seneschal in a local court of justice, perhaps because the lord, Louis-Célestin de Saint-Pern, was a remnant of the Beauforts like himself. Meanwhile at La Guérande his widower cousin Alexis, head of the senior line and guardian of the family pedigrees, enjoyed a life of drunken disorder, cohabiting with his farmgirls, and vehemently suspected of using the noblest parchments to cover his butter-jars. His favourite oath was: 'By the honour of Chateaubriand!'

Les Touches, which still survives as a farmhouse, was a modest, two-storied manor of massive stone, with oak-avenues, a moat, a courtyard, and carved chimney-tops, at the end of a sunken lane on the pastoral slope leading down to the Rance. Here the squire produced twelve children in fourteen years: eight shortlived daughters, who are never heard of again, and four sons. First came three girls, then François, born on 31 October 1717, René-Auguste, born on 23 September 1718, the future father of François-René, then five more girls, then Pierre, born on 23 January 1727, and Joseph, born on 22 March 1728. On 28 March 1729 the four little boys were orphaned by the death of their father. Jacques-François left the inadequate income of 5,000 livres,[3] or 3,332 livres for the eldest son and 556 each for the three younger. But the sons, from family solidarity and generosity to their mother, postponed this disastrous partition indefinitely; it was carried out only in

1761, when thanks to René-Auguste the fortunes of the fallen house seemed to have risen again.

The eldest son François, whether through self-sacrifice or indolence, relieved the family of the burden of his dues and support by entering the Church, but failed most annoyingly to seek the rich benefices which might have enabled him to aid the careers of his brothers. He was ordained priest on 10 March 1742, spent two years as vicar at Bourseul near Plancoët, eleven miles northwest of Dinan, and in 1744 was presented by the Marquis René-Célestin de Saint-Pern (whose cousin had assisted his father) to the humble rectorate of Saint-Launeuc some twelve miles west of his birthplace. Ten years later the helpful Marquis made him rector in the nearby small town of Merdrignac, where he died insolvent on 26 February 1776, leaving only a reputation for sanctity, a quantity of frivolous unpublished verses, and debts which his grateful peasantry insisted upon paying.

When François left home for school at Dinan the two youngest boys were still babes, and the little René-Auguste became acting head of the family. It was decided that he should enter the king's navy, the last resource of a penniless younger son in the Breton nobility. He needed subsistence-money for his training at Brest, a uniform, books, and a brevet from the Navy Minister in Paris. His mother Dame Perronnelle sold her linen, her lace, and even her wedding-ring, but money was still lacking; the brevet never came, for want of an influential friend at court —'in France', as the Bretons used to say; and the poor lady took to her bed, ill with anguish. One morning in the spring of 1734 the fifteen-year-old boy came to her bedside and sternly declared: 'I am not going to be a burden to you any longer.' 'René,' she answered, weeping, 'What wouldst thou do? Till thy field.' 'It isn't enough to feed us; let me go.' 'Very well,' said the mother, 'go where God wills thee to go.' And the orphan adventurer set out to conquer the world, on a road that begins and ends in defeat.

He slept that night in the house of an aunt at Dinan, who gave him a letter of introduction to a friend in Saint-Malo. A few days later, according to a family tradition which has been contested without good grounds, he sailed for the siege of Danzig as a volunteer with the fleet sent to support the young Louis de Bréhan, Comte de Plélo, a Breton, poet, and kinsman (as was René-Auguste himself) of Mme de Sévigné.[4]

Stanislas Leczinski, father of the Queen of France, had been elected King of Poland in the previous September, and was now besieged in Danzig by a Russian army. Plélo, then French ambassador in Denmark, was determined to save the honour of France, but more so than Louis XV's pacific minister Cardinal Fleury, who, as Voltaire wrote, 'was equally unwilling to bear the blame of abandoning Stanislas entirely, or to risk large forces in his support'. Plélo had asked for fifteen thousand men, Fleury sent fifteen hundred; and these, led by Plélo in person, stormed the Russian trenches on 27 May 1734 and were driven back after enormous losses. The corpses were restored by the Russians with eighteenth-century politeness, including Plélo's, which had its left leg broken by a bullet, its face slashed by a sabre, and fifteen bayonet-thrusts in its heroic belly. So ended a typically gallant, useless and Breton-like adventure. Was René-Auguste taken prisoner with the rest of the survivors when Danzig surrendered on 9 July (they were treated kindly, and exchanged for the crew of a captured Russian frigate); did he find his way home otherwise; or was he never really there at all? His son believed he was twice wounded in the battle, and remembered his father declaring, with grudging admiration, when he told the story in winter nights at Combourg: 'Forty thousand of those Russian scoundrels could march over the Janissaries' guts and take Constantinople!' But ex-King Stanislas escaped to France and lived happily ever after in his makebelieve court at Nancy in Lorraine.

Home again at Saint-Malo the boy René-Auguste resolved to take the honourable profession of sea-going trade, which by repeated royal edicts was permitted to noblemen without loss of privilege. In the next six years he learned business in a merchant's office, studied navigation in the municipal school, and made three voyages as ensign to Newfoundland. The codfishers left for the Grand Banks in April, fished, salted and dried their catch until the autumn, sold it at Marseilles or Genoa during the winter, returned with a cargo of olive-oil and wine for Le Havre, and reached Saint-Malo in February or March, when it was nearly time to sail again. On one of these voyages René-Auguste was shipwrecked in Spain and robbed by bandits; on another he saw Italy. He matriculated as ship's officer on 22 September 1740: 'since an early age,' his certificate declared, 'he has applied himself with all possible exactitude to learning the art of navigation.' This was a hard school, and made hard men. By the end of 1745, as first lieutenant with a minute share in the profits, he had sailed on three more Newfoundland voyages and one to the West Indies, rising at last to the meagre pay of one hundred livres a month.

It was the year of Fontenoy; France was now at war with England in the War of the Austrian Succession, and all Saint-Malo abandoned codfishing for corsairing. The sea warfare of the French and English privateers was profitable, gentlemanly, and not too bloody. If an enemy merchant-ship seemed stronger it was not attacked; if weaker it usually surrendered, and according to the victor's choice either paid ransom or was sailed home under a prize-crew; prisoners on both sides were humanely treated and exchanged as soon as possible. So René-Auguste went privateering, soon joined by his brothers Pierre and Joseph with their mother's blessing. He was captured in March 1747 after taking four prizes, but freed after seven weeks in gaol at Plymouth, whereas Joseph had to languish there until peace was declared in 1748. Meanwhile René-Auguste went over to the West Indies trade after taking his certificate of captaincy, which permitted him to do business for his own profit as well as to sell his owners' goods on commission. After five voyages he returned in December 1752 with a property of 15,000 livres in sugar, a diamond worth 500, and a negro slave named Eugène bought in San Domingo for 1,018 livres. On this modest fortune, with his previous savings and future expectations, he felt able to marry, and did so on 3 July 1753.

His bride was Apolline de Bédée, aged twenty-seven, third daughter of Ange-Annibal de Bédée, lord of the manor of La Bouëtardais at Bourseul, and his wife Bénigne de Ravenel. The Bédées and Ravenels were satisfactorily noble, though their families had never risen so high nor fallen so far as the Chateaubriands. René-Auguste's elder brother François no doubt played some part in the match, for the Bédées had been among his congregation at Bourseul, and he now signed the contract and the parish register. The bride was a lively, elegant-mannered and angelically pious girl, short, dark and plain, with large features but fine eyes. Her mother had been educated at Saint-Cyr in the last years of the foundress Mme de Maintenon; and Apolline, in the century of the French Revolution, had been brought up on Fénelon, Racine, Mme de Sévigné, and the interminable romance of *Le Grand Cyrus*, which she knew by heart. A spinster aunt gave a small dowry of 4,000 livres, which René-Auguste allowed her to keep; and her parents pledged themselves to lodge and feed the homeless couple, with their negro slave, for three years. However, René-Auguste had not married for money, nor for love, but to found a family. The humiliated child who had refused to 'till his field' was now a tall, rigid, menacing man of thirty-five, obsessed by his ruthless will to restore the fortune of the Chateaubriands. He had renounced happiness. René-Auguste was loved by no one and loved no one, excepting the abstract descendants for whom he must find a title, a castle, and wealth, and then die.

He stayed at La Bouëtardais until his wife was duly pregnant, attended the baptism of his blackamoor Eugène, who had been briskly converted by the pious Bédée ladies, and in September 1754 sailed for West Africa in command of the slaveship *Apollon*, taking his brother Pierre as first lieutenant. In return for the customary brandy, muskets, tobacco and cowrie-shells the King of Dahomey graciously parted with 414 of his subjects, whom René-Auguste treated so humanely that only sixteen died on the journey instead of the normal eighty. He sold the survivors in San Domingo, throwing in, strange to say, his poor Eugène, and returned three years later, in September 1757, with personal gains of about 30,000 livres, which was hardly good enough. But he never went to sea again, having made sufficient capital to start in business for himself. His first child, a daughter baptised Bénigne, had been born during his absence in December 1754 and died before his return.

The Seven Years War with England had begun in June 1756. Trade ceased and corsairing recommenced, more profitable than trade for the lucky, more disastrous for the unlucky. René-Auguste was intermittently lucky, but always prudent, resourceful and indomitable. He moved to Saint-Malo, taking a small lodging in the Rue du Pont-qui-tremble in 1758, and a third share in the small but fast-sailing *Villegénie*, under the captaincy of his brother Pierre. The English swooped upon Saint-Malo on 8 July and burned eighty ships in Saint-Servan, thus reducing René-Auguste's competitors. But their landing at Saint-Cast on 11 September was brilliantly repulsed, not so much by the Duc d'Aiguillon (who was unjustly thought to be engaged at the time of the battle in an important private interview with a miller's wife, thereby covering himself, as was wittily said, 'with more flour than glory'), as by the country gentlemen of Brittany, in whose ranks old Bédée and his son Antoine fought gallantly. Meanwhile Pierre was safe at sea off Newfoundland, where he captured a magnificent prize, on the strength of which he married Mlle Brignon de Lehen on 12 February 1760, while René-Auguste was enabled to buy the *Villegénie* and move, in September 1760, to a more dignified apartment in the Hôtel de la Plesse in the Rue de la Victoire.

After three more highly profitable privateering campaigns of the *Villegénie* René-Auguste bought the frigate *Amaranthe*, built the swift bark *Vautour*, added the prize-ship *Providence*, took shares in the *Renoncule* and *Jeune-Auguste*, and with this private navy captured a score of English merchant-ships. One of these prizes, the *Donkinfield*, with a rich cargo of codliver oil and furs, inspired him with his only recorded joke: he insisted upon calling it the *Cane dans le champ*, or *Duck-in-field*. When the war ended in 1762 he had made by legal piracy the handsome fortune of 565,000 livres, 370,000 of which he had paid in the previous year for the castle of Combourg, and the title of Count that went with it. He had resurrected the buried honour and wealth of the Chateaubriands, forfeited two centuries before by the murder of Guy de Guitté; but to what avail, if the family should perish for want of heirs?

A first son was born at Saint-Malo on 4 May 1758, and pathetically named Geoffroy, in remembrance of the great Chateaubriand barons; but the baby died soon after. The longed-for heir, Jean-Baptiste, appeared on 23 June 1759; but René-Auguste must still beget a second son, in case the first should follow Geoffroy. A daughter came next, Marie-Anne, born on 4 July 1760, who lived to be a hundred years old: 'It's only a girl,' he wrote in chagrin to a friend. The year after, on 11 August 1761, arrived another girl, Bénigne, who reached the age of eighty-six; in 1762 Mme de Chateaubriand had a miscarriage; and two more unwanted daughters followed, Julie on 2 September 1763, and Lucile on 7 August 1764.

Meanwhile, resolutely as ever but now almost in vain, the Count of Combourg pursued the receding phantom of wealth through trade. He built the *Jean-Baptiste* for a West Indies freightship, but freights were lacking; the *Renoncule* was reconstructed as a fast model slaver, but slaves were dearer to buy and cheaper to sell than ever before. He sent the *Paquet d'Afrique*, the *Apolline*, the *Providence* and the *Dauphin* cod-fishing to Newfoundland; but fish were scarce, Englishmen had seized the best stations, and the dainty negroes of Martinique declared: 'We only like English fish.' The perfidious English had won the peace, and the French colonies in America were lost for ever.

In 1766, after a dozen voyages with marginal gains or alarming losses, René-Auguste made ferocious economies, and codfishing improved. The long-desired second son, Auguste, was born on 28 May 1766, and another girl, Caliste, was baptised on 3 June 1767. But Caliste soon died, and in that December, towards the week in which François-René was conceived, the poor baby Auguste fell ill with teething-fever. The anxious father wrote urgently to his banker in Paris for 'a paternoster chaplet of which I was told yesterday, that when hung round a child's neck has the virtue of cutting his teeth, or at least of contributing thereto and relieving the sufferer's pain . . . I am told it costs from six to eight livres.' Perhaps this paternoster might have saved little Auguste, but he died on the very day when it arrived, 30 December 1767.

Meanwhile René-Auguste was agitated not only by the vexations of trade and the births and deaths of children, but by the public affairs of Brittany and the private affairs of Combourg. Both he and his wife (for Mme de Chateaubriand's yearly pregnancies did not keep her out of politics) were ardent Chalotists, that is, supporters of Louis de La Chalotais, procurator general of the Parlement of Rennes[5] and champion of all Brittany against the Duc d'Aiguillon, the king's governor. Aiguillon, it was true, had built roads and quays, organised coastal defences, and killed, covered with flour though he was, two thousand marauding English at Saint-Cast; but he represented the court, the taxes and the Jesuits. In 1762 La Chalotais induced Parlement to expel the Jesuits from Brittany; in 1764–5 the Estates[6] refused a new subsidy, which Parlement declined to register. The rebellious magistrates were summoned to Versailles to be scolded by the king in person, and on their return resigned in a body, excepting a timid dozen who were punningly nicknamed the Ifs, which stood equally well for 'yewtree' and for Jean Foutre.

René-Auguste had attended the turbulent Estates, where his rotund and admiring brother-in-law Antoine de Bédée, known to the family as

Big Bédée or Bédée the Artichoke, bawled louder than anyone. Three menacing anonymous letters were sent to the king's first minister, Saint-Florentin, Aiguillon's uncle, in June 1765, for which a young man named Bouquerel (who had in fact written one of them) and the fairly innocent La Chalotais himself were arrested. A special commission was rigged to judge the elderly hero at Saint-Malo, where he was incarcerated at Christmas in the castle dungeon. Here, much incommoded by damp, cold, and the reek of tar from winter caulking in the harbour below, La Chalotais wrote his defence with soot and toothpicks, and smuggled it out to his family for printing, while the pregnant Mme de Chateaubriand bustled about among the ladies of Saint-Malo, doing her bit. M. de Fontette the gaoler, they all agreed, was a monster; and the numbered components of a clandestine gallows had been seen, or almost seen, hurried over the castle drawbridge by night! Regular news of Rennes arrived from René-Auguste's remote cousin, the Abbé Charles de Chateaubriand de Bellestre,[7] rector of Saint-Étienne, where he waged a permanent war with the cathedral chapter and took occasional shares in René-Auguste's corsairing and slaving ventures. La Chalotais was moved to Rennes on 31 July 1766. His prosecution was quashed by the king on 22 December, but he was nonetheless banished from Brittany until the next reign.

The Bédées, too, were rabid Chalotists, and none more so than Mme de Chateaubriand's sister Julie, the wife of an elderly magistrate of Rennes, Jean Moreau, who had recently had two strokes. Mme Moreau was thought to console herself with M. des Fourneaux, a crazy lieutenant in the regiment of her son Annibal. 'I am Jesus Christ,' Des Fourneaux had informed a lady of Rennes, adding: 'I can see you are just as surprised as I am.' But the Moreaus were hardly less surprised when he gave them to understand that he had refused a purse of 100 louis from the ex-Jesuit Abbé Clémenceau to poison La Chalotais in prison.[8] When Mme Moreau told everyone in Rennes under vows of strictest secrecy, the uproar was tremendous. After a lingering enquiry and trial Mme Moreau and Annibal were condemned to public withdrawal of their charges, with damages of 4,000 livres. Mme Moreau said she was ruined; her husband died of grief; and everybody sympathised. René-Auguste cursed, his wife wept; but it was felt that the Moreaus had deserved well of Brittany, especially when Aiguillon, reduced to desperation at last, resigned in August 1768. His grateful successor, the Duc de Duras, made Mme Moreau a present of 2,400 livres, and the good king annulled the whole case.

It was the same Duc de Duras who had sold Combourg to René-Auguste for 370,000 livres[9] on 3 May 1761. The new Count of Combourg had never yet set eyes on his property, so dearly bought. He made a brief visit three weks after the sale; but it was his loyal brother-in-law,

Antoine de Bédée, who had signed the contract on his behalf, and in August took ceremonial possession in his name, entering every room in the castle, lighting fires, ringing the bells in the church, visiting the lake, the mill and the lord's fourteen fiefs within the parish, and repeating this exhausting process in each of the forty other parishes where the master of Combourg held jurisdiction or fiefs.

Combourg had come to Emmanuel de Durfort, Duc de Duras, through his wife Maclovie de Coëtquen, the last of her line, the hereditary governors of Saint-Malo, who had held Combourg since 1553. The Duke was a Marshal of France, first gentleman of the king's bed-chamber and ex-ambassador to Spain, and the proceeds of the sale were to settle his enormous debts contracted in the royal service. This dis-possession, no doubt, was a symptomatic victory for the new merchant nobility over the old nobility of the court; yet it might seem that the wily duke had the better of the bargain.

The domains of the Count of Combourg stretched from the estuary of the Couesnon opposite Mont Saint-Michel, twenty miles to the north-east, to the parishes of Québriac and Dingé, eight miles to the south. Within these borders he possessed rights of justice and police, with his own private gallows on the heath of Rochefort in the parish of Tréméheuc; dues on the entry and departure of merchandise on Monday market-days and at nine annual fairs, of which the greatest was the September Angevine at Combourg itself; and forestal, coastal and other rights, whether real or merely honorific. But these dues were difficult and expensive to collect; more by half was extorted from his reluctant vassals than ever reached the Count himself; and the fat years, when his revenues might rise to 70,000 livres, were far outnumbered by the lean. The peasantry were impoverished, hungry, illhoused, overtaxed, and subject to disastrous epidemics of typhoid, smallpox and dysentery.

The personal domain of the lord of Combourg was limited and un-productive. In Combourg he possessed, besides the castle and its park, only the lake and watermill, the townhall, prison and bakehouse, a granary, the great meadow and another, with a few farms, lakes and mills in neighbouring parishes, and the neglected timber-forests of Bourgouet and Tanouarn to the south, bringing in 9,000 livres a year in all. 'If I could find a tenant at 8,000 free of all charges,' declared René-Auguste, 'I'd take him on.'

For several years he was pressed on one side by the Duke's creditors and by the Duchesse de Mortemart, widow of Mme de Duras's brother Jules-Malo, the last male Coëtquen, who demanded her inalienable dower-rent; on the other by innumerable local proprietors, lords, abbeys and priories, who claimed their own phantasmagoric feudalities or denied René-Auguste's. M. de Duras evaded action with ducal courtesy, or refused it with ducal hauteur; but 'I'm not frightened by ducality!' cried René-Auguste. Dry land, it seemed, was no less perilous to harvest than the sea, but could be dominated by the same courage and cunning. René-Auguste relished the struggle, enjoyed writing hundreds of letters of exquisite politeness, irony, conciliation and menace, on the best paper, in neatly exuberant calligraphy, and always with identical egocentric spelling-mistakes (whereas his wife or Bédée the Artichoke never misspelt the same word in the same way twice). By 1765, two years before the stipulated six, he had paid nine-tenths of the purchase price, and his opponents were beaten or exhausted. But then, there was still the interminable, inextricable, damnable affair of M. de Trévégat's cow.

Long ago in the lordship of M. de Duras, on 7 September 1752, as dusk fell on the last day of the annual Angevine fair in the castle-meadow by the lake, an unknown peasant had refused to pay the exit-dues of four sous on a newly-purchased cow. The cow was detained; but two days later the chevalier Thépault de Trévégat arrived in person from his distant seat at Carentoir near Vannes, fifty miles away, to claim her, together with the costs of his journey and refreshments. The Duke's bailiff counter-offered to return the cow for the four sous, with the costs of his own pains and *her* refreshments. This difference was irreconcilable. M. de Trévégat went to law, pleading a decree of Jean II in 1301, and the Custom of Brittany, article 119: 'Let no man arrest the horse of a nobleman'. M. de Duras disputed the authenticity of Jean II's decree, and maintained that a cow was not a horse. The case went from the judge of Combourg to the Presidial or bourgeois court of Rennes, then to Parlement; when René-Auguste bought Combourg in 1761 it had reached the Estates of Brittany. The poor cow had been sold to cover her keep, for she ate a great deal and gave very little milk. At last she died, lamented by all, the bailiff died, even M. de Trévégat died in 1772, but the lawsuit remained immortal in the hands of his heirs.

The contract of sale had stipulated that M. de Duras should guarantee the lifting of all litigation affecting Combourg within three months. After three years, in 1764, he had done nothing whatever. René-Auguste then offered to take upon himself the Duke's lawsuits for a consideration, all except the intolerable affair of M. de Trévégat's cow. But it was not until 1773, after nine more years of masterly inactivity on the part of M. de Duras, that the transaction was completed: René-Auguste, in return for the waiving of 15,000 livres on his purchase, assumed responsibility for all outstanding lawsuits against Combourg, including the bitter pill of the deceased M. de Trévégat's deceased cow.

It was better so. Strife and perplexity were now his natural element, his reason for living. And these preposterous litigations were, in the feudal phrase, 'noble suits', not only a compulsory and pleasurable rural sport for aristocrats, more exciting and dangerous than hunting or shooting, but a source of prestige and self-content, a proof of the lost and found nobility which René-Auguste had bought Combourg and given his life to assert. He accepted and provoked new embroilments of his own; he was never quite to succeed, but no one was ever quite to have the better of him. The affair of M. de Trévégat's cow survived René-Auguste's death in 1786, and formed part of his legacy to his heir Jean-Baptiste. It vanished in the explosion of the Revolution, but cannot be said either legally or metaphysically to have ended. Indeed, the affair of M. de Trévégat's cow remains unsettled to this day.

1768 was a year of particular agitation. René-Auguste equipped the *Saint-René*, a new economical slaver on his new economical plan, with 40,000 cowrie-shells (for the blackamore kings now demanded cash in this form, having gone off brandy—'it melts like butter on a stove'). These shells took five months to arrive from Amsterdam under a drunken skipper. His little codfisher the *Paquet d'Afrique*, for which he had taken out insurance just in time, was never heard of again. In March his very life was endangered by a violent influenza, and his pregnant wife fell ill for two months. At Rennes in May the foolish Moreaus were on trial for having taken the crazy M. des Fourneaux seriously. In June René-Auguste's lawyers at last secured the forty dossiers of the Combourg lawsuits, which M. de Duras could not be persuaded for five more years to sell; and in July began the rains which were to destroy the harvest and culminate in the great gale.

So, for René-Auguste, the land proved tempestuous as the sea. The pitiless storm of September 1768 was an emblem of the father's past and of the naked newborn babe's future. And while the father dwindled and the child grew, slowly gathering for more than twenty years, over the roofs of Paris and the avenues of Versailles as over the ramparts of Saint-Malo and the beeches of Combourg, a greater storm was brewing.

2

THE RAMPARTS OF SAINT-MALO

SOON after his birth the new and last baby was separated from home
and parents, and sent to live or die with his grandmother Bédée at
Plancoët. 'On leaving my mother's womb I underwent my first exile,'
wrote Chateaubriand in his Memoirs. For a banishment that later
seemed harsh there were no doubt excellent reasons. It was not customary for an eighteenth-century noblewoman to suckle her child, and
the overworn Mme de Chateaubriand, now aged forty-two, ill last
spring, released at last from eleven pregnancies in fifteen years, was
perhaps unable or reluctant to do so. Winter was coming, her favourite
season of society, religious observance, politics and gossip, the season
also when little Auguste had died only last year, in the cruel winds of
Saint-Malo, for want of a paternoster. The four girls had moved into
the nursery, and there was no room in the house for another baby. To
René-Auguste, who had begotten so pertinaciously and till now in vain
in quest of a possible replacement for his heir Jean-Baptiste, the survival of François-René seemed more important than his presence. The
child needed country air, the milk of a strong peasant wetnurse, the
care of his adoring grandmother.

Ange-Annibal de Bédée had died at the age of sixty-five in January
1761, less than three years after helping to defeat the English at Saint-
Cast. His widow Bénigne had moved from their manor-house of La
Bouëtardais to the little market-town of Plancoët, only two miles to
the north, twelve miles southwest of Saint-Malo, at the head of the
drowned-valley estuary of the Arguenon. In time of spring-tides the
river, true to its name (*Ar gwenn avon*, the White River), brims white
with foam from the sea. The quiet pretty town, with its weavers,
tanners, shipbuilders and country lawyers, lay on the left bank, em-
bowered to north and south by twin hills, each crowned with a windmill, the gorseclad La Janière, and wooded Brandefer with rust-red
springs. On the right bank the Rue de l'Abbaye sloped upward from
the bridge, past the church of Our Lady of Nazareth with its convent
of Dominican friars, and on to Corseul and Dinan.[1] In this uphill
street of gentlefolk the seventy-year-old Mme de Bédée lived with her
spinster sister Mlle du Boisteilleul at the Maison Notre-Dame, a large
two-storied cottage which she held on lease from the Dominicans, facing south, with attics, shuttered windows, and front door opening
down four semicircular stone steps directly into the street; at the back

was a terraced garden looking over the valley to the gorse of La Janière. Next door lived three old maids, the Demoiselles Loaisel de Villedeneu, Mme de Bédée's childhood friends; and she was often visited from his nearby château of Monchoix by her jolly son Antoine and his four children, then aged from ten to two. The banished baby did not lack the society of kind old ladies and happy fellow-infants. He only lacked a mother.

François-René remained inexplicably puny and nearly died, until it was found that his wetnurse was dry. Providentially she had a still-suckling friend, the farmer's wife at the Porte au Rocher across the street, who had enough milk for two. Over the altar in a side-chapel at the Dominicans' church of Notre-Dame de Nazareth stood a miraculous statue of the Virgin and Child both crowned in majesty. This Virgin had laid forgotten for many centuries at the bottom of a neighbouring pond, till discovered by her supernatural radiance and wailings in 1621, whereafter the little baroque church was built by the local citizens in 1647 to house her. Since then she had performed innumerable miracles, and specialised, as she does to this day, in the rescue of ailing babies. The nameless fostermother devoted François-René to the Blessed Virgin of Nazareth: if she saved his life, he should wear her colours, blue and white, till he was seven years old. The distant Mme de Chateaubriand, when asked to approve this vow, was all for it. From that day François-René mended, and three years later, in the autumn of 1771, returned fat and strong to Saint-Malo.

The three-year-old child was too young to have memories; but within him, deeper and vaster than any memory, was an unassuaged, irremediable, unidentified love. His family, whom he now saw for the first time, were strangers. A hireling had called several times a day to give him half her milk; his absent mother had done only her eighteenth-century duty, which was not enough, to a child of the nineteenth century. Now Mme de Chateaubriand was present, but still remote, devoted only to his elder brother, busy if at all with the upbringing of his sisters. Brisk, discontented, intermittently wellmeaning, she left him to the servants.

A servant had nurtured him, and now another servant gave him love, which he passionately returned. The family housekeeper, La Villeneuve, was a Bédée discovery, from the hamlet of Villeneuve at Pluduno, the next parish west of Plancoët and the site of uncle Antoine's château of Monchoix, and like many a Breton domestic she was called after her birthplace.[2] This good woman carried him in her warm arms from room to room, dumped him in a corner and hurried to pick him up, dried his tears and hugged him, muttering all the while: 'There's one who won't be proud and haughty, who has a good heart, who doesn't despise poor people; here, little lad!—' and she gave him a sip of wine in the larder, or stuffed him with sugar. 'I loved her madly,' he wrote. He screamed when separated from her, and once, when Mme de Chateaubriand saw fit to dismiss her rival, François-René fell into a speechless stupor of grief and refused to eat for a whole day, until La Villeneuve was reinstated. His father's goodnatured manservant La France also won his affection. But soon he turned to a companion nearer his own age.

His sisters Marie-Anne, Bénigne, Julie and Lucile were respectively eight, seven, five, and four years older than François-René. They carried him again and again in their arms to the room where he was born, showed him the ramparts and the reefs, and told him of the great storm. He never forgot these eery tidings of a violent destiny. Sea and world might now be calm, but to no avail, for the storm was in his heart, and would travel with him through space and time to the end.

The three eldest girls were cherished, prim and ordinary; but the youngest was neglected and strange like himself. Lucile was a thin, timid, unhappy child, too tall for her age, speaking and learning with difficulty, wearing threadbare dresses that did not fit, the castoff clothes of her sisters. Her ribs were galled by the rods of her stays, her long neck held cruelly erect by an iron collar masked with brown velvet, her dark hair combed and quiffed to the top of her head, relentlessly powdered and pomaded, and tied with a black ribbon. The busy mother abandoned Lucile as a toy and a menial to François-René. But the boy did not take advantage of his power; instead, recognising a victim still more forlorn than himself, feeling for the first time the horror of oppression and the compulsion to enlist in a lost cause which were to be leading motives of his whole life, he became the protector of his protectress. His heart bled when he compared Lucile's shabby gowns with the fine attire of his other sisters. If she was punished, the house was filled with the noise of his weeping until her sentence was rescinded. When her writing-master rapped her chilblained knuckles with his ruler, François-René hurled himself upon the tyrant. After he was five they were both taken every morning to the infant school kept by two aged hunchbacked sisters clad in black, the Mlles Couppart, who scolded Lucile for her backwardness in writing, and were assailed with scratches and slaps by her indignant brother.

François-René was no more forward than Lucile at reading and writing. The writing-master M. Després, an interloper from Normandy who wore a sailor's pigtailed wig, made him copy out endlessly a couplet of Boileau which he loathed not merely for its glaring fault in grammar:

> *'My mind, it is to you to whom I'll speak,*
> *For you in faults I cannot hide are weak!'*

At each error M. Després punched the boy in the neck, with unintelligible cries of '*Tête d'achôcre!*'³—but with impunity, for when oppression was directed only against himself, François-René did not retaliate.

Meanwhile the child had begun to discover his native city. Saint-Malo lies on a sea-bared rock, one of many that were once green hills in the lost woodland of Lyonnesse. Others are scattered round it near and far, a ring of fortified outcrops on the lowtide sands, a barrier of islets on the sea horizon, the pyramid of Mont Saint-Michel hidden to the east, Mont-Dol stranded high and dry by the road to Combourg. At its southeastern point Saint-Malo is linked to the mainland by the sandspit of the Sillon, thus enclosing, between its landward shore and the town of Saint-Servan on the opposite coast, a long wide tidal basin, deep at high tide, dry at low. On that granite plateau the hermit Aaron was joined in the sixth century by the good bishop Saint Malo; the cathedral of Saint-Vincent was built in the twelfth and its lantern tower in the fifteenth; Duchess Anne added in 1498 her keeps of Grumble-Who-May and La Générale to the square castle guarding the entry to the Sillon; and during the long wars of Louis XIV and Louis XV a sea-chivalry of trading, codfishing, shipbuilding, slaving and corsairing gentlemen grew rich and raised, in an unbroken circuit within the ramparts, their tall grey palaces of granite. All is gone today, gone and risen again. Saint-Malo, bombed and burned by the American liberators in August 1944, but since so admirably rebuilt in the image of the past magnificence of the corsairs, might seem almost unchanged to Chateaubriand gazing from his tomb. Yet nothing remains of his city but a corner in the east with his birthplace, another fragment in the west, the shell of the shattered cathedral in the centre, the unbroken castle and the infrangible ramparts.

La Villeneuve pinned a cheap print of his protectress the Blessed Virgin above his bed, and took him to mass at Saint-Vincent. In the winter night the cathedral was thronged with a dim multitude of aged kneeling sailors, of young women and children holding tapers to light their prayerbooks; the sea-gusts of Christmas rattled the stained-glass windows and shook the nave; and as the priest rang the holy bell François-René saw the real God descending upon the altar, the heavens opening to welcome their worship. He bowed his head. If God was present in the cathedral of Saint-Malo, then He might indeed be everywhere. 'Nothing is far from God,' his mother told him. On the great feasts of the Church he was taken with his sisters to all the sanctuaries of the city, from the magnificent hospital of Saint-Sauveur in the west to the little seventeenth-century chapel of Saint-Aaron on the highest point of the rock above his home. Nearer still, between the Rue de la Victoire and the ramparts, was the Benedictine nunnery of La Victoire, with its famous painting of the Battle of Lepanto and the victory over the Turks, in honour of which it was named and founded in 1611 as a refuge for nobly-born widows, and maidens who could not or would not marry. The nuns sat behind their grill out of view, and François-René was doubly stirred to hear the sweet chanting of invisible women and the bellowing of the waves below.

As the kneeling sailors prepared for sea others beyond the reefs steered their course for port by the cathedral tower. The ideas of God and danger, religion and the sea, became inseparable in the boy's mind. Among his earliest memories was the sound at night of a handbell rung from street to street, 'to tell Christians they must pray,' he was informed, 'for one of their brothers who has died'. A year rarely passed without his seeing a ship carried on the rocks or, rolled by the breakers to his feet as he wandered on the sands, the drowned corpse of a foreign sailor.

At first, guarded by La Villeneuve or La France, he played alone on those sandy beaches with his fosterbrothers the sea and gale. One of his first great pleasures was to run down after a receding wave, and back again as the next arrived to pursue him. Then he joined the other children, among them his cousins Stanislas and Armand,[4] the sons of his father's brother Pierre, to build sandcastles—'varying in size or elaboration according to the strength or taste of the little architects'— against the incoming tide. The first wave flowed through the cunning tunnels they had devised to admit it; the second sapped the foundations; the third, amid their shouts of joy, left not a trace of their fortress. 'How often since then,' wrote Chateaubriand, 'have I thought myself building for all eternity castles that have crumbled faster than my palaces of sand!' At low tide they played in the shattered wreckage of the infernal machine, exploded, happily in vain, by an English fleet on the night of 29 November 1693. Sometimes, on the sand-dune called La Hoguette in Paramé at the further end of the Sillon, they had games of touch between four upright posts supporting a square of oaken beams. The perching gulls flapped away as, with a feeling of inner terror, the boys approached. This was the ancient gibbet of the lords of Le Plessis-Bertrand, whose long-vanished seigneury had passed nearly four centuries before into his own family, till that had all but vanished too.[5]

But the days of the annual fairs were unhappy for him. One of these, the Petite Saint-Ouine, otherwise known as Foire des Bigorneaux or Periwinkle Fair, was held near the chapel of Saint-Ouen at the northern point of the Grand-Bé. All Saint-Malo trooped out over the sands, with covered wagons, long files of horses and donkeys, and processions of religious fraternities winding with cross and banners through the multitude. But François-René heard with heavy heart the clangour of joy-bells in the distant churches, the salvoes of festal cannon, the cries of the stall-keepers whose cakes and toys his parents had given him no pennies to buy. His clothes were ragged and shabby, while other children wore their best finery. He wandered aloof and ashamed among the rockpools, with their constellations of plum-green and fire-red sea-anemones, gathering the seashells that lie in jewelled swathes, opal, topaz and pearl-white, at each fringe of the receding tide, and crouched at last on a rock, gazing past the flying gulls at the bluish distances of the sea-horizon, listening to the song of waves on distant reefs. Behind him the final northward cliff of the Grand-Bé, below the summit gorse and the grey fort, plunged in a cascade of sea-pinks to the sands. The boy sat brooding only a few yards and a little more than seventy years from his grave.

From these joys or sorrows he came reluctantly home, sometimes alone and crestfallen, sometimes riotously accompanied by all the infant ruffians of Saint-Malo, his dearest friends. His shirts were torn, his stockings holed, his shoes down at heel, his face grimy; often he had lost his hat, sometimes even his coat. And yet, inconsistently, he longed to be otherwise: 'I already loved, and have always loved, cleanliness and even elegance'. No doubt, since he incorrigibly spoiled his clothes, his mother was justified in omitting to repair or replace them. But he suffered bitterly, with the unreasoning resentment of a child who feels unloved, from this half-fancied, half-selfincurred neglect. At night, aided by La Villeneuve and Lucile, he tried to mend the damage, but next day, after their desperate patchings and darnings, his appearance was only the more odd. Mme de Chateaubriand sighed and scolded, and then, overcome by the strange expression of his face, scratched, bruised and smeared with dirt, burst into laughter. 'How ugly he is,' she cried, and compared François-René adversely with his virtuous elder brother: Jean-Baptiste, she declared, was a Cato, a hero.[6] René-Auguste, with the not unamiable mingling of sternness and indulgence which he always showed to the shortcomings of his younger son and other subordinates, only shook his head and sententiously remarked: 'The Chevaliers of Chateaubriand have always been thrashers of hares,[7] drunkards and brawlers.' He had in mind, no doubt, two recent examples of this sad rule, in the death two years before of his own unsatisfactory youngest brother Joseph,[8] and the disgraceful incarceration in this very year, 1774, of the blackest sheep in all the family, the youngest brother of his cousin the Abbé.[9] But François-René was outraged by his parents' verdicts and felt inclined, as he remembered long afterwards, 'to commit all the crimes that they seemed to expect of me.'

The Chevalier's conduct was not improved by two further events in the autumn of 1774. The lease of their home in the dark Rue des Juifs was terminable (in accordance with the Saint-Malo custom by which tenancies were held in multiples of three years) at the beginning of that

September, six years after their moving in at the time of François-René's birth. The last phase of René-Auguste's activity in commerce was now at its height; he seized the opportunity to move into a finer mansion in the merchant quarter, the Maison White, at no. 4, Place Saint-Vincent. The ground-floor, with its handsome doorway flanked by two Doric pillars, was shared by the widow Leroux's grocery and René-Auguste's business offices; the Chateaubriands occupied the first floor, looking over the ramparts upon the inner harbour; on the second floor was René-Auguste's friend M. Gesril du Papeu, who had been godfather in 1767 of his soon-dead daughter Caliste; and on the third floor lived the proprietor, M. White de Boisglé, mayor of Saint-Malo. Opposite was the Porte Saint-Vincent, the chief gateway of the city, leading to the causeway of the Sillon and the mainland, with the castle to the left and the quays to the right. Near by, in the house of the merchant Charles Dolley, lived Pierre de Chateaubriand and his family.

François-René now attended the day-school kept by Father Chopin in the Rue Saint-Benoît, near the Benedictine monastery and the northern ramparts. The Chopins, as the worthy priest's pupils were called, were children of the aristocracy and rich merchants, and traditional enemies of the equally tough Casse-Bras or Arm-breakers, sons of the poor who were educated at the rival school of the Brothers of the Christian Doctrine. François-René found himself in familiar company. His schoolfellows were his playmates of the sands and ramparts, including his cousins Stanislas and Armand. But he also made a formidable new friend in Joseph Gesril, his neighbours' son and heir, the ringleader of all the Chopins.

Joson, as his doting father called him, or Gesril, as he was more respectfully known to his comrades, was one of those tragic and romantic leader-figures, like the Steerforth of Dickens or the Dargélos of Cocteau, who are thrown up by the Darwinian struggle for life of every school community, but attain immortality only when one of their companions is destined to creative genius. In the fascination exercised by such child heroes there is something sinister, almost supernatural, some daemonic image, not necessarily of evil or cruelty, but rather of the hidden side of the human situation that rejects the commonplace and responds to peril and the unforeseen. Gesril, although reckless in personal courage, took his chief delight as an instigator of daring in others. He revelled in crowds and combats; François-René, who loved solitude and never picked a quarrel in his life, was his contrary and yet his counterpart. 'Are you going to take that lying down?', enquired Gesril, when some older and bigger urchin dared to contradict François-René; and a fight to the finish ensued, in which Gesril praised his friend's bravery, but made no effort to avert his defeat. Sometimes he raised an army of child rascals, divided his conscripts into two bands, and organised a pitched battle of stone-throwing on the sands. Another deadly sport was the crossing, when wind and tide were high, of a narrow downward-sloping parapet, twenty feet above the seaward base of the Tour des Dames in the castle. A bellowing mountain of water approached as each player hurried over; if caught, he would either be crushed against the wall, or dragged into the raging sea. 'Not one of us refused this venture,' wrote Chateaubriand, 'but I have seen many a child turn pale before attempting it.'

François-René and Gesril, who was eighteen months his senior,[10] became intimate friends. The younger boy was an apt pupil for this teacher of audacity and the absurd; but their union was not the ordinary schoolboy relationship of master and servant, tempter and dupe. 'We were both misjudged in childhood, and formed our attachment from an instinctive knowledge of what one day we might be worth,' he wrote. Each was destined to live in the quest, confrontation, and conquest of death, each recognised and accepted in the other an individuality marked out from the crowd. Meanwhile, however, François-René became no less notorious than Gesril among the nursemaids of Saint-Malo, whose highborn charges they led into mischief and danger, as an exceptionally naughty little boy. His exploits in the spring of 1775 were so heinous that even René-Auguste decided something must be done.

Along the shore of the castle end of the Sillon a row of oaken piles—the same that are seen to this day, now gnarled, split, and corroded with brine, but then new—protected the causeway from the force of the sea. Here one Sunday, as the incoming tide swept beneath them, the children sat, boys and girls, one on each pillar, watched by their anxious attendants. Gesril was posted at one end, François-René last but one at the other, with only a pretty girl beyond him, little Hervine Magon, half laughing in her pleasure, half weeping in fear. The wind rose, the waves grew fiercer. 'Get down, Mademoiselle, come back, Monsieur,' cried the servants. Suddenly the pitiless Gesril shoved his neighbour, the whole row toppled one by one like a pack of cards, François-René hurtled involuntarily into Hervine Magon, and Hervine Magon tumbled into the water. The nursemaids waded out, hoisting their petticoats, each seizing and smacking her ward. Little Hervine was fished out, drenched, just as she was being carried out to sea. 'François pushed me,' she declared. The culprit was chased all the way to the Maison White, where his parents were luckily out. La Villeneuve stoutly defended the door, and slapped the foremost of his pursuers in the face. Even Gesril, for once, lent a hand; from his second-floor windows, aided by his two sisters, he threw saucepans of water on the enemy, and pelted them with baked potatoes. The siege continued till nightfall, and next day it was known throughout Saint-Malo that the Chevalier de Chateaubriand, aged not quite seven, was turning out to be a thorough scoundrel.

Disgrace was soon followed by bodily harm. One day at low tide François-René and Gesril made their way towards Saint-Servan across the dry inner harbour, accompanied by La France and Gesril's own servant, fording the tidal runnels over the narrow causeways of stepping-stones. As they neared one of these, two sturdy cabin-boys approached from the other side. 'Are we going to let these villains cross?' exclaimed Gesril. 'Into the water, puddle-ducks!' he shouted, and assailed the enemy with a shower of pebbles. But Gesril had now met his match: the cabin-boys charged, drove them back upon their servants, and threw stones with better aim. François-René was struck on his left ear, which hung half-severed and bleeding over his shoulder. But he feared no wound so much as his parents' anger; La France with all his entreaties could not bring him home, and he hid till nightfall in Gesril's quarters on the second floor. Gesril dressed his head in a napkin, which made him look for all the world like the venerable Mgr. des Laurents in his episcopal mitre, and they passed the evening with Angélique and Gesril's other sister in a graceless game of high mass. But even François-René dared not evade his compulsory attendance at family supper. The bloodstained bishop crept downstairs with beating heart; his mother screamed; his father, though much amazed, said not a word. La France tried in vain to prove that the boy was more to be pitied than blamed. His ear was tended, and healed very well; but M. and Mme de Chateaubriand decided in consultation that he must be separated from Gesril. School holidays were near, and in September François-René would have to be released from his vow to the Blessed Virgin of Nazareth. In July they sent their unruly son to spend the rest of the summer at Plancoët.

The lucky boy was exiled into paradise. No cult of danger and violence was practised at Plancoët; there was no necessity of living up to Gesril, no ramparts, no storms, no drowned sailors; the stern atmosphere of duty and disapproval in his parents' home was exchanged for the affection and timeless tranquillity of the old ladies, the ebullient cheerfulness of Uncle Antoine and his children. He walked in a calm village, sat in green gardens, wandered through a smiling inland countryside.

Mme de Bédée, his mother's mother, was now aged seventy-seven, and would live to be ninety-seven. She was a plump, agreeable old lady, tall, cleanly and serious, with the noble manners and cultured mind of a country gentlewoman who had been to school at Saint-Cyr. She wore oldfashioned pleated gowns and a widow's bonnet of black lace tied under her chin. Her unmarried sister, Suzanne de Ravenel du Boisteilleul, resembled her only in having a heart of gold. In one of those amicable transactions through which the priests or spinsters of a noble family did their duty by their more worldly kindred, she had resigned her inheritance in return for her lifelong keep; it was her money that had furnished La Bouëtardais long ago, and provided the modest dowry of her niece, François-René's mother. Mlle du Boisteilleul was now seventy-one, and lived to be ninety; she was tiny and thin, talkative and mocking. In youth she had been betrothed to a Comte de Trémigon, who had preferred to marry someone else; and now she hummed through her spectacled nose, as she embroidered two-tiered sleeve-cuffs for her sister, a song which the boy supposed to be of her own composition:

> *'A hawk once loved a little bird,*
> *And, so folk say, the bird loved him . . .'*

ending with the refrain:

> *'Ah! Trémigon, the fable seems obscure?*
> *Turelure!'*

This, he thought, was peculiar conduct for a hawk; and, what was stranger still, the Maison du Dôme a few doors further down the hill—so called from the rounded superstructure of its attic—with the garden pond by which Mme de Bédée was allowed to sit each afternoon, was occupied by none other than a M. de Trémigon![11]

Every delicious uneventful day was the same. Mlle du Boisteilleul looked after the housekeeping. Mme de Bédée rose late and dined early at eleven, had a nap, and at one in the afternoon—for though hale enough, she was past walking—was carried down the terraces in her chair to the banks of M. de Trémigon's pond, where she sat knitting under the willows, with her sister and grandchildren round her. At four she was carried back to her drawing-room, where her manservant Pierre set out a card-table. Mlle du Boisteilleul rapped with the fire-tongs on the granite chimney-back (it is still there), and a few moments later, summoned by this signal, in trooped the Mlles de Villedeneu from next door for their game of quadrille. No sooner were the cards dealt than the ladies began to quarrel; this indispensable tiff was the only event of their day. Peace was restored with eight o'clock supper, and the arrival from Monchoix, only two miles away, of her son Antoine and his daughters, Caroline, Marie, and Flore. Antoine told for the thousandth time how he had seen the Battle of Fontenoy[12] as a page to King Louis XV, thirty years ago when he was eighteen, and capped his boastings with naughty stories that made the good spinsters die laughing. At nine the servants entered, everyone kneeled while Mlle du Boisteilleul said prayers; and at ten the whole household was asleep except Mme de Bédée, whose maidservant read aloud to her till one in the morning.

Monchoix—My Choice, as Antoine named it—was and is a fine mid-eighteenth century mansion of smallish size, begun in 1759 and finished in 1767, on the Bédée estate of La Mettrie-Martin in the parish of Pluduno. It has two tall-windowed stories, with attics above and cellars below, a pedimented west front with a state entrance above twin horse-shoe stairways, and towering chimney-stacks at each corner. One of these, with good reason, leans outwards; for the Bédées were immeasurably fond of dancing, and one summer evening, when no fiddler was to hand, a stranger had to be called in from the highroad. He played very well, too well. The dancers began to cut the oddest capers, leaped high in the air, sweated and gasped, could not stop, begged for mercy, and noticed that the mysterious fiddler had cloven feet. Abbé Loyer was fetched in haste from Pluduno. 'Ah! It's you again!' grumbled the Devil, for it was he—'Are you going to follow me everywhere?'; and seeing that the game was up, he sportingly offered to disappear in fire, water or air, at the good priest's choice. The Abbé chose air, the fiend vanished in a sudden tempest up the fireplace, and that is why the south-east chimney-stack over the drawing-room at Monchoix is out of per-pendicular, and is supported to this day by an iron stanchion.

François-René's room was the northeastern attic, with views along the oak-avenue and eastward to the hill of Brandefer. But his chimney, too, was put to no virtuous use. He hid in it pots of his aunt's delicious jam, stolen from the dining-room cupboard; and his cousin Caroline robbed the thief, taking away the jam and stuffing the jars with tow. His aunt Marie-Angélique, born a Ginguené from Rennes, sounded the only discordant note in the Bédée merriment. Her husband, she declared, 'was squandering his capital along with his revenue'; but no one paid attention to her complaints, for she had eccentricities of her own. A savage hunting-dog lay always in her lap, and a tame boar-pig followed her everywhere and filled Monchoix with his gruntings.

René-Auguste, after escorting François-René from Saint-Malo in July, had returned to Combourg to supervise his four daughters ('too old to be abandoned to the charge of servants, and too young to be left in their own', he explained to a friend), and to release his fretful wife, who hated Combourg, to take the waters at Dinan. The time of François-René's seventh birthday on 4 September 1775, when he would be redeemed from his vow to the Blessed Virgin of Nazareth, was approaching. There were two great annual pilgrimages at Notre-Dame de Nazareth: one, for the Assumption of the Virgin on 15 August, was too early, but the other, for her Nativity on 8 September, was just right.

Mme de Chateaubriand arrived, fresh from her blissful month at Dinan. They dressed him for the last time in the Virgin's colours, in white coat, shoes, gloves and hat, and a blue sash;[13] and at ten o'clock

in the morning he climbed the hill to Notre-Dame with his mother, all
the Bédées, his wetnurse and foster-brother, followed by half the people
of Plancoët. They passed through the quincunx of immemorial elms,
older than the church, and entered a dim blaze of candles and lamps,
where the monks were already in their stalls. The beadles led him to
three chairs in the choir, where he sat between his nurse and her child.
'The great lady my mother was left at the door, the peasant-woman was
taken into the sanctuary': of the two, which was his real mother? Mass
was said, his white wear was hung *ex voto* beneath the Virgin's statue,[14]
and he put on a violet coat instead. The Prior of the Dominicans, well
primed with Chateaubriand history, spoke in his address of the ancestral
Baron Geoffroy who had gone to the Holy Land with Saint Louis.
'Perhaps you too,' he said, 'will visit Palestine and Nazareth, and see
the Virgin to whom you owe your life, through the intercession and
prayers of the poor, which are always most powerful in the ear of God.'
So it was to be, thirty-one years later. Lastly Mme de Chateaubriand
took holy communion, and prayed that its grace should fall upon her
graceless boy. With all her good intentions she could never understand
that a child needs love as well as religion. Henceforth, however,
although too late, having seen herself and François-René at the centre
of this imposing public ceremony, she began to feel a pious affection
for him. Perhaps, she thought, she might even have the joy of steering
him into the priesthood.

They returned to Saint-Malo in October. The winter was hard, and
kitchen-fires were banked high. At three o'clock in the frosty morning
of 17 February 1776 the driver of the public coach to Rennes, who
providentially happened to be waiting for his passengers in the Place
Saint-Vincent, noticed that Widow Leroux's grocery was ablaze, and
raised the alarm. Oil and tallow from her marine stores fed the flames.
René-Auguste had just time to call his daughters, who slept next to his
own room and exactly above the burning grocery. Four minutes later
their bedroom floor fell in; another six minutes, and the whole first-
floor apartment was gutted. Nothing could be done to stop the con-
flagration, for the water in the castle moat was frozen hard. Young
Gilbert, their former neighbour in the Rue des Juifs, hurried to the
scene, and helped the eldest daughter Marie-Anne to escort François-
René wrapped in a blanket to his own home.

There had been time to save only the family silver and some, but not
all, of René-Auguste's business papers and ledgers. Their furniture and
the contents of his ample wine-cellar were destroyed, and even a bundle
of his best cambric handkerchiefs from the West Indies, which someone
had thrown from the window, could never be found again. Philo-
sophically he began at once to make good his losses, ordering 'a dozen
bamboo armchairs, upholstered in yellow Siamese cotton striped with

white' from Rouen, and three hogsheads of wine from Bordeaux. 'I am not the sort of person to repair my damages by retrenching on everyday expenditure,' he remarked.

M. Magon de Boisgarein was able to offer the homeless Chateaubriands their old lodging in his Hôtel de la Gicquelais in the Rue des Juifs, next door to the Gilberts. Here they remained for fifteen months. François-René's parents had decided that he should go to boarding-school next year at the college of Dol, to learn mathematics, drawing, the use of arms, and English in preparation for a career in the king's navy. So at least his father hoped, remembering how more than forty years ago he had waited in vain for the brevet from Paris. But Mme de Chateaubriand plotted that her son should also be taught Latin and Greek in secret, and then feel a vocation for the Church. Perhaps François-René was given a private tutor during this year, possibly the Nicolas Savary with whom he later lodged. But his conduct was not altogether reformed, for the Gilberts remembered him at this period locked in disgrace in the garret of no. 4, lit only by the skylight to which he climbed, and gazed at the immense sea-horizon, and the cliff of the Grand-Bé his grave.

René-Auguste was now fifty-eight. 'M. de Chateaubriand was tall and cold,' wrote his son, 'his nose was aquiline, his lips thin and pale, his eyes deepset and small, green-blue or glaucous, like the eyes of lions or of ancient barbarians. I have never seen such a look as his; when anger rose in it his flashing eyeballs seemed to leave their sockets and shoot out to strike you, like bullets . . . One's feeling on seeing him was of fear.' Except in such explosions of fury René-Auguste was habitually silent, and his profound sadness only increased with age. His face wore the bewildered look of a man who has done his utmost and has found it not enough.

The eight years since François-René's birth had been a time of gradual failure and relinquishment of old enterprises, and desperate, unsuccessful efforts in new. René-Auguste decided to send no more ships to the Grand Banks, and found after balancing his books in 1770 that the six fishing campaigns of 1764–9 had resulted in a loss of 41,855 livres.

Slave-trading, despite the zealous captaincy of his brother Pierre, was little less disappointing. The sugar-planters of San Domingo paid partly in cash but mostly in promises to be redeemed on the next voyage, or the one after, or later still. The *Saint-René*'s campaign of 1768–9 still showed a loss when accounts were closed seventeen years later, after René-Auguste's death in 1786. A superb profit of 111,000 livres was made in 1770–1, the best in all his career as a slaver, but only 57,000 in 1772–3, when the returning *Saint-René* was driven by storm to Le Havre and had to be sold there.

Meanwhile he had sold the old *Jean-Baptiste* in 1769, and built another, to exchange slaves from Mozambique for coffee at the Ile-Bourbon in the Indian Ocean. But on its second voyage in 1773 this new *Jean-Baptiste* was driven ashore in a hurricane; the honest and foolish skipper was drowned, and the wily second-in-command proved to be a rogue, having engaged in private trade in collusion with René-Auguste's chief clerk. When the enterprise of the *Jean-Baptiste* was finally liquidated in 1785 it showed a loss of 93,000 livres.

In a last burst of activity René-Auguste bought the large *Roi de Juda* in 1773, with room, if one could call it room, for 500 slaves. But how was a profit to be made from slaving when, as happened in the *Roi de Juda*'s campaign of 1774–6, only 394 negroes could be bought for a ship made to hold 500, and of these 89 died of smallpox on the voyage? Even so, Pierre could only arrange for the sale of the survivors by employing a commission agent, against René-Auguste's strict orders and greatly to the annoyance of his accredited agents, MM Blanchardon and Bellot. When Pierre returned to Saint-Malo on 16 June 1776, disappointed and broken in health, René-Auguste tactlessly but not unkindly showed him their angry letters. Pierre flew into a white rage and left, slamming the door. He never went to sea again, and though René-Auguste refrained from further reproach the rift between the brothers was never quite healed.

René-Auguste surveyed the fifteen years of toil and anxiety since the purchase of Combourg in 1761. Corsairing had brought him wealth: already in that last year but one of the Seven Years' War he had possessed some 565,000 livres, of which Combourg cost 370,000.[15] But his subsequent profits had gone mostly to cancel his losses. He was now worth 235,000 livres in capital, together with other sums invested with his old friends, the merchant house of Villesboinet at Nantes; in fifteen years he had gained less than 100,000 livres. Destiny had mocked him; such a success was indistinguishable from failure; he had come to the end of the road on which he had set out forty-two years before, when his mother said: 'Till thy field.'

War with England was brewing and would put an end to trade, though he thought for a moment of turning to corsairing again. Heaven indeed, if he might judge by results, sternly condemned fishing and honest trade, favoured even slaving only once in four times, and reserved its blessing for licensed piracy! But where was his vanished youth, and where his lost ships? No, the game was up, he would retire, live as a country nobleman at Combourg, marry his daughters, establish his sons, and wait for death. Still, it was desirable for both parties, he reflected, that Mme de Chateaubriand should be able to spend the winters without him in Saint-Malo, and that even he should go there for Lent in order to eat fresh fish. He bought a small house at 479, Rue des Grands-Degrés, with panelled drawing-room and dining-room for her modest sociabilities, but no business offices for himself. M. Desportes, his last clerk, could forward his diminished correspondence.

Ever since 1763 René-Auguste had made brief summer visits to Combourg, where M. de Duras had left the castle in decay and the seigneury in disorder. In those days there were only three beds in the castle, and when the Count brought a friend to stay the bailiff had to sleep out. He harried his peasants, drove their pigs from his woods, stopped their fishing in his lake, gaoled them for bribing his game-keepers, ejected bad tenants and engaged new, enclosed waste land and made enfeoffments from it in scores, gave minute sums to charity; and yet the wretched creatures persisted in dying of starvation from the succession of bad harvests which followed the great storm, and the consequent epidemics of smallpox and dysentery. In the one year 1773 there were 330 deaths, a tenth of the parish of Combourg. The pave-ment of the main street was in urgent need of renewal, but who was to pay, the townsfolk, the lord, or the province? A four-cornered legal wrangle with the town council, the Estates, and the highways commiss-ioners began in 1766 and continued for twenty years; it was as exas-perating, delightful and insoluble as the affair of M. de Trévégat's cow; neither René-Auguste nor any other party won or lost, but the pave-ment was never mended. These rural pursuits convinced him that Combourg might be as pleasant and bracing as Saint-Malo. In the stricken year of 1773, and again in 1775 and 1776, he spent summer and autumn there, occasionally accompanied by his wife, supervising the renovation and refurnishing of the castle. Their last winter in Saint-Malo was busy with final preparations; he announced their removal for the spring of 1777. A place was booked for François-René at the College of Dol. With a child's egocentricity he interpreted this change of home and school as a punishment for his misbehaviour.

Pierre, not to be outdone, bought a château of his own for 98,000 livres on 18 October 1777. Val-Guildo with its estate of nine farms lay on the left bank of the Arguenon estuary, six miles north of Plancoët. The manor-house had been burned by the marauding English from Saint-Cast in 1758, and only the west wing remained habitable. Pierre rebuilt the blackened ruins, and removed to this new home in 1779. François-René's grandmother Dame Perronnelle, 'our old Mama', as René-Auguste wrote tenderly of her to Pierre, died there on 22 October 1781, aged eighty-nine; she had left Dinan in 1775 to live with Pierre's family in Saint-Malo, where François-René remembered the old lady, 'still with fine eyes smiling in the twilight of her youth'. So he lost for a time his cousin playmates. Stanislas became a page of the young queen, Marie-Antoinette, in 1779, and Armand was sent to college at Dinan to study unwillingly for the priesthood.

René-Auguste went to Combourg early in April, before the trees were green. Mme de Chateaubriand and the children lingered in Saint-Malo for the state visit of the king's youngest brother, the Comte d'Artois, from 11 to 13 May. 'Your Highness, the visits of princes are very dear,' said the bishop Mgr. des Laurents, and it was felt that his words contained an innuendo. The town spared no expense in entertaining the royal spendthrift with a mock seafight, which François-René watched from the northern ramparts opposite the Grand-Bé. The eight-year-old boy saw the nineteen-year-old prince, last and most insolent of the doomed Bourbons, walking in the crowd on the sands below: 'in his brilliance and my obscurity, what destinies lay hidden!'

At sunrise on 14 May 1777, in the great family coach with gilded mouldings, upholstered in crimson velvet, drawn by eight horses with jingling bells, they left for Combourg.

3

COMBOURG CASTLE

A S THEY drove through the Breton spring the four girls chattered
breathlessly, Mme de Chateaubriand heaved deep sighs of grief
and resentment for the loss of Saint-Malo, and the chevalier remained
silent, all eyes and ears in rapture at his journey into the unknown.
They crossed the Sillon, passed the gibbet of Paramé, changed horizons
as they climbed the plateau to the bay of Cancale, saw the dim pyramid
of Mont Saint-Michel far in the east, and halted to rest the horses and
dine at Le Vivier by the sandy shore. Then they turned southward
inland, through the fevered marshlands of Dol with their osiered rhines
and reedbeds below sea-level, past the mysterious red cliff of Mont-Dol,
once an islet in the sea, now wreathed in blossoming apple trees 'like
the nosegays of village brides'. At Dol they rolled by the prison-gate of
the college which François-René was condemned to enter a fortnight
later. The landscape rose and harshened, through heaths and woods,
gorse and broom, with patches of neglected fallow and starved oat-
fields. Charcoal-burners led files of shaggy ponies with tangled manes;
longhaired peasants in goatskins drove gaunt oxen with shrill cries, or
plodded behind lumbering wagons. At last, by the crossroads called
Terre-Rouge on the uplands of Les Fresches, they paused on the crest
of a downward slope: they saw below them, still four miles away, a
little town, a church-spire, a lake, a mound with a beechgrove lit by the
setting sun, and rising from these trees the four towers of a feudal castle.

'I have been obliged to stop,' wrote Chateaubriand, 'my heart was
beating so violently that it thrust away the table on which I am writing,
and made my hand tremble. The memories now awakening in my mind
overwhelm me with their force and multitude; and yet, what are they
to the rest of the world?'

Half an hour later they left the highroad and turned right, up an
alley of overarching hornbeams, so dark that the boy never forgot his
sensation of fear as they entered and joy when they emerged. They
drove past the bailiff's house, through a gateway in the wall, and left
up a sloping oblong lawn, the Green Court; and there before them was
the stern north front of Combourg castle, between two great round
towers capped by conical roofs, with a steep flight of twenty-nine steps
leading over the dry moat to the entrance doorway. René-Auguste hurried down in the twilight to meet them, his sad face wreathed in unaccustomed smiles. They climbed the stairway, passed through the

echoing vestibule and a gloomy inner courtyard, and sat down to supper in the guardroom. At Saint-Malo François-René would be sent hungry to bed if he refused to eat what he was given; when his father's eyes were turned he would beg La France with an imploring gaze to take his plate away. Now he ate without constraint and decided, forgetting Plancoët, that this had been the first journey and the first happy day of his life. Ever afterwards he was to seek happiness, and stranger still to find it, in travel. Next morning as soon as he woke he went out to explore his new domain.

The castle of Combourg[1] was founded in 1037 by Ginguené, arch-bishop of Dol, who gave it to his brother Rivallon Grey-Goat to pro-tect the southern approaches of his bishopric in the marches between Normandy and Brittany. Rivallon was a lucky lord. When besieged at Dol by Conan Duke of Brittany in 1064 he was rescued by none other than William of Normandy, as the whole world has seen in the Bayeux Tapestry.When Conan sacked Combourg next year in reprisal Rivallon escaped with his life. One day he was luckier still. As he walked by the Fontaine de Margatte, a spring which feeds the lake of Combourg from the northeast, he found a little old gentleman only twelve inches high, with his beard entangled in a thornbush. In return for his release the gnome confided that a white stone lay there, which had the property of quelling the waters. Soon afterwards Rivallon Grey-Goat spoke harshly to an old woman, who declared she would flood the valley for ven-geance. The lake rose as a violent torrent gushed from the Fontaine de Margatte; but Rivallon hastened to the thornbush, hurled the white stone into the fountain, and the waters subsided. No inundations have occurred since then, but if anyone should remove the magic stone from the Fontaine de Margatte the valley of Combourg would be flooded again. The seigneury remained with the house of Dol-Combour until 1162, and passed by marriage through the families of Combour-Soligné (1162–1340), Châteaugiron-Malestroit (1340–1506), and Montejean-Acigné (1506–53), before reaching the Coëtquens in 1553. The Duc de Duras married Maclovie, last of the Coëtquens and thirty-first owner of Combourg since Rivallon, in 1739,[2] and sold it to René-Auguste de Chateaubriand in 1761. This was the first and last time that Combourg has changed hands by sale.

François-René later believed, exaggeratedly but not quite incorrectly, that Combourg had once belonged to the Chateaubriands of Beaufort by intermarriage with the Coëtquens, and that it was for this reason his father had chosen to buy it.[3] In fact, no male Chateaubriand had ever owned Combourg; yet the family archives showed that from the four-teenth to the sixteenth centuries the Chateaubriands had frequently been linked, both feudally and by marriage, with the Coëtquens and earlier lords of Combourg.[4] It need not be doubted that René-Auguste (though he declared he bought it without seeing it or even knowing where it was) acquired Combourg with particular pride in its former connections with his ancestors.

Surprised by joy at living in a castle, the chevalier went out into the May morning. His new home, he found, consisted of four round towers joined by curtain-walls, 'like a cart with four wheels', inside which the living and other rooms formed a hollow square around the inner court-yard. The main front, battlemented, crumbling and lichened, faced northwest between the two highest towers, looking down the stairway over the walled Green Court to the kitchen-garden and the surrounding mysterious woods. The wood on the right was the Petit Mail or Little Mall, through which he had driven yesterday evening along the horn-beam arcade. The wood on the left, of oaks, beeches, sycamores, elms and chestnuts, was the Grand Mail or Great Mall, 'in which,' he wrote, 'I spent my youth'.

The north tower or Tour de l'Horloge, built in the thirteenth century as the original donjon-keep, was the oldest and highest of all and con-tained, halfway up its interior staircase, a clock that struck the hours. The west tower, or Tour du Marquis, built by Geoffroy de Malestroit towards 1450 and named after a later Coëtquen, was nearly as high and stouter still. The two smaller towers on the far side, facing southeast over the lake, were both of the fourteenth century; the one on the east corner was called Tour Madame or Lady's Tower, the one on the south Tour du Garde-Meuble or Wardrobe Tower.[5] All was granite, and built on a rock of granite. 'Everywhere silence, darkness, and face of stone: that was the castle of Combourg.'

Above the doorway were the sculptured arms of the lords of Com-bourg and the slits through which had passed, long ago, the chains of their drawbridge. To the left of the vestibule as one entered was the chapel, where Mme de Chateaubriand prayed every afternoon between dinner and supper, and René-Auguste heard mass every Sunday served by his chaplain, Abbé Chalmel; to the right was the square dark kitchen. The inner courtyard, forty feet by twenty-two and surrounded by blank fifty-foot walls, contained a well, 'of immeasurable depth', piercing the rock down to water-level, and to the left of the entrance, a spiral stair-case of granite leading to the upper floors. On the far side of the court-yard, between the two lesser towers, was the former guardroom, used as both the dining-room and the drawing-room of the family; they dined and supped at the east or left end, and then sat by the huge fire-place at the right or west end. This enormous room was dimly lit by four wedgeshaped alcoves, one at each end and two in the long outer wall, cut ten feet deep through the masonry and ending in narrow windows, which looked east over the town, west upon the stables and a terrace bordered with trimmed box-trees, and south over the lake and the highroad to Rennes. It was panelled with oak painted grey-white, and adorned with ancient portraits, a relic of the Coëtquens, including the great captains of Louis XIV, Condé and Turenne; over the chimney-piece hung a picture of Achilles slaying Hector under the walls of Troy. At either end were sloping corridors, 'like the corridor in the Great Pyramid', one ascending to René-Auguste's austere bedroom in the east tower, the other to his study in the south tower, above which was a bedroom reserved for Uncle Antoine de Bédée on his visits.

Over the great living-room, from which it was reached by a narrow winding staircase in the east tower, was Mme de Chateaubriand's own luxurious bedroom, adjoined by smaller rooms for the girls. François-René slept far from all these in an eery cell between the top of the spiral staircase in the courtyard and the east tower. From his window could be seen only the opposite crenellated wall of the court, where a wild plumtree grew among pendulous hart's-tongue ferns. At night the wind bellowed in the cellars beneath, and then roared up the twisting funnel of the stairs to beat against his door. Somewhere below him was the bedroom kept for Jean-Baptiste on his rare visits home from his law-school at Rennes. On the first floor at the north front was Queen Christine's Room, a state bedroom for guests in the north tower; another guest-room above the chapel, with a ceiling painted with birds and coats of arms, variously called the Armorial Room, the Bird Room, or the Knights' Room; a billiard-room above the kitchen; and in the west tower (which was hence sometimes called Tour des Archives), a room with six iron cupboards where René-Auguste kept and lovingly perused his seigneurial documents.

Far above by the eaves one could walk all round the castle along the outer battlements. From here, with only turrets, swallows and clouds above him, the chevalier looked down on the woods, the roofs of the town, the lake and its swans, the watermill, the castle meadow dotted with cows, the priory with the tomb of its founder Rivallon Grey-Goat, the woods again. Beyond all these the landscape rose in a shallow amphitheatre, green with pastures, blue with forests, purple and yellow with heaths, pricked with village spires and chimney-tops of the local gentry's manor-houses, to a near horizon of low hills. The furthest landmark, only fifteen miles away, was the domed crest and church-tower of Bécherel to the southwest, not far from his father's birthplace at Guitté. But every horizon, however near, calls the gazing young to the ends of the world. Past those placid hills to the north was the sea, Jersey, England; to the west, the ocean and America; to the south, Spain and Italy and North Africa; to the east, Flanders, Prague, Jerusalem. Perhaps he would see all those places one day. A fortnight later Abbé Portier, headmaster of the college, arrived and took him, weeping, to Dol.

As he soon found, there was no great cause for tears. The pleasant town of Dol, walled and moated, with its great cathedral, stands on the first ridge of the inland plateau, at the edge of vast marshlands stretching northward to the sea, east to Mont Saint-Michel, west to the Rance at Chateauneuf within ten miles of Saint-Malo. The bishop, Mgr. de Hercé, was a friend of the family, and in the cathedral itself was a front stall, next to the bishop's own, founded by Guillaume de Chateaubriand de Beaufort in 1529 and bearing his gold lily arms.[6] The college was built in 1728–37 in Saint-Jacques's Fields, just outside the southern wall of the town on the right of the highroad to Rennes. The main building, containing the rooms of staff and boarders, had two forward wings, with classrooms in the left wing and chapel and refectory in the right, forming a square entrance-court with two fine acacias on either side of the gate. At the back was a garden with flower-beds, enclosed by a hornbeam hedge trimmed into arbours. The school year lasted from October to the end of July. There were six teachers, all in holy orders, one each for the two top classes in philosophy and rhetoric and the second to fourth classes, while the junior master took the little boys in the fifth and sixth together. There were about a hundred day-boys, but fewer than a dozen boarders, whose parents paid a fee of 230 livres a year.

His masters, he found, were youngish, amiable and cultivated priests, who well understood boys and the art of discipline through kindness. His headmaster, Abbé Joseph Portier, aged thirty-eight, who was also a canon of the cathedral, was learned, gentle and simple-hearted. François-René, having missed all but two months of the school year, needed special instruction to fit him for promotion from the sixth to the fifth class next October. He was put in the charge of Abbé Joseph Leprince, master of the rhetoric class and an accomplished geometrician, who taught him mathematics from the manuals of the famous Bezout. M. Leprince was witty and handsome, fond of the arts, and a passable portrait-painter, though afflicted, poor man, with a weak chest. Abbé Julien Égault, regent of the third class, taught him Latin; M. Égault was a disciplinarian with a sense of humour, newly ordained, aged only twenty-five, and despite some differences of opinion on matters of conduct they got on very well together.

His schoolfellows were peaceable enough; if they had been otherwise, they would not have daunted the child warrior who, at Gesril's side, had fought the Arm-Breakers beneath the ramparts of Saint-Malo. In their games he refused to lead or be led: 'I was incapable of being either tyrant or slave, and so I have always remained.' He lacked the advantages of wealth in making friends, for his small allowance was soon spent, and he had no weekly pocket-money like the day-boys. And yet, to his astonishment, he found himself popular, a centre of

attraction, and modestly attributed this success to his 'ability to enter
the minds and adopt the ways of others'. But schoolboys, in fact, are as
quick as grown men to detect the presence in their midst of a veiled
wanderer. He was equally surprised to find that work, for him, was a
delight, that his memory was exceptionally powerful. The rudiments of
Latin cost him no pains, and he made swift progress in mathematics,
amazing Abbé Leprince by his 'clarity of conception'. As for discipline,
'it took some time for an owl of my species to grow used to the cage of
school, and to regulate his flight to the sound of a bell'; but he grew
used nevertheless. All this was enough for one term.

His school-holidays at Combourg were 'one long bout of play', for
Combourg was not always dark and solitary. He made his first acquaintance with the local notables, who came to dinner in the castle after
attending Sunday morning mass in the parish church. There was the
bailiff, François Maillard de la Morandais, whose wife was a cousin of
Mme de Chateaubriand; the seneschal, M. Gesbert de la Noé-Seiche;
the procurator fiscal René Petit; M. Petit's future father-in-law the
excise-officer M. Launay de la Bliardière,[7] who had thirteen children, so
that his house was 'full of merriment and debts', and whose son David
became François-René's playmate;[8] the notary Julien Le Corvaisier,
who was to salvage the wreck of Combourg in the Revolution at the
risk of his life; and the squires of neighbouring manors, René-Auguste's
vassals, MM. du Petitbois, de Château-d'Assis, and de Trémaudan.
François-René noticed that M. de Trémaudan had an extremely pretty
wife. The rector of Combourg, Abbé Sévin, took him on his lap after
his Sunday sermons, and could not believe, many years later, that the
celebrated defender of the Christian religion was none other than the
young rascal and companion of peasant boys whom they had all called
the Little Chevalier; however, once convinced, he made a point of
quoting the *Génie du Christianisme* in his homilies. The wealthiest citizen
of Combourg was M. Potelet, a retired India merchant, whose wife had
once been engaged to Gesril's uncle. At dinner in the castle M. Potelet
enthralled François-René with tales of Pondicherry and the marvels of
the East, but infuriated his host by always leaning his elbows on the
table. 'I'd like to throw my plate in his face!' declared René-Auguste.

One new friendship of this summer left a darker memory. The gamekeeper Raulx took a fancy to the little chevalier and led him about the
woods of Combourg, but not long after was shot by a poacher. Raulx
gathered his gushing entrails in his hands and crawled to a nearby
cottage, where he died. François-René imagined this hideous scene
with grief and anger, and longed to take vengeance on the murderer.
He decided, to his horror, that he brought misfortune upon his friends,
and that he had a revengeful nature, truly enough. And yet, he could no
more have averted the later calamities of his friends than he could have

prevented the murder of Raulx, while his desires of vengeance were generally roused by the wrongs of others, not his own, and he never put them into action. 'I am unforgiving, but I am not vindictive,' he wrote. However, the reality of death and violence had entered, from the beginning, the dream world of Combourg.

Like many other feudal lords during the last generation before the Revolution, René-Auguste thought it his right and duty to revive the waning country sports of the Middle Ages. On Easter Monday the vendors of Lenten fish from his lake had to jump into its waters and wrestle waist-deep, watched by peasants in sabots and sheepskins, with long flowing hair. On Whit Tuesday, along a sunken lane in the Great Mall, newly married husbands tilted on horseback at the quintain, supervised by the bailiff, with prizes for winners and forfeits for losers, while their wives vaulted over the cemetery wall in the priory below, singing:

> *'If I am married, that you know well;*
> *If I am happy, that I shan't tell;*
> *My song is o'er,*
> *I owe you no more.'*

These folk amusements were no doubt much enjoyed by spectators and participants alike.

But the great festivity of the year at Combourg was the immemorial fair of L'Angevine, held in the castle meadow below the lake, and so called because merchants came all the way from Anjou to attend it. By a happy coincidence it began on François-René's birthday, 4 September, and ended on the 7th, eve of the Nativity of the Blessed Virgin and anniversary of his release from his vow. As he wandered through the stalls, amid cider and sweetmeats, sausages and pig's fry, acrobats and fortune-tellers, greeted by all the townsfolk as the little Chevalier, the fair seemed almost his own. The vassals paraded at the castle to raise the lord's banner, then dispersed to keep the peace and enforce collection of the lord's dues; torches blazed every night outside the house of the Lantern in the main street. René-Auguste kept open table, and admitted all to his gardens and woods. For three days everyone sang, cheered, fired guns, and danced, the gentry in the guardroom to a violin, the peasantry in the Green Court to bagpipes. 'Once a year, at least, something like joy could be seen at Combourg.'

In October he returned regretfully to Dol, obtained his promotion from sixth class to fifth, and early in 1778 was top of the form. During the next summer holidays at Combourg he made a delightful journey to Saint-Malo with the bailiff, M. de la Morandais, the impoverished but wellborn cousin by marriage of Mme de Chateaubriand, whom René-Auguste had appointed to this post out of family goodwill in

1768. France had joined the American War of Independence against England, and an army was encamped on the sand-dunes of Rochebonne near Paramé. The good bailiff, in his grey felt cap and humble coat of shoddy with a single silver galloon on the collar, sat the enraptured François-René astride on the crupper of his yellow mare, clinging to the belt of his hunting-knife. They rode along the bridleway through Lanhélin and Miniac-Morvan to Chateauneuf, and stopped to dine, ten miles northwest of Combourg, at the ancient Benedictine abbey of Le Tronchet. Even here they were on home ground, for Le Tronchet had been founded by the lords of Combourg in the twelfth century, and René-Auguste counted as an honorary founder-benefactor; too late, for in that age of enlightenment the abbey was closing for want of monks. Only a single sad father remained, charged with selling furniture and timber. He gave them a sumptuous meal of newlaid eggs, carp and pike, in the prior's deserted library; and as they ate the boy saw with a pang, through a cloister arch and beyond the lake, the tall sycamores quiver one by one, bow their crests, and roar to the ground. The camp at Rochebonne was better fun; he saw the streets of tents, stacked muskets, tethered cavalry-horses, fighting men waiting for the English who never came, and in the distance the spires of Saint-Malo and the glittering sea.

After two terms in the fourth form at Dol he spent the Easter holidays of 1779 with his mother and sisters at Saint-Malo, where on 13 April he attended the wedding of his beloved Villeneuve, now aged forty, to an honest plumber, Julien Odap, a widower with four children, and signed the register, along with his sister Bénigne. The boy was too ailing to return to college, and the others had to leave at René-Auguste's order for Combourg; so against his will they boarded him out, lest his education should suffer, with a writing-master, Nicolas Savary. In June, as if in self-defence, he fell ill with measles followed by swollen glands, and was nursed by Mme Odap in her new home. The doctor, M. de la Chapelle, declared he must do no work for two months, and abetted him, along with René-Auguste's clerk M. Desportes, in thwarting his aunt Mme du Plessis's efforts to send him back to M. Savary.

Saint-Malo was more amusing than ever in that summer. The Prince de Nassau arrived with fifteen hundred men for a raid on Jersey, followed by the Comte de Vaux with thirty thousand for the invasion of England. Jersey was not raided, because of bad weather; England was not invaded, because the Spanish fleet failed to keep its rendezvous with the French; but every day by the seafront there were mock landings and sham attacks, watched by fine ladies from Paris on their chairs along the ramparts. One day he saw a rider in hussar's uniform galloping past on a Barbary charger: it was that great warrior and lover the Duc de Lauzun, 'one of those men in whom a world was ending'.[9]

Even Jean-Baptiste came to see the sport from Rennes, where his student days were now over; René-Auguste had just bought him a post as counsellor in Parlement for 29,000 livres. One evening in July this kind stuffy elder brother said to his junior: 'Get your hat, I'm taking you to the play!' François-René was so bewildered with joy that he went down to the cellar to fetch his hat, before remembering he had left it in the attic. The old theatre of Saint-Malo had been burned down on 27 October 1778, and it was in a temporary wooden building that they passed through alarming dark corridors, opened a little door, and found themselves in a half-filled box by the stage. He waited impatiently for the marionette-show to begin; for having hitherto seen only Punch and Judy, he supposed that a theatre was a place where one could watch much finer puppets than in the streets. To his annoyance and embarrassment the stage was occupied only by two men who walked up and down talking in loud voices about their own private affairs; others came in, including ladies, and made extraordinary gesticulations; one began to cry, and soon all were sobbing. The curtain fell, leaving him still baffled. He had witnessed a performance of Diderot's senti-mental drama of middle-class life, Le Père de famille.

Early in August he returned to Combourg castle. Part of the regiment of Conti, under its second-in-command the Marquis de Wignacourt, was billeted all that summer of 1779 at Combourg. Twenty gallant officers dined every day with the family, and every morning to François-René's delight the guard was ceremonially mounted in the Green Court, drum and fifes marching at the head, while he watched from the top of the stairway. But he was displeased to find his woods full of soldiers, and astonished by their strange accents of Auvergne or Gascony: these men must have come, he thought, from the ends of the earth. The officers pained him with their incomprehensible banter, troubled his mind with their talk of Paris and the court. For the first time his inno-cence was disturbed by the glimpse of another world, enticing and terrible in its unknown pleasures and perils. One day as he watched Wignacourt galloping under the trees he felt again the lure of travel, whether to discover this new world, or to find another solitude in place of the one thus marred. Then, with a sense of vertigo as over an abyss, he recoiled in fear, relieved to find he was 'still little François, in the seclusion of my woods, sheltered by my sisters' affection, and under my mother's wing'. The soldiers brought dysentery to Combourg; poor M. de la Morandais died of it on 30 August, and René-Auguste gave the post of bailiff to Julien Le Corvaisier.

After his missed term he worked at Dol in the third form with re-doubled vigour. He began to learn Greek; he composed Latin penta-meters with such facility that Abbé Égault nicknamed him The Elegiac; he knew his tables of logarithms by heart: 'that is to say that, given a number in geometrical proportion, I could produce its exponent in arithmetical proportion from memory, and vice versa'. Another triumph of memory made him the envy of the whole college. Every evening in chapel their headmaster Abbé Portier read a sermon, which he would then call upon some pupil taken at random to summarise. The drowsy boys drooped on their benches, each trying to seem invisible; and a lucky one, who had fought the rest for this coveted refuge and won, was always invisible indeed, fast asleep in the darkest and remotest confession-box. One evening the Abbé detected François-René so ensconced, and determined to make an example of him. 'Monsieur de Chateaubriand,' he demanded, 'what have I just read?' But the culprit, warned by merciful providence or instinct, had stayed awake, and was able to repeat, word for word, Massillon's long and intricate list of the various ways in which God may be offended. Amid a discreet murmur of applause the good man called him up, gave him a tap on the cheek, and announced, by way of making the recompense fit the crime, that he might stay in bed next morning till breakfast-time. 'I modestly withdrew from the admiration of my comrades,' says Chateaubriand, 'and took full advantage of the grace bestowed'.

Early in the new year, on 11 January 1780, François-René attended the double wedding of his two eldest sisters in the chapel of the castle of Combourg. Marie-Anne, aged nineteen, married François-Jean-Joseph Geffelot, Comte de Marigny, aged twenty-five, and Bénigne, aged eighteen, married Jean-François-Xavier, Comte de Québriac, aged thirty-eight. Both gentlemen were captains in the dragoons, amply noble, and resided in fine town mansions (which still survive) at Fougères, thirty miles east of Combourg. René-Auguste gave each bride the handsome dowry of an income of 1,500 livres, the interest at 5 per cent on two capitals of 30,000 livres. On this happy occasion François-René was surprised to see the fortunate girls, and his mother also, in floods of tears. It was true that his sisters were leaving home for ever, and this was the beginning of the end of family union for them all; but for the second time, as when he had listened last summer to the officers from Paris, he felt himself on the brink of the mystery of the adult world. What is the real difference between grown-ups and children?

His question soon began to be answered. The extraordinary but banal chain of events which changes every human boy into a man—the same for any, yet different in each, and for each perhaps the most important happening, the most irreversible and fraught with destiny, of all between birth and death—commenced for him at the unusually early age of eleven and a half. The revelation began with two books which he found by chance at Dol. The first was an unexpurgated Horace; the other was one of the many manuals of confession, elaborated century after century by the mediaeval Church and not intended for lay persons, which classify and describe, with a scientific accuracy unsurpassed till Freud, the immense variety of sexual desires and acts that a good priest must detect and a bad penitent may try to conceal. Thus instructed he knew everything and understood nothing. What were these strange enchantments 'of a sex in which I had hitherto seen only my mother and sisters'?—and why were these multitudes of ghosts burning in eternal hell for the concealment of one sin? As he lay sleepless in the dormitory François-René saw white and black unhallowed hands stealing through the curtains of his bed, and recognised them for the white hands of the temptress and the black hands of the damned. He fell asleep, and soon, in the first dream orgasm of puberty, 'felt the explosion of some sparks from the fire that transmits life'.

In class he was then construing Book Four of the Aeneid and reading Fénelon's *Télémaque*. Suddenly he found himself ravished by Dido's beauty and the charm of Calypso's nymph Eucharis, enraptured too by the harmony of Virgil's hexameters and Fénelon's prose, whose golden cadences would one day resound in his own. One day he translated aloud Lucretius's invocation to Venus—

> '*Aeneadum genetrix, hominum divumque voluptas . . .*'[10]

—with such alarming ardour, that Abbé Égault snatched the book from his hands, and set him to learn Greek verbs. He stole a Tibullus, and found there the image of his own desires in his storm-beaten bedroom under the eaves at Combourg:

> '*Quam juvat inmites ventos audire cubantem*
> *Et dominam tenero detinuisse sinu*'[11]

—except that the Roman's longing was fulfilled, and his own was not. There was no such ban on the edifying works of Massillon; but François-René found beauties unsuspected by his teachers in the lenten sermons on the Prodigal Son and the converted harlot Mary Magdalen,[12] which he read feverishly in his bed by the light of candle-ends robbed from the chapel. Such is the power of Massillon's eloquence that the sins of the flesh seem hardly less seductive than the bliss of repentance, for which, or so an unwary reader might suppose, these sins are shown to be an indispensable preliminary. The story of *René*, indeed, even the whole life of Chateaubriand himself, is already implicit in the romantic agony of Massillon's Prodigal Son. Another primrose bypath was revealed by Virgil's Second Eclogue:

> '*For fair Alexis shepherd Corydon burned . . .*'

Alexis, Abbé Égault lamely explained when the whole class demanded an elucidation, was an unruly pupil, who refused to obey the exhortations of his affectionate teacher! François-René was not convinced by this interpretation, but the subject did not really interest him.

In the same spring he became aware of another of the passions of awakening manhood. On fine Thursdays and Sundays the boys were escorted on walks into the countryside. Sometimes they went to the rocky hillock of Mont-Dol, two miles to the north, and played on the summit turf among prehistoric and Roman remains. A gigantic footprint on a stone near the northern precipice marks the spot whence the Archangel Michael sprang with one leap to Mont Saint-Michel, which they saw far to the east, along the fringe of the sparkling sea. Sometimes they were taken to the meadows of the Eudist seminary at Abbaye-sous-Dol, half a mile southwest of the town on the road to Dinan, by the banks of the little river Guioult.[13] Here one afternoon in May 1780 the prefect for the week, who happened to be Abbé Égault, left them in a grassy lane, with instructions to play as they pleased but on no account to climb trees, while he retired to read his breviary.

The lane was bordered by elms, and far aloft in the highest of these they saw a magpie's nest, with the mother sitting on her eggs. All eyes turned on François-René who, seized by love of glory, took off his coat and began to climb. The poor mother flew away, he seized her six eggs and put them in the bosom of his shirt, and found himself caught in the fork of the tree, fifty feet above ground. A terrible cry arose: 'Here comes the prefect!' All fled, except a boy named Le Gobbien from Saint-Malo, who tried in vain to rescue him, and then joined the rest. Desperately François-René hung from the fork, grasped the trunk with his legs, and slid to the ground, grazing knees and hands and smashing the eggs. He wiped away the blood, but could not hide the vivid yellow stain of egg-yolk. 'Well, sir,' said Abbé Égault, 'you shall be whipped.' 'Neither you nor any other man,' declared François-René, 'shall ever raise a hand against me.' The angry priest called him rebel, and vowed to make an example of him. 'We shall see,' replied the proud culprit, and with pretended indifference joined his friends in their ball-game. But back in college, in the Abbé's room, he broke down in uncontrollable tears. The Abbé, he pointed out, had taught him Latin; François-René was his pupil, his child; he might confine him on bread and water, load him with impositions, and he would thank him for his mercy and love him the more; but he could not dishonour him so! The Abbé remained implacable; François-René kicked him on the shins with all his might and then, while the worthy priest, limping heavily, aimed ineffectual blows across the bed with his cane, wrapped himself in the coverlet and shouted:

'*Macte animo, generose puer!*'[14]

This display of erudition tickled M. Égault's sense of humour. He laughed and proposed an armistice: they should submit their difference of opinion to the headmaster. That indulgent man, without positively declaring that François-René was in the right, decided he should be spared his richly deserved caning; and when the boy kissed the sleeve of his gown in a passion of gratitude, he could not forbear giving him his blessing. It might be argued that the teacher stood in greater need of protection against the pupil than the pupil against the teacher. However, in this burlesque incident François-René recognised a second stage in the advent of manhood, the resolve not to be put to shame. 'Such was the first battle I fought in defence of that honour which has become the idol of my life, and for which I have so many times sacrificed my repose, my happiness, and my fortune.'

His summer holidays at Combourg were less merry than before. Abbé Leprince was invited to give him extra tuition in mathematics, and followed him everywhere, melancholy and taciturn, for the unfortunate man was now dying of consumption.[15] One evening, after walking side by side for hours without a word, they found themselves lost in the forest northwest of Combourg. 'Which way shall we go?' asked M. Leprince, and François-René answered without hesitation: 'The sun is setting; at this moment it will be striking the window of the west tower; we must go this way!' The delighted M. Leprince made a point of telling René-Auguste of his son's feat of navigation; but the stern father rejected his proposal that François-René should be given a horse, considering that a future naval officer need only know how to manage a ship. So the boy was reduced to stolen rides on their fat carriage-horses, and on Piebald, a vicious black and white mare, who kicked when trotting, and turned round to bite him in the legs when asked to jump a ditch. He never learned to ride well; 'my seat,' he confesses, 'is elegant rather than secure'; and in his accounts of his travels it may be noticed that, although he rode many thousands of miles on horseback, he fell off rather frequently.

Soon François-René was liberated from M. Leprince by a sharp attack of malaria, which he had brought home with him from the marshlands of Dol. René-Auguste had no faith in doctors but believed firmly in quacks. He took the opportunity of sending for a particularly blatant impostor, Pierre Fournet, newly arrived in Combourg during the previous winter with his apparent wife, who had produced a boy baby in May. M. Fournet, jabbering away in the patois of his native Dauphiny, and dressed in a goldtrimmed green coat with slightly soiled muslin sleeves, a huge powdered wig, and loads of false diamond rings, swore to cure him within twenty-four hours. He flung wide the bedcurtains, felt François-René's pulse, made him put his tongue out, said he needed purging, and popped a morsel of medicated caramel into his mouth.

René-Auguste was delighted, convinced as he was that all illness was caused by indigestion, and could be cured by purging till the blood came. Half an hour later François-René was seized with dreadful vomitings. M. Fournet waved his arms in wild despair, while his wig spun round like a teetotum; every time François-René screamed he screamed too, till René-Auguste threatened to have him thrown out of the window. At last he burbled: *'Che, monsou Lavandier?'* M. Le Lavandier, the long-established apothecary-surgeon of Combourg, was sent for in haste, and soon set François-René to rights. But poor M. Fournet had to be investigated; it was discovered that he was not really married, so the rector, having already baptised his bastard, made good this omission. In the wedding-register the belated bridegroom is described as 'herbal doctor', but an unknown hand has written 'Charlatan' in the margin.

François-René, now aged twelve, spent his fifth and last school-year at Dol in the second form, working hard at mathematics, Greek and Latin, and playing no less strenuously at the same games of ball and hoop which he later found among the Red Indian and Bedouin young. One winter morning the school porter summoned him to the gate from an animated game of prisoner's base in the front court. In the highroad stood a big redfaced priest, with a walking-staff in his hand, wearing an unkempt black wig, a torn soutane tucked up into his pockets, dusty shoes, and stockings with holes in the heels. 'Little rascal,' cried this irascible man, 'are you not the Chevalier de Chateaubriand of Combourg?' 'Yes, Monsieur,' replied François-René, polite and puzzled. 'And I,' bawled the stranger, foaming with inexplicable rage, 'am the last of the senior line of your family; I am the Abbé de Chateaubriand de Bellestre; take a good look at me!' And from the waist-pocket of his threadbare plush breeches he produced a mouldering six-franc piece wrapped in dirty paper, hurled it in his wondering nephew's face, and plodded off on his way, muttering his matins with the same air of furious wrath. René-Auguste, not content with helping in the incarceration of the Abbé's ne'erdowell brother in 1774 to oblige him, had canvassed his application to the Estates of 1778–9 for a retirement pension, which the Estates of 1780–1 had just granted; hence Charles-Hilaire's indignant desire to show that he, too, knew how to do the handsome thing, and that the Chateaubriands of Bellestre were every bit as good as the Chateaubriands of Combourg. They were certainly as proud. According to family rumour, the Abbé had been invited by the Prince de Condé some fifteen years before to become the tutor of his little son, the Duc de Bourbon; to which the outraged Charles-Hilaire had replied that the Prince, of all people—seeing that the barony of Chateaubriand had passed into his family[16]—ought to be aware that a Chateaubriand could *have* a tutor, but could not possibly *be* one. 'This

haughtiness,' confesses Chateaubriand with irony, 'was our family failing; it was odious in my father, absurd in my elder brother, and I am
not altogether sure, despite my republican leanings, that I have entirely
succeeded in shedding it myself, though I have taken pains to conceal
it.'[17]

The time of his first communion, the precursory coming of age when
the child is declared old enough to eat the flesh of his Saviour, was
drawing near. François-René's abstinences that Lent were thought wellnigh excessive; the whole college was edified, and his teachers tried to
curb the fervour of his devotion. But his confessor, Father Pierre
Delaunay, the fifty-year-old and stern-seeming superior of the Eudist
seminary, had doubts, for the boy's air of anxious guilt seemed incompatible with the trivial nature of the faults he admitted. 'Are you hiding
anything from me, my son?' 'No, father.' 'Have you committed this
fault, or that?' 'No, father.' The priest dismissed him with a sigh, and
a gaze that seemed to pierce to the depths of his soul; and François-
René left with the pale, distorted face of a criminal.

On Tuesday in Holy Week, 10 April 1781, Mme de Chateaubriand
arrived to witness the Christian triumph of her son. François-René
spent the night in hopeless prayer and a terrified reperusal of the forbidden confession manual, this time in order to discover not the sins he
might wish to commit, but the eternal punishments on whose brink he
now stood. Next afternoon, when the schoolboy communicants set off
with their parents to Abbaye-sous-Dol for the final confession and
absolution, Mme de Chateaubriand walked beside him, displaying the
love and pride in her son which she manifested only in such moments
of intersection between his worldly life and the mysteries of religion.
He trudged guilty through the innocent spring. Father Delaunay
awaited him in the sacristy, where he confessed as imperfectly as before,
with halting voice and trembling knees. 'Well, have you not forgotten
anything?'; and: 'No, father,' he still repeated. The troubled priest had
already raised his hand in the absolving gesture which to François-René
signified endless damnation, when at last he cried: 'I have not told
everything!' His terrible judge, melting into tears, embraced him and
said: 'Now, my dear son, have courage.' So François-René told all,
sobbing with happy relief. The wise priest was not surprised by his sins,
which were the same as any other boy's, but by the depth of ardour
with which this extraordinary boy had pursued them at so tender an
age, by the obstinate pride of his concealment, and the violence of his
shame. 'He was the first to detect the secret of what I might one day be.
He divined my future passions and, without hiding the good he thought
he saw in me, warned me of the ills to come.' Father Delaunay, still
doubtful, pronounced an absolution he would have preferred to post-
pone, and François-René emerged with head held high, buoyant step

and radiant air, to fling himself into his mother's arms. Next day, on Maundy Thursday 12 April 1781, he took his first communion. His unregenerate self retired, after noticing with resentment that his comrades' clothes and nosegays were finer than his own; and now his one care was to avoid profaning the holy wafer by letting it cleave to his palate. God had forgiven him. At that blissful moment, as he wrote, he 'understood the courage of the martyrs, and would have proclaimed Christ on the rack or among the lions in the arena'. Strangely enough, however, his first full confession was also his last. It was as though the living God, in pardoning his first adolescent desires, had accepted in advance the lifelong passions to which they would lead. It would be blasphemy to suppose that God could change His mind, or ever require a renewal of this licence. Their next settling of accounts would be beyond the grave, and he would await it without dread. Meanwhile, for nearly twenty years to come, he allowed the fervour of his faith to wane, secure in his immunity.

A last sacrament remained before he entered the longed-for storms of early manhood. His father had decided that he must attend the more advanced college of Rennes in the final stages of his education for the navy; so he left Dol, with affectionate regret for the kindly priests and his schoolmates,[18] several weeks before the end of the summer term. A confirmation mission was held at Combourg from 1 to 23 July 1781; he joined the classes, and on the last day was confirmed, along with the peasant boys and girls his contemporaries, by Mgr. des Laurents, Bishop of Saint-Malo, at the top of the stairway above the Green Court.[19] Then they all trooped along the edge of the moat to the foot of the east tower, where opposite his father's bedroom, a few paces down the steep bank overlooking the highroad and the lake, they raised a tall commemorative cross of wood. François-René helped to steady it while the socket was filled in; his father saw it every morning when he woke, no doubt with mixed feelings, for this was his son's cross, but his son was *his* cross; it survived the Revolution and still remained, toppling outward and mossgrown, for Baron Taylor to see and draw during his picturesque tour of France towards 1830. On this occasion, in accordance with custom, François-René was given an additional christian name: Auguste, after his father, or, as he himself sadly believed, after the little brother who had died in the winter before his own birth. He later used all three names in legal documents,[20] and signed his works as François-Auguste;[21] but he kept René as the name of his secret self, as the name of his future hero. At the beginning of October, a few weeks after his thirteenth birthday, thus renamed and confirmed, he went to Rennes.

4

RENNES AND BREST

'RENNES seemed a Babylon, the college a world,' he wrote. The capital of Brittany since before the Romans came, the seat of Parlement and more often than not of the Estates, the fifteenth most populous town in France, was the first big city he had seen. Rennes was square and walled, bisected by the Vilaine, nowadays embanked between straight quays, but then a serpentine stream, overflowing in winter, dwindled and mephitic in summer. The citizens were proud of their modernity, for the medieval town, burned down in the great fire of 1720 except for a few old houses near the cathedral, had been entirely rebuilt, with wide parallel streets, and high grim mansions of reddish granite. Cold Rennes had lost its past and seemed then, as it is still, severely legal, sad beneath the sunless skies of inland Brittany, and yet endearing in its rectilinear staidness, and fortunate in possessing the paradisal Mont Thabor, one of the most beautiful public gardens in France.[1]

The college of Rennes, with its three courtyards and magnificent chapel, had been built with characteristic splendour by the Jesuits in the seventeenth century, south of the Vilaine near the eastern edge of the town.[2] After the expulsion of the Jesuits by Parlement and La Chalotais in 1762 the college was reorganised by the municipality, but the new staff (a principal, two sub-principals, and nine masters) was still chosen from the priesthood. The principal was Abbé de Fayolle; his birthday was a school holiday, when his pupils sang at the tops of their voices songs of praise of their own composition:

> 'Terpsichore, Polymnia dear,
> Come, come, in answer to our prayer,
> Reason itself invites you here! . . .'

But perhaps the Muses, even in the Age of Reason, would not listen to reason. Abbé de Chateaugiron taught the second class, Abbé Germer, who had a particular liking for classical allusions,[3] took rhetoric, and Abbé Marchand taught 'physics' (which then consisted chiefly of mechanics, mensuration, and other branches of applied mathematics required of candidates for the navy or the military engineers).[4]

The college had produced not long ago, before the departure of the Jesuits, three famous authors: the literary and dramatic critic Geoffroy, who later praised *Atala*; the poet and critic Ginguené, who was a cousin of Uncle Antoine de Bédée's wife, and later attacked *Le Génie du Christianisme*; and the Chevalier de Parny, poet of love, in whose dormitory and very bed François-René was proud to find himself sleeping. He was just in time to glimpse the future General Moreau, victor of Hohenlinden, rival and enemy of the great Napoleon; Victor Moreau was then a day-boy, but already aged eighteen and about to leave. Another celebrated foe of Napoleon (François-René himself was destined to be yet a third) shared his dormitory: Limoëlan, who with Cadoudal organised the bomb-plot of 24 December 1800 against the First Consul. His other bedfellows were the illfated Saint-Riveul, who eight years later became the first Breton noble to die in the Revolution, and—none other than Gesril himself, still up to his old trick of picking quarrels for other people.

The collegians of Rennes were fond of brawling; they challenged one another to duels on half-holidays in the gardens of Mont Thabor, and there fought it out under Gesril's presidency, fencing with mathematical compasses tied to walking-sticks, or battling still more bloodily hand to hand, until one or the other owned himself beaten. François-René soon gained the same ascendancy over his comrades as at Dol, but at Rennes he had to fight for it. One day among the fallen leaves, while Gesril graciously looked on as his second, he fell before Saint-Riveul and paid dearly for his refusal to surrender. The ferocious conqueror tore his hair out by handfuls, and then, of course, they became the best of friends.

Every night there were high jinks in their dormitory, when they jumped over their beds and smashed the chairs. The supervising master of the week found the spyhole in their door stuffed with paper, but pushed it out with his finger and caught them in the act. Next night he poked his finger into something else, for Limoëlan had stopped the hole with the more solid contents of his chamberpot. 'Who did that?', he cried, bursting into the room and finding them all ostentatiously asleep. 'What on earth is the matter, Monsieur le Préfet?', enquired Gesril, emerging in his nightshirt and offering the use of his waterjug and basin with polite concern, while the others, dramatically holding their noses, vanished under the bedclothes in fits of mirth. They were all imprisoned in the cellars, where Gesril broached a winebarrel, Limoëlan demolished a wall, Saint-Riveul tunnelled to the kitchen yard and was nearly devoured by a resident pig, and François-René climbed to a grating and harangued the populace in the street outside. No one owned up, not even the conspirator Limoëlan; 'we were heroic,' says Chateaubriand simply. A malodorous story!

Gesril left for Brest at the end of 1781, thus improving the tone of the college and the conduct of François-René. During next year he became proficient in Latin, took immensely to Greek, and was top in mathematics, 'for which,' he says, 'I always had a decided leaning'. But his religious fervour diminished, owing 'to the great number of my teachers and comrades, which multiplied opportunities for distraction'. This relapse was not for want of devotional practice in the college, where mass was celebrated daily after morning school, a Latin prayer was repeated aloud before and after each class, and monthly certificates of confession were compulsory. But in this rebellious young generation of the future revolutionaries incredulity was rife among the schoolboys of Rennes, and Parlement itself felt obliged to issue decrees, all in vain, for the amendment of their faith.[5]

On 23 April 1782 he was summoned from Rennes to attend the marriage of his third sister, Julie, in the castle chapel at Combourg. Julie, always his favourite next to Lucile, was now eighteen and prettiest of all. Her bridegroom, the Chevalier Annibal de Farcy, aged thirty-two, was a captain in the infantry regiment of Condé, and belonged to a good Breton family; indeed, he was a remote cousin of the bride and the other young Chateaubriands on their mother's side.[6] M. de Farcy lived only a few yards from Julie's married sisters at Fougères, in the Hôtel de Farcy, where she went to join him. Now only Lucile remained with the ageing parents at Combourg; the stage was being set for the great drama of François-René's youth, which would begin in the next year. At the wedding he was overcome by the beauty of Thérèse de Moëlien, Comtesse de Trojolif, and heard, as he says, 'the bewitching faraway voice of the passions that were drawing near me; I hurried to meet these sirens, allured by their unknown music that troubled my heart and called me to my ruin.' The countess was twenty-two, and her beauty was still admired on the scaffold eleven years later, when she was guillotined for her part in the royalist conspiracy of her cousin the Marquis de la Rouërie.

Summer holidays began and ended late at the college of Rennes. Prize-giving was on 24 August, and the autumn term opened on St. Luke's Day, 18 October, with a public mass in the chapel, when the principal presented the municipal officials each with a tall white candle adorned with the arms of the town. But François-René arrived a few days late, for on 22 October 1782 he was at Bécherel to witness, along with his brother Jean-Baptiste, the marriage of M. Gesbert de la Noé-Seiche, seneschal of Combourg, to Mlle Faisant de la Gautraie. This time it was the bride who impressed him with her charms. In January 1783 he went to Brest, without returning home, and without the regret with which he had left Dol; 'perhaps,' he says, 'I had lost that flower of innocence which makes us delight in everything that is innocent like ourselves.'

Jean-Baptiste fraternally saw him into the public coach for Brest, where he was met, after the long journey of 160 miles which took three

days, by his mother's cousin, the Chevalier de Ravenel, who had promised to keep an eye on him. This bluff sailor of the family, after
gloriously capturing the English frigate *Unicorn* off San Domingo in
1780, had retired with the rank of ship's captain. He installed François-
René at a lodging-house for navy candidates in the magnificent Rue de
Siam, found him a fencing-master, a drawing-master and a teacher of
mathematics, and presented him to the famous Comte d'Hector, victor
in numberless seafights, and now commandant of the port of Brest.
François-René's examiner would be the great mathematician Bezout,
whose textbooks he had studied ever since his early years at Dol; the
examinations would be strict now the war was nearly over, and many
would be ploughed; but with such friends in court, how could he
fail?

Fifty years ago in 1733, at the same age of fourteen, his father had
waited at Guitté in vain for the brevet from Versailles, without which
no candidate for the royal navy could sit his examination. History
repeats itself, but always with a difference. François-René's brevet had
not yet arrived, although Jean-Baptiste had used his influence in Paris;
but no doubt it would come in time for the next examination in April,
or the second and last in August. René-Auguste, a proud orphan who
would not till his field, had waited in despair; disappointment had
deranged his whole life, and empty success had left him forever unhealed. François-René, still not at all sure what he wished to be, secure
in a prosperous father, felt only philosophical boredom. Meanwhile, as
he was not yet an official candidate, he could not attend the official
classes. He idled for a month, and then worked hard with his three
private teachers, or hidden alone in his bedroom. For the first time in
his life he had free choice between company or solitude; he chose
solitude, perhaps because he felt ashamed before his breveted comrades,
perhaps because the manners of naval cadets were not to his taste, but
most of all for the melancholy delight of being able to be alone. On
13 March a business correspondent of René-Auguste reported meeting
him with M. de Ravenel; 'the boy is working well and fruitfully,' he
wrote, 'as he did not do in the first month. It remains only to encourage
his zeal and good intentions.'

Brest lies at the end of France and the world, on the northwest shore
of a landlocked haven. Without hinterland or land communications,
far away from any other large town, it was little used for commerce
except as a port of call; but strategically it had remained, since Vauban
fortified it for Louis XIV, the great headquarters of the French fighting
navy, the gateway to America and India. From the ramparts François-
René gazed over a vast inland sea, gleaming and deep, reaching ten
miles southward and fifteen miles east to distant blue hills; looking west
he saw the passage to the open Atlantic, the mile-wide Gullet of Brest.

Below to the right was Vauban's granite fortress, by the winding estuary of the Penfeld; on the opposite bank, to be reached by ferry from the foot of the Rue de Siam, was the new quarter of Recouvrance with its turmoil of quays and shipyards and men incomprehensibly labouring. The ecstasies of solitude, he found, were as keen in a crowd as in a wilderness.

He sat brooding on a disused mast by the quayside of Recouvrance. Shipwrights and sailors, soldiers and gangs of convicts passed to and fro unseeing before him. He was invisible and alone. Here carpenters were planing planks, ropemakers twisting a cable, shipboys lighting fires under cauldrons of tar; there a pilot shouted his vessel into dock, carts backed into the water, bales of merchandise and sacks of provisions and trains of cannon lumbered from stores to ships, from ships to stores. Voyagers came ashore; other voyagers embarked. Pulleys unloaded holds, great wooden cranes lifted blocks of masonry. Strange vague thoughts invaded him, of the structure of society, its blessings and curses: these labourers were toiling till death for those employers; these good sailors had risked their lives to kill and plunder, so also had those wicked convicts. How sublime or base were men's achievements, how unfathomable their purpose!

A different solitude was not far away. He rose and followed the Penfeld, which curved till the port was hidden, and became a muddy stream in a narrow marshy valley. He lay on the bank, watching the gliding choughs, the eddying water, listening to distant cries of men, the muffled beat of caulking hammers, and sank into a still profounder revery. Suddenly guns boomed far away, the farewell salute of a ship putting to sea; François-René shuddered, and his eyes filled with tears.

Spring went by, and the April examinations, but still no brevet came. Another young Chateaubriand was a candidate at Brest, cousin Stanislas, François-René's playmate long ago under the ramparts of Saint-Malo, who had gone to be Marie-Antoinette's page at Versailles, and now longed to join the navy. Stanislas, at least, had a brevet, and could sit; Bezout ploughed him, but he would try again in August.

On 17 June 1783 François-René wandered west along the shore to within sight of the open sea. The sun beat down; with thoughts of the ocean's infinite spaces and unknown worlds beyond, he lay on the hot beach and slept. Again he was roused by gunfire, but now by multitudinous detonations. The strait was thronged with gallant ships, pennants flying, signals hoisted, cannon thundering; some dropped anchor and stood abruptly still, as if by enchantment, others scudded by on glittering wakes. The Marquis de Vaudreuil's squadron was home triumphant from the West Indies. The war with England was over.

Cutters put out, laden with officers, whose faces were burned with the sun of strange seas, joyful and fierce with the pride of victory. All Brest ran to meet them at the mole. As the heroes marched by, one broke ranks and rushed to throw his arms round the astonished François-René. He recognised Gesril, Gesril again, grown extraordinarily tall, still pale from a swordthrust in the chest. He was leaving that very evening, he explained, to join his family in Saint-Malo. All summer François-René was haunted by the vision of Gesril so suddenly reappearing, so swiftly vanishing, so enviable in both. Which of Gesril's examples should he follow: to go to sea, if the navy would have him, as was doubtful, or go home, as he easily could?

Others remained, and others departed, but not for home. M. de Ravenel took him to Comte d'Hector's house, where he heard the tales of sailors old and young, their battles in mid-ocean, their foreign landfalls. One had arrived from India, one from America; another was leaving to circumnavigate the world, another for the isles of Greece. 'Look, there's La Pérouse,' said his uncle. La Pérouse, 'whose death is the secret of the tempests', had returned from destroying the English fur traders' posts in Hudson Bay, and would sail from Brest two years later to disappear in the Pacific. The boy watched and listened, and then, sleepless all night, fought exultantly against tremendous odds, discovered vast new lands, in waking dreams.

His brevet never came. The inexorable Bezout failed Stanislas again, and he was sent down on 30 August with five comrades, 'for having taken two examinations without success'.[7] With the end of hostilities recruitment lapsed, few were appointed, none could expect the rapid promotion of wartime. Royal France had created a great republic beyond the sea, and gained nothing but the liberty of America, the hatred of England, and the seeds of her own revolution.

François-René felt a growing revulsion. If the navy did not want him, why should he want the navy? He would like to fight, but there was no more fighting; he longed to travel, but to travel alone, at his own free will. 'My spirit of independence made service of any kind repulsive; I have in me an impossibility of obeying.' The thought of Gesril's appearance and disappearance returned, and 'made me come to a resolution that changed the course of my life; it was written that this young man would have an absolute empire over my destiny'. Deepest of all, no doubt, was the consciousness that he had not yet found his identity, that a rendezvous with his unknown self awaited him in the solitude of Combourg.

One morning, without telling his uncle Ravenel, without asking anyone's permission or even writing to his parents, he left for Combourg. Aghast at his own temerity, in fear of his father, he expected to be received with outbursts of violent rage. Instead, despite their amazement, his family welcomed this prodigal return. Even René-Auguste only shook his head as if to say: 'Here's a pretty kettle of fish!' His mother scolded, and then kissed him with all her heart. But Lucile kissed him in an ecstasy of joy.

SISTER AND SYLPHIDE

ONLY his father and mother and Lucile were left at Combourg, with a cook, a chambermaid, two lackeys and a coachman. When these few masters and menials dispersed over the vast castle, all seemed deserted, as though not a living soul were there. The married girls came sometimes from Fougères with their husbands and children; Marie-Anne, Comtesse de Marigny, had a little girl, Élisabeth, aged two, Bénigne, Comtesse de Québriac, had two little boys, and Julie, Mme de Farcy, would bear her only child, Zoé, in June next year. But on 8 August 1783, a few weeks before François-René's arrival, M. de Québriac, Bénigne's husband, had died at Combourg, and on the 27th their elder son, César-Auguste, not quite three, died also. Now the girls were back at Fougères, comforting Bénigne.

Lucile, on 12 May 1783, had become an honorary, non-resident canoness in the chapter of l'Argentière, near Lyons. For admission it was necessary to prove eight generations of nobility on the father's side, and three on the mother's; but René-Auguste could do a great better than that, and the royal genealogist Chérin declared, with professional connoisseurship, that he had never seen a finer or fuller pedigree. No vows of celibacy or reclusion were demanded, though at twenty-five a canoness could take up residence, if she chose, with a private apartment and a modest prebend. Meanwhile one had only to promise not to wear red or use rouge, and to avoid reading naughty books. Membership of l'Argentière conferred the title of countess, so that Lucile was henceforth known in the family as Madame la Chanoinesse, or Comtesse Lucile. Altogether, being a canoness was a tremendously grand status, equally suitable for acquiring a husband, or for a life of refined spinsterhood, supposing, as already seemed possible for Lucile, now just nineteen, one was not the marrying kind. There was even talk of getting her into Remiremont, which was grander still. It could never be said that René-Auguste did not do his best for his children. And so, when her tempestuous younger brother returned to Combourg, Lucile seemed already almost a nun—like their cousin Marie-Anne-Renée, Pierre's eldest daughter, whom on 5 May 1781 François-René had witnessed, awestricken, taking the veil in the convent of La Victoire at Saint-Malo, where she now lived for ever under her name in religion as Soeur des Séraphins.

As if to show he could go one better, François-René suddenly

announced his determination to enter the Church. Perhaps remnants of
his faith still lingered, or he wildly hoped for a refuge in the priesthood
from the rising storm of his passions; but also, as he later admitted, 'the
truth was that I was only trying to gain time, for I had no idea what I
wanted'. His mother was delighted; she had longed for this ever since
he went to Dol. 'Perhaps the navy won't suit him,' she had often provokingly remarked. Even René-Auguste was not displeased. He knew
what it was to wait for a brevet that never came, and the Church was
considered a very proper career for the younger son of a noble family.
So they sent him to the College of Dinan.

The college, with 250 pupils, was halfway in size between his former
schools of little Dol and huge Rennes, resembled these in being an
ancient institution staffed by priests and recently renovated, and was
particularly favoured by the richest merchants of Saint-Malo, where
there was no high-school. The bishop, Mgr. des Laurents himself, had
re-endowed it in 1777, and moved it to a derelict convent of starving
and elderly Benedictine nuns (whom he pensioned off, much to their
pleasure) in the Rue de Lehon, near the southeast edge of the town walls
and the precipitous gorge of the Rance. This college was almost a
seminary, for in deference to the bishop the town council had agreed
to the inclusion of a top class in theology, whose superior the Abbé de
Rouillac held precedence over the nominal principal, the erudite and
urbane Abbé Puel de Saint-Simon, who took rhetoric. No school could
have been more suitable for making a priest of François-René, if he had
ever risen to the theology class. There were two masters of philosophy,
another Abbé de Rouillac, the director's nephew, who spoke exquisite
Latin in school, and Abbé Duhamel, who taught François-René. The
boarders enjoyed separate bedroom studies in the cells of the vanished
nuns above the cloisters.

His last schooldays commenced at the opening of the autumn term,
which began as at Rennes on St. Luke's Day, 18 October. He decided
he knew more Latin than his teachers (a common illusion in boys chang-
ing school), and learned a little Hebrew (so perhaps, after all, he did
touch upon the theology class). He was afflicted with useful fits of nose-
bleeding, which forced him to leave the classroom and take long solitary
walks in the wooded valley of the Rance. But he was still boyish enough
to play prisoner's base with his companions, as at Dol, in the meadows
by the river. In those very fields, he boasted to them, several of his
ancestors had fought beside their cousin Du Guesclin at the siege of
Dinan in 1364; there too (but this was rather an anticlimax), one of his
great-uncles, René de Chateaubriand, a captain in the tobacco excise,
had been murdered by smugglers in 1722.

He stayed at Dinan, on and off, until the summer of 1784. In the warm
season they were taken down to the river on Thursday and Sunday

afternoons; he learned to swim for the first time, and once narrowly escaped drowning, not for the last time. His schoolfellow little Broussais was attacked 'by ungrateful leeches, who could not foresee the future' —very appropriately, for Broussais later became a celebrated physician, and always prescribed leeches for the reduction of fever. To another comrade, Lecourt de la Villehassetz, he wrote nostalgically fifty years later, recalling his own pet name 'Francillon', and 'my dear heaths of Brittany, which I shall see no more': 'you must admit, Monsieur, that we were very happy urchins at Dinan, and that glory (if there is such a thing), and its pretentions, and our old age, and all we have seen, are nothing compared with a game of prisoner's base on the bank of the Rance'. But Combourg and Uncle Bédée's Monchoix were temptingly near, Combourg only fifteen miles southeast, Monchoix twelve miles northwest. He began to make truant visits to each, at this parting of the ways.

Uncle Antoine de Bédée had bought the lordship of Plancoët two years before, gaining dues on the seignorial butchery, bakery and market, with the title of Baron de Plancoët. Bédée the Artichoke was a benevolent lord, who paved his streets, unlike René-Auguste, threw his granary open to the poor in time of famine, and arranged that the new highroad from Dinan to Lamballe should pass through Plancoët; though all this was not to save him in the Revolution. Monchoix was full of revelry as ever. The most ardent of its dancers was François-René's cousin Caroline, aged twenty-two, a nice, ugly girl, but with fine eyes and a pretty figure, who liked to pretend he was smitten with her, while he preferred to believe she was smitten with him. He was struck by the contrast between the dark silence of Combourg and the festive din of Monchoix; when he moved from one to the other, 'it was like exchanging the desert for the world, the castle-keep of a medieval baron for the villa of a Roman prince'. But he did not choose Monchoix.

Towards the summer holidays of 1784, by imperceptible degrees, he found himself fixed at Combourg, with no more question of Dinan. René-Auguste acquiesced, less for reasons of parsimony, as his son ungraciously supposed, than because he had decided to keep a personal eye on this irresolute youth. Mme de Chateaubriand, rather than force her boy into a false vocation, resigned herself to wait and hope.

A complex but unerring instinct had led him back to Combourg. Here alone he could find the mingling of external order and inner tumult which he needed in his perilous quest for himself. Here his daily routine was divided into hours of intolerable yet reassuring constraint, and hours of total yet terrifying freedom. Every morning in the rigid monotony of a strange family life he accumulated longings for rebellion, which he assuaged every afternoon with paroxysms of liberation in the pent solitude of his turret room, or the limitless solitude of the woods.

Each evening he returned, alarmed by his own anarchy and isolation, to a prison which already seemed a refuge. So he repeated day by day in miniature the prodigal son's escape, his wandering, his despair, his homecoming, his welcome, if only to the banal agape of family supper. In his Memoirs he called this crucial period, between his return in the summer of 1784 and his departure in the summer of 1786, 'my two years of madness'. 'It was in the woods of Combourg that I became what I am.'

René-Auguste was a country gentleman of very regular habits. He rose at four, winter and summer, crossed the inner courtyard to rouse his manservant, who slept in the vaulted cellars below François-René's turret staircase, and took his morning coffee, with sugar which he prudently kept locked with his moneybags and silver in his bedroom cupboard, at five sharp. Then he worked till noon in his study in the south tower, on the remnants of affairs left unsettled at his retirement from trade, on feudal lawsuits, the endless quarrel over the pavement of Combourg town, the pedigree of his family, and any other business. This room contained three black leather chairs and a table littered with parchment deeds; over the mantelpiece hung the enormous family tree of the Chateaubriands, covering seven centuries from Brien the First to his own grandchildren. Mme de Chateaubriand and Lucile took breakfast in their rooms at eight. François-René had no fixed time for rising or breakfasting; he was supposed to work in his bedroom until midday, but usually he did nothing at all.

At half past eleven the bell was rung for noonday dinner in the guard-room. Having eaten, they stayed together in uneasy silence until two. Then, in those last days of summer, René-Auguste went fishing on the lake, inspected his kitchen-garden, or strolled within a stone's-throw of his castle. Mme de Chateaubriand prayed in the chapel, Lucile shut herself in her room, François-René roamed the countryside in a savage ecstasy of freedom. After eight o'clock supper, when the evening was fine, all four sat out on the stairhead above the Green Court. René-Auguste had his gun; he banged away, taking potshots at the owls as they glided from the battlements in the gathering dusk. The others watched the sky, the trees, the last rays of sunset, the first stars. At ten o'clock all dispersed to bed.

But autumn came, and the year's death entered into Combourg evenings. Four living phantoms left the supper table and gathered round the great fireplace. Mme de Chateaubriand sank in spectral sighs upon her chaise-longue; the servants brought her a single candle on a stand, cleared the table, and retired; François-René and Lucile huddled in their chairs close to the blaze. Then René-Auguste, cloaked in a long white woollen dressing-gown, with an erect white nightcap on his half-bald head, began his nightly walk, to and fro, the length of the guardroom.

At midway he vanished into the gloom, and only his slow tread could be heard, till he reached the end, turned, and reappeared, with his white gown and white cap and long pale face. While he was far off François-René and Lucile had whispered a few words together; as he approached, they fell silent. 'What were you talking about?' he enquired in a stern voice; but seized with terror, they made no reply. He continued his walk, and for the rest of the evening no sound was heard but his measured footfalls, his wife's sighing, the murmur of the wind.

On some rare evenings, however, René-Auguste paused, sat with his family by the fire, and spoke with bitter concision of the distresses of his boyhood, the adversities of his fortune. He told of storms and perils, of the siege of Danzig and the scoundrel Russians, his voyages to America, Africa and Italy, his shipwreck in Spain, his one visit to Paris —'a place of abomination,' he said, and Paris seemed, in the voice of his old memory, the strangest and furthest of all the lands he had seen. 'I have not done enough for my family!' he concluded, and resumed his walk. François-René had listened with absorption, and now his eyes brimmed with tears of filial love. His father's sufferings and despair, he thought, should have fallen upon himself alone.

The castle clock struck ten. René-Auguste halted abruptly, as though arrested by the same mechanism that had chimed the bell. He drew out his watch, wound it, took his great silver candlestick with tall candle, visited his study in the south tower for a moment, and then returned, candlestick in hand, making for his bedroom in the east tower. Lucile and François-René stood in his way, trembling with fear and respect, to kiss him goodnight. He bent his withered, sunken cheek to their lips, without a word, receded into the shadows, entered the corridor. They heard his door close.

The spell was broken. The three captives burst into a torrent of talk, making up in a quarter of an hour for all the silence of the day. Then François-René called the chambermaid, and escorted mother and sister to their bedrooms above. At their request he examined the dark stair-ways and flickering passages, looked under their beds and up their chimneys, in search of marauders or ghosts. Nine summers ago, in 1775, when François-René was at Plancoët in blissful disgrace and Mme de Chateaubriand at Dinan taking the waters, the four little girls had sat up in the small hours clandestinely reading the death of Clarissa in Richardson's novel. They heard footsteps on the stairs, supposed it was their father come to surprise them, blew out their candle and dashed panicstricken into their beds. The steps paused by their bedroom door as if to listen, then receded towards their father's tower. Next morning René-Auguste asked if they had heard anything in the night! Someone had tried to open the door leading to his staircase, and would have suc-ceeded but for a chest that happened to be in the way. He had woken with a start, seized his pistols and then, hearing no more and thinking he was mistaken, had gone to sleep again. The wouldbe murderer or thief was never discovered, but a servant was suspected. Another time, one December evening when René-Auguste was writing by the logfire in the guardroom, he heard the door opening behind him, and turned to see a tall shape like a goblin, watching him with ebony face and haggard, rolling eyes. He grasped the redhot tongs from the fire and advanced; the intruder backed away, fled across the inner court and escaped into the night. Robber or demon, who could tell? Combourg also had its indubitable ghosts. Every Christmas Eve at midnight the spirit of Malo de Coëtquen walked the castle, identifiable by its wooden leg; for the last marquis had indeed lost a leg at Malplaquet in 1709, although he died safe in his bed at Combourg in 1727 eighteen years later, and ought to have lain quiet in his family vault in the Jacobins' church at Dinan, where he was buried. This apparition had been seen several times on the spiral staircase of François-René's turret. Sometimes by way of a change the wooden leg wandered about by itself, followed by a black cat, upstairs and down; it knocked on the doors, pushed them open, stumped away, and was heard vanishing into the cellars at daybreak.

Such were the bedtime stories of Combourg. Mme de Chateaubriand and Lucile lay down for the night, half dead with terror, but François-René sought his lonely turret with perfect equanimity. Instead of trying to convince him that ghosts did not exist, his parents had trained him to defy them. When his father enquired with an ironic smile: 'Can it be that Monsieur le Chevalier is afraid?' he would willingly have gone to bed with a corpse. All the arguments of philosophy could not have reassured him more convincingly than his mother's remark: 'My child, nothing happens unless God allows it; you have nothing to fear from evil spirits, so long as you are a good Christian.' Thus emboldened he had forgotten the fears of his childhood, when the uncanny noises of the castle night had pierced him with terror, till he hid sweating under his coverlet and lay awake till morning. Sleepless still, but long since unafraid, he listened to the cries of the screech-owls as they flitted from tower to tower, outlining the shadows of their wings on his window curtains in the light of the westering moon. He exulted in the sounds of the wind, now seeming to run with light steps, now lamenting, now roaring in the cellars and hurtling against his door. The nightwinds of Combourg became playthings for his fancies and wings for his dreams, till at four o'clock he heard the distant shout of René-Auguste calling his manservant in the courtyard below, like the voice of the last phantom of the night. Then he slept.

In counterpart to the nocturnal hours of freedom for the imagination came the afternoon hours of freedom for the body. When he escaped at last from the silence of midday dinner, where he had dared neither speak nor eat in his father's presence, he forced himself to sit for a moment on the topmost step of the perron and calm his agitation; if he had run straight down, he would have fallen headlong. Then he crossed the Green Court into the woods, and ran and leaped until he dropped exhausted, panting for breath, drunk with liberty and delight.

His father gave him an old gun, and sometimes, handsomely enough, took him shooting. Soon the huntsman's passion seized him to the point of frenzy, and he went out alone. He never forgot the field where he shot his first hare; he stood for hours up to his waist in the lake, waiting for wild duck. But he loved this murderous pastime not so much for its own sake, as for the joy of independence: 'leaping a ditch, tramping over fields, marshes, moors, feeling myself in possession of power and solitude with my gun in a wilderness, was my natural way of being'. Sometimes he wandered so far that he could walk no more, and the gamekeepers carried him home on a litter of branches. But before long the pleasures of hunting failed to satisfy him. Freedom and isolation were not enough; he was troubled by a longing for happiness which he could neither control nor understand. What did he want? Who could reveal him to himself? He turned to Lucile.

Lucile was now twenty and he sixteen. Like all her sisters and brothers she had the Chateaubriand long nose, oval face, lofty forehead, strong round chin, blueblack eyes and dark brown hair, with the Bédée shortness of stature. She was five foot three in height, although to François-René, who had not yet reached his full growth of a mere five foot four, her statuesque figure made her seem tall. She wore her hair long, framing her pale face and brought forward to hang in serpentine locks between forearms and virginal bosom. Lucile was strikingly beautiful without being at all pretty. Her movements, voice, smile, and facial expression seemed indefinably pensive, absent, mournful, perhaps even a little odd. As she brooded motionless, appearing not to breathe, with one arm clasped behind her head, she reminded the classical François-René of a funereal goddess on a Greek stele. But her pious mother, when Lucile on their evening walks halted to read some devotional work at a favourite spot, where two country lanes met by a stone crucifix and a tall poplar, would declare with enthusiasm: 'She's like a Christian of the early Church!' Awake or in her dreams Lucile saw the future. At night she would sit with her lamp on the stairway of the great north tower, watching the castle clock; when the two hands of the dial drew upright together, a moment before the stroke of midnight, she heard sounds that informed her of deaths far away. And then, Lucile had fits of melancholy, in which no matter what became an occasion for anxiety, or sorrow, or injured feelings. A phrase that would not come, a baseless fantasy, would torment her for months.

She gazed at the sky, or round about her, with eyes full of dejection or ardour. François-René tried to console her, and fell as he spoke into gulfs of inexplicable despair. Lucile was a difficult girl, and to all but him might have seemed a tiresome one, had it not been for her innocence, her sincerity, and a touch of genius. Everyone always admired and liked her.

Recently Jean-Baptiste had brought with him on his visits home a young gentleman from Normandy, Alexandre-Henri de Malfilâtre, aged twenty-seven, a cousin of the illfated poet of that name.[1] Jean-Baptiste, ever-helpful, arranged for him to be appointed councillor, like himself, in the Parlement of Rennes, where he was installed on 3 May 1784; he would have made an excellent match. But nothing came of it. Perhaps M. de Malfilâtre found Lucile too alarming, or was himself not inclined to marriage—he became a priest in London during the emigration, and died at Somerstown in 1803. François-René believed that Lucile's melancholy was due to an unrequited passion for this reluctant suitor; but then, Lucile had always been melancholy, although she was still more so now. Perhaps she was distressed not only by a failure in love, but by a calamitous realisation that she would never love any man but her younger brother.

Winter drew near, and guests became rarer still at Combourg. Two venerable bearded Capuchin friars with staffs and knapsacks came on All Souls' Eve, while the dead men's wind was roaring in the battlements and rain beat the windows. They told stories at supper of their missionary days in Tartary or among the Red Indians of America, praised Lucile's beauty and modesty, said prayers to family and servants assembled, and next morning had vanished. Or two elderly country gentlemen arrived on horseback, with hunting-knife in belt and pistols slung to their saddlebow, to ask a bed for the night on their way to plead their lawsuits in the Parlement of Rennes. One was the Comte de Montlouet, René-Auguste's vassal from the manor of Gaugray at Roz-sur-Couesnon, opposite the mudflats of Mont Saint-Michel, at the furthest limits of his lordship; he had been godfather to Bénigne's second son François in 1782, and René-Auguste occasionally procured him a barrel of best wine from a correspondent at Bordeaux. The other was the Comte Goyon de Beaufort, whose first wife, another Goyon, had presented him in dying with the longlost Chateaubriand seigneury of Beaufort.[2] René-Auguste welcomed them with his usual punctilious ceremony on the perron, bareheaded in the rain and wind. At supper they discussed family affairs, explained their lawsuits, or repeated yet again the tale of their campaigns in Hanover during the Seven Years War; then they slept in the state fourposter, with its double curtains of green muslin and crimson silk, in Queen Christine's room in the north tower. Next morning, when François-René and Lucile came down to the guardroom, and gazed on the castle meadow, flooded or white with hoarfrost, they saw two horsemen on the lakeside causeway, receding towards Rennes. They were alone again.

Alone again, they became inseparable during all that winter and the following spring. For François-René it was the first profoundly intimate relationship of his life, for Lucile it was the only one. Every day, till these months seemed endless and marked them for ever, they walked side by side in the woodland of the Great Mall, engrossed in one another. The leafless beeches sighed above them, the deep dead leaves rustled and crackled under their step. The winter of 1784–5 was cruel, and brought misery or death to the peasants of Combourg; but brother and sister trod in bliss over the dazzling snow, fretted with the prints of woodbirds, squirrels, hurrying stoats. Spring came, the beeches budded green, and still they paced, still talking, over a carpet of rathe primroses. 'Young as the primroses, sad as the withered leaves, pure as the new-fallen snow, we felt in harmony with our recreations.' The forest shared and kept their secrets.

Of what did they speak? 'What were you talking about?', their father had asked, but did not stay for an answer. René-Auguste may well have been perplexed by his children's excessive absorption in one another; but as this stern and virtuous man took no action to separate them, he can hardly have detected any monstrous complicity. Indeed, no one would ever have suspected the possibility of an incestuous relationship between this devoted brother and sister, had it not been for the literary indiscretion of François-René himself. Some twelve years later during his exile in England he described with instantly recognisable detail in his story René the intimacy of their youth at Combourg, and the hero's discovery that his sister Amélie has loved him all too dearly. 'God of pity,' prays Amélie, at the moment of entering a nunnery and dying to this world, 'grant that I may never rise from this funereal bed, and load with Thy blessings a brother who did not share my criminal passion!' The mystery of her strange behaviour, her melancholy, her alternations of fondness and avoidance, is thus retrospectively explained. René, appalled by this terrible revelation, leaves his native land to seek death among the Red Indians of the New World.

It may be argued, truly enough, that incest between brother and sister was a literary commonplace in the last generation of the French pre-romantics; indeed, all the incidents in René which might seem to belong to conventional melodrama, and not to the actual life of François-René and Lucile, have been identified in popular novels of the period. And yet, in that age of the rending of taboos and rebellion of the unconscious, when the same insurgent forces of love and death produced revolution and war in nations and sexual lawlessness in individuals, the themes of romantic fiction were sometimes the realities of experience.

Byron and Shelley, a generation later, wrote obsessively of incestuous love because they had felt and known it; then why not Chateaubriand?

The question is not idle; for it we duly respect and revere this noble and illstarred couple, François-René and Lucile, we owe them the truth, and shall not admire them the less if their destiny was shadowed by a guilty passion. But this truth is hard to seek. The errors of forbidden love, unless witnessed or confessed, are difficult to prove, but always impossible to disprove. No evidence of their incest exists, except the symbolic fiction of *René*. No evidence of their innocence exists, except their own asseverations in later years; and these, it might be thought, would have been the same in the case of guilt as in the case of innocence. We shall never know beyond all doubt, however long we ponder, whether brother and sister lay together in the towers or woods of Combourg.

Nevertheless, their later words and conduct show no certain trace of the lingering obsession, the over-compensation, the excessive emphasis with which the conscious or unconscious mind admits or rejects its own guilt. Byron and Shelley wrote again and again of incest, Chateaubriand never again. In the coming six years before his exile, in the four years between his return from exile and the death of Lucile, their relationship was affectionate and natural, without the significant reservations which spring from a past complicity. Lucile, recalling their youth in a last letter before her death, reminded her brother of 'the innocence of our thoughts and our joys'; Chateaubriand in his Memoirs reproached himself for ever having left the friendship of 'this celestial creature', when both were 'pure as the newfallen snow', for the love of other women; and their veracity seems honest and simple, with no sign of over-insistence, no undertone of concealment. They looked back to their young days as a Time Lost when each was without sin. And in this year of 1785 at Combourg it seems that their intimacy gradually waned, not because it was inordinate or criminal, but because it was disappointing. They had come together because they were unloved, alike, and alone, because Lucile had rejected the world, and François-René was not yet bold enough to enter it. They drew apart because he outgrew her. Poor Lucile was, after all, only a stage in his approach to manhood, his escape from the prison of family, his quest for his own individuality.

Already in the autumn of 1784 their companionship had taken the turn that led to the beginning of the end. One day as they walked in the woods, and François-René spoke with lyric praise of solitude, Lucile said: 'You ought to write all that.' Her words were a revelation. He felt, as he says, 'the divine breath of the Muse'; a new life appeared to open before him, a void within him seemed to be filled. He set to work to compose verses, night and day, 'a multitude of little idylls or pictures of nature', 'about my pleasures, that is to say, my woods and valleys'. He persuaded Lucile to follow his example. Every day they inspected and discussed one another's work, or together translated their favourite passages, 'the finest and saddest', from the Book of Job or Lucretius. So their secret conversation as they paced the woods was of poetry, their own poetry.

François-René continued to write his 'multitude of little idylls' from 1784 until 1790. Unfortunately, nearly all were lost during the ensuing years of exile, and no more than ten survived to be published in 1828, in the first edition of his collected works, under the title of *Tableaux de la Nature*.[3] Only two of the ten, the lines beginning *'Forêt silencieuse'*, and *'Nuit d'automne'*, seem to belong to his earliest period, from the autumn of 1784 to the spring of 1785.[4] These agreeable juvenilia—

> *'O silent forest, pleasing solitude,*
> *How sweet to roam through your sequestered shade!'*

and so forth—show remarkable talent in a sixteen-year-old, a genuine love of nature, even, here and there, a touch of exact observation, of momentary contact with reality. But the reader is taken aback, knowing the furious young man from whom they came, by their gentleness verging on insipidity, by the elegant tameness of their diction. François-René, obedient to Lucile's command, wrote only of the joys of solitude, not of its anguish; there is nothing here of his savage exaltations and despairs, his unfulfilled passions, his longed-for tempests, which he had not yet discovered to be suitable subjects for literature. Like other writers of genius in immature youth, his ambition was not to explore his true self, not even to emulate the writers he most admired,[5] but to copy the literary magazines of the day, in his case the *Mercure de France* and *Almanach des Muses*, which were full of verses just like his. Instinct had warned him to save his deeper experience for the time when he would be fit to deal with it. He already had the feelings of genius, but did not yet know the words which, once he wrote them, would become his own and no one else's. He was still unaware that his destined medium (though he always liked to believe he was proficient in both) was to be prose, not verse.

Meanwhile Lucile was equally busy, perhaps to better purpose. 'Lucile's thoughts were nothing but feelings; they issued from her soul not without difficulty, but when she succeeded in expressing them the result was unsurpassable.' Her five surviving prose poems may have been written several or even many years later. But if her Combourg compositions were like these in quality and manner, then she resembled François-René more than he yet resembled himself. Lucile's addresses to the Dawn, the Moon, Innocence, virginal symbols which she invokes with voluptuous purity, already foretell the new music and rhythms of the mature prose which he would not begin to write until ten or fifteen years after.

Soon François-René's lyric fervour abated. He had believed in his talent, and saw he had none; he had dreamed of future fame, and now wept for the loss of his unborn glory. Poetry, he decided, was not the answer to the riddle of his unidentified desires, but an evil temptation. He bore resentment against Lucile for leading him astray. Lucile herself receded into her melancholy, perhaps haunted again by thoughts of the elusive M. de Malfilâtre. François-René wrote no more, and resumed his solitary idleness.

Now he must ask again, where would he find himself? Not, as it seemed, in Lucile, still less in any other woman. He was timid in any company, most of all in a woman's; he could not see one without embarrassment, blushed if she spoke to him, would have preferred any other torture to that of being left alone with her, and yet, once she was gone, he longed for her to come back. He summoned again the radiant visions of his schooldays, the heroines of Virgil, Tibullus, or Massillon; they returned, unresponsive, with the faces of his mother or sister, appearing to ask only his protection and respect. Even so, he seemed to glimpse behind the veil another face, a different request. Soon chance enlightened him.

One of the local gentry came to stay for a few days in the castle, with his pretty wife—she may have been either Mme de Trémaudan, or the Combourg seneschal's wife, Mme Gesbert de la Noé-Seiche,[6] both of whom he praises for their good looks. Some disturbance happened in the street below, everyone hurried to the eastern window of the great guardroom to watch, François-René arrived first, and the lady scampered in a close second. He turned politely to let her by, but found her barring his way in the deep dark granite alcove. She pressed on, their bodies met, and once, twice, thrice, she leaned her bosom upon his breast and enquired, gazing into his distraught face: 'What is the matter? Are you ill?' 'From that moment I became aware that supreme felicity must consist in loving, and being loved, in a manner that was still unknown to me.' Yet his desire, then and perhaps ever after, was not for a mortal woman of flesh and blood, but for an ideal phantom.

'Accordingly I created for myself a woman made up of all the women I had ever seen.' This imaginary companion appeared, at first, with the genius and innocence of Lucile, the tender affection of his mother in the moments when she happened to notice him, the yielding figure and hair and smile of the adorable guest who had pressed him to her bosom, the eyes of some Combourg village girl, the freshness of another. Other features were borrowed from the portraits in the castle guardroom of great ladies from the time of François I, Henri IV, Louis XIV, even from paintings in churches of the Blessed Virgin, protectress of his childhood. But soon all these were not enough. Rejecting the known, he began to compose his dear ghost from the unknown, taking her face and dress from everywhere in space and time, 'from all lands, all centuries, all arts, and all religions'. She became a Celtic chieftainess, daughter of Morven, from Ossian, a sultan's wife from the gardens of Baghdad or Granada, the lady of a medieval manor. She was Aphrodite, naked and passionate, severe Diana dressed in azure sky and dew, laughing Thalia, Hebe with the cup of youth, a fairy who brought him power over all nature.

Now he possessed the creature of his love; she followed him always and everywhere, seen by him, invisible to others. But how could she love him, when he owned none of the qualities which are necessary for being loved? He solved this problem in the same manner, by lavishing upon himself all the accomplishments he lacked. In the dream world where he met his enchantress he rode like the Heavenly Twins, struck a lyre like Apollo, wielded sword or lance like Mars, was gallant and knightly as Bayard. Now she loved him in return.

In the moonlight of midnight, through gardens of orange-trees, along the marble galleries of her palace on the seaverge of Naples, past motionless statues and silent moonpaled frescoes, a young queen advanced to meet him, decked in diamonds and flowers. He heard the light fall of her step on the mosaic floor, mingling with the faint murmur of the waves; he felt the undulant silk of her headscarf caressing his forehead; he fell at her knees. She bent her face towards his, and pressed her hands on his heart. She was sixteen years old, like himself.

The dream vanished. He was lying on his bed, not hers, in his dark turret room, a poor insignificant little Breton, without looks or glory or talent. No one would ever look at him, he would go through life unknown, no woman would ever love him. Despair took possession of him, he no longer dared to raise his eyes upon the dazzling image he had created.

But the Sylphide, unaware of his deficiencies, was faithful in love. She came at his call, or came uncalled. He spoke to her, and to no other. He grew thin, hollow-eyed, sleepless, with all the symptoms of a man sick with passion, as indeed he was. His look became vacant and sullen, ardent and unhappy. He avoided even Lucile, with whom he had shared all secrets, but could not share this, partly from shame of his folly, partly from jealousy for his phantom: might she not cease to exist, if he revealed her existence? 'My days flowed by in a way of life that was wild, uncanny, insensate, yet full of delight.'

'I do not know,' he wrote, 'if the history of the human heart offers any other example of such a kind.' This belief in his singularity was not altogether mistaken, even though the self-induced hallucinations which he supposed to be unique are in fact wellnigh universal. Nature prefers, for her own ends, that every adolescent should explore his desires in the daydreams and nightdreams of imagination before fixing and fulfilling

them, more perilously, in a real object. Rousseau before him, a predecessor whom he at first admired but later repudiated, had invented his
own Sylphides, and even called them by that magic name.[7] But few
have sought their Sylphide with such anguish, such lifelong intensity
and persistence, as Chateaubriand. In the phantom he pursued, unawares and in vain, his lost birthright, the love of the mother who had
abandoned him in infancy and remained, even when he regained her,
indifferent and unidentifiable. His attachment to Lucile, obsessive in
childhood and renewed in mid-adolescence, had never answered his
need. Accordingly, at the very moment when he outgrew and rejected
Lucile, the Sylphide had appeared.

But the ghostly girl, although for a while she had seemed masked in
their faces, was more than a disembodied reincarnation of an actual
mother and sister. She was, deeper still, the response to an archetypal
and anonymous deprivation; she was the love which, as a weeping
newborn babe, he had never received; she rose from the buried time
when the suckling has not yet distinguished the ministering mother
from its own need. She was not entirely a lying fantasy, but rather a
symbol of the truth or part truth, that reality itself is only an inadequate
projection of the ideal; that in the love of oneself for others, of others
for oneself, there is always something false or factitious, a response that
is never quite identical with the longing that demands it. The Sylphide,
only now summoned and recognised, had grown up with him and
within him, and would never forsake him. She was his loneliness, she
was the romantic tragedy, she was himself.

He resumed his wanderings in the haunted landscape of Combourg.
The heaths rising northward were scattered with the dolmen tombs and
menhirs of prehistoric stone-men. On one of their granite slabs[8] he used
to sit at sunset and watch, with the Sylphide beside him, the sungold
crest of the woods, the fields in glory, the evening star shimmering
through pink clouds. A heathlark settling on a pebble, a gust of the
evening breeze rending a spiderweb stretched between grass-stalks,
recalled him to reality. Sick at heart, with face awry, suddenly alone, he
took his hangdog way back to the castle.

The stormclouds of summer afternoons rose slowly over the heights
of Bécherel, mounted the sky, encroached eastward and overhead,
darkened the valley, the meadows, the lake. He watched in exultation
from the great west tower, as the thunderclaps rolled and roared in the
eaves, rain crashed on the pyramid roofs of the turrets, and the brass
weathervanes flared in the lightning. He called aloud to the longed-for
tempest, to bring him his Sylphide!

On fine days he hurried across the beechwood of the Great Mall
down to the meadows by the Linon. Here in the poll of a willow, in a
secret seat between earth and sky, he passed the sultry hours with no

companion but the little birds and the ghost. He wandered along the rivulet, rippling downstream through its waterweeds, listened intently to the faint, inexplicable sounds of those desert places. Night fell. She was the rustle of the breeze, the coolness of the dew, the shining stars, the lamenting nightingales, the scent of unseen flowers. As reality and vision merged, so too did the senses that perceived them. He thought he heard the moonlight singing in the woods! He tried to find expression for these new joys, but the words died on his lips.

Hand in hand they visited cities of illustrious ruin, Venice, Rome, Athens, Jerusalem, Memphis, Carthage, which one day he would see in living fact, but now trod in a waking dream, spectral and unpeopled, alone with the Sylphide. They crossed the seas, implored happiness from the palms of Tahiti, the spicegroves of Amboina. They waited for dawn on a peak of Himalaya. They floated down sacred rivers, past pagodas crowned with spheres of gold, and slept on the banks of Ganges, while a gaudy waxbill perched warbling on the bamboo mast of their skiff.

In the midst of this phantasmagoria the real world, if it could be called real, continued to exist. Even François-René himself sometimes left his land of dreams; on 18 February 1785 he is found dining at Saint-Malo with M. Magon de la Villehuchet, who reported next morning by letter to René-Auguste: 'The Chevalier is in the best of health!' His father, mother and Lucile eyed him curiously, saw no Sylphide, sighed, and went about their own affairs. René-Auguste, although he still pottered at his lawsuits, quarrelled with neighbours, refused to pave the town or give an inch in the matter of M. de Trévégat's cow, and wrote occasional business letters in a pathetically laboured hand, was preparing for death. On 5 May 1785 he appointed his brother Pierre sole agent for the recovery of his bad debts in the West Indies, where 248,000 livres in 'money of the Isles' (or 166,000 in good French money) were still owing from the slavetrading enterprises which he had abandoned nine years before. On this occasion he cast up his last balance. His entire fortune, including 330,000 for Combourg, amounted to 630,000 livres, or only 65,000 more than at the end of his corsairing in the Seven Years War, twenty-four years ago. Truly, felt René-Auguste, although he had done so much, he had not done enough for his family.

Jean-Baptiste, not content with Rennes, was beginning a new career in Paris, at the centre of things. René-Auguste made over to this beloved, unprodigal son the sum of 160,000 livres in advance on his legacy. But he did not feel the time was yet ripe for deciding the destiny of his wayward younger boy. On 13 August 1785 M. Restif, a merchant of Saint-Malo, offered a berth as ensign for François-René on one of his ships bound for India, in return for an investment of 6,000 livres. This was a quite usual transaction, subject of course to the commercial capacity of M. Restif, who had heard, he said, that 'Mme de Chateaubriand was enquiring at Saint-Malo after a post for your son'. But René-Auguste replied that he had no spare funds at his disposal. He was not in the giving vein that day.

Autumn came, François-René's favourite season, the time of his birth in the great storm. Wedges of swans throbbed overhead, coveys of woodpigeons clattered down, arriving for winter. Black battalions of rooks gathered in the meadow by the lake, to perch in the highest oaks of the Grand Mall at dusk, while blue mists rose along the woodland rides. 'I saw with inexpressible delight the return of the season of tempests.' He was now seventeen, and on the edge of the abyss.

Every evening he rowed across the lake in his father's boat, which René-Auguste was now too old and gouty to use. He glided through the bulrushes and the round floating leaves of the waterlilies. Swallows tirelessly soared and swooped, dipping their breasts in the mirroring water, clamouring harshly, suddenly clinging to the reeds, in their ritual dance of farewell. Twilight came, the lake chopped and slapped against its brinks, rushes shook their swords and spindles, moorhens and mallards fell silent. 'The great voices of autumn issued from marshes and woods.' He rowed back to mooring, climbed to the castle, sat haggard through supper, and at the stroke of ten ran to his turret, opened the windows, and recited the spell that would bring the Sylphide.

She came, more obedient than ever now, when she was about to leave him. Wound in her hair and robes he rode with her on the clouds that hurried over the courtyard; flying together they stirred the tree-tops, grazed the peaks of mountains, whirled over wavecrests of unknown seas. They swam through the worlds of space, soared to the throne of heaven and plunged to the gates of the pit. In these last visions, more perilous both in seeming and in fact than any that had gone before, he returned to the philosophy of Gesril. 'I wedded in ecstasy the idea of danger to the idea of pleasure.' The gusts of the gale became the sighs of their delight, as the enchantress drew him on her lap, and the breath of her lips ran through his veins like blood. Then in his final exaltation the Sylphide became more a moral than a sensual image; she was glory and honour, the lonely virtue of dedication to the noblest cause, genius in the eternal moment of inspiration. His own sense of identity vanished; he was the cloud, the gale, a bodiless spirit singing the supreme felicity. Consciously and deliberately he discarded his separate being and transformed himself into the Sylphide. Now at last he possessed her beauty, he was at once desire communicated and desire gratified, love and the object of love.

Awareness of his insanity struck him like a blow. He hurled himself shouting on his bed, writhed in grief, wept scalding tears that no one saw, meaningless tears shed for nothing, for a nothingness. The Sylphide was gone, the world was empty of her. She did not exist.

He could not stay in his room. He tiptoed down through the blank darkness, opened the door of the perron furtively, like a murderer escaping from his crime, and stumbled to the great wood. He strode in circles, waving his arms, clasping the wind that fled as the witch had fled. He leaned against the trunk of a beech, watching the rooks he had wakened flapping sleepily to another tree, the moon crawling through the leafless boughs, a dead world mirroring the whiteness of a tomb: he would like to live there. The night was cold and raw; he knew it, without feeling it. The sky paled. He was roused at last from his thoughts not by the icy breath of dawn, but by the sound of a bell.

The bell of Combourg church was tolling for the newly dead at break of day, as Breton custom demanded, in a three-note tune, monotonous, plaintive, and rural. Some shepherd had died in his unknown cabin, and soon would be laid in his unknown grave. For what purpose had that man lived? What was he himself, François-René, doing in this world; and since in the end he must leave it, would it not be better to set out in the cool of the morning and arrive early, than to finish the journey under the burden and the heat of the day? A red flush of desire rose to his face, and the idea of death seized on his heart like a sudden joy.

He had returned to the real world cured of his frenzy, but without recovering his sanity. For a while he observed and reflected. Lucile was sunk in her misery, his mother was no consolation, his father made life a torment. René-Auguste, moved no doubt not by any intention of cruelty but by compulsion to discharge his last duties as a parent, now spied on his son incessantly in order to rebuke him. When François-René returned from his savage wanderings and found his father waiting at the stairhead, he dared not go in. But his ordeal was only deferred, for even the heroic ex-lover of the Sylphide could not avoid family supper. He sat on the edge of his chair motionless and speechless, in tattered clothes, with hair unkempt and cheeks lashed with rain, under the unblinking gaze of René-Auguste. Sweat trickled on his forehead, and the last glimmerings of reason abandoned him.

He still possessed his father's old fowling-piece; the trigger was worn, and often went off without being pulled. He loaded with three bullets, made his way to the densest thicket of the Great Mall, put the muzzle in his mouth, and struck the butt against the ground three times. Nothing happened. He repeated the test twice more—three bullets, three knocks, three trials, magic numbers!—still without result. A gamekeeper approached. He desisted, since evidently he was not meant to die at that moment, and put off the execution of his project until another day.

A sudden illness rescued him from these disorders. Body and soul had fought their duel, had struggled each to destroy the other, and now fell apart exhausted. 'My lungs became swollen and inflamed, I was seized by a violent and irregular fever.' His parents thought the emergency too serious for the local doctors Préciaux and Le Lavandier, and sent to Bazouges-la-Pérouse, a village ten miles east of Combourg, for the eminent Chèvetel, a gentleman-physician favoured by the rich and noble of the entire region. Chèvetel examined the patient attentively, prescribed remedies, but saw his malady was spiritual as well as physical. 'The essential thing,' he declared, 'is to uproot him from his present way of life. You must see he leaves Combourg as soon as he recovers.'

François-René lay in danger for six weeks, nursed by Lucile, whose loving care saved his life. One morning during his convalescence, towards the end of December 1785, his mother came to sit at his bedside and improve the occasion. 'My son,' said she, 'the time has come for you to make your decision. Your brother is in a position to get you a benefice, but before going into the seminary you must think seriously. Much as I should like you to enter the Church, I would far rather see you a man of the world than a scandalous and sacrilegious priest.'

François-René felt with compunction that his mother had put the alternatives only too clearly. Suppose he became an abbé: how absurd he would be, how could he win a woman's love if he wore neckbands? If he rose to be a bishop, he must either acquire virtues or hide his vices; but he felt himself too frail for the one, too incapable of concealment for the other. He informed his mother that his vocation for the priesthood was not strong enough. How similar was this situation, and yet how different, to the moment fifty-one years before when René-Auguste had gone to Dame Perronnelle's bedside and refused to till his field; how like, and how unlike, the forces of ambition or self-realisation that had arisen in the father, and were now rising in the son!

What then was he to do? It was too late to enter the king's navy, for the ever serviceable and well-connected Jean-Baptiste had recently approached the navy minister himself, the Prince de Montmorency-Tingry, only to be informed that cadetships would shortly be restricted to boys aged between thirteen and fifteen. But the merchant marine, as the family's enquiries of last August had shown, would require capital investments for which René-Auguste was disinclined. Only the army remained, which François-René liked well enough, for it promised him glory and a handsome uniform; and yet, he felt he could never endure the loss of his independence or the constraint of military discipline. In a last tergiversation he produced two new and fantastic ideas. He would like to go to Canada, he announced, to chop down forests and farm his clearings; or else he would sail to India and take service with one of the native rajahs. Oddly but characteristically, René-Auguste was far from displeased. For all his stern practicality, he was never unduly shocked by an adventurous proposal, and his own distant youth, as codfisher to Newfoundland, slaver between Africa and the West Indies, corsair on the high seas, had been spent in hazards not so remote from these. He upbraided Mme de Chateaubriand for her son's change of purpose, but yes, he said, the boy should have his passage to India. And so, combining the needs of François-René's career with obedience to Dr. Chèvetel's orders, they packed him off to Saint-Malo, where an Indiaman was reported to be fitting out for Pondicherry.[9]

The ship did not sail, or perhaps he let it sail without him. His birthplace was strange to him, and he a stranger there. When people met him, they asked who he was. His playmates had gone out into the world. He looked through the harbour in vain for the ships in whose rigging he had played; they were far at sea, or had been broken up. None of his family was left, for Uncle Pierre had moved seven years ago to his manor of Val Guildo. The house in the Rue des Juifs was now an inn.[10] Probably he stayed in his mother's little home from home in the Rue des Grands-Degrés, and perhaps she also came on and off, when René-Auguste's health allowed it, for her usual winter and lenten holidays from the gloom of Combourg.

She was there for business on 24 January 1786, when she signed on her husband's behalf a receipt for the sum of nearly 25,000 livres, which the villainous Drieux, captain of the lost *Jean-Baptiste*, had embezzled thirteen years before, and which his children had at last repaid. For the last fortnight René-Auguste had been confined to his bed in the east tower with gout. On that evening at Combourg the old man had a slight stroke. Doctors Préciaux and Le Lavandier hurried to the castle and spent the night by him. Mme de Chateaubriand returned, perhaps the still-ailing François-René too for a few weeks. On 28 February a doctor's bill from Préciaux shows him at Combourg, taking a dose of Corsican moss, in those days a favourite remedy for threadworm.

René-Auguste, ever indomitable, partly recovered the use of his limbs. But his left arm now quivered in an unceasing palsy, which he restrained by gripping it with his right hand. At his doctor's orders he went for the last time to take the waters at Dinan, so sovereign against gout—for what other than gout could any malady of an eighteenth-century gentleman be? Yet in his heart René-Auguste knew that the end was near; the warning finger of death had tapped his left shoulder, lifted and retired, but not for long.

Death would soon return, so be it. But first he must see that he left his family secure and rising. Bénigne, three years a widow and with a little son aged four, remarried on 24 April 1786 at Fougères, attended by the Marignys and Jean-Baptiste. Her new husband, the fourth military nobleman of Fougères to marry into the family, was Paul-François de la Celle, Vicomte de Chateaubourg, aged thirty-four, a lieutenant in the regiment of Condé. M. de Chateaubourg had good expectations, for only a child nephew, who duly died unmarried a few years later, stood between him and the headship of his line, with the title of Count. Jean-

Baptiste himself was preparing a decisive step upward in his legal career; in July he bought an influential post as Master of Requests[11] in the Parlement of Paris, and moved from Rennes to the capital. Mme de Chateaubriand, no doubt, after weeping a little, would live agreeably enough as widow and dowager in her beloved Saint-Malo. The loyal steward Le Corvaisier would look after Combourg until Jean-Baptiste chose to marry. But for René-Auguste his wild younger son was still an unsolved problem. François-René's flight to India, if the young scapegrace really intended it, was satisfactorily bold, and reminded him of his own young days; but exile was not a career, and would benefit neither the boy nor the family. Early in the spring, without informing François-René, he ordered Jean-Baptiste to find him a post in the army. Jean-Baptiste, never at a loss for wires to pull, applied to M. du Boberil de Cherville, the procurator general of the Estates of Brittany.

Meanwhile François-René again wandered desperate in Saint-Malo. He visited his old nurse La Villeneuve, and was touched to find she had kept the little wickerwork frame on wheels in which he had learned to walk at Plancoët. Where could he walk now, and expect to find love? He roamed along the desert sands, where long ago he had built his childish castles. When the tide was low, the vast empty expanse seemed like his own desolate heart, from which hope had ebbed. When the gale blew and breakers rose, he remembered how he had dared them in sport with Gesril; but now he was tempted to yield to them in earnest. Cape La Varde checked his course, three miles east of the city, where the crescent of whitegold sands ends in a harsh granite promontory. He sat on the furthest seaward cliff. Here, on fairdays long ago, had been one of his hiding-places, where he swallowed his tears while his playmates revelled far away in their joy. Now that he was a man, he felt neither happier nor more loved. Soon he would leave his country and cross the ocean; how should he hope to find in an alien land the love that was absent from here and from Combourg? The midsummer sun shone on the sea; but once again, like a visitant from the castle woods, longing for death rose in him and seemed to impel his limbs. He need only let himself drop into the waves, now or tomorrow.

Tomorrow brought a letter from his mother: he was to come home at once. He obeyed instantly, and arrived in time for family supper, where his father said not a word, his mother sighed unremittingly, and Lucile seemed lost in consternation. At ten o'clock, when his parents dispersed, he questioned Lucile. 'I don't know what they are going to do with you,' she said, 'except that they're going to make you leave home.' Sure enough, next morning at eight he was summoned to his father's study. 'Monsieur le Chevalier,' announced René-Auguste, rigid and swaying, 'I have decided on your fate; you must say goodbye to your follies. Your brother has found you a brevet as sublieutenant in the regiment of Navarre. You will be stationed at Cambrai, and you will leave in a few days.'

M. du Boberil de Cherville had acted quickly and done very well. He had written to Comte d'Andrezel, major in the regiment of Navarre, who had proposed the new recruit to his colonel-in-chief, the Marquis de Mortemart. Yes, M. de Mortemart would be delighted. On 24 and 30 June M. d'Andrezel wrote direct to Jean-Baptiste, in the most obliging terms. He would do all he could to see that the Chevalier de Chateaubriand should be nominated for his commission during the next winter; he would watch the young man's expenses, be his mentor; and in order the better to do so, he would be glad to receive information concerning 'his moral nature, his character, the studies he has followed, those for which he shows particular preference, his other interests, etc.' The departure of the subaltern was planned for 10 or 15 July.

Even so, he still lingered for a few weeks more at Combourg, preparing his baggage, or pleading for time. On 2 August together with Lucile he stood as godparent—a feudal duty to their servants, vassals or neighbours which the whole family took in turns—at the baptism of the latest male child of their gardener, Aumont. But early on the morning of 9 August René-Auguste sent for him again. 'You will leave immediately for Rennes,' said he, 'and from there for Cambrai. Here are a hundred louis; make them last. I'm old and ill, I haven't long to live. Conduct yourself like a gentleman, and never dishonour your name or my memory.' He clasped his boy in his arms, and François-René felt that stern and wrinkled face pressing with emotion against his own. Once again, as in the castle nights when René-Auguste had said: 'I haven't done enough for my family,' the son was overwhelmed by love, pity, gratitude and remorse towards the father he had always feared. He threw himself weeping upon the aged man's fleshless hand, and kissed it. 'You had better have my old sword,' said René-Auguste, and gave it him. Then, holding his palsied left arm with his right hand, without giving him time to recover, as though even now the lad might succeed in escaping, he led him to a one-horse chaise that waited in the Green Court, and watched him climb in. The coachman drove off, and they swung down the drive and into the avenue.

François-René had just time to wave his hand to his mother and Lucile, bathed in tears on the stairway. Then he was bowling along the causeway by the lake, past the bulrushes where his swallows had clung, the millstream, the meadow. He looked back at the castle, where the four towers rose to peer after him, and the beechwoods sighed. At the next slope all disappeared. And yet, in this moment of farewell, when he was banished for ever from Eden for his sins, he felt a new exultation to which, as he remembered it thirty years later, the closing words of *Paradise Lost* seemed appropriate. The world was all before him.

PART TWO

The Judgement of Paris

6

ROYAL HUNT

FRANÇOIS-RENÉ reached Rennes in time to dine with his father's friend, M. Duparquet-Louyer, a procurator in Parlement, whose family came from Combourg. Next day M. Duparquet-Louyer sent the young ladies his nieces out shopping for the rest of the Chevalier's outfit, including 'two pairs of finest cotton stockings, a real bargain', and proceeded to find him an agreeable travelling-companion. The pretty wife of M. Todon, mercer of Rennes, a grand-daughter of a former official at Combourg, was leaving for Paris by post-chaise; if the young couple went shares it would be more economical, more comfortable, and so much more enjoyable than the mail-coach! Mme Rose eyed the Chevalier, burst into trills of laughter, and consented. 'They met, spoke, agreed, and left at seven-thirty this evening,' wrote M. Duparquet-Louyer to René-Auguste. Perhaps as he read, knowing his son, the father's face was creased with his last grim smile.

So the former lover of the Sylphide, who never yet had set eyes on a real woman without blushing, found himself driving through the summer night with a lively little milliner. He huddled into a corner of the carriage, for fear of brushing against her gown. When she spoke, he mumbled without answering. He was utterly useless; at the end of each stage it was she who had to get out to pay the postillion. In the light of dawn, as she stared at this ninny again, the expression on her face was of amazement.

The landscape had changed; the dress and voices of the peasants were no longer those of Brittany. François-René, feeling uprooted and absurd, sat in deep dejection. He knew himself to be wild and shy, but he was not an oaf; how unjust, that he should be despised for the virtue of his modesty! In the next few years he acquired social courage and aplomb in plenty. Yet this first contact with the world of men and women left in him, as he acknowledged, 'an impression that time has never completely effaced'. His alienation from his fellow-creatures, or the difference between any mortal woman and the Sylphide, were not the mere illusions of an awkward boy, but the truth itself.

Early in the morning of the second day they approached Paris. As they drove downhill from Saint-Cyr he was struck by the wideness of the highway, the neat regularity of the fields. They passed the orangery at Versailles; surely the King, victorious from the War of American Independence, the Queen, dazzling in the height of her youth and beauty, would tread those marble stairways in triumph for ever! They entered Paris, where all the faces seemed to be sneering at him, and drew up at the Hôtel de l'Europe in the Rue du Mail.[1] 'Give this gentleman a room,' said Mme Rose to the doorman, and added to François-René, with only the vaguest suggestion of a curtsey: 'Your servant, sir.' He did not see Mme Rose again.

He climbed a dark steep stair to the third floor, preceded by a chambermaid with a labelled key, followed by a porter carrying his exiguous trunk. Three blasts of a whistle sounded, the maid shouted: 'Coming!', and both hurtled downstairs. Finding himself thus alone he felt strongly inclined to return to Brittany. He was hungry; but how did one ask for food in Paris without showing that one did not know how to behave? He opened his window, and saw nothing but an inner yard, deep as a well, and servants bustling across it to and fro, who would never in all their lives give a thought to their prisoner on the third floor. He sat opposite the grimy alcove with unmade bed where he would be doomed to sleep, and stared at the mannikins painted on its wallpaper.

A distant noise of voices grew louder and nearer; his door flew open; in came his brother, and a huge fat man with open mouth and protruding tongue, puffing and blowing, smeared with snuff, chattering incessantly. It was none other than cousin Annibal, son of his mother's sister Julie Moreau, the comic hero and victim of the Clémenceau Affair nineteen years before—now a goodnatured ogre, the prosperous absentee keeper of the tobacco warehouse at Fougères, who frequented every anteroom and drawingroom and gambling-den in Paris, and 'knew everybody'. Jean-Baptiste embraced François-René affectionately. 'Well, now, Chevalier,' bawled Cousin Moreau, 'so here you are in Paris! I'll take you to call on Mme de Chastenay straight away!' François-René recoiled in horror. 'I'm sure the Chevalier needs to rest,' said Jean-Baptiste, 'we'll go and see Mme de Farcy, and then he can come back for dinner and go to bed.' On the way down Cousin Moreau gave the proprietor a thorough wigging: 'It's a horrible room and much too high up! You're to give him a better one, *at least* one floor lower!'

As they climbed into Jean-Baptiste's carriage, on their way to see dear Julie, François-René felt bliss returning to his heart: so, in the midst of an indifferent world, Brittany and his family were with him after all! Julie, as was correct for respectable spinsters or unattached wives, was staying in a convent. M. de Farcy was a man of action and strong character, something of a spendthrift, but neither tyrant nor fool. Julie, fourteen years younger than her husband, was gay, independent, and ambitious. Like Jean-Baptiste she had felt the call of Paris, though for her elder brother Paris meant his career, while Julie was lured by the charm of its cultured society. Very sensibly, after four years of marriage, M. and Mme de Farcy had decided on an amicable parting. Julie had been in Paris since the spring, on the pretext of consulting its doctors for her health. Henceforth she spent half the year in Paris and half in Brittany; but when she resided in the Hôtel de Farcy at Fougères, or in the neighbouring châteaux of her elder sisters, M. de Farcy was always tactfully elsewhere.

Julie, François-René's favourite sister next to Lucile, welcomed him with sisterly tenderness. She was less beautiful than Lucile but much prettier, with her caressing blue eyes, long brown hair crimped and waved, shapely arms and white hands with which she gestured so charmingly. Julie was brilliant and animated, and laughed a great deal, unaffectedly, showing her pearly teeth. As she clasped him in her perfumed embrace, with her ribbons and laces and rose bouquet, François-René felt a sense of protection which he had scarcely known since his childhood summer at Plancoët.

At eight o'clock next morning the fat cousin returned. 'Well now, Chevalier,' cried he, 'we'll go out and have breakfast, then we'll dine with Pommereul, and in the evening I'll take you to see Mme de Chastenay!' François-René resigned himself to this unavoidable fate. After breakfast Moreau insisted on leading him through all the seediest streets in the neighbourhood of the Palais Royal, 'so that you can see the dangers to which a young man might expose himself'. This was a notorious district of brothels and gaming-hells, and Moreau was evidently an expert on the subject. They dined at a restaurant, where the food was awful, with a crowd of fellow-Bretons, who talked about the court, stocks and shares, women, the most recent public love-affairs, the latest meeting of the Academy, the new play, actors, actresses, and authors. Among the guests were two Bretons of Moreau's generation, whom François-René would meet again: the tiny madcap Chevalier de Guer, who was to fight the Revolution, and the thoroughly progressive Baron de Pommereul, who was to join it. Pommereul was against the entire nobility, excepting of course his own family which, as he justly pointed out, was mentioned with approval in Mme de Sevigné's letters.[2] After dinner Jean-Baptiste did his best to take François-René to the theatre, but no; Cousin Moreau thought it more urgent that he should come and see Mme de Chastenay.

Mme de Chastenay turned out to be a lady not in her first youth, but still quite attractive enough to inspire an attachment. She welcomed him affably, did her best to put him at his ease, and asked polite questions about his provincial home and his regiment. François-René, overcome with embarrassment, made signs to Cousin Moreau to cut the visit short; but Cousin Moreau, unseeing, went on singing his praises. 'He's a most remarkable young man,' he affirmed, 'he used to make up poetry when he was still in his mother's lap!—why don't you write some now,' he added, 'about Mme de Chastenay?' Mme de Chastenay, taking pity, suddenly remembered that she had an appointment. 'Come and see me again tomorrow morning,' said she, in a voice so gentle that François-René found himself promising to obey.

He obeyed, and this time found her in bed, in a most elegant bedroom. She was a little indisposed that morning, she explained, and besides, she had the bad habit of getting up late. She set herself to overcome his timidity, and soon he found himself talking with utter abandon. He could not remember what he said, but never forgot her look of astonishment. 'We will tame you,' she said with a smile, stretching out a half-bare arm and the prettiest hand he had ever seen. He left, not daring to kiss that hand; he never saw her again, and never even knew who Mme de Chastenay was.[3]

Next day he set out by mailcoach for Cambrai, once the archbishopric of his beloved Fénelon. His regiment of Navarre, first mustered in 1515 for François I, was one of the oldest in the French army. His uniform, as M. d'Andrezel had promised Jean-Baptiste, was 'ready in twenty-four hours'; its colours were white trimmed with skyblue, the very hues he had worn in childhood for his protectress the Blessed Virgin, and it seemed as though he had worn it always.

His new brother-in-law Chateaubourg, pleased to show himself a useful member of the family so promptly, had given him letters of recommendation to the officers. The wellbred Chevalier de Guénan, first lieutenant, invited him to his own mess, where he dined every day with second lieutenant La Martinière, and sublieutenant Achard, a wealthy young Breton with an estate near Fougères. His major, Comte d'Andrezel, was as fatherly as could be wished, though not to the detriment of discipline. Once again to his surprise, as in his schooldays at Dol and Rennes, he found himself inexplicably accepted and even sought after by his companions. No one ever thought of subjecting him to the usual rough ceremonies of initiation, and within a fortnight he was treated like a veteran. Elderly captains and young sublieutenants deserted their favourite coffeehouses to resort to his humble room. The old ones confided in him about their campaigns, the young about their amours.

La Martinière was strikingly ugly, and his face was pitted with smallpox. But the poor man was smitten with love for a fair native of Cambrai, who did not requite his passion, and half a dozen times every day he took François-René to stroll in front of her unkind street-door. Then he discussed his feelings over large glasses of gooseberry cordial, for which François-René paid. Perhaps François-René could do still more to assist him?

François-René had suddenly become a dandy. According to standing orders they must dress with the strictest military formality: small hat, hair frizzed close to the head, stiff pigtail behind, coat buttoned tight.

He submitted by day, but at night he ordered his barber to let down his
locks and uncomb his pigtail, donned a hat of exuberant amplitude, and
with coat unbuttoned and lapels spread sallied out to plead his friend's
cause with the cruel charmer. In this fetching négligé he ran face to face
into M. d'Andrezel. 'What is the meaning of this, sir? Consider yourself under three days' arrest!' François-René felt a little abashed; but
then he reflected that at least he was now released from responsibility
for his comrade's wooing. He occupied his confinement in rereading
Télémaque in the author's own city, and during his hours of duty made
swift progress in drill and the theory and practice of arms. Within a few
days of his arrival he had heard news of the death of Frederick the
Great, King of Prussia, which occurred on 17 August 1786. A few
weeks later, soon after his own eighteenth birthday, he learned of the
death of someone else.

Towards eight o'clock on the evening of 6 September, quite suddenly,
René-Auguste de Chateaubriand, Count of Combourg, had suffered a
second stroke and died. Down in the castle meadow the Angevine fair
was in full swing. He was aged sixty-eight all but a fortnight. That night
the chaplain Abbé Chalmel and the bailiff Le Corvaisier kept vigil over
his body in his bedroom in the east tower, while in her bedroom over
the guardroom the griefstricken Mme de Chateaubriand was tended by
Lucile and Dr. Préciaux, who stayed till two in the morning. On the
8th René-Auguste was buried in the seigneurial vault of the Lords of
Combourg at Combourg church, in an old disused lead coffin. The local
nobility, MM. de Petit-Bois, de Montlouet, de Chateau-d'Assis, the
officials Launay de la Bliardière, Noury de Mauny, Petit, and the clergy
Le Douarin and Sévin, attended and signed the register. Mme de
Chateaubriand fled to Saint-Malo, leaving the modest sum of 240 livres
as alms for the poor. Antoine de Bédée arrived, too late to see even the
body of his brother-in-law, but in time to receive on the 12th the
official visit of M. Labbé, the royal notary resident at Combourg. Together they made ritual procession through the three-dimensional
labyrinth of the deserted castle, climbing every stair, threading every
corridor, securing every door with crowned paper and sealing-wax. As
they prepared to seal the great door of the perron, Abbé Chalmel
objected that it was still his duty to serve the chapel; so they left chapel
door and great door unsealed, and handed him the keys of both. Bédée
the Artichoke as proxy had seen his sister's husband into the castle
twenty-five years before, and now he had seen him out.

A letter from Lucile told François-René the news, and summoned
him to Saint-Malo. He wept, remembering the old man as he paced the
castle guardroom in the winter nights, and forgetting his severity. He
had loved his father, and his father, he rightly decided, had loved him.
Then he realised with alarm that henceforth he would be his own

master: what would he do with his liberty? 'I doubted my strength; I recoiled from my own image.' He was granted leave; M. d'Andrezel had been promoted lieutenant-colonel of the regiment of Picardy, and took him to Paris as his courier. Without lingering in the great city he left immediately for Saint-Malo, where he perhaps arrived in time to witness the next episode in the legal consequences of his father's death.

On 23 September M. Labbé reappeared, to make an inventory of furniture and effects at 479 Rue des Grands-Degrés and apply yet more seals. A curious scene ensued, in which an uninstructed bystander might have thought the elder son's attitude unfilial and the mother's unmotherly. Jean-Baptiste announced that by the custom of Brittany he was now the lawful owner of his father's entire property, subject to settlement of his juniors' shares in proper time and form. He refused consent to the sealing of his father's town house, and demanded removal of the seals placed on Combourg in his absence. Mme de Chateaubriand countered by producing the deed of mutual donation of property made by René-Auguste and herself on 4 July 1753, the day after their marriage, which left the surviving partner in sole possession by usufruct until his or her decease, together with the right of applying seals, which she now claimed![4] In fact, of course, this legal quibbling did not imply any actual discord between the fond mother and her favourite child. It was the duty of each, in the regulation of so complex an inheritance, first to stand upon their utmost rights, and later to work out an equitable agreement. But the matter of seals was allowed to lapse; evidently, Mme de Chateaubriand could not really wish her only home to be barred, nor could Jean-Baptiste, who had no intention of residing at Combourg, really want the castle left open to thieves. On 17 October, at the joint request of both, M. Labbé unsealed the guardroom at Combourg, and the housekeeper Mlle La Salle was reinstalled there as custodian.

François-René returned to Cambrai to complete his first three months' term of duty. He passed rapidly to the nominal grade of corporal, then of sergeant, with the applause of his instructors. In that declining peacetime army furlough was liberal, and only six months of actual service were required of him in each year. Towards December he went on leave to Fougères, an ancient rose-grey fortress town, with a walled medieval castle on one side of the deep valley of the little river Nançon, and on the other terraced gardens ('like shelves laden with flowers', wrote Balzac) rising to the 'high town' where his sisters lived.

Julie had returned from Paris, and invited Lucile to join her in the Hôtel de Farcy; now Lucile too was free, like François-René, for the first time in her life. The Hôtel de Farcy was demolished in 1847, but the little terrace garden remains, still known as 'Lucile's garden', where Lucile would read and meditate, alone and out of sight, and gaze across the misty valley at the castle. François-René stayed partly with Julie, partly with Marie-Anne in the nearby Hôtel de Marigny, and partly with Bénigne, who continued to live in her first husband's Hôtel de Québriac. Everyone knew everyone at Fougères. In the winter season there were dances, dinners, assemblies; François-René found himself taking part in all these pleasures, feeling that as a professed solitary he ought not to enjoy them, but enjoying them nevertheless.

Towards the end of January 1787 a letter came from Jean-Baptiste in Paris. He himself, he explained, was unfortunately not eligible for presentation at court, since he was still a man of law, though he meant to remedy this before long. So he had decided in the meantime to have François-René presented instead. The proofs of noble descent made four years before for Lucile, when she was received as canoness of l'Argentière, would serve just as well for him. The Duc de Duras (who had never ceased to feel a feudal benevolence towards the Chateaubriands since he sold them Combourg) had consented to be his sponsor. The lucky François-René would instantly receive the honorary rank of captain of cavalry;[5] and next, Jean-Baptiste saw his way to having him made a Knight of Malta, with a splendid benefice. He was on the road to fortune, he must come at once!

François-René was thunderstruck. He, whose one ambition (as he thought) was to live alone and forgotten, he, who was taken ill when he found himself with three or four strangers in a drawingroom, was now expected to meet the King! He ungratefully drafted an ungracious reply, pointing out that Jean-Baptiste was the elder brother, that it was for him to uphold the family name, that His Majesty might well have use for a soldier in his army, but could not possibly need an impoverished young nobleman at his court. He read this romantic epistle to Marie-Anne, who uttered shrieks of horror and sent for Julie, who laughed him to scorn. Lucile would have liked to take his side, but dared not oppose her sisters. Crestfallen, he wrote that he would come, and left as if summoned to the gallows.

He stayed at the same hotel, as he knew no other, in a room next door to his old one, but a little larger and with a window on the street. Jean-Baptiste, embarrassed by his awkwardness or merciful to his timidity, introduced him to no one; but he had François-René to dinner at his lodgings in the Rue des Fossés-Montmartre every afternoon at three (for of course one dined later in Paris than at Combourg), and enquired: 'What have you done? What have you seen?' 'Nothing,' was the invariable reply, and Jean-Baptiste shrugged his shoulders and turned his back. Once, when he called François-René to the window to watch something in the street, the apathetic young man would not leave the armchair where he lay sprawled at the other end of the room. 'You will die unknown, and useless to yourself and your family,' predicted the elder brother, despairingly rather than unkindly. Then they parted till the same hour next day.

Cousin Moreau was no longer in Paris. François-René walked more than once past Mme de Chastenay's house, but never dared ask the porter if she was still at home. His only company was two young girls who every day at four o'clock, the very moment when he returned from dinner with his brother, sat down to draw at their window in the house opposite. From time to time they sedately raised their heads to look at him, and for once he was grateful to be noticed. In the evening he went alone to the Opéra or Théâtre Français, and felt at home in the desert of the crowd. He saw Mme Saint-Huberti in Gluck's *Armide*; so beautiful was this enchantress, as she tempted the paladin Rinaldo to linger for ever in her arms, that he decided there had been something lacking even in his own witch, the Sylphide. On other evenings he walked from street to street or along the quays. Then, back in his room, he sat staring at his fire. The distant rolling of carriages sounded like the nocturnal murmur of the seas of Brittany or the woods of Combourg, and he remembered, without feeling it anew, his old unhappy passion. He imagined the people in those carriages, driving to bright-lit drawing-rooms, to balls, to love, and victory in love. Then he came to himself, abandoned in a hired room, seeing the world through his window, hearing its sounds through his walls.

The dreadful day of his presentation drew near. Jean-Baptiste escorted him to Versailles, and he never afterwards saw the long line of street-lamps from the Place Louis XV to the Passy barrier without recalling his anguish. Jean-Baptiste introduced him to the Duc de Duras, an obliging old gentleman who despite his exquisite manners seemed disconcertingly homely when one noticed the commonplaceness of his mind; even so, the good duke scared François-René terribly. Next morning he waited with the throng of courtiers outside the King's bed-chamber in the Oeil-de-Boeuf, the tall anteroom with a bull's-eye window. They gazed at him, with discreet murmurs of: 'Do you know who he is?' But he observed that, of the two characteristics which composed the demeanour of a great lord towards an unknown inferior, they displayed only one, the air of extreme politeness; the other, the air of protective disdain, they eschewed, for who could tell whether, if His Majesty took a fancy to the young upstart, he might not be on the threshold of power?

'The King has risen!' The door opened, Louis XVI was seen taking his hat from the gentleman-in-waiting, and emerged on his way to morning mass. François-René bowed; the Duc de Duras said: 'Sire, the Chevalier de Chateaubriand.' The King stared, seemed about to speak, could think of nothing to say, and passed on. They hurried to await the Queen in the Galerie des Glaces, where in the vast mirrors the looking-

glass world of the park lay reflected, sloping ever downward by fountains, avenues of leafless beeches, a great oblong water, to a vague,
infinite, bluegrey vista of paradisal peace and eternal security. Marie-
Antoinette swept by, attended by a radiant procession, curtseying nobly
as she passed, full of delight in life.

He rejoined his brother who, as an unpresented and unpresentable
man of law, had been unable to accompany him. Jean-Baptiste entreated
him, almost pathetically, to stay in Versailles for the Queen's evening
game of cards: 'you will be presented to Her Majesty,' he urged, 'and
the King will talk to you.' François-René declined, thanking him for
the warning, and fled to Paris and his lonely hotel.

But his ordeal was not over. A few days later, on 19 February 1787,
he was summoned to attend the King's hunt in the forest of Saint-
Germain. He dressed in the correct uniform, grey coat, pink waistcoat
and breeches, topboots, and hunting-knife slung to the belt, and re-
paired to Versailles. The Duc de Coigny, the chief royal equerry, gave
instructions, of which the most important was: 'Mind you don't cut
across the hunt, because the King flies into a rage if anyone gets between him and the quarry!' Drums beat the salute, the guards presented
arms, a voice cried: 'The King.' The King entered his carriage, and the
long line of hunting courtiers drove off behind him to the rendezvous.

Under the trees were neighing horses, yelling hounds straining at
the leash, fine gentlemen and ladies, and horns blowing. François-René
presented his invitation-card and was allotted a skittish, hardmouthed
mare called l'Heureuse. The scene seized his historical imagination; he
thought of royal mistresses at the chase, of Louis XIV's Mme de
Montespan, Henri IV's Gabrielle d'Estrées, his own collateral ancestress
Françoise de Chateaubriand, whom François I had briefly loved.[6]
Besides, he was in a forest, and therefore felt at home.

King, hunters and huntresses rode off, leaving him alone with
l'Heureuse, who defied his efforts to mount. At last he succeeded in
hurling himself upon her back, and head down, foaming at the bit, she
advanced crabwise with sidelong bounds. Then she galloped head out,
full tilt into a group of riders, scattering them amid laughter and
screams, stopping only when she collided with the horse of a lady, who
accepted his excuses very politely. He heard a murmur everywhere:
'Did you see the debutant's adventure?' Half an hour later, as he was
cantering down a long avenue towards a mysterious pavilion, a gun-
shot rang out, l'Heureuse dashed aside through a thicket, and he found
himself by the newly slain buck, closely followed by the King himself.
Alas for the Duc de Coigny's warning! He leapt to the ground, pushing
l'Heureuse back with one hand, bowing low with hat in the other. The
King glared, seemed about to 'fly into a rage', but instead remarked
goodhumouredly and with a loud laugh: 'He didn't last long.' Such

were the only words ever addressed by this harmless monarch to
François-René. The others came up, astonished to find the strange
debutant involved in yet another 'adventure', and even 'talking to the
King'. Perhaps he was on the brink of fame and fortune; but rather
than stay for His Majesty's ceremonial unbooting he retreated again
to Paris. Even Jean-Baptiste gave up the struggle, consoled only by
the reflection that now, at least, the court had heard the name of
Chateaubriand.

Louis XVI was within six years of the guillotine; it would be very
long indeed before the hour of favour at court struck again for
François-René.

In any case, it was now time for them both to return to Combourg
for the final division of their father's property. On Saturday 3 March
the whole family assembled: the mother, the two sons, and the four
daughters. Marie-Anne's and Bénigne's husbands came too, to see fair
play for their wives; M. de Farcy tactfully preferred to stay away, but
had given Julie power of attorney; and since the two younger children
were still minors,[7] François-René was accompanied by his trustee, M.
Gesbert de la Noé-Seiche, seneschal of Combourg, and Lucile by hers,
M. des Bouillons de la Loriais, barrister in the Parlement of Rennes.

The long ritual of inventory proceeded throughout the following
week, until every article in every room had been meticulously listed and
valued. The Chateaubriands did it in style, for divisions of inheritance,
even more than baptisms, marriage-contracts, or funerals, were the most
delectably prestigious of ceremonies in a noble family under the old
regime. Everything was as correct as correct could be, almost, in matters
of sixpenny fire-shovels or fourpenny porringers, to the point of
absurdity. Jean-Baptiste has been blamed for these exigences, quite
unjustly, for in this and all occasions of his meritorious existence he was
merely acting his part, a little pompously but never ungenerously, as
eldest son and feudal head of the family. In fact, not only were the rights
of each at stake, together with the fiscal dues of the crown (as the
vigilant presence of M. Labbé indicated), but all were enjoying themselves thoroughly.

The inventory survives, and by this strange chance the world may
even now know the presence and price of every bed, chair, table in every
room, each pot and pan in the kitchen of the castle of Combourg.
Various unjustifiable inferences have been drawn, and must be rejected:
for example, that René-Auguste deprived his family of sugar and
candles, or that François-René's room was meanly furnished and fire-
less.[8] It is more interesting to glimpse so many of the objects made
familiar by the *Memoirs*: the coach upholstered in crimson velvet,
the clock in the north tower by which Lucile had midnight visions, the
genealogical tree of the Chateaubriands in René-Auguste's study, the

couch where Mme de Chateaubriand lay sighing in the guardroom on winter evenings. Perhaps she was not a very downtrodden wife after all; at least, her bedroom is by far the most expensively furnished in all the castle. Her husband's is of monastic simplicity, his bed (60 livres) the cheapest in the whole household. But René-Auguste compensated for this frugality by the splendour of his wardrobe, which included eighty-six shirts, sixty-two pairs of stockings, and a dozen suits of silk, velvet, or satin, yellow, grey, black, maroon, or sprigged with flowers. Locked in his cupboard with the sugar and candles they found 31,152 livres in ready cash, the family silver (7,369 livres by weight), a gold watch, and a gold snuffbox. Mme de Chateaubriand presented an account of her furniture at 479 rue des Grands-Degrés (1,925 livres), which no one disputed. She handed over the proceeds of her debt-collecting since her husband's death (13,979 livres), together with the latest instalments recovered by Uncle Pierre from the West Indies (1,972 livres). Then at last, to the relief of all, she dramatically declared her renunciation of the old vexatious 'mutual donation' of 4 July 1753.

Next day, 14 March, they proceeded to the division of spoils. First the widow's dower must be decided. Mme de Chateaubriand's sacrifice still left her with a second line of defence, for her marriage contract stipulated that after her husband's decease she should enjoy half the usufruct in rents and interests upon his entire property. However, she gracefully consented to resign this secondary but still enormous claim in consideration of a life pension of 8,000 livres, payable quarterly in advance; and the first year's instalment was handed to her on the spot.

So far everything had passed off amicably, but now came a hint of unpleasantness. The Custom of Brittany prescribed that two-thirds of a nobleman's property must go to the eldest son, and the remaining third be divided between the other children; a plebeian's estate, on the other hand, was shared equally by all his offspring. Marie-Anne and Bénigne, primed by their lawyers, pointed out that René-Auguste's fortune had nothing to do with his rank, since it had been gained by trade; it was therefore, they maintained, a plebeian estate, and they claimed equal shares for all. Some high words ensued. Mme de Chateaubriand was scandalised, and never quite forgave her elder daughters, not so much for their greed as for their outrage to family pride. A plebeian estate! Fortunately the law was perfectly clear; ordinances of Louis XIV and Louis XV laid down that large-scale commerce, especially in the merchant marine, was no derogation of nobility; so René-Auguste's was a noble estate, after all. However, to compensate for any imaginable stain of retail trade in their legacy, Jean-Baptiste urbanely and more than generously proposed to distribute 25,000 livres among his five juniors, or 5,000 each, as a personal gift; and this too was counted out on the spot. Then, at last, the final division was made.

It is unlikely that any of the heirs had expected to come into a fortune; but if any had nurtured such a hope, then he or she was grievously mistaken. René-Auguste's personal estate was found to be barely over 300,000 livres. Jean-Baptiste's two thirds would therefore amount to 200,000, while the five younger children would get 20,000 each. But Jean-Baptiste had already received from his father 160,000 in advance three years before; so he gained little, except the lordship of Combourg with its feudal dues. The shares of the three elder girls were smaller than their marriage-portions, so they profited less than nothing. Jean-Baptiste, as was his right and duty, retained control of Lucile's and François-René's shares until their coming of age; so they too gained nothing for the time being. Only Mme de Chateaubriand, with her handsome little pension, her freedom and her town-house, had reason to be satisfied.

It was with this disappointing outcome in mind that René-Auguste had lamented, in the winter evenings, that he 'had not done enough for his family'. In fact the old man was not personally to blame. His mysterious failure to improve his fortune, despite all his energy, prudence, courage and final exhaustion, was predestined by the same economic decline of France, the unprofitable wars and loss of empire, which were among the causes of the coming Revolution. In that universal and now imminent catastrophe all he had left behind him was doomed to perish. Combourg, feudal dues, noble rank and noble estates, would vanish away; in their place the Chateaubriands would inherit ruin, the guillotine, prison, destitution and exile.

So the family dispersed in discontent—Jean-Baptiste to Paris, the girls to Fougères, their mother to Saint-Malo—unaware that even this unsatisfactory pittance of wealth was dust and ashes, fairy gold.

Only François-René, though none the richer, was none the sadder. Money would be delightful to spend, but sordid to seek; why should he miss what he never had? He returned to his military service. The regiment of Navarre had moved from Cambrai and divided; the first battalion was stationed at Le Havre, the second, his own, at Dieppe. Thanks to his presentation at court he was now considered quite a personage. In May M. de Mortemart, a little belatedly, applied for his appointment as acting sublieutenant, but the War Ministry omitted to reply. He took a new fancy to his profession, worked hard at drill, and was given a platoon of recruits, whom he marched to and fro on the pebbles by his old friend the sea. La Martinière, he found, was in love again. Parted from his beauty of Cambrai, he was now languishing at the big feet of a not very young beauty of Dieppe, with coif and coiffure half a yard high, named Mlle Cauchie.

Was it not time he himself should be in love? In July, after completing his second period of three months' service, he went on long leave to Fougères. The queen of the town, he found, was Mlle de la Bélinaye, an elderly spinster who lived in her family mansion next door to the Hôtel de Marigny; her sister Thérèse was the mother of Armand de la Rouërie, the future royalist conspirator, and her other sister Perrine was mother of Thérèse de Moëlien, whose presence at Julie's wedding in 1782 had given François-René his first impression of female beauty. Among Mlle de la Bélinaye's neighbours was another maiden lady, Mlle Victoire des Alleuz, on whom he decided to practise his arts of love. This 'agreeable frump', as he ungallantly describes her, was aged thirty-one, thirteen years older than himself, and twice the age of the Sylphide; so he mistakenly imagined there could be no risk for either of being taken seriously. To his horror the senior lady capitulated to his advances; to her horror, she realised too late that he was not in earnest. Mlle des Alleuz never married, never forgave or forgot her deceiver, and spoke of him with unfading resentment until her death in 1858, at the age of a hundred and two. It is said her last request was for 'a glass of water from the Fountain of Youth'. From this contretemps François-René learned, or ought to have learned, the extraordinary difficulty of behaving well in affairs of 'love'—his conduct had, in fact, been abominable—and that success is sometimes even more embarrassing than failure.

Soon he moved with his sisters to the country, to Marie-Anne's Château de Marigny, or Bénigne's Le Plessis-Pillet, or the Marquis de Langan's Bois-Février. This new solitude in Brittany, he felt, was less complete, solemn, enforced, and therefore less meaningful than that of Combourg. Besides, his sisters brought provincial society with them into the fields. The five young people went from one neighbour's house to another, dancing at balls, or taking part in amateur theatricals, in which, as he tells us, he was a bad actor.

Although Marie-Anne was not his favourite sister, hers was his favourite château. Marigny, six miles northwest of Fougères, was a sixteenth-century manorhouse with moats, towers and chapel, between two lakes, in a quiet countryside of woods, meadows, and outcrops of granite. Under the still waters lay a submerged town, whose bells could sometimes be heard chiming; on the hillside above was a supernatural boulder which, every Christmas Eve at the moment of midnight mass, rolled down to drink from the stream. Near by rose a dolmen, the very one on which the priestess Velléda in *Les Martyrs* was to harangue her savage tribesmen. François-René began to write verses again, in a little room at the foot of the drawingroom staircase, where Lucile, as was just like her, had insisted on erecting an altar to Friendship. Bénigne's Le Plessis-Pillet, towered and moated like Marigny but not so grand, was seventeen miles southwest of Fougères, in the parish of Dourdain, surrounded by heaths and forests. Marigny, except for its chapel, and

Le Plessis-Pillet, except for the keep and a few ruined arches, have long since been demolished, but Bois-Février survives.

M. de Langan's wife was a Farcy twice over, through both father and mother. Hence she was a cousin not only of Julie's husband but also of the young Chateaubriands, in the manner of Brittany, where everyone was everyone else's more or less distant relative; and as no one disapproved of Julie's separation, the connection was not allowed to lapse. Bois-Février became a particular resort of Lucile, and François-René made frequent visits, often staying for weeks at a time. The château had been rebuilt in mid-eighteenth century style, with two forward wings, a formal garden and fountain, and avenues through the woods behind. A contemporary drawing shows the Marquis and his wife dignifiedly strolling by the fountain, with their small daughters Camille and Émilie, and their son Eugène, who was to perish at bloody Quiberon in 1795. Long afterwards, in 1826, Émilie wrote memoirs which give an unexpected though not very vivid glimpse of François-René ('the first celebrated person I ever met'), as he appeared at that time, when he was nearly nineteen, to a rather trite little girl of twelve. He was 'as gay and amiable as could be', she declares; he 'gave an original turn to everything he said', although unfortunately his most amusing remarks 'lost their charm when one tried to repeat them', because it wasn't so much what he said as the way he said it. Then again, he was 'very good-hearted, easy to get on with, and fond of children, to whom he gave his whole attention with all his amiability'. Little Émilie believed quite incorrectly that he had 'done absolutely nothing at school', and that it was not until he entered the army that 'his taste for literature declared itself to such a degree that he thought of nothing else'. But now, she noticed, 'he had run right through the French poets, and was studying hard to read the rest, with all the courage born of great desire'. 'Mark my words,' her father used to say, 'that young man's imagination will make a stir in the world, and M. de Chateaubriand will end up by being a writer!'

Meanwhile the sagacious Jean-Baptiste, true to his promise, had decided to abandon his magistracy in the Parlement of Paris in order to be presented at court. He sold his post as Master of Requests, and joined the King's own cavalry regiment; for in his new position as Comte de Chateaubriand and head of an ancient family, inheritor of a feudal estate and its revenues, the nobility of the sword was clearly preferable to the nobility of the robe. Jean-Baptiste appeared to have chosen his moment doubly well. The Paris Parlement was in dire trouble that summer, outrageously declining to register the King's edicts for taxes and loans, even suicidally demanding the convocation of States General. But in August, when the new prime minister Loménie de Brienne exiled the rebels to Troyes, Jean-Baptiste was no longer with them; in the coming struggle it seemed perfectly obvious that the safe way to preferment lay with the court. Old Lamoignon de Malesherbes, the friend of Rousseau and the philosophers, much respected as an honest and moderate reformer, had joined the incoming government as minister without portfolio; and his son-in-law the Président de Rosanbo had been a colleague of Jean-Baptiste in the lawcourts of Parlement. In November 1787 Jean-Baptiste married M. de Rosanbo's sixteen-year-old daughter Aline, Malesherbes's grand-daughter; it was, for him, a sensationally brilliant match, and indeed, but for the irony of history which was to make it calamitous, would have been the first and only really clever thing he ever did. He was duly presented at court, after submitting the ready-made proofs of nobility that had already served for Lucile and François-René, and on 21 February 1788 he attended the royal hunt, like his younger brother just a year before. But it is exceedingly unlikely that Jean-Baptiste rode between His Majesty and the buck.

Julie, seeing the promise of further social success in her brother's advancement, told everyone that Paris was necessary for her health. François-René's experience of army and court had changed him without satisfying him; he had become uncomfortably aware of stirrings within him which ran counter to his love of solitude and impelled him to emerge from obscurity. Perhaps destiny called him to Paris; in any case, he thought he would like to meet some poets. Even Lucile, since the death of her inhibiting father, was showing signs of opening out, and all agreed that her genius and beauty deserved a wider field. So Julie persuaded Lucile, and Lucile persuaded François-René. Early in December 1787, a few weeks after Jean-Baptiste's amazing marriage, they set off together in 'an agreeable association of the three youngest fledglings of the nest'.

7

SWORDS IN THE STREETS

THE philosopher Delisle de Sales, a new friend of Julie and an old friend of Malesherbes, had found them an apartment near his own in the Pavillons Saint-Lazare, in a pleasant suburb a quarter-mile north of the Porte Saint-Denis, conveniently close to the Hôtel de Rosanbo in the Rue de Bondy, where Jean-Baptiste lived with his wife's parents. So François-René now had a man of letters on the premises. Delisle de Sales was a celebrated, dishevelled mediocrity, still living on the reputation of his tedious *Philosophie de la nature* (1769), in seven volumes, which had been burned by the public hangman and gained him a glorious imprisonment. But nobody had troubled to burn his even more tedious *Histoire des hommes* (1779–85), a history of the world in no fewer than fifty-two volumes. On the marble bust of himself in his room he had written: 'God, Man, and Nature, he explained them all!', a motto more appropriate to the great Buffon from whom he had cribbed it, than to Delisle who, although he had certainly discussed these subjects, could hardly be said to have thrown light on any of them. A grimy roll of paper protruded from his pocket, on which he would write his sudden inspirations, standing at the street-corners. However, Delisle was a decent chap enough, and to the innocent François-René he seemed a demigod.

Among the laws of the natural history of men of letters, François-René found, is that to meet one is to meet his friends, and then the friends' friends, until very soon the admiring aspirant knows as many of the species as he could possibly wish, or even more. Delisle introduced him to little Carbon de Flins des Oliviers, Flins for short, of whom his rival Le Brun wrote:

> '*Carbon de Flins des Oliviers*
> *Possesses far more names than bays.*'

Flins wrote comedies in verse, lived on tick, and kept two footmen. He fell in love with Julie, who solved this problem in her usual way, by bursting into fits of laughter; but Flins, who prided himself on knowing how to behave in polite society, took his rebuff like a gentleman.

Flins, in turn, presented François-René to the poet Fontanes and the critic La Harpe. Fontanes, a rising new light of the classicist didactic school, was to have a salutary influence in later years upon François-René as an intimate friend, an encouraging mentor, and a powerful protector; but at this early time it is doubtful whether even the most perspicacious of these Parisian men of letters saw in this obscure young Chateaubriand anything more than the little brother of the charming Mme de Farcy. La Harpe, he too, took it upon himself to become enamoured of Julie, and was amazed, when he stalked into her drawing-room with three huge volumes of his own works tucked under his tiny arms, to find himself no more successful than Flins, for all his glory. In youth he had been a protégé of Voltaire; indeed, Voltaire had called him 'my son', and he had called Voltaire 'Papa'; and when he amended the poet's feebler lines in the dramatics at Ferney, Voltaire would humbly admit: 'The boy is right, it does sound better like that.' La Harpe was loudmouthed, blustering, but quite genuine, with a keen eye for talent, and still able to shed sincere tears at a beautiful verse or a virtuous deed. He dined with ministers, and harangued them on the abuses of the times, eating with his fingers and trailing his lace sleeves in the plate, sending for an omelette if the dinner seemed insufficient, and thundering the most violent left-wing enormities to great lords, who were only too delighted to feel they were entertaining a real philosopher.

The poet, critic and journalist Ginguené, on the other hand, was recruited to Julie's salon by the ramifications of cousinship which linked all Bretons, for he was a relative of the disgruntled and animal-loving wife of Uncle Antoine de Bédée, née Ginguené. He was also one of the most distinguished old boys of the college of Rennes, where he had studied twenty years before François-René, in the time of the Jesuits. Ginguené, who wrote heavy prose and correct, occasionally agreeable verse, was a careerist with sufficient talent to find jobs, but not quite enough to keep them. Later he and François-René disliked one another heartily, owing to political and literary differences—for Ginguené, not content with having done very well for himself in the Revolution, wrote three violent articles against Le Génie du Christianisme in 1802—but for the time being they dined out together or supped in cabarets amicably enough.

With Ginguené came his inseparable friend Lebrun, generally known as 'Pindar' Lebrun, more on the strength of his appearance in fancy dress as the Theban lyrist at Mme Vigée-Lebrun's famous 'antique supper' than from any actual resemblance in merit or style, though Lebrun did write odes. The symbiosis of Ginguené and Lebrun, in which Ginguené as an experienced man of talent shielded the guileless genius of Lebrun, while Lebrun in turn beamed the rays of his glory on the wordly eminence of Ginguené, was an unspeakably comic spectacle. Lebrun was tall, thin, pale, bald in front, and angry-eyed. He lived in the Rue Montmartre, in a garret furnished with an armchair that had lost its stuffing, four broken pots for water and other purposes, books heaped pellmell on the floor, and a truckle-bed curtained with soiled napkins; but this frugality was due less to poverty than to avarice, and to fondness for ladies who had to be remunerated cash down. It was in the same sordid bed that a chaster Muse visited him, punctually, from three to four every morning, for he never went to sleep without composing a few verses. François-René used to call on him at his toilet in the forenoon. 'Ah! My dear fellow,' exclaimed Lebrun, 'I did such a piece last night! Oh! You really ought to hear it!' And he intoned his latest lines in a voice of thunder, while his exasperated wig-dresser cried: 'Monsieur, will you or will you not turn your head round!', and forcibly grabbed the divine head of Lebrun with both hands; but the poet soon forgot, and wagged it as wildly as ever. Lebrun's odes were vigorous, his elegies soulless, but he excelled in satire and epigrams, especially when his victim was Flins or La Harpe—'*La Harpe, whose face demands a slap*'.

But it was through his own daring, without previous introduction, that François-René became acquainted with the most illustrious of his predecessors at Rennes, where he had felt so proud to sleep in the former bed of Parny. With uncharacteristic forwardness he wrote to the great man, asking permission to call, declaring truthfully that the *Poésies érotiques* were his delight, and he knew them by heart. Parny civilly acceded, returned his visit, and even allowed himself to be presented to Julie and Lucile. He was tall and slender, still only thirty-five, brownskinned and pitted with smallpox, with deepsunk flashing black eyes, and the remote air of a captive feline whose true home is the tropics. The indolent and solitary Parny loved pleasure but disliked society; in polite company he was punctiliously wellbred, but without amenity or desire to charm in conversation. Here, at least, was a man with a character of his own, however ineffectual, one who preferred to be himself, provided it was not too much trouble, and not a mere copy of all the others. 'I never saw a writer so like his own works,' wrote Chateaubriand long afterwards, 'he wanted nothing but the sky of the Indies, a cool stream, a palmtree, and a woman'; but unfortunately only the last of these cravings could be fulfilled in Paris, and without the rest seemed unavailing. Parny was born in the Ile Bourbon, and had returned there after his schooldays at Rennes to fall in love with the creole Eléonore. In the famous lovepoems that told their story could sometimes be heard, despite the obligatory faded elegance of that era, a line or two with preromantic undertones of real voluptuousness and despair, the distant music of equatorial seas, the nostalgia of his lost paradise, a faint prophecy of Lamartine, even of Baudelaire. Eléonore was tall and goldenhaired, he told François-René, not beautiful, but alluring, and the very spirit of sensuous charm. 'On my last visit to the island she sent for me, and her messenger was the same negress who had summoned me to our blissful meetings twelve years before! Imagine my feelings! But I couldn't go, my ship was in the harbour, and I had to sail that very night.' Then François-René spoke to Parny of the marvellous *Paul et Virginie* of Bernardin de Saint-Pierre, which had appeared only the year before, in 1787. This tragic idyll of two children in love on a tropical island had reminded him, no doubt, of his own adolescent amours with the Sylphide, and his prose would bear for ever the traces of Bernardin's exotic imagery, the sweetness and melancholy of his diction and cadences. But Parny considered Bernardin (who had spent only three years in the neighbouring Ile de France) as a trespasser in his natal climes, and would have none of him. 'His descriptions of places are all wrong,' he said.

However, one of François-René's acquaintances in this decadent and dying age possessed the quality of genius, or at least of permanent relevance. The moralist Chamfort was brought to Julie's little suppers by Ginguené. He was tall and stooping, with a face of sickly pallor, dilated energetic nostrils, and glacial blue eyes which in moments of animation seemed to dart streaks of lightning. His conversation was as brilliant as his writings, and delivered in a flexible voice that followed the turns of his feelings; and he told, a little too often, a series of extraordinary anecdotes about the nobility, who welcomed him for his fame, but whom he hated because of his own illegitimate low birth. François-René was deeply impressed by his tale of a noble courtier, who amused himself by pointing out to his innocent daughter-in-law the fellow-courtiers who drove by in their carriages, describing the intrigues of each with this or that great lady, and inviting her to choose whichever she fancied for her lover. 'And do you think,' concluded Chamfort, 'that a moral order of this kind could exist much longer?' It could not, indeed, but Chamfort was to die with it, by his own hand.

Such were the men of letters who were François-René's daily companions during the following three years, at their morning uprising, in Julie's evening salon, and at midnight cafés. He never met Marmontel, nor Beaumarchais, nor, greatest of all, André Chénier, who was absent in London during this period, and whose poems remained unpublished during his brief lifetime. Even so François-René, and Julie with him, could now claim a high score both numerically and qualitatively in this indoor game of literary society. They had succeeded in gaining admission, albeit only as lay member or hostess, to a group which included half of the most conspicuous names of the day. In the literature and thought of the prerevolutionary decade Delisle, La Harpe, Ginguené and the rest formed the left or progressive wing. They derived, however degenerately, from the philosophers and encyclopaedists of the previous age, whose great men had been Voltaire and Rousseau and Diderot. The ideas which in that dawn had been so novel and vivifying were now trite and stagnant; one of the great intellectual renewals in

human history had declined into a mere climate of opinion; and yet it
was this climate, rather than the secondrate men of letters who sat sun-
ning themselves therein, that provided the popular philosophy of the
coming Revolution.

Without apparent inner conflict, impelled by deference and protective
mimicry, François-René adopted the doctrines of his new literary companions. He too found it agreeable to believe, ethically, in universal
brotherhood, the perfectibility of man, the noble savage; metaphysically,
in the remote existence of a benevolent God Who asked only that all
men should do as they pleased and therefore be totally happy; politic-
ally, in an urgent but painless reform which would begin with the
liberalisation of court, aristocracy and Church, and end with a stable
limited monarchy and a contented nation. The millennium was just
round the corner, and could be hastened by incessantly talking about it.
'I thought myself a little philosopher,' he decided in later years, and
could explain his submission to these insipid talents only by 'the kind
of dominion which any literary renown exercised upon me'. In fact
François-René's new views, although neither reprehensible nor altogether erroneous, were second-hand, factitious, and foreign to his
deeper nature. This interval of quiescence and acquiescence, however
retrograde, was salutary for his future development; beneath the mask
of conformity, which he would never wear again, his true self continued
to evolve. But meanwhile the precocious boy genius of Combourg disguised himself unrecognisably as an ordinary eighteenth-century young
man about town.

Fortunately, however, a benigner influence mitigated the perils of
François-René's period of latency. He found, while still left vulnerable
by the loss of his father and his home, a new family in the Rosanbos, a
new father in old Malesherbes.

Jean-Baptiste was now twenty-nine, thirteen years older than his
child bride, yet only three years younger than his mother-in-law, for the
Lamoignons and Rosanbos wedded early. Although he had married for
advancement rather than love, he tenderly adored his wife, and addressed her in letters, during the long periods of absence which were
necessitated by his career, as his *petit loup* or *petit chou*. Aline had two
younger sisters, Louise and Guillemette, and an eleven-year-old brother
Louis, known as 'his lordship Lolo'. The house was full of the offspring
of aunts and cousins, and François-René delighted to see the great
Malesherbes arrive, hot and weary from the royal council, hurling his
wig into a corner of Mme de Rosanbo's boudoir, and lying on the
carpet amid a stupendous din to be assaulted by the infant mob. 'M. de
Malesherbes,' as one of his playmates told Sainte-Beuve sixty years
later, 'made his little friends feel he enjoyed these games just as much as
they did.'

Malesherbes was a burly old man, with a frank bulging face radiating humour and energy, bushy grey eyebrows, wig set askew, and shirt-front smeared with snuff. He talked passionately, intelligently and copiously, in a brusque voice rendered indistinct by lack of teeth, seizing his companion by the top coat-button; when the monologue ended, three hours later, every button in the listener's coat and waistcoat had been successively undone. He took a fancy to Lucile when she acted with touching grace, after being induced to sip a little champagne, in a family play in honour of his birthday. L'Argentière was not good enough for Canoness Lucile, he declared, and became even more pressing than Jean-Baptiste for her transference to Remiremont, with its 'sixteen quarters'; for M. de Malesherbes, philosopher though he was, and lifelong opponent of the aristocracy as a force of reaction, was still imbued with the principles of noble birth.

He noticed in François-René signs of cultivated interests which were sadly to seek in his worthy grandson-in-law Jean-Baptiste. Soon he began to talk of his own favourite topics, of Rousseau, botany, and the geography of distant lands. François-René in turn was won over by his evident predilection for Lucile, and by the outspoken simplicity of manner which took away his own shyness. 'In the presence of this virtuous man I seemed to become stronger and more free.' The great minister was gratified to find that this promising boy, nearly fifty years his junior, already shared his own political views, like his favourite daughter Mme de Rosanbo, but unlike the rest of his family. For his other daughter Mme de Montboissier and Jean-Baptiste were rabid absolutists, while the Président de Rosanbo ('a model of levity', wrote Chateaubriand) cared for nothing but the power of Parlement.

Malesherbes's creed was not very different from that of François-René's literary friends; but he had battled all his life for progress which they only chattered about. He stood for freedom of the press, abolition of *lettres de cachet*, judiciary, penal and police reform, emancipation of Protestants and Jews; yet these limited ends were only means to the utopian goal of a constitutional monarchy in which the king would obey the wishes of a beloved and loving nation. Already, in his previous ministry under Turgot in 1776, he had ominously referred to His Majesty as 'the sovereign of a free people', and dared to recommend the summoning of States General. When Turgot fell Malesherbes had resigned, with none of his aims accomplished. 'You're luckier than me,' remarked the good king, half wistfully, half in mild rebuke, 'you can abdicate'. Now he was minister for the second and last time, as a liberal figurehead in a reactionary government. He was permitted, almost in mockery, to bring about only the most innocuous and least popular of his lifelong policies, the emancipation of the Protestants—exactly a century after the revocation of the Edict of Nantes which had made

their worship clandestine, their marriages illegal, their children illegitimate. Then he was graciously invited to proceed with the emancipation
of the Jews. 'You have made yourself a Protestant,' said the king, who
could be witty on occasion, 'I hereby make you a Jew.' So Malesherbes
pressed on, dutifully and in spite of himself delightedly, with this just
and desirable but not very urgent reform, for all the world as though
the time were still mid-century, and France could still be saved by a
leisurely programme of enlightened half-measures.

In his pertinacity of honourable effort, his underlying despair, his
final failure which was also a tragic victory, this jolly rubicund man was
not unlike his opposite, the pale severe Count of Combourg. Malesherbes was almost the same age as François-René's lost father, whose
place he now briefly yet everlastingly shared. Over the undying image
of René-Auguste, so discouraging and forbidding and hard to please,
François-René received the imprint of a new father-figure who welcomed his company, admired his unfledged talents, and was himself
admirable. Three men revealed to the young Chateaubriand the patterns
which were already implicit in his deepest nature and would direct him
throughout his life. Gesril showed him the bright eyes of danger, René-
Auguste gave him melancholy and isolation, and Malesherbes brought
the ideal of a selfless and selfdoomed statesman. For despite his seeming
commonplaceness old Malesherbes, as history would show, was unique
in his generation as Chateaubriand would be in his. Alone of Louis
XVI's ministers Malesherbes felt an impossible loyalty to both king and
nation; he was a non-authoritarian idealist, indifferent (fatally so) to
personal power, dedicated to the impracticable task of steering the past
into the future by saving the monarchy from itself; and he alone faith-
fully shared the fate of his thankless royal master, which through his
one-man opposition he had striven to avert and helped to cause.
Malesherbes as an eighteenth-century philosopher gave the political
example which Chateaubriand would follow, thirty and forty years
later, as a nineteenth-century romantic, until the Bourbons fell again
for ever.

Even so, in the society of literary gentlemen and of his new family
François-René had not forgotten to be alone. He read history and Greek
in his room every morning after riding-school, translating the *Odyssey*
and Xenophon's *Cyropaedia*—'fortunately at that time I was mad about
Greek'. Then, because he could not travel in space to distant lands, he
travelled in time through medieval Paris. In the crypt of Saint-Denis, in
Sainte-Chapelle and Notre-Dame, in alleys of the Ile de la Cité where
Héloise had lived with her uncle Fulbert, for the first time since
Combourg he saw the Sylphide. But under the gothic arches, among the
tombs, she wore the hue of death. 'She was pale, she gazed at me with
sad eyes, she was only the shadow or ghost of the dream I had loved.'

He wandered through the desert of the crowd, shuddering with horror at the famished whores who clutched at passers-by. 'I was too timid and too highminded to let myself be tempted,' he says, no doubt truly. But his denial suggests that at this time—not unduly soon, for he was nearly twenty—he surrendered his early-resented and long-preserved virginity to some woman or women who asked neither to be paid nor to be loved. Then in the spring of 1788 both he and Jean-Baptiste left Paris, for different ends.

In March, soon after his status-enhancing presentation at court and scarcely four months since his marriage, Jean-Baptiste joined the recently appointed French ambassador in London, who was none other than his new uncle Anne-César de la Luzerne. La Luzerne, youngest son of Malesherbes's sister, had served as ambassador to the United States during the American Revolution in 1779–83, and made himself so popular that a county in Pennsylvania is named after him to this day. His brother César-Henri was now navy minister, and was related to the foreign minister M. de Montmorin by the marriage of his son Guillaume to Montmorin's daughter Victoire. Three ministers and an ambassador! —Jean-Baptiste could hardly have married into a more seemingly influential family. Although no official post in the London embassy was available, everyone felt it would be an excellent opportunity for the Comte de Chateaubriand to learn diplomacy from the top; and among the secretaries Jean-Baptiste (who himself wrote pretty verses in spare moments) had the privilege, forever denied to François-René, of meeting André Chénier. But his absence was diplomatic in two senses. The struggle between the prime minister Loménie de Brienne and Parlement was now nearing its crisis. If Jean-Baptiste sided with Parlement, his career at court would be ruined; if he sided against, his father-in-law the President would be furious; and Malesherbes, who was playing a waiting game, would be equally embarrassed whichever he did. Trouble was brewing even in the provinces, and if he returned to Brittany Jean-Baptiste would be compromised by having to do his bit as a Breton nobleman. It would be best for everyone that he should be out of the country altogether; but none of these considerations applied to François-René.

François-René gleefully returned to Brittany when the disturbances were just about to begin. There can be little doubt that Jean-Baptiste had invited him to act as his deputy in the name of Chateaubriand; that Uncle Antoine de Bédée had summoned his aid in the good cause; and that even Malesherbes, whose only hope for States General lay in the victory of the Parlements over his own prime minister, had encouraged the young hopeful to go as observer and agitator. All through the winter the Paris Parlement had refused to register Loménie de Brienne's edicts for new taxes, and called louder than ever for States General; the survival of his ministry and the solvency of France depended on the desperate Loménie's victory over these rebels. Aided by Privy Seal Lamoignon, a distant cousin of Malesherbes, he prepared a coup d'état for the suppression of the Paris and the eleven provincial Parlements. It was a last attempt to rule by absolute monarchy, to avert revolution by a show of strength. 'I've made arrangements for *everything*, including civil war!' said Loménie complacently. But the news leaked out before the appointed day of 8 May, and everywhere Parlements and townsfolk were prepared for resistance. Already on 5 May an extraordinary diet of Breton noblemen met at Rennes to show solidarity with their own Parlement. François-René, after seeing Julie and Lucile safely to Fougères, was there, full of delighted anticipation.

What a commotion! 'It was the first political meeting I ever attended,' he wrote thirty-three years later, 'I was deafened and amused by the shouting.' All the noblemen waved their arms and bawled at once, standing on their chairs or climbing on the tables. Foremost was the Marquis de Trémargat, known as Wooden-Leg, for he had lost a gallant limb in the navy. 'Let us all go to the Commandant,' he roared, 'We'll say to him: "The noblemen of Brittany are at your door; they demand to speak to you; the King himself would not refuse to hear them!" ' 'The King himself would not refuse!' he repeated, amid redoubled huzzas and stamping of feet, and off they all went to the residence of M. de Thiard, the new Governor of Brittany, from whom no thought could have been further than that of declining to listen. M. de Thiard was a polite, frivolous, elderly, love-verse-writing courtier, who had taken over this thankless post in succession to M. de Montmorin himself, and already regretted it; but he showed tact and courage during the ensuing month of moderately goodhumoured rioting and fraternisation between citizens and troops, and no one was killed. He heard out the noblemen of Brittany with exquisite respect. Next morning they met again to pass a resolution of infamy upon all who might accept places in the new administration, and sent this terrible manifesto to press complete with the list of its 1,429 signatories, among whom François-René ('F. de Chateaubriand') saw his name in print for the first time.

Next day, nothing daunted, accompanied by his unpopular colleague the Intendant M. de Molleville, by his personal guard under its sexagenarian captain M. de Caud—who eight years later was to become the shortlived husband of Lucile—and by the regiment of Rohan in garrison at Rennes, M. de Thiard enforced upon the protesting Parlement the registration of the edicts for its own suppression. He emerged from the Palais de Justice amid a menacing populace, whose dreadful roar of 'Haro!' he at first optimistically mistook for the patriotic cry of 'Vive le Roi'; but a running noose was flung after him, as a token of what he might expect, followed by a hail of brickbats and bottles; his sedan-chair was torn to pieces, a billet of wood (intended, it was said in excuse, for M. de Molleville) struck him on the head; and bloodshed between soldiers and crowd was only averted by a young officer who cried: 'My friends, why cut one another's throats? I'm a citizen like yourselves!', and halted his men.

Three weeks of protests followed—from Parlement, the noble diet, the interim commission of the Estates of Brittany, the municipality of Rennes, even the law-students under their leader Victor Moreau, François-René's former schoolfellow—addressed to the King, his brothers, the prime minister (with copy to Malesherbes, whose sympathy was wellknown). At last on 2 June, amid further rioting, in which the noblemen drew their swords upon the army officers but did not use them, and a young girl challenged their embarrassed colonel to a duel, M. de Thiard brought out his sackful of *lettres de cachet*. Parlement sat illegally for a final resolution, declaring the ministers and all who abetted the new laws 'guilty of treason against King and Nation', and then dissolved under duresse into house-arrest or exile to country estates.

On 5 July the nobles met once more to draw up a petition to the King, again with more than 1,400 signatures, demanding revocation of the edicts and the calling of States General. This time, by way of making sure, they sent a deputation of twelve to Versailles to deliver their message, including Trémargat Wooden-Leg, the dashing Armand de la Rouërie, Cousin Annibal Moreau's friend the little spitfire Chevalier de Guer, nicknamed César-Gargantuaël, and the Marquis de Bédée de Visdelou, a distant cousin of Uncle Antoine. But His Majesty refused to see them, and on 14 July, after being banqueted by all the Bretons in Paris, they were thrown into the Bastille to cool off. Here, in the sombre fortress which on the same day a year later was to witness so different a scene, the twelve heroes were afflicted neither by thirst, nor discomfort, nor boredom, for sympathisers sent them wine of the best, armchairs, and a billiard-table. Meanwhile François-René and his fellows at Rennes sported big beautiful coatbuttons of mother-of-pearl, engraved with the ermines of Brittany and the motto: 'Death rather than dishonour!' It was all very exciting, entertaining, and gratifying. Everywhere in France the populace had rioted in support of the Parlements, the taxes remained unpaid, and Loménie was dismissed on 24 August. François-René had done his duty for Jean-Baptiste, for Malesherbes, Brittany, liberty, his own noble rank, his own progressive ideals. They had won, Necker was prime minister, States General were announced for next May, the millennium was about to begin! But in fact the noblemen of Brittany had unwittingly begun the now irreversible Revolution. 'We triumphed over the Court, as did everyone else,' he wrote long afterwards, 'and we fell with it into the same abyss.'

His army career was in abeyance. M. de Mortemart had succeeded
last September in finding him an acting sublieutenancy, but in March
1788 the war minister (Loménie de Brienne's brother) had abolished all
such substitute posts, and he was removed from active service. On
10 September he was reinstated in the wellnigh imperceptible rank of
'volunteer nobleman-cadet'. However, the regiment still found him
something to do. After he had watched the triumphal homecoming of
the twelve heroes from the Bastille on 12 September, with laurel-
wreaths and free wine and fireworks, he was sent to nurse a brainsick
Breton officer in a Normandy village. They were billeted in a peasant's
cottage, in a room partitioned by a tattered tapestry curtain lent by the
lord of the manor, behind which the patient was first bled and next, by
way of relaxation, plunged into icecold baths. Lugubrious and shivering the poor man sat, with blue fingernails and violet face, his long
beard straggling over his emaciated, dripping torso; then he sobbed
under an umbrella which, he believed, would shelter him from his own
tears. Truly, thought François-René, if this simple device were indeed
a sure shield against sorrow, then a statue ought to be raised to the
inventor of umbrellas. During his only bearable moments he walked in
the hilltop village graveyard, dreaming of all his life, his Paris friends,
the woods of Combourg, 'so near in space, so distant in time', and the
lost Sylphide. It was a case of the blind leading the blind, he reflected,
for was not he as crazy as his patient?—more so, indeed, for he brought
the good man back to his regiment completely cured.

Jean-Baptiste had left London for Brussels in July, and then proceeded to Spa to take the waters. 'I'm in the plight of the Wandering
Jew,' he wrote to his girl wife, 'and my travels and vexations far from
my *petit loup* can only end with the troubles of Parlement.' Did she
happen to know, he enquired with more trust than tact, 'of any fair
ladies from Paris' who might help to rescue him from boredom at Spa?
But his *petit loup* did not take their separation lightly. Julie, with all the
worldly sagacity of one who had been blissfully parted from her own
husband for two years, wrote to her from Bois-Février to preach
patience, and aunt Montboissier explained that 'as he's lucky enough
to be out of public affairs in this stormy moment, it's all for the best that
he should keep away'; 'I'm sure he's enjoying himself tremendously at
Spa!' she added consolingly. In September, when the coast was clear at
last, the prodigal spouse returned. There was talk of his bringing Aline
to Combourg, for a belated honeymoon in the shooting season and to
start a family. Mme de Chateaubriand and François-René visited the
deserted castle to make it fit for their habitation, but they never came.

Jean-Baptiste had not forgotten his scheme for having François-René
made a Knight of Malta, in anticipation of a rich benefice. Because the
Knights were a religious as well as a military body it was first necessary

for him to take minor holy orders, and the candidate joined his mother at 479, rue des Grands-Degrés to await the bishop's pleasure. For the first time François-René found his hitherto crossgrained parent delightful. In her widowed old age and the retirement of her beloved Saint-Malo, where she now spent her days in church and her evenings gossiping and knitting with her friends, Mme de Chateaubriand had mellowed but grown absentminded. One morning he met the old lady in the street with a slipper under her arm, which she had snatched up in mistake for her prayerbook. He rejoiced to hear her reciting folk tales in verse of her own composition, and always remembered one absurd quatrain from a story of a demon vanishing up a chimney, which evidently belonged to the legend of the satanic fiddler at Monchoix:

> 'The Devil flew so fast
> Along the avenue
> That scarce an hour had passed
> Ere he was lost to view.'

'Really, mother,' he objected, 'it seems to me that the Devil didn't go so very quickly.' 'Nonsense, boy, you don't know anything about it!' Then there was the duck-princess, who prayed to Saint Nicolas to preserve her from a cruel ravisher, and so gave her name to the village of Montfort-la-Cane in the marshes south of Saint-Malo:

> 'A duck the fair maid changed into,
> Duck she became, and by this means
> Straight through her prison-bars she flew
> Into a duckpond full of beans!'

Soon it was time for him to meet the bishop, not the old bishop Mgr. des Laurents, who had quelled the great storm in 1768 and confirmed him in 1781 and was now dead,[1] but the new bishop Mgr. de Pressigny, who was a favourite of the Queen and a youngish man of forty-three. On 16 December 1788, in the chapel of the episcopal palace, François-René in full regimentals with sword knelt before him, while the reluctant prelate, feeling that to bestow orders upon a layman and soldier was a profanation savouring of simony, but yielding to the saintly reputation of Mme de Chateaubriand, cut a lock of hair from the crown of his head and handed him a certificate of tonsure in ecclesiastical Latin. But even this manoeuvre, like so many of Jean-Baptiste's little schemes for the advancement of himself or his family, was as illtimed as it was ingenious. The much used Chateaubriand pedigree was sent to Malta, the chapter of Aquitaine declared in June and confirmed in November 1789 that François-René was 'worthy on considerations of greatest weight to be granted the grace he solicits', but all in vain. By then the Bastille had fallen, and soon there would be no more nobles nor wealthy orders to give them sinecures. Everything in that epoch of catastrophe came too late for those who behaved, like Jean-Baptiste, as if the future would resemble the past.

While his topknot was growing again François-René took to riding, for he now had no father to grudge him horses. He galloped along the sands of Paramé by the fringe of the waves, then dismounted to play kneedeep with these old friends as in the days of Gesril. He cantered by the shores of Saint-Servan and the gracious declivities of the Rance, where seagoing gentry had built their country mansions in the lost days of prosperity. Exotic plants and trees from the distant lands where they found their fortunes decked their terraces and lined their avenues. In spring one could gaze over the swaying heads of a tulip-bed at the endless sea with its ships and calms and tempests. Every whitewashed cottage of the peasant sailors had its garden where, among gooseberries and marigolds, flourished a spicebush from Cayenne, a tobacco-plant from Virginia, a strange flower from China, like a chart of its master's voyages. These coastdwellers had come long ago from Normandy. Their wives and daughters were tall, slender, and nimble, wore peaked cambric coifs, grey woollen bodices, short petticoats of striped silk and white stockings with coloured clocks, and silver chains looped from their waists. Every spring morning these girls of the North brought baskets of fruit and scallopshells of curds to market, leaping from their wherries as if they had sailed in to invade Brittany once more. Blue-eyed and rosy-faced, carrying jars of milk or flowers on their heads of yellow hair dewpearled, they seemed to François-René comelier than Valkyries or the basketbearing maidens of the Parthenon.

Very soon, long before the season of tulips and market-going Valkyries, it was time for him to attend the crucial Estates of Brittany at Rennes. Every Breton nobleman, even those who like François-René were under twenty-five and not entitled to vote, had received a personal summons from M. de Boisgelin, president of their order; for trouble was expected, and the number of swords would signify more than the number of votes. Their meetings to decide policy, before the formal opening, seemed splendid fun, just like last May. Trémargat and Guer and Antoine de Bédée broke chair after chair when they climbed on them to orate. The chairs shattered with particular readiness under the weight of Bédée the Artichoke. But François-René became aware of a curious trait in his own character. The more excited his companions grew, the cooler he himself became. In later years he felt the same incongruous indifference when a soldier under fire, later still as a statesman in times of stress.

Soon, however, he saw that nothing had remained the same since May, except the exuberant intransigence of his fellow-nobles. In that merry month, when all Bretons united against the hated Loménie for the freedom of their province, when nobles and commons fought shoulder to shoulder in the streets (except that the nobles had only shown their swords, whereas the commoners had used their cudgels and brickbats), the noblemen of Brittany had felt themselves popular for ever. But now the commons had learned, from the example of the nobles themselves, that power in the coming age was promised to the violent; they had demands of their own, and only the nobility stood in their way. Even the new minister favoured their cause, for only by playing the Third Estate against the nobles could Necker hope to get his taxes in. The noblemen of Brittany, with astonished indignation, found themselves regarded as public enemies.

This disagreeable change in the wind was made manifest by the incident of M. de Becdelièvre's hat. On Sunday evening, 28 December, M. de Becdelièvre put on his hat in his box at the theatre; he was one of the twelve heroes incarcerated in the Bastille last summer, and thought nothing forbidden to his imperishable popularity. A cry of 'Off with your hat!' rose from below. Becdelièvre rashly hurled his headgear into the pit, saying loudly: 'Let the bravest man among you bring it me back!' Such a knightly challenge might have done very well in the court of François I above the lion's den, but in Rennes at the end of 1788 it fell flat. Becdelièvre's hat, trampled and torn to pieces, was returned to him by a mere usher, quite unfit for wear. A score of fellow-nobles defiantly clapped their hats on. 'Come down here,' yelled the pit; the curtain was lowered, young plebeians went out for weapons, and a bloody end to the play was averted only by the arrival of M. de Thiard, who persuaded the gentlemen to let the quarrel drop.

Next day the last Estates of Brittany began their session in the disused refectory of the Cordeliers. Nine hundred nobles were present, not counting the five hundred non-voting minors; they vastly outnumbered the other two orders, for every Breton nobleman was entitled to attend by right of birth, without election. The Third Estate numbered forty-nine representatives of the towns, unofficially reinforced by one hundred and fifty supernumerary delegates sent to encourage or if need be intimidate them. By the constitution of Brittany each order must vote separately, so that nobility and clergy had always commanded a majority of two to one over the commons. But on the following day, Tuesday 30 December, the commons revealed their machiavellian plans for the breaking of this immemorial deadlock.

Their demands were first and foremost for 'double representation', or equality of numbers with the other two orders combined, and for 'vote by heads', that is, voting in full session instead of by order. If these revolutionary claims were granted the tables would be turned for ever, for by winning supporters among the moderate minority of their opponents the Third would enjoy a permanent majority over both nobles and clergy. They furthermore demanded the abolition of the nobility's and clergy's feudal privilege of exemption from taxes,[2] in particular the oppressive Breton hearth tax, to which only plebeians were liable.[3] The justice of this programme was as exasperating as its enormity. Indeed the moderate nobles were thought willing to concede, but the diehards under Trémargat Wooden-Leg and little Guer ('the craziest madman in the whole province', said M. de Thiard) shouted them down. The commons refused to sit until their claims were heard; the nobles and clergy could only counter by refusing to hear their claims until business was opened. Ageold feudalism and newborn democracy were in immovable confrontation. On 7 January 1789 an order from Versailles suspended the session for a month. The commons slyly obeyed and withdrew. Nobles and clergy, suspecting darkly but not unjustly that Necker and commons were in league to disrupt the Estates, solemnly vowed never to accept any change in the constitution, and declared themselves in permanent session. An awkward squad of gentlemen kept guard in the hall through the nights of that bitter winter, and passed the long hours (or so a satirical newspaper of the time alleged) in playing leapfrog, blind man's buff, and hunt the slipper.

At last, on 26 January, the infatuated diehards proceeded to an act of fatal rashness. A public meeting was called in the open space of the Champ Montmorin,[4] attended mostly by their own tradesmen and lackeys, and by such honest workmen as could be bribed to come for free drinks and forty sous apiece. A few nobles lurked on the fringes. 'My friends,' cried the speaker, 'don't you want the constitution of Brittany to stay unchanged, and your masters to keep their privileges, and the price of bread to go down?' Shouts of 'Vive la noblesse!' greeted these stirring words, and the rioters marched (rather like the mob in *Sylvie and Bruno* roaring for 'Less bread! More taxes!') to present their manifesto to Parlement.[5] At the door of the Café de l'Union they encountered a group of jeering students under their leader Moreau,[6] and hunted them through the streets with a hail of stones and billets of firewood. One of the city watch seized a footman running with a huge cudgel, when up popped M. de Trémargat and pushed a pistol in his face: 'Release my servant, or I'll blow your brains out!' After three hours of fighting M. de Thiard succeeded in clearing the streets.

That night the angry students of Rennes gathered under Moreau at the Café de l'Union. The noblemen had bribed their lackeys to massacre them, they decided; they must arm immediately for selfdefence and vengeance.

Next day, 27 January 1789, the streets were deceptively quiet. The nobles met, ashamed of their sordid victory, but in no spirit of conciliation. Many had been unaware of yesterday's plot, or disapproved and ordered their servants not to take part; even the instigators had, perhaps, intended a manifestation rather than a riot. But all now felt valiant apprehensions: their landlords, it was rumoured, had sworn to murder them in their beds; the students were wearing hidden body-armour, proof against noble swords; they must fight for their lives and honour!

At three in the afternoon a bleeding youth approached the Café de l'Union: a gang of footmen had stabbed him for testifying against their part in yesterday's tumult. Five hundred students poured into the square, appealing to Parlement for justice on the evildoers, menacing the nobles who lounged haughtily in the Cordeliers' doorway. 'Murderers,' cried the students; 'Liars,' retorted the nobles, rather lamely. Meanwhile other gentlemen strolled back from dinner in their lodgings, hastened as they heard the uproar, and were assailed in the streets leading to the Place du Palais. Those in the hall formed ranks to clear the square and rescue their comrades. On the word of command from M. de Boisgelin they drew their bright swords, shouting 'Long live Brittany!', and charged, François-René among them; 'it was rather a fine sight,' he remembered thirty years after, not without irony. Instantly surrounded, beset with cudgels and brickbats, standing and returning pistol-fire, pummelled and scratched and bruised, they could not break out, but could only with difficulty break back in again.

Single combats, not without chivalry and some remnant of the etiquette of duelling, continued in the sidestreets. 'I suppose you won't deign to measure swords with a member of the Third Estate?' enquired Moreau's henchman Ulliac of the Marquis de Montbourcher; but Montbourcher, not being in the least snobbish, set to with a will just as he would have fought a social equal. He soon sent the young man's sword flying in the air, but picked it up and handed it back, remarking: 'Ah, Monsieur, if we knew one another better we'd hate one another less!'; and the combatants embraced amid the applause of the crowd. Another cheering group watched M. de Kersalaün, a middleaged ex-navy officer, and a student named Blin, cutting and thrusting with extraordinary courage and fury, till they had to be parted and led away; Blin was badly wounded. But not all these encounters were so courteous. Young Louis-Pierre de Boishue, aged twenty-one, emerged from an alley and fell upon a group of students, wounding one in the thigh; but another felled him to his knees, and another, alas, shot him dead, His father arrived too late to save him, his mother at her window saw his corpse carried by. And little Saint-Riveul, fighting with the same impetuosity as when he had torn François-René's hair out by the roots at Mont-Thabor, died instantly with a bullet through his heart.

M. de Thiard hurried up, tactful and intrepid as ever, pleading, soothing, and blandly ignoring the bullets that whistled past his ears. Tragedy turned into farce when Bédée de Visdelou (he, not improbably, was the tall thin Bédée who, as Chateaubriand says, was nicknamed Bédée the Asparagus in contradistinction to Bédée the Artichoke) was seen bustling by with a double-barrelled gun on his shoulder; at Thiard's orders it was wrested from him despite his expostulations ('But I was going to help my son!'), and its two shots were fired into the air. Gradually the streets were cleared. The nobility carried bedding, food and arms into the hall and refused to emerge until, three days later, paroles of non-aggression had been exchanged on both sides. Five hundred young men marched in from Nantes, sixty from Saint-Malo, sworn 'to avenge our brothers massacred at Rennes;' they were rapturously welcomed, feasted, and marched away again without incident. But a mass meeting of the populace had been called for 3 February, the day on which the prorogued Estates were due to reassemble, with the intention of backing the Tiers by force. Foreseeing inevitable civil war, Thiard obtained from the King an order for indefinite suspension of the Estates. Nobility and clergy met unilaterally to sanction Necker's taxes, confident that the Third Estate would put itself in the wrong by refusing; but the Third, not to be out-manoeuvred, voted the taxes in its turn, with shouts of 'Vive le Roi! Vive Necker! Vive M. de Thiard!', and stole all the credit. Then the Three Orders dispersed for ever. There would never again be Estates of Brittany.

On 10 March Necker issued a special edict for the election of Breton delegates to the States General. The Tiers, in accordance with 'double representation', were allotted forty-four, the nobility and clergy only twenty-two each. Nobles and clergy assembled at Saint-Brieuc in April, without François-René and the other non-voting young. Many of the saner gentlemen were in favour of an election, and some, including Armand de la Rouërie, would very much have liked to be elected; but, as M. de Thiard reported, 'Guer spoke oftener and louder than anyone else', 'reason was smothered by shouting', and both orders irrevocably declined to send delegates. They confidently expected that Necker would give way, but in fact he was only too delighted to be rid of them. Thus the nobles of Brittany deprived themselves of political representation in the assembly which would decide the destiny of France.

So ended François-René's first lesson in politics. He had drawn his sword, with mixed feelings but without misgivings, in loyalty to his own reactionary class and the cause of Brittany, against the angry mob who shared his own newfangled notions of the equality and brotherhood of man. The arrogant folly of the Breton nobles had brought their own downfall, the victory and undying resentment of their adversaries. And yet, to do them justice, their intentions had not been altogether selfish. They had fought, alone and in vain, to avert the abolition of the Estates on which the last vestiges of the old independence of Brittany were based. They had sacrificed their power and popularity; but was it not absurdly fine that they had kept their honour? François-René retained a sense of the futility of violence, and a preference for lost rather than for successful causes.

He was more personally impressed by the fate of Saint-Riveul. How strange, that his bosom friend at the college of Rennes had been slain by the gunmen of their senior schoolfellow Moreau! Thirty years later, when he meditated in his Memoirs on the day of 27 January 1789, he saw a still more mysterious significance in this boy's death. Whether by the caprice of chance or by the will of heaven, his friend had been the first victim of the Revolution; all that vast stream of murder took its source from the bullet-pierced heart of Saint-Riveul!

'Now proceed, reader,' he concluded, in words which have renewed their terrible relevance in every generation of human history since his own, 'cross the river of blood which separates for ever the old world in which you were born from the new world on whose frontier you will die.'

8

LOVE AMONG THE RUINS

FRANÇOIS-RENÉ returned to Saint-Malo, resumed his seashore
riding, and began writing again; for two poems about sunset on the
winter sea which survive in *Tableaux de la nature* were no doubt composed towards this time. From his reading of Bernardin de Saint-Pierre
he had begun to discover his own ability to see the natural world in
colour and shape, and the possibility of conveying his vision in words.
In these verses of a boy of twenty a line or couplet which no predecessor
could have written begins here and there to sing and shine, and gives a
promise which he would fulfil only in prose—

'The whitening reef beneath a pure horizon'

or

'The ageing sun congeals with gold and purple
The variable green of glittering seas'.[1]

His thoughts turned also to the West Indies, for there was some prospect of Jean-Baptiste's sending him to San Domingo to collect the
fourteen-year-old bad debts of some 166,000 livres left there from their
father's slave-trading. René-Auguste had made Pierre his deputy for
this purpose in 1785, but Pierre was now an ailing old man of sixty-
three. The task required a member of the family to go out in person for
several years, and excellent introductions could be expected from the
navy and colonies minister M. de la Luzerne, Malesherbes's nephew,
who had been governor of the island in 1786–7. So François-René
dreamed and wrote of *'happy isles'*, of

'enchanted worlds
Bathed in the waters of an unknown sea'.[2]

Sometimes, as he reined his horse through the fringes of 'my old
mistress, the sea', he noticed a pretty girl striding along the Sillon, with
pink cloak, white gown, and yellow hair billowing in the wind. He
vaguely recognised little Céleste Buisson de la Vigne, an orphan grand-
daughter of a wealthy merchant, then just fifteen and still a schoolgirl
at the convent of La Victoire, where his cousin Marie-Anne-Renée,
Soeur des Séraphins, was a nun. Then he turned away and rode on, his
thoughts elsewhere. He did not know that the Ironic Spirit had shown
him his future wife.

He thought instead, with more gallantry than genuine feeling, of

M. du Châtenet's sister Eugénie. Châtenet, a captain in the artillery then on leave in Saint-Malo at his family mansion near the Porte de Dinan, was his latest friend, a 'philosopher' like himself but six years older. They called one another '*tu*' and planned to live together, 'deep in the country near Paris', with, as François-René put it, 'two or three persons like yourself, and a mistress (for that is a necessary evil)'. Possibly Eugénie might come too? And as Châtenet had been so obliging with regard to her, François-René could do no less than promise to introduce him to 'Countess Lucile' at the earliest opportunity.

Early in March 1789 he moved to Fougères to stay with Marianne in the Hôtel de Marigny. Would not Châtenet have been surprised to receive a letter from the next world, he enquired, in the first surviving letter of all his multitudinous correspondence; for he had met with an accident between Dol and Antrain, and narrowly escaped drowning in a pond, 'carriage, horses, postillions and all'. He invited his friend ('don't deceive me, Châtenet, remember we are philosophers') to give Eugénie 'a thousand tender and witty messages from me, which won't cost you much effort'. As for Lucile, who was staying with Julie at the Hôtel de Farcy, he had made Châtenet's declaration to her, to such good effect that she was 'longing to make his acquaintance', he reported perhaps with exaggeration. She was 'determined to meet him and continue the romance' as soon as they foregathered in Paris, but: 'Respect her if you win her fancy, my dear Châtenet, remember she is a virgin'. François-René's language is reminiscent of *Les Liaisons dangereuses*; his plot to involve his 'philosophical' friend and innocent sister might recall the young Shelley's semi-incestuous match-making between his sister Elizabeth and his fellow-infidel Hogg. But this almost odious letter should not be taken too seriously. It has always been the custom of callow young men to disguise their timidity with a mask of cynical levity, and even to flirt with one another's sisters. Besides, it was surely high time, five years after her fiasco with M. de Malfilâtre, for Lucile to meet more suitors. If François-René found her a good match the whole family would thank him. However, neither good nor ill came of it, for Lucile was for no man.

His mood soon changed. Julie fell ill, and he watched by her bed day and night with stricken heart. Now their visit to Paris would have to be postponed until May, he wrote to Châtenet on 28 March. Meanwhile he was obliged to make a trip to the south of France, and before he could settle for ever in Paris he might be kept 'by unforeseen business for five or six years in exile from my country'. The long absence is no doubt in the West Indies; the other journey, which he apparently did not make, was perhaps connected with the intended move to Nice of Jean-Baptiste's elderly client and distant relative, the Comtesse de Calan.[3] He appealed to Châtenet's sympathy in the name of 'the propensity

towards melancholy which we have in common'. Even Eugénie's response to his long-distance wooing had been unsatisfactory, though
hardly unprovoked. 'I'm sorry Eugénie has misjudged me; she is the
first person who has ever reproached me with lack of sensibility,' he
grumbled.

The coxcomb of these letters is mirrored by a pastel portrait of this
time, the earliest, like the letters, to survive. François-René wears his
own hair long, to indicate advanced opinions, but curled in a roll and
powdered grey in token of fashionable nobility; he sports the unbuttoned English-style riding-coat, the elegant shirt with frilled open neck,
in which he had gone wooing for La Martinière. Fortunately beneath
the silly Bédée softness budding power still looms, in the resolute
Chateaubriand chin, the formidable dark eyes.

Leaving Lucile and Marianne to nurse Julie he went to stay with
Bénigne at Le Plessis-Pillet and La Sécardais, or Lascardais as the
family always called it after the local pronunciation. Lascardais, the
chief seat of the Chateaubourgs, was eight miles north of Le Plessis-
Pillet, in a similar country of oak-forests, heaths, rocky hills, and
menhirs. The old Count had converted the medieval manor-house into
the new château in 1760, and died in 1770, bequeathing Le Plessis-
Pillet to his second son Paul (who married Bénigne in 1786), and
Lascardais to his eldest son Charles. Charles died in 1777, leaving
Lascardais to his infant son François, now a boy of fifteen under the
guardianship of his uncle Paul, who was thus equally at home in either
domain. The bailiff was M. Livorel, who had once managed the country
estate of the college of Rennes. When the Fathers were expelled by La
Chalotais in 1762 M. Livorel had the good sense to cease to be a Jesuit
but to continue to be a bailiff.

Even so, new Lascardais was no less haunted than ancient Combourg,
and its ghost was seen by none other than M. Livorel, the most practical and unimaginative of all possible ex-Jesuits. On his first night at
Lascardais a death-pale old man in nightcap and dressing-gown glided
into his bedroom, lighted candle in hand, sat for two hours speechless
by the fireside, while M. Livorel lay trembling in every limb, then rose
and departed, candle and all. He described the apparition to his farmers
next day: 'That was the old master,' they affirmed. Thenceforth whenever M. Livorel looked behind him in a dark wood, the phantom was
there; whenever he made to climb a stile, the late Count was sitting
astride of it. 'M. de Chateaubourg, leave me be,' he once made so bold
as to plead, but the spectre only answered: 'No!' M. Livorel told this
alarming tale as often as asked, always in the same words and with the
same tone of conviction.

Meanwhile François-René continued to write verses, for his one
ambition now was not to rise in the army, still less to win the unrespon-

1 Chateaubriand, his only
authentic portrait in youth

His sister Lucile

2 (*top*) Céleste, Chateaubriand's wife, in 1812, aged 38
(*left*) His sister Julie, Mme de Farcy
(*right*) His sister Bénigne, Comtesse de Chateaubourg
(*centre*) His eldest sister Marie-Anne, Comtesse de Marigny

sive Eugénie, but to have a poem printed in the *Almanach des Muses*.
Several of the ten *Tableaux de la nature* describe, in their imagery at once
generalised and precise, the rocky heaths and green meadows, the firs
and sycamores, the tumbling or placid streams of Lascardais or Bois-
Février.[4] A grassgrown ride in the park at Lascardais is still called
Avenue Chateaubriand in his honour, and tradition points out a lime-
tree bower on the garden terraces, an immemorial chestnut-tree by a
path through the home-fields, where he used to sit with Lucile.

He returned to Fougères, where a young female friend of this time
remembered sixty years later how Lucile, 'beautiful without being
pretty', 'noble in heart and manner', would relax into childish merriment in the intimacy of her own circle. François-René, she recalled,
was less amiable; all evening he would remain mute amid the general
conversation, and then see her home in the same inexorable silence, 'till
I began to suspect he did it on purpose to annoy me!' Mlle de Langan
also, now aged fourteen, found him changed when he revisited Bois-
Février, still kind and witty, but less agreeable. This deterioration was
not difficult to explain, she decided: 'after reading all the authors, he
wanted to meet them, and made friends with those of his time, very
dangerous persons who gravely weakened his principles'. Hence he
now thought of nothing but deserts, solitudes, and meditations, she
complained, rather inconsistently, would hardly let himself smile, and
left their company to sit dreaming on rocks and by stream-banks.[5] Both
these young ladies thought, by a natural error, that in their presence no
young man could possibly think of anything else, or wish to be
elsewhere.

At Bois-Février he no doubt saw again the Marquis de la Rouërie,
and his inseparable American friend, the big handsome Major Chafner,
who smiled so broadly and jabbered so oddly, for he would never consent to learn proper French. The Marquis came to preach the impera-
tive need for representation of the Breton nobility at the States General,
preferably in his own person; Chateaubriand is certainly thinking of
him when he speculates on the possibility that the Revolution might
have taken a different turn, if Brittany had elected 'a man of Mirabeau's
genius but with contrary opinions'. However, La Rouërie's genius was
not for words; he failed to convince M. de Langan or anyone else, and
so, remarked the pert little Émilie, 'had to go back to La Rouërie to
cultivate his cabbages'. The Marquis had built new stables with carved
oak mangers and frescoed walls, cut a vista through his park towards
the distant spired peak of Mont Saint-Michel and the blue sea, and
'turned the whole place upside-down', said envious neighbours. But he
had not returned to grow cabbages. He sent for his cousin Thérèse de
Moëlien, whose beauty had ravished François-René at Julie's wedding
seven years before. She was now thirty, old enough to do as she pleased;

5

she became the mistress of La Rouërie, rumour said, or of Chafner, or of both, or of neither. Together they were seen galloping through the woods, the lovely Amazon, the burly major, the slim, haggard La Rouërie, with his long, pointed nose and chin, and wild eyes—a romantic trio, or rather quartet; for behind the Marquis, clinging to his saddle-back, rode a little pet monkey. If Breton gentlemen refused to speak to the nation, perhaps they might be persuaded to express their views in action; perhaps, if need be, in civil war?

Meanwhile Uncle Antoine was in trouble at Plancoët. Last year's harvest had been poor throughout France, and the winter severe. The quiet Rue de l'Abbaye (where François-René's aged grandmother and greataunt still lingered on, though long since deprived of their partners at quadrille by the reaper Death)[6] saw scenes of unaccustomed violence. Whenever a wagon was loaded for market, a mob hurled the corn-sacks to the ground, and molested farmers and millers, who threatened in return 'to exterminate the people and burn the street down'! This was the famous occasion when Antoine de Bédée threw open the granaries of Monchoix and offered 'a horseload of wheat for each family as long as any is left'. But Uncle Antoine also arranged, in his capacity as sheriff of Plancoët, for mounted constables to come from Dinan and arrest the ringleaders. Soon Plancoët market was orderly and full of grain. 'I hope the rest of the kingdom may be as quiet,' he reported complacently, and added: 'When the government decides to enforce the laws from the very beginning, and to repress those who infringe them, it will be easy to prevent the disorders which arise from the contempt in which they are held.' Bédée the Artichoke's golden recipe would doubtless have averted the Revolution, if the soldiers had not been about to join the rioters.

Day by day through that spring, as the three young Chateaubriands waited to depart for their promised city, came news of tremendous events in Paris. The first was bloody, and worse still, prophetic. On 28 April the Faubourg Saint-Antoine rabble sacked the house of M. Réveillon, a liberal-minded paper-manufacturer, who paid the highest wages in town but had made a tactless remark on the cost of living.[7] Several hundred rioters were killed or wounded when the reluctant French Guards opened fire; but this bloodshed demonstrated the readiness of the mob to fight, and the horror and shame of it weakened the nerve of both soldiers and authorities. Henceforth all attempts to restrain the mob would be halfhearted, and fail.

Then, none too soon, the age of brotherhood and equality seemed to dawn. The twelve hundred delegates of the States General assembled, bearing Cahiers of pleas from all districts of France, including Combourg.[8] They filed past the smiling, embarrassed King in the Palace of Versailles on 2 May. Louis XVI, anxious to appear democratic, ignored the bishops in their violet robes, the nobles with their plumed hats, and spoke only to Papa Gérard, a Breton farmer who had turned up in peasant costume. 'Good morning, good fellow!' said His Majesty. The absence of the noblemen of Brittany went unnoticed and unregretted; but Bretons were strong in the Tiers, and its policy was evidently modelled on the delaying tactics of the commons in the Estates of Brittany four months before. It, too, refused to begin business until the nobles and clergy consented to join it, but this time with success. After six weeks of deadlock the opposition was seen to be crumbling; on 17 June the Tiers declared itself to represent the entire nation, and renamed itself as the National Assembly; on the 20th it swore the Tennis Court Oath, never to disperse until it had made the new Constitution of France; and next day it was joined by the clergy, whom the liberal minority of nobles agreed to follow.

Court and government were taken by surprise. They had planned to allow the Third Estate to coerce the nobility and clergy, not to absorb them. Pressed by his brother Artois the King announced on 23 June that the Estates must sit in separate chambers, and confine their debates to the problems of taxation. He promised all manner of liberal measures —equal liability to taxes, freedom of the press, abolition of *lettres de cachet*, judicial reform—but meanwhile the National Assembly must consider itself dismissed.

Nobles and clergy departed, but the Tiers remained. 'Go tell your master,' cried Mirabeau, 'that nothing but the force of bayonets can remove us!' 'They want to stay,' said the King with an oath, 'Eh! *foutre*, let them stay!' They stayed, declared again that they were the National Assembly, and added that their persons were henceforth inviolable. The King, since no one would obey his wishes, could only order them to obey their own. He wrote on 27 June to 'his loyal clergy and loyal nobility', requesting them to join the Tiers. 'The Revolution is over,' wrote one over-optimistic delegate, 'and without one drop of blood being shed!'

On that day, a happy one for all true philosophers, François-René set out for Paris in charge of Julie and Lucile, not without adventures on the way. This time of great hope was also called the summer of the Great Fear. From April onwards, summoned by the mysterious underground leaders of the Revolution, bands of sallow-faced, club-bearing ruffians—the celebrated Brigands, who were later dismissed as a myth, but have been reinstated by modern historians as a reality—had been seen or imagined everywhere in France, marauding towards the capital. Now peasant vigilantes stopped the young Chateaubriands' carriage at every village, demanded passports, questioned the travellers. When they reached Versailles, no longer a palace of eternal delight, they saw troops quartered in the Orangery, trains of artillery parked in the palace yards, deputies and soldiers and courtiers jostling to and fro. In Paris they found their way blocked by hungry crowds queueing outside bakers' shops, by loiterers discussing politics at every corner. Camille Desmoulins was orating at the Palais Royal. When they alighted at their hotel in the Rue de Richelieu on 30 June, they saw an insurrection in progress. The French Guards had refused duty, a dozen ringleaders had been confined in the Abbaye prison at Saint-Germain-des-Prés, and the mob had risen to release them. The liberated mutineers, regaled with drinks at the Palais Royal, cried: 'Don't be afraid, do as you please! We're the Nation's soldiers.'

Two other Bretons had arrived in Paris, a nameless poet, and none other than François-René's old sweetheart Mlle des Alleuz, the 'agreeable frump'. On Sunday 12 July he escorted them to Versailles to see the fountains, and then, as he was privileged to do by his presentation at court, waited with them in the long gallery for the Queen's return from mass. She came, with her goldenhaired children, the eleven-year-old princess and the doomed little Dauphin, followed by his tutor M. du Touchet. The tutor noticed François-René, and obligingly pointed him out to the Queen; she darted towards him the same dazzling smile as before, so unforgettable that when he attended her exhumation twenty-five years after, he believed he recognised the same expression on the white teeth in the massive Hapsburg jawbone of her severed skull. 'He's not telling the truth!' cried Mlle des Alleuz when she heard this passage in his Memoirs at the age of ninety, 'I was there myself, and the Queen took no notice!' But perhaps the agreeable frump had forgotten, or perhaps her eyes had not been on Marie-Antoinette. The Queen was radiant, her courtiers beamed, as well they might; for Necker had been dismissed, old Marshal de Broglie was war minister, and now the King would surely come to his own again. The Ministry of the Hundred Hours had begun, so called because that was how long it lasted.

Like other returning excursionists on that Sunday, the young Bretons found their way home encumbered by a vast multitude in procession, carrying busts of Necker and the King's mob-wooing cousin the Duc d'Orléans, borrowed from a waxworks museum. The Prince de Lambesc's German dragoons pursued the demonstrators through the holiday crowd in the Tuileries gardens, were pelted with stones, fired upon by their faithless brother-soldiers the French Guard, and withdrawn to the Champ de Mars. The tocsin rang. Paris was now delivered to the rioters.

'To arms!' cried Camille Desmoulins. Gunsmiths' shops were looted, 30,000 muskets seized from the armoury of Les Invalides. The middle class armed against the mob, the mob against all forces of order; but both joined, along with the French Guard and the Brigands, in the siege of the Bastille on the 14th. This baleful fortress, under its amiable governor the Marquis de Launay, was then a mere rest-home for a few select social misfits, containing four forgers awaiting trial, two lunatics, and a young gentleman put away at the request of his family for various unnatural vices. François-René joined the fashionable spectators and lovely ladies who drove up in their carriages; among them, leaning against the fence of Beaumarchais's garden, was one of his favourite actresses, Mlle Contat, tenderly escorted by a young man of his own age whom he would know long after, Étienne Pasquier, the future duke and statesman. Launay dutifully parleyed, conciliated, resisted with brisk fire, then capitulated to save the lives of his little garrison of elderly pensioners and his own. But the roaring mob lynched him, desperately struggling—'Kill me quickly, good friends!'—and his three officers, and three wretched pensioners, and M. de Flesselles, the provost of the city council, and once Intendant of Brittany. The severed heads of all these were paraded through the streets by drunken heroes, while all prudent bystanders took off their hats, not to the dead but in reverence to the murderers. François-René looking aloft saw rebel French Guards firing triumphal cannon from the Bastille towers, with dreadful faces thronged and fiery arms.

'It's a revolt,' cried the King, when he heard the news in bed that night, and was answered: 'Sire, it's a Revolution!' No choice remained for His Majesty but to sanction what he could not resist. He dismissed his disastrous new ministers, recalled Necker, and with him reinstated (to the gratification of all Chateaubriands) Malesherbes's nephews Montmorin and La Luzerne. On 17 July François-René saw the precarious monarch visiting his beloved people of Paris, under the protection of the Mayor of the new city council, the astronomer Bailly, and the commander of the new National Guard, the Marquis de Lafayette. 'Paris has conquered its King,' declared Bailly with audacious double meaning; 'I don't think I ought to hear,' muttered the embarrassed Louis. When he reached Versailles, still wearing the enormous cockade of the new red, white and blue tricolour which Bailly had thrust in his hat, the Queen remarked: 'I didn't know I had married a commoner!' The first emigration began; Artois fled, and the three Condé princes, the Queen's favourite friend the Duchesse de Polignac, and the outgoing ministers. All philosophers of good will, and François-René among them, could not but rejoice, for had not their philanthropic dream come true? Within one day the King had been transformed into a virtuous constitutional ruler, and it only remained for the National Assembly to supply him with a virtuous Constitution. Yet their hearts misgave them; for the victory of liberty and brotherhood, if such it was, had been won not by themselves with reason and fine feelings, but by a furious rabble with atrocious murder.

A week later, on 23 July, as François-René and his sisters sat with their Breton friends, they heard cries of 'Shut your doors!' from distant neighbours. Looking from the window he saw a ragged, exultant multitude pouring into the Rue de Richelieu; they brandished, as it seemed, two banners, which as they rushed nearer could be seen to be two human heads on pikes. His friends withdrew, but François-René lingered, fascinated by horror. The foremost ruffians noticed him and halted, jovially thrusting their pallid trophies in his face, capering and leaping to reach him. One had its mouth stuffed with hay, like a comic moustache: it was Foulon, the recently dismissed Minister of Finance, who was rumoured to have remarked: 'If they have no bread, let them eat hay.' The other, with half its face torn away, one eyeball hanging loose, its teeth biting the iron of the pike thrust through its mouth, was Foulon's son-in-law Bertier, the Intendant of Paris. Ever and anon the revellers brought the two dead mouths together: 'Kiss Papa!' they cried. In a paroxysm of revulsion, with words which were addressed not only to the assassins but to himself, François-René shouted: 'Brigands, is this what you mean by liberty?' They howled with rage, and battered on the street-door, while his sisters swooned and his fellow-lodgers upbraided him in terror. Then the mob surged past towards the rear entrance of the Palais Royal, there to deliver those grisly remnants to its masters and paymasters.

François-René began to reconsider his political ideas. The rivulet of blood that had sprung from the heart of Saint-Riveul was broadening, the Revolution of brotherly love was poisoned at its source. This was not what *he* meant by liberty. However, as a good liberal he attended on 30 July the Marquise de Villette's dinner in celebration of Necker's return. His hostess, the 'Beautiful and Good' and adopted greatniece of Voltaire, had taken a fancy to him. Mirabeau was there, ablaze with impudent genius, with his huge squashed vertical face, on which the marks of smallpox seemed scars of hellfire, roaring like the muzzle of a blackmaned lion. François-René remained speechless as usual, but Mirabeau took note of him.

The Revolution continued its course of highminded legislation from above and (in Taine's phrase) 'spontaneous anarchy' from below. In the all-night sitting of 4 August, in a frenzy of self-sacrifice and appeasement, the noble and clerical right wing of the Assembly abolished their own immemorial privileges of feudal dues, exemption from taxation, game preservation, and tithes.[9] Towns and provinces renounced their millennial prerogatives; so perished for ever the lost cause of the independence of Brittany, for which François-René had drawn his sword in the streets. His birthrights as nobleman and Breton were gone, he noted with wry approval, and soon he was relieved of his honour as a soldier. On 10 August fidelity to the King was replaced by a new oath of loyalty 'to Nation, Law, and King', to be sworn by all army officers, 'with the

most august solemnity', in the presence of their own troops on parade.
So the Monarch now took third place, and the mob would henceforth
be unhindered by the military. François-René learned with pride that
his own regiment of Navarre, then in garrison at Rouen without him,
was just in time to be the last to quell a riot.[10] Next the Assembly ratified the Declaration of the Rights of Man, marking an epoch in the
aspirations though not in the actions of sinful humanity. Neither the
admirable Article Four ('Liberty consists in being able to do anything
that does not injure others'), nor the equally admirable Article Ten
('No one may be molested for his opinions, even in matters of religion'),
would save any man from the guillotine. The King was granted only a
choice between sanction or veto, which his bewildered Majesty seemed
likely to use. He summoned the loyal regiment of Flanders; this was to
be his last act as a free monarch.

Before long François-René saw more heads. At noon on 6 October
the news reached Paris: 'The King is paying us a visit!' He hurried to
the Champs-Elysées, and witnessed the triumphal procession of thirty
thousand, menacing and jubilant, trudging home from Versailles. Past
him paraded terrible market-women carrying loaves stuck on pikes,
male cut-throats firing pistols in the air, obscenely gesturing whores
astride on cannon, neatly complacent national guardsmen, crestfallen
gentlemen of the King's bodyguard who had saved themselves, all but
two, but could not save their master. Jeering ruffians rode footboard and
roof of the royal carriage, where King, Queen, royal children, and the
King's sister Madame Élisabeth sat impassive. 'We made the bugger
sanction!' yelled the harridans, and 'Courage, friends, you shall not
want for bread; we bring you the Baker, the Baker's wife, and the little
Baker's boy!' Before all, by way of oriflamme, marched the familiar
double standard of the Revolution, two severed heads on captured
Swiss halberds. But these, he saw, were no unkempt heads like Foulon's
and Bertier's. They had been freshly curled and powdered in mockery
by M. Gelée, wigmaker at the bridge of Sèvres.[11] One was young Des
Huttes's, the other had belonged to François de Varicourt, Beautiful
and Good's little brother. These had faced the rabble alone last night,
as sentries on the royal staircase. 'What have you come for?'—'We want
the King's heart, and the Queen's, and their tripes, to make us cockades!'
The moment in which the gallant pair were hacked to pieces had given
their comrades time to flee and be rescued by the somnolent Lafayette.[12]
Their Majesties were installed in the Tuileries. Louis, decked yet again
with a huge tricolour in his hat, unconvincingly announced that it was
with pleasure—'and with trust,' added the Queen eagerly—that he
revisited his beloved people of Paris. The King was now not only
powerless, but a prisoner and hostage. The shutters closed in the ghost-
palace of Versailles. The Assembly moved to the royal riding-school

next door to their captive; they too, did they but know it, were prisoners. 'The deputies are in the riding-school,' it was facetiously said, 'but the riders are in the Palais-Royal.' Many of right and centre emigrated, including the president Mounier and the tearful Lally-Tollendal. In the three months since Mounier had carried the Tennis Court Oath, and Lally had wept for joy on being crowned with a classical wreath of uncooked parsley after the storming of the Bastille, the Revolution had moved so dizzily leftward that their liberal heads seemed forfeit.

'The severed heads changed my political dispositions; these cannibal[13] feasts filled me with horror, and the idea of leaving France for some distant land took root in my mind.' The Chevalier de Panat, Fontanes's friend, even proposed that he and François-René should emigrate together. Panat, a staunchly royalist navy captain with two elder brothers in the right wing of the Assembly, was one of those witty buffoons, of greedy table-manners and slightly soiled appearance, who turn up repeatedly during half a century, always teased and always welcome. 'My life-witness,' Chateaubriand called him, one evening forty years later when he had him to dinner, and Panat, on their way home, gave his reminiscences of this very time to his fellow-guest Villemain. 'I guessed his quality from the start,' declared Panat, 'and told Fontanes, who thought as I did. When Lally and Mounier left I tried to persuade him to emigrate with me, but he hesitated; he was in love, and besides, he was already a victim of melancholy, sister of inaction. But from that time he seemed to me full of genius, although half crazy.'

So the wilder self of François-René had not entirely disappeared beneath the political philosopher. Panat's diagnosis was doubtless correct, but no one will ever know with whom François-René was at that time in love, or with how many. 'Tied to no woman,' he says, 'the Sylphide still obsessed my imagination.' And yet, 'It was a time of duels and love-affairs, of mysterious trysts among ruins, under a cloudless sky, amid the peace and poetry of nature; of sequestered, silent, solitary walks, interspersed with eternal vows and indefinable endearments; one heard meanwhile the rumbling of a world in flight, the distant reverberation of a crumbling society, which menaced with its downfall these felicities cowering at the foot of the precipice of history. When two people lost sight of one another for twenty-four hours, they could not be sure of ever meeting again.' What two people? He confesses, with irony at the thought of all he omits, only that he went to the theatre with Mlle Monnet and her father, Malesherbes's protégé, professor of mineralogy at the Jardin des Plantes, to whom the matchmaking Mme Ginguené had introduced him. The girl sat at the front of their box, and he close behind her, half grumbling, half delighted. 'I don't know whether I liked or loved her, but I was certainly scared of her. When

she had gone I wanted her back again, though full of joy to be relieved
of the sight of her.' Sometimes he called, 'sweating at the brow', to take
her for a walk arm in arm; 'I seem to remember squeezing hers a little'.
And sometimes he went to the theatre alone, 'in search of boredom to
ease me from boredom, like an owl in a cranny in a wall'. The teeming
auditorium became a wilderness of solitude where his thoughts could
stray to the voice of Talma in Racine, the music of Sacchini, the motions
of the ballet at the Opéra, even the 'caterwauling of a vaudeville' or a
popular ditty of country lovers, heard half unconsciously yet remembered all his life:

> *'Though long the night in rain, wind, snow,*
> *We know a way to make it go!'*

But he frequented more attentively another theatre where, as he truly
says, 'one of the greatest dramas in the world was being played'. One
had to get up early to find a seat in the crowded public gallery at the
Manège, and wait till the deputies arrived, deep in conversation,
gesticulating, still munching breakfast. François-René sat behind the
royalist opposition. The topic for debate, he noticed, was nearly always
a proposal for abolishing something. The speeches for and against became ever more stormy, the public joined in with applause or hooting,
the president of the day (who was often his own Breton acquaintance,
Isaac Le Chapelier, the deputy for Rennes) rang his bell, while members
shouted at one another from bench to bench. One morning he found
himself just behind a swarthy little gentleman-deputy from Dauphiny,
bounding with rage in his seat, pointing to the left-wing majority and
saying to his neighbours: 'Let's draw our swords and fall on those
ruffians!' The market-ladies overheard him, knitting in the gallery as
they would knit three years later round the guillotine; they rose to their
feet, foaming at the mouth, each clutching her unfinished stocking in
upraised fist, and screamed: '*A la lanterne!*' But the candle-lit evenings
were even more dramatic than the mornings, for one glimpsed in the
wings the obscure and terrible men of the future, the tragic villains who
would rise to play their part in the last act but one, the destined murderers of those who now held the front of the stage. Once, after the
close of a particularly frenzied debate, François-René took note of one
such nonentity mounting the rostrum. His face was lifeless and grey
(posterity would call it seagreen), his dress and manner neat and vulgar;
he might have been the bailiff in a respectable family, like M. Livorel,
or a village notary scrupulous of his appearance. He proceeded to read
an excruciatingly boring report, to which no one listened. 'Who is that?'
asked François-René. 'That's Robespierre,' he was told.

How much more dangerous seemed the leonine Mirabeau, when he
halted the rabble with a toss of his mane and a glare of his savage eyes!

Once, at a session of terrifying disorder, François-René saw him towering on the rostrum, sombre, impassive and misshapen, and thought of
Milton's Chaos, enthroned above

> 'Tumult and Confusion all embroiled,
> And Discord with a thousand various mouths'.

But Mirabeau had taken Robespierre's measure. 'That man will go far,'
he prophesied, 'because he believes every word he says.'

Amid this collapsing world François-René had not forgotten his first
and wildest ambition, to have a poem printed in the *Almanach des
Muses*. 'By dint of intrigues and anxieties', as he confesses, he induced
Delisle de Sales to arrange for 'L'Amour de la campagne, par M. le
Chevalier de C * * *.' to appear in the issue for 1790 of that elegant pocket annual. The sight of his own verses on pages 205–6 made
him 'all but die of fear and hope'. 'My poem,' he boasted, 'was discussed
in the society of Ginguené, Lebrun, Chamfort, Parny, Flins, La Harpe
and Fontanes', as well it might be, for nearly all these literary friends
had turned up as usual in the same number.[14] Ginguené, with his flair
for never keeping quite up with the vanguard of progress, had contributed two odes in ecstatic praise of the soon to be discredited Necker,
addressing him in one as the Swan of Lake Leman, in the other, by way
of variety, as the Swan of Lake Geneva.

But François-René's brief first published work was neither political
nor topical. The poet joyfully revisits in springtime, after a sojourn
'mid palaces, in cold men's company', the beloved rivulet last seen at the
beginning of winter, and vows to live and die by its side. The situation,
perhaps even the actual time of composition, belongs to the spring of
1787, when he returned to Fougères after his abortive presentation at
court and the settlement of his father's estate at Combourg. His fellow
contributors no doubt appreciated a tasteful allusion to Gray's *Elegy* in
the shepherds' epitaph for the poet. Perhaps they also uneasily detected
through the sentimental tinsel of the Chevalier's verses some signs of a
freshness lacking in their own, and sensed the first faint tapping of the
young nineteenth century on their old eighteenth-century door.

9

THE STOCKING-SELLER

MEANWHILE, in the dangerous company of politicians, poets, demure young ladies, and the scapegraces of his regiment, François-René had spent beyond his means. In February 1790 he found himself obliged to raise 4,500 livres by 25 March. This was no ordinary debt, but a debt of honour, and his thoughts turned to the heroic duty of self-slaughter which loss of honour would entail. Luckily his distant cousin Félix de la Morandais, eldest son of the kindly bailiff who had taken him as a child to Saint-Malo on his yellow mare, was in Paris and came to the rescue. This providential relative owned a stocking factory at Angers; he offered to lend François-René the equivalent of his debt in stockings, and instruct him in the art of selling them. La Morandais notified his manager M. Piochon, supplied a batch of samples and a list of suitable dealers, drew up a note of hand for the loan, and then disappeared to spend the summer at Lausanne.

François-René's anguish was real. 'I am bound to settle my debt under pain of being dishonoured and blowing my brains out on the spot,' he reminded his saviour, and repeated: 'My position as an officer, my honour, and perhaps my life are at stake.' But soon he warmed to his task, left the samples with the merchants, collected orders, searched for a guarantor, pacified his creditor, and carried on an energetic correspondence with La Morandais and Piochon. His business prose is unexpectedly deficient in orthography, but crystal clear, for he said everything twice over. Like father, like son; René-Auguste, too, had been known to sell haberdashery in his time, and had written to his agents and captains with the same odd spelling, the same commercial guile and lordly affability. Perhaps, François-René suggested, he could avoid customs dues by pretending the stockings were for the King's service and the use of his regiment? One good turn deserved another; he was 'on the point of getting a good post in the West Indies', and if La Morandais would care to put his younger brother in his hands, he promised airily, he would 'find him advancement there or the means of making his fortune'. How lucky meanwhile was La Morandais, 'enjoying peace and nature in Switzerland, while we inhabitants of France are again plunged in chaos!'

Five huge bales, containing 165 dozen pairs of cotton stockings, white, grey, plain, sprinkled or ribbed, arrived from Angers on 5 April, addressed to 'the Chevalier de Chateaubriand, officer in the regiment of

Navarre, infantry' at 4, Petite rue Saint-Roche, where Julie, Lucile and he had moved in the previous autumn.[1] The consignment was valued at 4,534 livres, enough to cover his debt; yet so far was François-René from finding his trade distasteful that he was only too pleased to accept two bales more, to the value of 1,200 livres, which M. Piochon had packed by accident and begged him to take. He ordered these to be sent to Marianne's Hôtel de Marigny at Fougères to await his arrival.

La Morandais had prudently insisted on his obtaining a guarantor, and hoped even for the surety of Jean-Baptiste himself. Strictly speaking, François-René as a minor was not at liberty to contract a debt without the consent of his elder brother as his legal guardian. But the culprit dared not approach Jean-Baptiste, for fear not only of his wrath and the humiliation of it, but of the conditions of reform and economy which he would certainly impose. 'I've told him nothing about it,' he pleaded, 'I can't make use of him in business affairs, because I should have my hands tied!' However, François-René had by no means lost face in his regiment, where his broadminded companions felt that nothing could be more honourable than to have a debt of honour, unless to acquit it by a stroke of honourable trade. So his old comrade of Cambrai days, Lieutenant Achard, obliged with his signature—'a very good gentleman, though that doesn't count for much nowadays', blessed with 13,000 a year, a recently deceased father, and an estate near Fougères—'my sisters know him well and can tell you about him'. Another friend even envied his good fortune, and urged that he, too, should be accommodated with some of these wonder-working stockings; but François-René recommended that this candidate should be informed, with expressions of regret, that for the moment all were sold. 'He is under twenty-five,[2] in debt, and gambles,' he warned La Morandais with virtuous disapproval.

He arrived at Fougères in the last week in April, and found his second batch of stockings already delivered. Enough was enough: 'I don't need anything more for the moment,' he told M. Piochon on 7 May.[3] No doubt he found a satisfactory sale among his own and his sisters' friends, or with the shopkeepers in that busy market-town. But traffic in stockings was not the original purpose of his visit, for even before there was any question of selling his wares in Brittany, on 23 March, he had notified M. Piochon of his coming departure 'on pressing business'. This business, as it appears from his letter to La Morandais of 14 April, was the collection of 'funds I have there' which conveniently fell due 'more or less in the month of March', and from which he would arrange for Marianne to pay the interest on his loan every year 'during my absence in America'. Thus he had spoken for the first time of his intended journey as being to the continent of America, and not merely to the West Indies.

Jean-Baptiste himself was now in diminished circumstances, though through no fault of his own. Since the abolition of feudal rights last August the peasants of Brittany had been busier in burning châteaux and molesting aristocrats than in paying rents. Combourg itself was still unharmed under the ward of the good steward Le Corvaisier, but their cousin Flore de Bédée and her husband M. de Blossac de Châteaud'Assis had been alarmingly maltreated at their château of Launay-Blot near Dol. Uncle Antoine had fled to Saint-Malo, so had their visitor of winter evenings at Combourg M. Goyon de Beaufort, and such magnates as MM. de Botherel, Bédée de Visdelou and Magon de la Villehuchet had even languished in prison. No gentleman was safe who had drawn his sword in the streets at Rennes during last year's troubles, and the family made François-René swear not to set foot there. On 25 February 1790, to Jean-Baptiste's disgust, the Assembly made the abolition of feudalism permanent by embodying it in the new Constitution, but declined to discuss the promised compensation. 'I lose nearly half the revenues of my Combourg estate, which unfortunately were entirely in dues,' wrote Jean-Baptiste to his client Mme de Calan on 16 March, 'and I can't say much better for my government bonds.' Creditors of the State were already being paid in *assignats*, the new, rapidly inflating paper money financed by the confiscated property of the Church. 'In fact,' Jean-Baptiste added—with the elegant irony which was a French gentleman's only resource against a plebeian Revolution, and which one day would help to bring himself and others of his family to the guillotine—'I am fully entitled to regard myself as one of the principal victims of the great work of regeneration!' Where now was the glorious career he had prepared by marrying into relationship with three powerful ministers? His relatives had lost not only power but even influence, for the National Assembly, not the King's government, ruled France. However, M. de Montmorin was still in nominal charge of foreign affairs. Jean-Baptiste hinted that he would like a diplomatic appointment at Constantinople, then a key post, for the Sultan was at war with Russia and Austria, and France must have a finger in the pie. But Mirabeau in a moment of caprice had the same idea, reached over Montmorin's head, and Jean-Baptiste's chance was gone.[4]

François-René fared no better from M. de la Luzerne, who as navy minister was also responsible for the colonies, including San Domingo, where he himself had so recently been governor, and a pro-revolutionary assembly of colonists was now defying his successor. It was evidently the minister's duty to restore the King's authority in the colony, if the deputies his masters would allow him. François-René's 'good post in the West Indies' would have included not only collection of the family's longlost credits but special duties as an agent for his uncle-in-law La Luzerne. But their plans were spoiled by the Assembly's decree of

8 March, by which the sister assembly of San Domingo was granted full recognition, and invited to submit its own proposals for its own future constitution. François-René's mission to the 'happy isles' was thwarted. The liberated islanders would be less likely than ever to welcome an emissary of La Luzerne, or to surrender 166,000 livres of obsolete bad debts to the younger son of a deceased nobleman. 'The colonists are very lucky, they'll be able to do just as they please to get rich,' he lamented to La Morandais, and it was on this painful occasion that he added the remark about France being 'plunged into chaos again'. Between his first letter to La Morandais, of towards 9 March, and the second, of 14 April, his 'good post in the West Indies' had been transformed into a long 'absence in America'. This random eddy in the torrent of the Revolution had altered the course of his destiny.

Early in June 1790 he was back in Paris, completing his trade in stockings, meditating his new journey, but also determined to enjoy the first and last occasion of general gaiety provided by the Revolution. A Feast of Federation was announced for the anniversary of the Fall of the Bastille on 14 July, and the prospect seemed to unite all parties in a wave of hope and joy. On that great day delegates from all over France would join with puppet Monarch and ruined Church, mutinous Army and complacent National Guard, disintegrating Assembly and louring Mob, to swear indissoluble brotherhood to one another and eternal fealty to Nation, Law, and King. Fifteen thousand dawdling workmen were digging on the Champ de Mars a vast turf amphitheatre to receive them, half a mile long, complete with lath and plaster Arch of Triumph and pyramidal Altar of the Country, where the scandalous bishop Talleyrand and two hundred priests in tricolour sashes would ascend to consecrate the Nation's oath with high mass.

At moments, now he was resolved to depart, François-René found himself relishing the heady air of factitious optimism and liberated energy. He saw the answer to a riddle which had baffled him in his studies of history three years before. How, during times of the breaking of nations, had people managed to go on living? 'In a society that is being shattered and rebuilt the struggle of two spiritual powers, the clash of past and future, the interaction of old ways and new, form a transitory combination which leaves not a moment for boredom. Passions and characters set free display themselves with a vigour which they lack in the well regulated city. Infraction of laws, emancipation from duties, conventions and decencies, the very presence of danger, add to the interest of this disorder. The human race walks on holiday in the streets, rid of its schoolmasters, restored momentarily to a state of nature.'

Soon he found himself a little nearer to this state of nature in his quality as a gentleman born. On 19 June 1790 the Assembly abolished titles, armorial bearings, and liveries. Suddenly François-René was Chevalier no more, and Jean-Baptiste ceased to be a Count; instead, each was henceforth plain Monsieur Chateaubriand! Some even lost their names. When a nobleman's appellation had derived from his fief, he must now revert to his forgotten family surname, which often had an embarrassingly bourgeois sound. Lafayette himself became M. Motier. 'M. Vignerot's carriage!' bawled a clump of idlers outside the Opéra, and split their sides when the Duc d'Aiguillon's coachman failed to understand that his master was ready for home. Most infuriating of all, the *Moniteur* used these unknown names in its daily reports of the Assembly; so whenever a progressive aristocrat, devoted to the Revolution, made an important speech, none of its readers could guess who had spoken. Mirabeau (now Riquet) collared the unfortunate reporter and enquired, in his voice of bronze: 'Are you aware, sir, that with your *Monsieur Riquet* you have set all Europe at cross-purposes for three days?' The Duc de Chabot wittily had the arms on his coach painted over with the emblem of a cloud; surely, when the passing cloud of the Revolution chose to melt away, his scutcheon would reappear bright as ever?

Jean-Baptiste reported these mishaps to Mme de Calan with his usual wry gusto. He adhered to the *politique du pire,* to the school of thought which maintained that the worse things got, the better. According to this line of reasoning, the Revolution was so inherently unstable that its victories were really defeats. Judicious non-resistance would soon lure this rash movement over the brink, and then quite suddenly everything would be the same again. People called him the fanatic Chateaubriand, Chateaubriand *l'enragé.* Jean-Baptiste was hand in glove with his father-in-law. M. de Rosanbo, when the Assembly sent the Paris Parlement into compulsory recess on 5 November 1789, had happened to be president of its vacation chamber. He drew up a secret protest, signed unanimously by himself and his colleagues, pointing out that such a dismissal, and indeed the Assembly itself, had no basis in law, and repeated this ingenious stratagem when Parlement was abolished altogether in October 1790. Before long, seizing the moment when everyone was thoroughly tired of the Revolution, M. de Rosanbo planned to produce these pulverising cantrips from their hiding-place in the woodwork of his beautiful new English water-closet in the Rue de Bondy. Then Parlement would instantaneously spring to life and declare the Revolution null and void. The King would come to his own again. The President de Rosanbo and his water-closet would have saved France!

François-René had more than one sharp tiff with Jean-Baptiste and M. de Rosanbo. How, they scolded, could he be so culpably impartial as to be a moderate? How could he associate with such villains as Mirabeau, who had stolen Jean-Baptiste's embassy, or Le Chapelier the

renegade Breton, founder of the Jacobin Club, who had abolished noble
privileges, feudal dues, the independence of Brittany, the Parlement of
Rennes, the just hopes of gentlemen with credits in San Domingo, and
now their very titles! But his moderatism was attacked no less acrimoniously from the other side by his literary friends Ginguené, La
Harpe and Chamfort, who were now thoroughly committed to the
Revolution. In his growing sense of alienation from family, friends and
fellow men François-René longed more than ever to see the stable
Revolution and established liberty of the United States, the uncon-
taminated solitude of the American wilderness, the noble Redskins in
their original state of nature.

His final moment of choice had arrived only two days before the
abolition of titles. Le Chapelier was now in uneasy coalition with
Mirabeau and the constitutional liberals, in a belated effort to halt
Robespierre by supporting the court. He had seceded from the Jacobin
Club, his own creation, to form the rival Club of 1789, dedicated to the
proposition that in that late glorious year the Revolution had gone far
enough. He invited François-René to a banquet of these Eighty-Niners
at the Palais-Royal on 17 June. Perhaps this lively and well-connected
young man could be persuaded to join them for more than dinner?
The banqueters drank toasts to the coming Feast of Federation, the
National Guard, the memory of Benjamin Franklin, and many other
worthy causes. Mirabeau talked expansively, mostly about himself.
François-René listened spellbound and silent to his romantic tales of
love, of his lost Sophie ('a soul framed by nature's hands in a moment
of magnificence!'), his expressions of longing, genuine, but not genuine
enough to be fulfilled, to retire from politics into the solitary world of
the imagination. Mirabeau, too, he noted with fellow-feeling, had been
oppressed in youth by a severe father, was nurtured (in that father's
own words) as 'a night-fowl between four turrets', and had a diehard
royalist brother to whom he felt immeasurably superior! 'In any other
family,' Mirabeau insolently boasted, 'my brother would be the black
sheep and the one with the brains; in mine, he's the prig and the fool.'
As the guests departed the subject turned to Mirabeau's enemies.
François-René still remained speechless. Suddenly he felt the great
man's exquisitely manicured hand resting on his thin shoulders; 'I feel
the pressure still, as if Satan had touched me with his fiery talon,' he
wrote thirty years later. Mirabeau stared him full in the face, his yellow
eyes aglare with vainglory, vice, and genius. 'They will never forgive
me my superiority,' he said. A rebel archangel thus deliberately tempted
François-René. An amenable reply ('But I forgive it!') would have
altered his destiny. The moment passed, he kept his silence and freedom.

The labourers in the Champ de Mars were going slow. At the end of
June all Paris realised with consternation that the huge amphitheatre

might not be ready in time for the Feast of Federation. Everyone joined in with wheelbarrow and shovel, shopkeepers and deputies, polished abbés, sturdy monks, tender nuns, progressive nobles, and beautiful ladies. François-René himself, perhaps recruited by these last, toiled with a will. But a sudden illness confined him to bed and kept him from attending the Feast. He went to Fougères to recuperate and finish his business, and was already there on 15 July, if the date on a letter to La Morandais can be trusted.[5]

During his absence, on 6 August 1790, Jean-Baptiste lent 17,191 livres in his name—all but one sixth of the capital which François-René had inherited from his father's estate and which Jean-Baptiste controlled on his behalf—to a former colleague in the Parlement of Rennes, the Marquis de Montaigu, under promise of repayment on the same day three years later. By a normal legal fiction the loan was declared to be 'without interest', which was presumably subtracted before handing over the money. By this ingenious transaction Jean-Baptiste enabled his young brother to eat his cake and have it, to raise ready cash without breaking into his capital, and to save this capital from the hazards of the Revolution, which would surely be over when the time came for repayment in 1793. The opportunity seemed so advantageous that Jean-Baptiste arranged for Montaigu to borrow 15,083 livres of Lucile's little nest-egg on the same day. The Marquis emigrated not long afterwards. Jean-Baptiste had made another of his wellmeaning miscalculations. However, François-René was now financed, by his brother's assistance but not at his cost, for his journey to America.

In mid-September Jean-Baptiste, summoned, as he told Mme de Calan, by 'the dilapidation of my affairs caused by the decrees of the august Assembly', made his first trip to Brittany since 1787. He found the tradesfolk of Rennes in consternation at the loss of their Parlement. 'A numerous populace, who gained their livelihood from it, and whom the charms of liberty will not save from dying of hunger, regret today the chains that bound them,' he wrote to his mother-in-law, Mme de Rosanbo, in words which were underlined in red by a clerk of the Committee of Public Security three years later and used in evidence against him. But the Revolution could not be halted by expressions of urbane disapproval. The revenues of Combourg, which in exceptionally good years under René-Auguste had risen to 70,000 livres, had now dropped to 10,000. Jean-Baptiste visited his old mother at Saint-Malo. Perhaps he also presided over a family council at which François-René's journey was finally sanctioned.

François-René had still to settle his stocking-debt, of which Jean-Baptiste apparently remained forever unaware. La Morandais was now back at Rennes, staying with his uncle M. Dastin, Mme de Chateaubriand's cousin by marriage, a procurator in the defunct Parlement. In his letter from Fougères marked 15 July François-René had offered to meet him 'to finish our business', and quaintly suggested a rendezvous —'without fail, even if it rains'—at Saint-Aubin-du-Cormier, near Bénigne's château of Lascardais, since the family would not allow him to set foot in Rennes. The letter marked 21 September shows that La Morandais had demanded payment of interest due on 1 September. In the last, marked October 1790, François-René is found on the point of repaying the principal of his debt with money forwarded from Paris, and asking him to restore his note of hand guaranteed by Achard's signature 'so that I may return it to my friend'. His debt of honour and part, at least, of his debt to La Morandais were now liquidated, and he was free to think of nothing but America.

His army career had melted away in the Revolution, and ceased to be a hindrance. He had not served with his regiment, as it seems, for two years, since he nursed his poor mad colleague in the autumn of 1788. In August 1790, immediately after the feast of universal brotherhood, half the French army mutinied against its officers. In September his own rank of gentleman cadet was abolished, and François-René found himself compulsorily retired on half pay to await a new appointment. Sub-lieutenancies would be scarcer than ever, for a quarter of all vacancies must now be filled by the promotion of N.C.O.s. For an indefinite period his presence was not required, and his absence would pass unnoticed. Apparently he did not officially announce his intention of leaving France: 'François de Chateaubriand de Combourg,' wrote a regimental clerk on 13 March 1791, guessing rather wildly at his address, 'has retired pending reappointment to Chateaubriant in Brittany'.

The amiable and unkempt Panat tackled him again. Perhaps they might revive the idea of emigrating together? Panat took François-René for solitary walks, and even dined him at Saint-Cloud with Fontanes and Rivarol,[6] but found him unforthcoming. Now more than ever the young man seemed 'full of genius, though half crazy'. He would not join the émigrés, he declared, because he was going to America to discover the Northwest Passage! Panat, 'pointing out that I'd been a sailor myself and knew the map', made various objections, to no avail. 'I'm looking for something new,' cried the impetuous François-René, 'there's nothing to be done here; the King is ruined, and you've no hope of a counter-revolution. I'm doing like the seventeenth-century Puritans who emigrated to Virginia, I'm off to the forests: that's better than going to Coblentz.[7] What's the use of emigrating from France? I'm emigrating from the world! Either I'll die on the way, or I'll come back bigger than I left!' 'And 'pon my soul, he kept his promise,' added Panat, when he told the story long afterwards. But his decision to go to America combined even more complex motives and causes than he revealed to Panat, and these must now be examined.

PART THREE

The Noble Savage

10

HYPERBOREAN STRANDS

ALTHOUGH François-René had lived with the prospect of a
lengthy absence from France for at least eighteen months, ever
since his letter to Châtenet in March 1789, and his poem about the
'happy isles', only in March 1790 had his destination changed from
San Domingo to the United States. But the new plan touched older
memories. He had dreamed long before of travelling to America, on
All Souls' Eve at Combourg in 1784, when the Capuchin missionaries
told of their life among the Red Indians, and again in the spring of
1786, when he announced to his acquiescent father his intention to 'go
and clear forests in Canada'. Such aspirations were in the family. Both
René-Auguste and Uncle Pierre had crossed the Atlantic many times,
cod-fishing, slave-trading, plundering the English. They had even seen
Quebec when it was still French, each on his first voyage as captain and
corsair; René-Auguste in 1747, when he returned with beaver-pelts and
whale-oil, Pierre in 1758, when he took a cargo of provisions to re-
plenish the citadel which Wolfe stormed a year later. How could his
father have refused him then, or his brother deny him now?—so long
as Jean-Baptiste remained unaware that his chief purpose was to write
a book.

In old age René-Auguste sat in his tower and read Abbé Raynal's
Histoire philosophique des deux Indes (1770); the author, he was fond of
declaring, was 'a master-mind'. François-René, as a Combourg tradition
affirmed, was punished for boyhood misdeeds by being locked in his
father's study, and took the opportunity to read books which it would
have been better for him not to read. He had certainly perused at a
tender age not only the freethinking *Gazette de Leyde* and *Journal de
Francfort*, to which René-Auguste as a freemason and court-despiser
subscribed, but Abbé Raynal's philosophic and Voltairean lament on
the two lost empires of France in India and America. It was Raynal,
among others, who had shown him the dream landscapes of Himalaya
and the sultry banks of Ganges, to which he had flown on the storm-
winds, from his troubled bed in the northeast turret, in the arms of the
Sylphide. But he also first learned from Raynal of the Natchez Indians
of Louisiana and the Iroquois of Canada, the Eskimos of Labrador, the
virtuous Quakers of Philadelphia, the apparently indubitable reasons
for believing in the existence of a Northwest Passage, and the urgency
of pursuing the quest for it, for all these matters were in Raynal.

His thoughts were thus early directed by family tradition, and by boyhood memories and reading, towards the very aspects of the New World which held his imagination ever after. So there is no need to doubt his statement in the preface to *Atala*, that he had begun to write about the Red Indians of North America even before he had any prospect of visiting them, 'I was still very young,' he says, 'when I conceived the idea of writing the epic of the man of nature, or describing the manners of savages by linking them to some known event.' A later stage of the same work is mentioned in a passage of *Essai sur les révolutions* written in 1796, where he includes, in a list of early compositions left behind in France at the time of his emigration in July 1792, 'the History of a savage nation in Canada, of which the setting, totally new, and descriptions of nature, foreign to our clime, might have merited the reader's indulgence'.

He felt at no loss for a plot. He would bring his noble Redskin to Paris in the reign of Louis XIV, like the Huron in Voltaire's *L'Ingénu*, to whom he felt much akin. Voltaire's hero was a Breton orphan, born in Canada of parents from Saint-Malo, nurtured among the savages, plunged like himself in a state of youthful innocence into a corrupt and bewildering Paris, falling in love with Mlle de Saint-Yves as he had, or almost, with Mlle des Alleuz or Mlle Monnet, meeting men of letters, and becoming a disillusioned philosopher. But perhaps, better still, his own 'man of nature' could love, instead of a white lady, a red maiden. Even Voltaire's Ingénu had adored the fair Abacaba, than whom 'sheep are less gentle, eagles less proud, deer less nimble', until she was unfortunately 'eaten by a bear'. But his own work would be serious where Voltaire's had been satirical, both in social comment and as a tale of love. His own heroine would be pure as Lucile, passionate and unattainable as the Sylphide; the lovers would be parted in death by the destiny of their own chastity, like Paul and Virginie. Of all this, or most of this, François-René could already write from experience. For the 'known event' on which his action would hinge, and even, as he hoped, for convincing local colour, he could resort to Raynal and other books.

In the year 1687 the Marquis de Denonville, governor of French Canada, had perfidiously arrested a group of Iroquois chieftains whom he had invited to a friendly council, and sent them to France to labour in the King's galleys. But Louis XIV, scandalised by this flagrant breach of protocol against fellow monarchs, ordered their instant release, their entertainment as distinguished visitors, and their honourable repatriation. The incident was briefly mentioned by Raynal, and told with more detail in Raynal's source, Charlevoix's *Histoire de la Nouvelle France* (1744). Here ready to hand was the historical event which would root François-René's tale in reality, and bring his hero captive from Canada to Paris and home again.

And yet, in the final form of *Les Natchez*, as completed towards 1798 and published in 1826, the sojourn of Chactas in the land of the Iroquois and his captivity in France are a mere subplot, a tale within a tale, memories of the blind chief's youth narrated in old age. The main action is set among the Natchez of Louisiana, fifteen hundred miles southward and forty years later, and hinges upon a different 'known event', the rebellion of the Natchez against the French colonists in 1729. Perhaps, as has sometimes been argued, Chactas was originally an Iroquois born, and the Natchez setting was a later afterthought. Certainly this would explain how Chateaubriand could describe his tale as being, in 1792, 'the history of a savage nation in Canada'. Even so, if his own account is to be taken literally, he had already chosen the Natchez rather than the Iroquois for his main setting earlier still, at the very beginning of his composition towards 1788 or 1789, before he had even thought of his journey to America. 'After the discovery of America,' he says, in the preface to *Atala*, 'I could see no subject more interesting, especially for Frenchmen, than the massacre in 1727[1] of the Natchez colony in Louisiana. All the Indian tribes conspiring, after two centuries of oppression, to restore liberty to the New World, seemed to offer as happy a topic to my pencil as the conquest of Mexico.' Perhaps he is here conflating two stages in the evolution of his work, either from lapse of memory or for the sake of simplification. But perhaps the author himself knows best, and his words ought not to be so lightly dismissed; perhaps the Natchez were in fact from the very outset his main theme, and Chactas's narrative of his youth, though first to be written, was always a subsidiary episode. Once again Raynal supplies a clue. In his sixth and final volume, devoted to North America, Raynal relates the Natchez rebellion only fifty pages after his account of Denonville's stratagem. He unhistorically assigns to it (for in fact it was merely a regional uprising) the same continental significance as in Chateaubriand's epic: 'at the end of 1729 the Natchez succeeded in forming a universal league, with the intention of simultaneously ex-terminating all their oppressors.' And Raynal tells the same romantic tale, absent from Charlevoix, of the unavailing betrayal of the plot by an Indian woman who loves a Frenchman, and her theft of the sticks which mark the day fixed for the massacre, which Chateaubriand adapted for the dénouement of *Les Natchez*. So the kidnapped Iroquois and the rebellious Natchez had dwelt long in his mind, side by side and in the same order as in his future work, ever since his boyhood reading at Combourg.

Soon, however, when he had already composed a first version of Chactas's adventures in Paris and had run out of personal experience, he met a serious hitch. His own verses had convinced him that he could write of nature as genuinely as Bernardin de Saint-Pierre, or even more so; but could he convey the poetic reality of landscapes and beings he had never seen? 'I threw several fragments of this work on paper,' he says, 'but soon I saw I lacked the right colours, and that if I wished to paint a true likeness I must follow Homer's example, and visit the peoples I meant to portray.' Once again it would be unwise to disbelieve him. In the same way and for the same purpose, sixteen years later, having discovered that the first version of his classical epic *Les Martyrs* was unsatisfactory for want of having seen the places he wished to describe, he made an almost equally arduous and dangerous voyage, 'in quest of images', as he said, to Greece and Palestine and North Africa. So his primary motive for the journey to America was to write a book—or rather, to possess the places and peoples of his reveries by embodying experience of their reality in a work of imagination.

But the approval of his family was necessary, and he could hardly tell Jean-Baptiste that he was going to America to collect impressions for an epic on Red Indians. 'I needed a useful purpose for my journey,' he confesses naively, and devised a scheme so staggeringly impractical that it could not but appeal to the hardest heads in that enterprising age. He decided to discover the Northwest Passage on foot, by travelling across the American continent to the further sea, and then circling back along the Arctic coasts to Labrador, New York, home and glory. Jean-Baptiste made no demur. Old Malesherbes was delighted. Indeed, it was in his company, during one of their favourite conversations about geography, that François-René had first conceived this extraordinary plan.

M. de Malesherbes had spent two years in retirement, twice refusing the exalted office of Privy Seal, which in better times would have been the crown of his career, but now seemed only a temptation to be rejected.[2] Sometimes he presented admonitory memoranda to the King, which His Majesty 'put in his pocket with a look of kindness' but omitted to read. Malesherbes, ever more aghast, averted his eyes from calamities for which he felt personally to blame. Could not the beginning of catastrophe be traced back to his own liberalising ministry under Turgot, fifteen years before? 'M. Turgot and I,' he said, 'were honourable men, very cultivated, passionate lovers of virtue; who could have doubted we were the best possible choice? But our knowledge of the world came from books, we lacked skill in affairs, we were bad administrators; without intending or foreseeing it, we contributed to the Revolution.' Malesherbes had called throughout those years for States General and representative government, and now he beheld the appalling result. 'In a time of violent passions,' he declared with the irony of despair, 'one must take good care not to speak the voice of reason,' and: 'I hope to end my days in silence and obscurity.' He deplored equally his royalist daughter Montboissier's hasty emigration, and his liberal daughter Mme de Rosanbo's forwardness in taking the collection, dressed in full mourning, at the requiem mass for the 'heroes of the Bastille'. 'Mme de Rosanbo continues to be a demagogue,' reported Jean-Baptiste sardonically to the Comtesse de Calan, 'only M. de Malesherbes is becoming very aristocratic.' The day would come when Malesherbes would emerge from silence and obscurity, and speak reason at the cost of his life; meanwhile, it seemed, he had made the great refusal.

François-René's plan gave him new life. 'If I were younger,' he cried with sparkling eyes, 'I'd go with you, I'd spare myself the sight of all the crimes and perfidies and follies that assail one here! But at my age a man must die where he is.' All through the summer and autumn of 1790 François-René called on him every morning in his study; with their eyes glued to maps they compared the various delineations of the Arctic zone—various indeed, being drawn almost entirely from conflicting theory, guesswork and whimsy—or calculated the equally irreconcilable distances from Bering Straits to Hudson Bay. They read over one another's shoulders the sea and land journeys of his English, Dutch, Spanish, French, Russian and Danish predecessors, the lost adventurers his peers. They discussed the precautions he must take against the perils of cold, wild beasts, starvation. 'What a pity you don't know botany!' Old Malesherbes was an expert practical botanist, a prolific author of never-published treatises, a lifelong acclimatiser of exotic plants in his park at the Château de Malesherbes, specialising in the red cedars, magnolias, sugar maples, and liquidambars of North America. He had been a friend and pupil long ago of the naturalist Bernard de Jussieu, the dendrologist Duhamel, and the herborising Jean-Jacques Rousseau. Thus admonished, François-René ransacked the works of all these, and those of the botanists Tournefort, Grew, and Jacquin. 'I already thought myself a Linnaeus,' he says. He took long walks in the Jardin des Plantes, then the finest botanical garden in Europe, complete with a vast library and scientific collections, not to mention the budding charms of Mlle Monnet. In the formal labyrinths of herbarium and arboretum, the floral chessboard of parterres, he crossed paths with his fellow enthusiast Bernardin de Saint-Pierre, unawares, for neither as yet knew the other. In this botanical crash-course François-René began to master the loving yet scientific knowledge of growing nature which would enable him to recognise what he saw in the travels of all his life, and would vivify the landscapes of his writings with the poetry of truth. Soon his wise mentor, instead of deploring his ignorance, took to exclaiming: 'What plants you'll bring me home for my gardens at Malesherbes!'

At the same time, still more ardently and arduously, he studied the narratives and maps, the aims, methods and achievements, of earlier pioneers. The historical and geographical background of his would-be expedition has been neglected by Chateaubriandists, from economy of effort, or from an illogical feeling that their investigations, if they made any, would be wasted on an absurdity. His project was impossible, but by no means absurd. Its significance can only be understood in the light of the knowledge which he acquired in order to formulate it; and conversely, the extent and depth of his preparatory studies reveal the seriousness of his intentions.

He had no lack of books or guidance, for M. de Malesherbes was lavish of both, and regarded himself, justly, as an expert in American matters as in all other polite studies. Much of the credit for the theoretical merits of François-René's plan, as well as much of the responsibility for its fantastic impracticality, must be granted to that erudite old armchair-geographer; and the traveller himself in later years modestly referred to his journey as undertaken 'on the advice of M. de Malesherbes', or even 'in accordance with a plan supplied by M. de Malesherbes'. Then again, his patron's library (the contents of which can be reconstructed from records and even from surviving volumes) was as rich in the literature of American travel as in the classics of botany. Here François-René found the narratives of Hennepin, La Hontan, Charlevoix, Le Page du Pratz, Carver, Crèvecoeur, Chastellux,[3] and many others, not for the first time. He had ransacked them already for the local colour of his savage epic; indeed, the very idea of his journey of discovery must have sprung from the reading which he had at first intended for a stay-at-home work of fiction. Each was complete with its folding map, in which the frontier between reality and make-believe, sight, hearsay, and conjecture, crept painfully and deceptively westward.

For two centuries, until only five years before he was born, his countrymen had possessed a vast empire in North America, expanding west along the Saint-Lawrence to Lake Superior, south down the Mississippi to the Gulf of Mexico. England had held the east-coast colonies and Hudson Bay, Spain the southwest and Florida, but all the rest, New France or Canada in the north, governed from Quebec or Montreal, Louisiana in the south, governed from New Orleans, had belonged to the King of France. French fur-traders and Jesuit missionaries ventured still further westwards, along the Minnesota River, up the Missouri, over the Grand Portage to Lake Winnipeg and the Saskatchewan. Then, in the fatal gamble of the Seven Years War, France lost all. Perfidious England took Canada, the lakes, the Ohio; the Spaniards gained Louisiana and the Mississippi. Westward exploration ceased for two generations, deprived of French initiative, inhibited even more by the defeat of England in the American Revolution, the rise of Indian resistance, the unreadiness of the liberated Americans to pass the Ohio.

How glorious then, thought François-René, if *he* were destined to restore the presence of France in the Far West! 'In the event of success I should have had the honour of bestowing French names upon unknown regions, of endowing my country with a colony on the Pacific, of wresting the wealthy fur trade from a rival power, of preventing that rival from opening a shorter road to the Indies, by putting France herself in possession of that way.' His success could have had no such consequence, for neither England nor Spain, nor the new United States certain soon to arrive between them, would ever have allowed France a footing on the Northwest coast; but such was François-René's romantic dream, and even old Malesherbes's. 'Don't fail to write to me by every ship, keep me informed of your progress and discoveries, I'll see to it that they go down well with the ministers!'

What ministers? Necker had left in September 1790, insulted and injured, to spend the rest of his life in Switzerland, writing tracts to prove how right he had been. La Luzerne resigned the navy in October, abandoning a ministry 'hateful as sin', said his family.[4] But one minister remained, to whom that Pacific coast was of special and personal concern. In May 1790 England and Spain had been on the verge of war, after the Spanish governor had seized English fur-trading ships at Nootka Sound on Vancouver Island, and M. de Montmorin, seeing a last opportunity for France to regain power in America, informed the Assembly of his preparations for intervention on the side of Spain. The Assembly happened that month to be in a mood of universal brotherhood, and responded by decreeing that 'the French Nation will never undertake a war of conquest', and that henceforth the right to declare war rested with itself, and not with the King and his ministers. However, times might change. It was perhaps during the Nootka crisis that François-René decided to include the Northwest Coast in his itinerary; and it is likely that M. de Malesherbes gave his nephew and former colleague M. de Montmorin a glowing account of the plans of this enterprising young man, and obtained his assurances, however vague, of present interest and future aid.

At that same time France was also concerned in a less remote region of the West. In 1789 land-agents in Paris from the Scioto Company of New York had sold lots on the unoccupied west bank of the Ohio to the value, or rather price, of a million livres. Journalists with inside information had insinuated that the salesmen were swindlers and the promised land was a wilderness. Even so, five hundred wouldbe settlers, including noblemen and makers of carriages, jewellery, clocks and wigs, whose talents would no doubt be of particular value in the backwoods, had sailed from Le Havre in February 1790 for Alexandria on the Potomac, thence to cross the Alleghenies and live happily ever after in their free new city of Gallipolis. François-René was in two minds whether to despise them as frivolous visionaries, 'sending on ahead plans of châteaux to be built among the savages', or to admire them as heroes of an emigration 'more rational than the folly of Coblentz', leaving home, as he was about to do himself, in quest of liberty. But here was another matter on which this useful protégé of M. de Malesherbes could report to M. de Montmorin.

In its final, most elaborate form François-René's expedition fell into three sections, each designed to solve a major geographical problem, each involving the exploration of a vast unknown region which no European had ever seen. He proposed to be the first man to cross the North American continent, the first to trace the untrodden Pacific coast, and the first to discover the Northwest Passage from Pacific to Atlantic.

He would have to begin by journeying through the known to the edge of the unknown. He decided to follow the route of the last of his predecessors, the Connecticut Yankee Jonathan Carver in 1766, to Lake Erie via Albany and Niagara, and thence by the old, still-frequented way of the chain of Great Lakes to the western end of Lake Superior. Others from there had penetrated a few hundred miles further, northwest to Lake Winnipeg, or southwest to the Minnesota River or the Missouri. But none had yet gone, as he resolved to go, due west to the Mississippi, whose still undiscovered source, as he says in an elegantly regretful past conditional, 'I would have recognised'.

The thought of that mysterious place—though he never saw it any more than Carver, who had only described it from the tales of his Sioux hosts—was to haunt him ever after. There, on a low aqueous plateau at the centre of the continent, so close that you could stand with left foot in one and right foot in another, rose the sources of the four great rivers of America. Let your canoe drift at random, and it would float you north down the River Bourbon (which Englishmen called the Nelson) to Hudson Bay, or east along the Saint-Lawrence to the Atlantic, or south on the Mississippi to the Gulf of Mexico, or else, most thrilling of all, down the fabled river of the West to the Pacific.

Other geographers, still trusting perforce to the various tales of Indians, since no white man had yet been there, gave different accounts. Some, relying on the map drawn on birch-bark for La Vérendrye towards 1730 by the Cree Indian Ogacha, made the four rivers flow from Lake Winnipeg, others from a fabulous Mountain of Shining Stone. A Missouri Indian squaw, more reliable than most, had assured Father Charlevoix in 1721 that the Missouri rose 'in bare, very high mountains, behind which is a great river flowing west'. An aged and garrulous Yazoo chief named Moncacht-Apé had told Le Page du Pratz in 1730 of his five-year journey in the days of youth; he had ascended the Missouri and crossed the divide to the Beautiful River, which flowed west into a Great Water where bearded white men came every year in a big ship to steal Indian maidens. The truth of these stories is more surprising than their falsity, for they point to the shining snows of the Rockies, the waters of the Columbia and Fraser hurtling westward to Pacific coasts already visited by forgotten Spaniards from California and Russians from Kamchatka.

Moncacht-Apé gave him a new idea for his book: he would make his savage hero take a journey over the American continent, and tell the story of it in old age to a Frenchman by the Mississippi, just as Moncacht-Apé had done to Le Page du Pratz, in the country of the Natchez.

François-René now stood in fancy halfway across America, where the four great rivers flowed from a quivering morass, or a lake, or a shining mountain. Here, as all authorities agreed, he need only identify the River of the West and float down it to the sea. But no! rather than reach the Pacific too far north to unravel all the secrets of its unknown coast, he resolved, prompted by Malesherbes, upon an astonishing but scientifically motivated detour. 'From that point,' he recalled, still in his past conditional mood, 'I would have descended by the plains of Upper Louisiana to forty degrees north latitude, and there have resumed my journey west, so as to strike the coast of the South Sea a little above the head of the Gulf of California.' Forty degrees north was close to the latitude of the former French post of Saint-Louis, where remnants of his furtrading countrymen still lingered under a Spanish governor, and would no doubt be happy to refit him with fresh supplies. Then he would reach the ocean near Cape Mendocino, just past the northward limit of effective Spanish occupation, at the threshold of the unknown, where everything he saw would be new, and he could give all his discoveries to France. He foresaw no obstacle from natives or country. The Sioux and Pawnees, true to their role as noble savages, would be kind to him if he was kind to them. He was blissfully unaware, like everyone else at that time, of the very existence of the Rocky Mountains, which he would here have encountered at their broadest point, a thousand miles of badlands, desert, parallel north-south ridges, snowpeaks, and no passes.

The second section of his immense journey would now begin. The west coast was a labyrinth of mysteries, which he would unriddle by travelling along it. He would discover the outlet of the River of the West, whose source he had already visited. He would measure for the first time the width of the continent, which varied so bewilderingly from map to map of the theoretical geographers. Perhaps he would discover the inland Sea of the West, into which a Greek pilot in the service of Spain, Juan de Fuca, claimed to have sailed at 47° north in 1592. The French cartographers De l'Isle and Buache had revived this tale in the 1750s, and mapped that legendary sea in the neatest detail, conveniently stretching for 1,500 navigable miles from its twin openings on the Pacific to near the headwaters of the Mississippi. For good measure they had added an inland Northwest Passage by a sea strait through the heart of the continent, based on the still more apocryphal voyage of the Spanish admiral Bartolommeo de Fonte in 1640, leaving the Pacific in either 50° or 60° north to enter either Baffin Bay or Hudson Bay. To add to the confusion a map by the Russian Stählin published in 1774 showed Alaska as an island, providing a short cut from the Pacific to the Arctic many hundred miles east of Bering Strait.

For a time these riddles seemed solved by Cook's third voyage in 1778, which was published with enormous success in 1784, and was no doubt read by François-René in the equally popular French translation of 1785. Cook mapped a continuous coast from California to the Arctic Ocean, disposing at least of Stählin's fabrication. But doubts soon revived, for Cook had been prevented by obedience to his instructions ('to lose no time in exploring below 65° N.'), and by the accidents of mist and storm, from any thorough investigation south of Alaska, in the very area where De Fuca's Sea of the West and De Fonte's strait had been reported. For a few years and for the last time the question of the Northwest Coast was reopened.

Cook had at least discovered Nootka Sound, where his men made a discovery of their own. For a handful of blue beads or an iron marlin-spike the Nootka Indians were delighted to part with sea-otter skins which the jolly sailors later sold for a hundred dollars apiece to the Chinese at Canton. From 1785 onwards English and American mariners traded in furs from Nootka, and gradually became aware that the whole deceptive coast northward to the Alaskan Mount Saint Elias was only a screen of islands. Captain Barkley in 1787 sailed into an entrance south of Nootka leading to apparently open sea; evidently, they thought, this was the Strait of Juan de Fuca, whose name it bears to this day. Captain Dixon in the same summer found the Queen Charlotte Islands, which he identified with De Fonte's Archipelago of Saint Lazarus. No one, they rightly said, had ever seen the real coast, or knew how far back it lay. Was this unknown coast (as appeared so obvious to the English) the western boundary of Canada, and therefore part of an English colony?—or was it rather (as seemed so manifest to the Spanish) a northern extension of California, and therefore the property of Spain? It was to test this issue that the governor of the Spanish post established at Nootka in 1789 had arrested three English fur-trading ships, where-upon the Nootka crisis ensued, and momentarily, in the spring of 1790, to all Frenchmen and especially to all friends of M. de Montmorin, that false, impossible shore had seemed the most interesting point of the external globe.

Such was the position of the Northwest Mystery when François-René was planning his journey. 'Despite the efforts of Captain Cook and subsequent navigators,' he wrote in 1796, summarising from memory a manuscript notebook of early 1791, 'it is known that doubt still remains.[5] A merchant ship in 1786 claimed to have entered in 48° north a sea in the interior of North America, and it was asserted that what had been taken for the mainland north of California was only a long chain of closely contiguous islands.' This passage, although no commentator has paid attention to it or realised that it relates to any real and identifiable situation in geographical history, is vital evidence of the seriousness of his studies, the up-to-dateness of his information on the voyages of Captains Barkley and Dixon, and the nature of his purpose.

Yet another problem awaited him at the point of juncture between Pacific and Arctic. Cook, in the vain hope of discovering the impostor Stählin's strait dividing Alaska from Canada, had explored a deep inlet on the south Alaska coast which he mistook for a river. The Canadian fur-trader Peter Pond, who discovered the Great Slave Lake in 1786, optimistically mapped it seven hundred miles west of its true position, identified the river flowing westward from it (in fact the Mackenzie River) as Cook's River, and provided the same lake with a second outflow along Hearne's Coppermine River into the Arctic. Pond's theories were first published in the London *Gentleman's Magazine* of March 1790, and aroused wide interest; for here, from a man on the spot, was yet another prospect of an inland Northwest Passage by water. So François-René reserved the options of following Cook's River to the Arctic, or of pressing on to Bering Strait before turning east; he would decide when he arrived there.[6]

He stood at last on the Arctic shore, the true goal of his journey; for his original plan had been to strike northward from the source of the Mississippi, and his immense detour westward was due to the promptings of old Malesherbes. To those polar solitudes he would look back ever after with deeper longing and regret than to any other region of the travels he did not achieve. He need never have returned. Wandering there he would have escaped from history, have met instead the companion whom through all his life he most desired yet dreaded to see, himself. 'Lost on those wild seas, those hyperborean strands where no man has left his footprints, the years of discord which have crushed so many generations with so much uproar would have fallen silent on my head: the world would have changed in my absence. It is probable that I would never have incurred the misfortune of being a writer.' Since he could not see them himself, he would take his hero Chactas to those ends of the earth.

And yet, did an Arctic Ocean even exist, or was it merely a fable like Juan de Fuca's Sea of the West, or a figment of the theoretical

geographers lured by the incurable hope of a Northwest Passage? Many
cartographers, including the De Fonte enthusiasts, showed the American
continent reaching to the Pole, and joining the north of Greenland
round a landlocked Baffin Bay. Until very recently the entire area from
Bering Strait[7] to Hudson Bay had remained unknown, except for the
doubtful reports of Indians. One white man, indeed, had seen the
Arctic Ocean in one place, but his discovery had been kept secret for
many years, and did not suffice to show whether this new coast was
continuous. It was François-René's mission to go there and see for
himself.

Throughout the first half of the eighteenth century the Hudson Bay
Company had received reports from Indians of a 'Far-off Metal River'
which flowed, many hundred miles to the west, past copper mines into
a northern sea. In 1771 their employee Samuel Hearne succeeded at last
in reaching it. He travelled with a war-party of Chippewas, watched
with helpless disapproval their massacre of a wretched little tribe of
Eskimos at Bloody Falls, and found the Coppermine River flowing
through treeless tundra into the Arctic Ocean, which no European
before him had seen. Hearne's discovery strengthened the possibility of
a Northwest Passage through an Arctic Ocean, and at the same time,
as he himself pointed out, demonstrated the nonexistence of any sea
passage south of 72°,[8] since he had crossed no salt water on his way.
Hearne's own narrative was not published until 1795, and Chateaubriandists have assumed that François-René's claim to have known of
his discovery in 1790 must therefore be an untruthful anachronism.
But the Company, departing from its traditional policy of secrecy, had
made Hearne's reports available to Cook in 1776. Hearne's journey was
summarised and mapped in the official publication of Cook's third
voyage in 1784, and François-René doubtless studied it in the French
translation of 1785. So he had every right to declare that the object of
his own journey was 'to discover the sea seen by Hearne'.

By a vagary of fate Hearne was connected with another of François-
René's heroes, the glorious La Pérouse, whom his uncle Ravenel had
pointed out to him at Brest in the spring of 1783. La Pérouse had then
recently sailed home in triumph from the final exploit of the War of the
American Revolution, the sacking of the Hudson Bay forts, bringing
with him Samuel Hearne in person as prisoner of war, or rather as
honoured guest; for Hearne had surrendered with graceful tact, and
then captivated his captor with the sight of his thrilling journal. 'I'll let
you go if you promise to publish it,' said La Pérouse, and was as good
as his word, for Hearne was free at Gosport in November 1782, and
back at Hudson Bay ten months later. In August 1785 La Pérouse himself sailed from Brest to discover the Northwest Passage, cruised for
two seasons in the North Pacific without finding anything that had not

3 Saint-Malo from the
mainland, early 19th
century
  Chateaubriand's
birthplace, in use as
annexe to Hôtel de
France, Saint-Malo, early
19th century

  His grave on the
Grand-Bé, mid-19th
century

4 Combourg Castle, village, and lake

Winter evening at Combourg, a scene from
Chateaubriand's Memoirs

already been discovered by Cook, sent his journals and charts home from Botany Bay in 1788, and then disappeared for ever. The two heroes beckoned François-René to their oceans.

Another possibility of influence is still more curious. It can hardly be coincidence that another enthusiast had recently visited Paris to plan a one-man crossing of North America, with the support of friends of Malesherbes. John Ledyard, a Connecticut Yankee like Carver and Pond, had sailed under Cook as corporal of marines, and published in 1783 the first unofficial narrative of Cook's last voyage. Homesick at Nootka in March 1778, gazing eastward to his birthland, Ledyard had become obsessed with a romantic desire to cross the continent alone on foot from west to east, and a patriotic resolve to open the Pacific coast to the United States fur trade. He devoted the rest of his life to the ever frustrated hope of returning to Nootka and beginning his journey. He found backers, who invariably backed out, at New London, New York, Philadelphia, and (after crossing the Atlantic in 1784) at Lorient.[9] He moved to Paris and told his plans to the seadog John Paul Jones,[10] the American minister to France Benjamin Franklin, and Franklin's successor in 1785-9, Thomas Jefferson. Jefferson, 'our first geopolitician', as Bernard de Voto has called him, was a statesman of continental mind, and would make expansion to the trans-Mississippi West a ruling theme of his life. He had already proposed an east-west crossing to General George Rogers Clark in 1783, and would support yet another abortive solo-traveller, the French botanist and spy André Michaux, in 1793, before sending out, as President of the United States, the successful expedition of Meriwether Lewis and William Clark in 1804-6. Early in 1786, after Ledyard's partnerships with the Lorient merchants and with Jones had fallen through, Jefferson encouraged his alternative plan to reach Nootka through Siberia, recommended him to America's friend Lafayette, and assisted him with the small doles which Ledyard accepted with such ungrasping candour from so many patrons.[11] Ledyard left for London in August 1786, attempted to sail for Nootka in November in an unlicensed ship which was immediately seized by the Customs, and found a new patron in the benevolent geographical busybody Sir Joseph Banks. He never saw Nootka again. After trying to get there by way of Siberia in 1787 he died of rage at Cairo in November 1788, on his way to discover the source of the Niger for Banks. He had met Jefferson for the last time in Paris on his way out that June, and promised: 'If I escape through this journey I will go to Kentucky, and endeavour to penetrate westwardly to the South Sea.' For he had not abandoned his obsession, but had at last[12] reversed its direction to the westward crossing chosen soon after by François-René. 'He was a man of genius, of some science, and of fearless courage and enterprise,' wrote Jefferson for his epitaph.

6

So François-René took up the torch at the moment when it was dropped by Ledyard, and it is hardly possible that he did not do so consciously. Not only were Ledyard's plans well known in French governmental circles and elsewhere, but Jefferson himself was a particular friend of Malesherbes and Montmorin. He visited Malesherbes and his park (for both were ardent arboriculturists) as early as October 1785, continued to exchange with him American and European plants and seeds for acclimatisation, and, in Jefferson's own words, 'we established together the most unreserved intimacy'. So, while it is likely that Ledyard was among the inspirations of François-René, it also seems more than probable that Malesherbes's knowledge through Jefferson of the monomaniac American directed his steering of François-René's plans. François-René always referred to his Arctic journey in quest of the Northwest Passage as his own resolve, but to the appended transcontinental and Pacific coast explorations as 'the plan agreed between myself and M. de Malesherbes'. What the luckless Ledyard had failed to achieve for Jefferson and the United States would be won for the glory of France by the daring protégé of M. de Malesherbes.

Thus guided in spirit by Ledyard, La Pérouse and Samuel Hearne, François-René imagined himself standing on the hyperborean strands at the mouth of Hearne's Coppermine River, having reached it either by following the Arctic coast from Bering Straits or, more conveniently, by the nonexistent river misinterpreted by Cook and fabricated (with its 'falls said to be the largest in the known world') by Peter Pond. Even here he could not be sure what he would find, whether a continuous eastward shore, or a landlocked gulf which would lure him north into unretraceable Polar desolations. Hearne had caught a single glimpse of a dismal shallow sea, with islands, and packice only half a mile out, and then hurried back. One sight of sea did not make a Northwest Passage. 'If I succeeded nowhere in finding a passage,' François-René wrote, 'I would have returned to the United States by way of Hudson Bay, Labrador, and Canada.' So, if the Passage existed, he would discover it; if not, his way of retreat was clear, for Hearne himself had returned in safety to Hudson Bay, and the trail from the Bay to civilisation at Quebec, which had been pioneered by Frenchmen in the seventeenth century, was still used as a fur-trade route. From Boston or New York he would return to France and fame, a great man in the eyes of Malesherbes, Jean-Baptiste, and—oh, of whom? Love, as Panat knew, had prevented him from joining the royalist emigration, but not from the resolve to cross America and come home again.

Such, in their wellread theoretical elaboration and their total impracticability, were the designs of François-René egged on by Malesherbes, such the contents of his mind in the months before his departure. He vaguely acknowledged the odds against him, his youth and inexperience, his lack of companions and of official support, the unpredictable difficulties of unknown country, the perils, which he entirely underestimated and thought he could cure by kindness, from hostile Indians. But, he reflected, every discoverer was a greenhorn once; he would surely find European comrades and Indian friends; the reluctance of any French government to aid its explorers was a fact of life to which even a relative by marriage of three ministers must resign himself. 'One must bear in mind a circumstance peculiar to France,' he wrote later, 'its travellers have been solitary men, abandoned to their own energy and their own genius; only rarely have they been employed or assisted by the government or by private companies.' If he failed, he would return and try again. 'It was possible that this first journey might be the last, if I succeeded at the beginning in procuring all the resources I needed for my great discovery; but if I should find myself halted by unforeseen obstacles, it was to be only the prelude to a second, a kind of reconnaissance in the wilderness.'

His journey was doomed to failure by multiple impossibilities: the inconceivable distances, tripled by the wellmeant meddling of Malesherbes; the logistic necessity for an expedition large enough to carry its supplies and defend them from the Indians, the inevitability otherwise of being plundered and slain, the vast unsuspected deserts and Rocky Mountains which lay beyond 'the plains of Upper Louisiana', the impervious Pacific coast (which only the Alaska Highway of the mid-twentieth century was to make passable by land), the starvation and cold of the Arctic tundra. Yet the ideas that prompted his plans were in the air of his time; the historical, political, and economic pressures were mounting which would cause others to achieve them within a few years of his own impossible attempt. Even then, as François-René was soon to learn, Alexander Mackenzie the Scottish furtrader had already reached the Arctic Ocean in July 1789,[13] at the mouth of the Mackenzie River 600 miles west of Hearne's Coppermine, and would make the first continental crossing (from Fort Chipewyan on Lake Athabasca to the Salmon River north of Vancouver Island) in 1793. The American navigator Robert Gray discovered the outlet of the Columbia River, the long-sought River of the West, in 1792. In the same year and the next the English Vancouver solved the remaining mysteries of the Northwest Coast: Nootka was an island, Juan de Fuca's sea was only the broad strait behind it, there was no inland waterway of De Fonte, Cook's River was only a landlocked inlet. The American army expedition of Lewis and Clark, despatched by President Jefferson, crossed the United States from Saint-Louis to the mouth of the Columbia and back again in 1804–06, overcoming by disciplined numbers the obstacles of Indians and mountains which would have

defeated François-René. The English Franklin in the 1820s explored the
central part of the Arctic coast, from west of the Mackenzie to east of
the Coppermine; Parry discovered Fury and Hecla Strait, the missing
link between Hudson Bay and the Arctic gulfs; so here, too, François-
René's route was at last pioneered.

And so, within a generation, his ideas were achieved, his questions
answered, by other men. But Chateaubriand still deserves a place among
the heroes of the vast human movement which opened the wilderness
of North America. He was, albeit more in imagination than in action,
a last French successor of Charlevoix and La Vérendrye, a precursor of
the nineteenth-century Anglosaxons who followed in reality the footsteps of his dream. In later years, when he wistfully admired the
triumphs of these newcomers and looked back to the infatuated hopes
of his youth, he could not prevent himself from feeling that his failure
was among the causes of their success, almost, even, that they had
deprived him of a rightful glory.

SULPICIAN ARK

HE EMERGED bewildered, with lines of latitude and longitude, primeval forests and noble savages quivering before his eyes, from Malesherbes's house in the Rue des Martyrs into the streets of Revolutionary Paris. In the soft days of that autumn of 1790 he saw that history had again moved on. Expelled from their cloisters, a Capuchin friar newly cleanshaven sat reading the newspaper at an outdoor café table, a prim nun in a drawingroom joined a circle of hilarious ladies, her nieces and cousins. At the theatre a spruce abbé came on stage to shouts of 'Down with priests!'. 'Gentlemen, long live the Nation,' cried the mummer, and resumed his role. On winter evenings François-René passed the Tuileries, 'a huge gaol crammed with prisoners awaiting execution', which the royal family were no longer permitted to leave, and saw the Queen's windows ablaze with festal light.

In the salons of the liberal aristocracy he glimpsed unawares the same young women who, in another epoch, were to love him with a romantic frenzy which as yet had not even been invented—which he, in fact, was to invent! By this irony of fate he stood unnoticed in the soirées of the Princesse d'Hénin, in whose London circle he would find Mme du Belloy, of M. de Montmorin and his daughter Pauline de Beaumont, of the Princesse de Poix, whose son Charles de Noailles had just married Natalie de Laborde, of M. Necker (before his flight), through whose daughter Mme de Staël he would one day meet Juliette Récamier. Still nearer home, much disapproving, he saw or heard of Mme de Custine.

Villemain, no doubt on the good authority of Chateaubriand's 'life-witness' Panat, describes him significantly in those days as 'vexed by what seemed to him shocking, at such a time, in the careless frivolity of certain young women friends of his sister-in-law who moved in court circles'. For the irreproachable Aline, strangely enough, had two scandalously flighty bosom-friends. One was the blue-eyed 'Countess Alex', also nicknamed Frivolity or Rose Pompon, wife of Alexandre de la Rochefoucauld, who was ambassador at Dresden but, she complained, hardly ever wrote to her. The other was Mme de Custine, née Delphine de Sabran, daughter-in-law of the Marquis de Custine, the American war-hero and future Revolutionary general. She, too, felt released from duty to her husband, having presented him with two sons.

Little Gaston, aged three, was madly royalist, and insisted on kissing the tall grenadier on sentry-duty outside the King's palace—a desire which baby Astolphe (whom she had just finished rearing on Rousseauish principles with her own milk) would put into practice at a much later time of life. Young Victor de X.,[1] whom they called the Troubadour, fell in love with Countess Alex, so his intimate companion the Comte d'Esterno could do no less, leaving the Troubadour to confide his woes to Mme de Custine. But just when Mme de Custine seemed on the point of consoling him altogether, Countess Alex decided, as she could not make both her lovers happy in Paris, that she must make them both happy in Brussels. Even there she was not quite successful. Why, she wondered, as we may wonder also, did the young gentlemen persist in taking a little house in the middle of a wood three miles from town? It was, they explained, so that they might talk together about the object of their passion, undisturbed. 'Everything that is dear to him is dear to me,' wrote Mme de Custine, left desolate, 'even Countess Alex.'

François-René was shocked by these scandals, but not personally involved; at most, he may have sensed the possibility that the Sylphide, who even in Combourg days had sometimes visited him as a princess or chatelaine, might one day return in the mask of some such noble wanton as these made serious by suffering. And yet, although he cannot have consciously resolved it, he was to love them in succession long afterwards, in approximate order of their ages.[2] It was as though his heart became imprinted, in those months before his departure, with the programme of a lifetime's wanderings on the hyperborean strands of love.

Aline herself, however, was shielded by innocence and motherhood. Jean-Baptiste's reunion with her in the autumn of 1788 had at last resulted in the birth of a son and heir, named Louis after M. de Rosanbo and Geoffroy after the ancient Barons of Chateaubriand, on 13 February 1790. François-René had seen this baby baptised, and carried back amid tears of joy by its grandmother Mme de Rosanbo to the girl mother's bedside. The arrival of his nephew meant that he must abandon all hope of ever possessing Combourg. Aline was now pregnant again, with a child to be expected in April,[3] when he would already have taken ship for America. However, he would always be an affectionate uncle.

Up to the moment of leaving Paris he continued to see his literary friends. Perhaps a dinner given by Fontanes, which he remembered as 'one of the gayest in my life', took place in those last months, by way of a farewell. Ginguené, Flins, and Parny were among the guests, 'the food was choice, the wine good, and we didn't act the poet to excess, although we couldn't resist it altogether'. Fontanes, with true hospitality, had invited not only his mistress, the poetess Mme du Fresnoy,[4] but her husband as well, and M. du Fresnoy, not to be outdone in politeness, 'took no notice of anything, which I thought very French'. Once again he narrowly missed meeting Bernardin de Saint-Pierre, now more famous than ever, for he had just published *La Chaumière indienne*, the story of which—about a philosopher searching for truth, and finding it in the hut of a Hindu pariah—was not without affinity to the theme of the noble savage already chosen by François-René. Mme Ginguené invited him to dine with the great man, along with Julie and Lucile, on 15 January 1791, and to go on afterwards to the first night of the opera *Paul et Virginie* at the Théâtre Italien; but François-René was previously engaged. Bernardin, his sisters reported, seemed far from satisfied with the shipwreck scene. 'The tempest I experienced on the Ile de France was rather more formidable than *that*,' he grumbled. A few days later François-René left alone for Brittany, on his way to America.

At Fougères he stayed for a week or so with Marianne. Perhaps it was at her instigation that he took the opportunity of seeing Armand de la Rouërie, who knew America so well, having fought at Brandywine and Yorktown, and might be persuaded to give him a letter of introduction. Instead of fobbing him off with some mere nobody the Marquis obliged by offering to write to none other than the President of the United States! Washington and he had kept up an exchange of news and polite regards ever since they beat the English side by side; indeed, La Rouërie had just received a much belated letter sent by Washington in October 1789, and was about to reply to it. He was well pleased to make the young Chevalier his messenger, still more to do a good turn to a possible recruit, for the Marquis had schemes of his own.

Early in February François-René left Fougères for Saint-Malo to arrange his passage. Instead of taking the direct way through Antrain, he decided to stay the night with the bailiff Le Corvaisier at Combourg, and bid farewell to the empty castle. He approached along a dark avenue in the Great Mall, treading over the withered leaves as he had with Lucile beside him long ago. The north front came in view beyond the Green Court. That stony face had been melancholy then, when the frozen anger of René-Auguste and the desperate fantasy of the Sylphide awaited him within, but now it was a desolation. The castle had died with his father. Weeds grew rank in the gravel by the walls, the stairtop was buried in drifted leaves, the great door was locked to keep him out, the shuttered windows glared like sightless eyes. A swound came upon him, and warned him to leave this place. He staggered back to the bailiff's house, collected his horses and baggage, and rode away in the blank of night.

He learned from Le Corvaisier, if they had time to talk, that even Combourg was marching in step with the Revolution. His trustee M.

Gesbert de la Noé-Seiche, after addressing the Almighty on 14 July, as
first elected mayor of Combourg, in terms so patronising that even
Robespierre would have approved,[5] had moved up to an administrative
post at Dol. Abbé Sévin and M. Petit had left the town council, which
was now a nest of Jacobins, except for the moderate new mayor Noury
de Mauny, and Le Corvaisier himself, who had joined in the hope of
protecting the interests of the Chateaubriands. Sévin and Chalmel were
in trouble for lack of zeal in surrendering church property, and reluctance to swear the constitutional clergy's oath, and the kindhearted
Noury was getting black marks for trying to shield them. Le Corvaisier
had been ordered to have the Chateaubriands' family pew and escut-
cheons removed from the parish church, for these aristocratic eyesores
'exposed the community to the criticism of strangers and even of neighbours'. He pleaded to no avail, on Mme de Chateaubriand's orders, that
the family's privilege was inalienable, resting as it did on their position
as hereditary founders of Combourg church in succession from Rivallon
Grey-Goat. But François-René's philosophical principles did not permit him to lament the woes of priests or the trappings of nobility.

At Saint-Malo, after an exchange of affectionate embraces, his mother
had more such news to tell. The bishop M. de Pressigny, who had
shorn François-René's topknot two years before, had retreated to Paris,
after seeing his palace stormed by the rabble and his cathedral barred
to himself and his canons. The Dominicans at Plancoët, who had
absolved François-René from his infant vow to the Virgin, were expelled from Nazareth. Uncle Antoine, on a visit to his mother in the
Rue de l'Abbaye,[6] was greeted by a gang of ruffians who tried twice in
one night to break the door in. He entreated Mme de Bédée to join his
exile in Saint-Malo, but no: 'My age will make them respect me!', said
the indomitable old lady, knowing very well it was not she they were
after. She was ninety-two. Even nuns were not safe. Two municipal
councillors had called on the Benedictine sisters at La Victoire in Saint-
Malo, to notify them that conventual life was now prohibited, and
invite them to taste the joys of freedom. All refused to budge, from
Sœur Sainte-Félicité, aged eighty, to the youngest, Sœur des Séraphins,
aged twenty-nine, who was François-René's own cousin Marie-Anne-
Renée.

But he was still more closely affected by the arrival in Saint-Malo of
a shipload of emigrant priests looking for a passage to America. Mme
de Chateaubriand's friend Mme des Bassablons had taken them under
her wing; a word from her, and they might be persuaded to let him sail
with them? Perhaps François-René was astonished by this lucky chance;
but it is much more likely that he had learned of that sacred convoy,
and determined to join it, even before he left Paris.

His charming friend Mme de Villette had a second town house near the Luxembourg, on premises belonging to the Sulpician fathers at Saint-Sulpice, a teaching order founded to train the instructors of future priests. Their Superior General, Father Émery, was a favourite uncle of Beautiful and Good, or rather, to be exact, his mother was a cousin of her grandmother. Émery in his prophetic soul foresaw that the storm then raging against the Church would be unprecedentedly severe and long. He resolved to create a branch of the Sulpicians in America to ride the Deluge. He thought first of Canada, where a Sulpician mission still lingered under British domination at Montreal, then of Gallipolis, the new Cloudcuckootown of the French settlers on the Ohio. But the Pope's Nuncio in Paris, Cardinal Dugnani, drew his attention to the recently inaugurated Catholic diocese of Baltimore, a see then covering the entire territory of the United States, and the presence, near by in London, of its first bishop, John Carroll, in quest of teachers to open a seminary. Émery sent the director of his own seminary, Father Nagot, to London in September 1790 with a magnificent offer, for the Sulpicians did things in style. He would supply Mgr. Carroll with staff headed by Father Nagot himself, a batch of promising pupils, equipment complete with sacred vessels, vestments and library, to arrive in Baltimore next summer with passage paid and funds for maintenance. Only one thought marred the rapture of Mgr. Carroll. 'I feel great sorrow,' he wrote to his Papist patron Henry Lord Arundell, 'in the reflection that we owe such a benefit to the distressed state of Religion in France.' 'If you want to go to America,' Beautiful and Good must have said to François-René, 'why don't you join my uncle's priests?' But how did they choose so conveniently to sail from Saint-Malo? For this fortunate chance yet another intervention in the affairs of Mgr. Carroll was required, again from a source close to François-René.

The ex-Jesuit Father Pierre de Clorivière (1735–1820), a native of Saint-Malo, was a cousin of Mme des Bassablons, an uncle of young Limoëlan, François-René's roomfellow at the college of Rennes, a brother-in-law of the treasurer of La Rouërie's conspiracy, Marc Désilles of Paramé, and since 1786 (two years after François-René's final act of truancy) director of the college of Dinan. Previously, after education at the English Benedictine college of Douai and a long sojourn in London, he had been parish priest at Paramé, and specialised in the conversion of stranded English or American Protestant sailors. This ardent and anxious divine was afflicted with a painful stammer, and an inability to decide between the various incompatible schemes for saving the Church singlehanded with which he was directly inspired by Heaven. In June 1790 the Almighty had ordered him, subject to M. de Pressigny's permission, to resign from Dinan (where the Revolutionary mayor was making his position impossible) and go to Baltimore; so he wrote, beating M. Émery to it by three months, offering his services to Mgr. Carroll, an old friend of his Jesuit days. Unfortunately the Lord inspired him next month to found a new society for the preservation of the oppressed Church in France, and a few weeks later, still more ambitiously, to re-establish the forbidden order of Jesuits. Father Clorivière was disconcerted to find that, while no one objected to his saving the Church in America, few except M. de Pressigny were eager for him to do so in France, least of all Cardinal Dugnani. Nor could he quite abandon his longing for Baltimore. When he learned, perhaps from the Nuncio himself, that the Sulpicians, happier than he, were bound thither, he arranged with Father Nagot that they should sail from Saint-Malo, on a ship to be provided by himself through the good offices of Mme de Bassablons. Soon after inaugurating his Society of the Heart of Jesus in February 1791 he left for Saint-Malo. Perhaps God would order him to sail, after all; if not, at least he could see them off.

The ways of Providence are mysterious, and can sometimes only be interpreted by their result, which in this instance was to make Father Clorivière the humble instrument for directing the Sulpicians to Saint-Malo, rather than Bordeaux or Le Havre, and for sending François-René to join them. Nor had Providence, despite some initial vacillation, intended in the long run to thwart Father Clorivière's own intentions. His Société du Coeur de Jésus survived Revolution and Empire, and was highly successful after the Restoration. His nephew Limoëlan, after failing to kill Bonaparte with his bomb in 1800, became a priest and went to Baltimore in his stead. In the fullness of time Father Clorivière even succeeded in reviving the Jesuits.

François-René's anxious wait for the Sulpician Ark reminded him of another winter vigil at Saint-Malo, in 1786, when he had looked in vain for a passage to India; so much so that in his Memoirs he confused two visits to his beloved nurse La Villeneuve, and assigned her death to the former year, whereas records show that she was still alive when her husband the plumber Odap died in 1787. So it was perhaps now, in 1791,[7] that he learned of her demise, called at her poor bedroom and empty deathbed, and saw again the wicker frame in which he had learned to walk, on which she had chosen to rest her dying eyes, before she left Saint-Malo on an even longer journey than his own.

In the last week of March he received his letter of introduction to President Washington, dated from the château of La Rouërie near Fougères, 22 March 1791. The Marquis, writing with evident satisfaction in imperfect but quite creditable English, did him proud, but studiously omitted to breathe a word of his plans for exploration. He 'presumed' that the purpose of 'Mr. le chevalier de Combourg, a nobleman of the State of Brittany and a neighbourg of mine'[8] was 'to inrich his mind by the active contemplation of such a moving and happy

country and to satisfy his soul by seeing the extraordinary man and
thoses respectable citizens who, led by the hand of virtue through the
most difficult contest, have made their chief counsellor of her in estab-
lishing and enjoying their liberty—his relations, for whom I have a very
high regard, desire me to recommend him to the notice of your excellency. I do it with pleasure, because that gentleman has allways appeared
to me to have a good right to the commendable reputation which he
does enjoy—he is a man of wit and much of his time is taken up by the
cultivation of that natural gift.' So the Marquis presented his protégé as
a leisured dilettante, which was perhaps as he in fact saw him, and with
ironical discretion refrained from revealing that the young visitor, as
one of his aims, hoped to revive a French presence in the Far West of
the United States. He was equally silent about his own imminent plans
for his 'unhappy, and perhaps more guilty, country', though Washington, knowing him, might be expected to guess that he meant to do
something about it. He signed the letter 'Armand', in memory of old
times. Washington was never to hear from him again.

Father Clorivière reached Saint-Malo on 26 March. As it happened,
the Almighty did not command him to sail, although Mme des
Bassablons had now found a ship, and even the accommodating M. de
Pressigny had urged him to stay in Europe.

The *Saint-Pierre* was a Newfoundland codfisher, small (160 tons) but
fairly new (built in England in 1783, and hence perhaps a war prize).
M. Cannevas the owner was not licensed for passengers, and thought
this particular cargo, composed of a batch of refractory priests and a
young local aristocrat, almost as dangerous as it was profitable; so for
this voyage he registered his captain, Jacques Desjardins-Pintedevin, as
the owner. In fact, it seemed touch and go whether they would be
allowed to leave. The increasingly Jacobin council of Saint-Malo
laboured resentfully under an undeserved reputation for leniency,
owing to the influx of nobility and clergy to whom the previous more
liberal administration had granted refuge from burning châteaux and
confiscated livings. They were now in two minds whether to get rid of
the *Saint-Pierre*'s passengers by letting them go, or to persecute them by
throwing them into prison. The balance was swung by a constitutional
priest on the council, whom Mme de Bassablons had bribed to put in a
good word.[9] The Sulpicians went on board on 28 March to keep out of
harm's way and wait for a wind.

François-René stayed ashore until the last moment. A letter from
Jean-Baptiste to his mother arrived on 5 April, announcing the death
of Mirabeau on the 2nd. The lion was dead, whose paw had once
touched him and then withdrawn. The effort to halt the Revolution by
uniting all the parties he had betrayed, the necessity to overthrow both
Lafayette and Robespierre, the awareness that he had achieved 'nothing

but a vast destruction', had shattered him. 'The grave,' wrote Chateau-briand, 'released Mirabeau from his promises, and sheltered him from perils which he would probably have been unable to overcome.'

Late in the afternoon of 7 April 1791 François-René embraced his weeping mother and went on board with the captain and the pilot. The capstan crew hauled up the anchor, the pilot steered them through the narrow channel past the lizard-haunted islet of Cézembre, and returned ashore at sunset. The sky was overcast, the breeze slack, the swell beat sullenly against the nearby reefs. He looked back to the spires and domes beneath which he had prayed in childhood with Lucile, the ram-parts, the nunnery with cousin Marie-Anne-Renée, the Rue des Grands-Degrés where his mother lay still crying, the sands where he had sported with Gesril. Streetlamps began to shine, and the lighthouses. Beyond the seaward cliff of the Grand-Bé a light twinkled from the house where he was born, now an inn, and seemed to smile farewell.

The ebbtide drew them out to sea, the lights on shore dwindled and disappeared. Exhausted by his thoughts, with vague regrets and hopes vaguer still, he went below, and rocked in his hammock to the murmur of ripples on the hull. The wind rose, the sails swelled. When he came on deck next morning, the land of France was out of sight.

12

THE DISCOVERY OF AMERICA

THE wind grew to a gale, and the *Saint-Pierre* narrowly escaped
shipwreck soon after leaving port. After a stormbound fortnight
in the Channel, Atlantic headwinds beat them southward off course.
But the tempest-loving François-René, who had not brought his pocket
Homer with him for nothing, was in his element. Combining the wily
Odysseus's stratagem against the Sirens with his defiance of Aeolus or
Poseidon on other occasions, he had himself lashed to the mainmast,
where drenched by broaching waves and buffeted by roaring winds he
shouted (if his fellow-passenger Mondésir quoted him correctly fifty
years later): 'O Tempest, thou art still not so glorious as Homer por-
trays thee!' His delight in the storm was enhanced by the pleasure of
showing off to seasick Sulpicians. As the only gentleman philosopher
in a shipload of priests he felt it his duty to disapprove of his company.
They, in turn, thought him quite mad.

M. Nagot had brought three Sulpician teachers from provincial
seminaries, Fathers Tessier, Garnier, and Levadoux, as staff for his new
establishment in Baltimore. He could not bear to be parted by the
estranging sea from his lifelong friend M. Delavau, canon of Tours, so
M. Delavau came too, along with their manservants Nicolas and Louis.
As pupil-teachers and candidates for priesthood M. Nagot had selected
five promising young men (one to each priest) who seemed specially
suitable for service in America. Three were English-speaking converts
from Protestantism. John Caldwell was an American from Elizabeth-
town, New Jersey, whom Lafayette had brought to France and educated
after the war. Francis Tulloch and John Floyd were Britons discovered
by M. Nagot during his recent visit to London, with the aid of Bishop
Carroll and his friends in the well-organised underground of English
Catholics. Another, Jean Périnault, was a French Canadian from Montreal. Only one, Édouard de Mondésir, a seminarist from Chartres, was
a native Frenchman, but he was already a veteran of America. M.
Émery, who was sometimes too clever by half, had sent him to join the
Montreal Sulpicians the year before, dressed up as a French Revolutionary in red and blue, so that his ecclesiastical character would be
quite certain to escape the notice of the heretical British. But the British,
who would have minded a cleric hardly at all (for they tolerated the
Roman clergy in return for their usefulness in keeping their French
subjects quiet), were thrown into consternation by the arrival of an

obvious Jacobin spy. They arrested the innocent villain double quick, and sent him crestfallen back to France; so young Mondésir, eager to try again, was now making his third Atlantic crossing in eleven months. Last of the team was a stranded American sailor, John Risdell, aged thirty-five, whose ship had sailed without him long ago when he fell ill at Saint-Malo. Father Clorivière had promptly converted him, Mme des Bassablons sent him to school and married him to a respectable local maiden from Ploubalay, and now he was being repatriated as official interpreter and future teacher of the new Catholic lay school at Baltimore, which happened conveniently to be his birthplace. His wife was the only woman on board, but no one, thought the ungallant Mondésir, was likely to be tempted, for she was a year senior to her husband, and a real termagant. They had boarded with her before sailing, and when Father Garnier asked at table for 'just a little' (*un petit peu*) of this or that, she cried in a schoolmistressly rage: 'Why can't you say "a morsel"?' (*un brin*). Father Garnier said nothing, but thought more. 'I foresaw we should all suffer a *little* or a *morsel* from this daughter of Eve on the voyage,' says Mondésir, and piously adds: 'God preserve us from peril on the sea with women aboard!'

If any spiritual danger sailed with them, the Sulpicians decided, it would come not from Mrs Risdell, but from the Chevalier de Chateaubriand. They were rather impressed to find he was a fully fledged Knight of Malta, ordained and tonsured by M. de Pressigny himself. But François-René made no secret of his philosophical views. M. Nagot, who was no fool, sensed that 'our chivalrous Knight of Malta', as they took to calling him, might be as zealous as himself in seeking converts, but in the opposite direction. Young Tulloch showed signs of interest. M. Nagot warned him 'not to get too intimate'.

So François-René turned to the crew for company. He was charmed to find that the boatswain, Pierre Villeneuve, was a namesake of his beloved nurse. The old man had seen many a seafight under Suffren in India and Estaing in America. Lolling against the bulwarks by the bowsprit, his cheek bulging with a quid of tobacco, he told how they cleared the decks for action, how the guns thundered, how enemy cannonballs wrought havoc below, ricochetting off gun-carriages and shivering the timbers. Villeneuve's descriptions of the East were based on comparisons with every-day life. A palmtree, said he, was just like a big cabbage, a camel was a donkey with a hump, all Orientals were thieving cowards, especially Chinamen, and Brittany was the finest country in the world.

Their conversations were interrupted by the ship's bell. Every morning the crew paraded in a row, stripped off their blue shirts, put on clean ones that hung drying in the halyards, and laundered their castoffs for tomorrow. Then, in the same buckets, they soaped their swarthy faces and tarry flippers, splashing like a school of seals, for this was a clean ship. Their skin was brine-impregnated, rock-hard and red, like the sea-beaten granite reefs of Saint-Malo. They were awkward as sea-beasts, nimble as seabirds; their brows were seamed not by care or age, but by wind and salt water, like the furrowed mainsail or the wrinkled sea. They spoke a marine language of their own, and in it exchanged sea news, which was much more interesting than land news, since it always concerned one directly. 'They've cast the log, we're running ten knots.' 'See that clearing in the clouds to westward? That's the eye of the wind, there's where it'll blow tomorrow.' 'The sand won't run in the hourglass, rain's coming.' 'Flying fish to south, we're near the doldrums.'

The captain sighted another ship through his spy-glass, and all morning they watched her approaching, hoisting her flag, clewing up sail, heaving to alongside. Passengers and crews gazed in silence from either deck, while the two captains hailed one another through speaking-trumpets: 'Your ship's name? From what port? How many days out? Your bearings? Fare ye well!' Then they parted, for ever.

The ship was a world, the sea a universe. François-René believed their story of the London cabin-boy, born and bred on his ship, who wept in despair when first made to set foot on land. Even his own sailor friends would swear never to leave their families again, but find they could not live without the sea, 'just as'—for so he wrote, taking the comparison from the state in which Panat had recently seen him—'a young man is unable to tear himself from the arms of a stormy and fickle mistress'.

The most eminent, respected and indispensable member of the crew, senior in rank to all but the captain, scarred by more savage affrays than the boatswain, seasoned in all the nameless villainies of the seven seas, yet affable to the point of popularity, was the ship's cat. Old Tom was a green-striped tabby, with bald tail and walrus whiskers, and firm sea legs which balanced every motion of the ship's rolling. He was said to have sailed twice round the world, and to have saved himself from ship-wreck by riding in a barrel. Now he lived mostly below, ready to take instant command in the hour of danger, and enjoying the privilege of sleeping whenever he pleased in the second officer's furlined jacket.

The bell rang again at noon for the seamen's dinner, at sunset for their supper. François-René watched them sitting jovial round the mess-can, each dipping his tin spoon in turn, with no cheating. Then those whose hunger was satisfied swapped their ship's biscuit or hunk of salt pork for a plug of tobacco or a mug of brandy. The passengers dined in the captain's cabin or, in fair weather, under a sail spread for awning, open to a vista of blue sea flecked with the white of breaking wave-crests.

In those warmer nights he took to sleeping on deck, wrapped in his cloak. The soft breeze curved the sails and spilled downward to lull him, carrying him to new skies and new dreams. The *Saint-Pierre* swayed in the eternal Atlantic swell; a ripple of pale foam, a trail of phosphorescent sparks glided along her bows. Above him shone numberless stars in a dark azure dome; about him heaved a shoreless ocean; below him he looked into 'the serious face of the abyss'. For the first time since Combourg he felt the power of nature in solitude; for the first time in his life he became aware of the immanence within and beyond nature of a still more awful presence, a deeper reality than his boyhood pieties at Dol, or the ideologies of philosophic deism, or even the devotions of Sulpician priests. 'Never has God more stirred me with his grandeur than in those nights when I had immensity over my head and immensity under my feet.'

It was then that Francis Tulloch came at last to join him. Tulloch was a tall young Scot of only twenty, with a strikingly handsome face, well-born, cultivated, easy-mannered, of friendly disposition, in fact altogether a charmer. His father was a Protestant nonconformist clergyman, the Reverend William Tulloch of Woolwich, eldest son of Alexander Tulloch, last of the lairds of Tannachie in Morayshire, who had been compelled to part with the ancient family estate. Francis had received an excellent education in Woolwich as a gentleman cadet in the Royal Artillery at the Royal Military School, where the curriculum included foreign languages, art, music and mathematics. He spoke adequate French, drew and painted, played the organ, composed little songs, and was fond of nature. When Father Nagot picked him up in London last September, ripe for instant conversion, Francis had written a letter of resignation to his Master-General the Duke of Richmond, abandoned his sorrowing parents, and followed meekly first to Paris, now to America. His mother's letters had been heartrending, and made him cry. Francis Tulloch was a quite harmless youth, but easily led, and uncertain where he wished to go. Father Nagot had induced him to try the priesthood, and now he was willing to try romantic melancholy with the Chevalier de Chateaubriand.

François-René was at no loss for the right thing to say. 'If you've decided that the Catholic religion is better than the Protestant, I haven't a word of objection. But to forsake your country and family and career, and run away to the ends of the earth with a seminary of priests, is a glaring folly which you will bitterly repent!' Tulloch must go straight to M. Nagot and declare he wanted to have nothing more to do with him. 'But I gave him all my money, and I'm afraid he wouldn't let me have it back,' objected poor Francis. 'Then we'll go shares in mine,' exclaimed François-René, and revealed that, as soon as he had delivered his letter to President Washington, he was going to travel among the

Red Indians. If Francis would accompany him in 'this interesting caravan', they could return to Europe together, and he would take a personal pleasure in restoring him to the bosom of his family. Meanwhile he would write to Francis's mother to announce the good news. How relieved, how grateful she would be, to learn that he had saved her son from the danger of becoming a Catholic priest, and was taking him to discover the Northwest Passage instead! Nothing could be simpler. Francis promised all, and they swore a tender friendship.

M. Nagot could not have interfered even if he knew. He lay seasick in his bunk, 'like a carp out of water', said the immune Mondésir, who rather enjoyed the honour of nursing his superior and taking down edifying phrases to his dictation. 'Write, write,' cried the good man, when he heard the others singing vespers on deck, '*Vox Domini super aquas!*'[1] So, as priest and Chevalier contemplated the presence of God upon the deep waters, their thoughts nearly coincided. Father Garnier was dreadfully seasick too. 'But M. de Chateaubriand, swinging in his hammock, did not suffer like our gentlemen; he was in a kind of frenzy.'

He had taken to joining the Sulpicians in their devotional readings, partly, perhaps, because he suspected that their simple faith might after all lead towards the same God as his own midnight intimations, but also, no doubt, from desire to keep in with them, jealousy of their hold over Francis, and even, as Mondésir put it, 'because he didn't know how to kill time on board'. They were reading aloud from Rodríguez *On Christian Perfection*. When his turn came he wrung more fervour from it than anyone. M. Nagot, one morning when he happened to be up and about, decided to snub him. 'One doesn't declaim a devout book as if it was a tragedy in a theatre,' he said. 'I always put my soul into everything,' was the Chevalier's lame reply. He took the hint, stayed away from the readings, but could not resist trying again. On Good Friday, 22 April 1791, when everyone was feeling already quite sufficiently edified after M. Levadoux's sermon, he obtained M. Nagot's permission to address the sailors. Brandishing a crucifix, he harangued those simple souls on the Passion with such wild and whirling words that Mondésir felt, 'if there had chanced to be a Jew aboard, they would certainly have thrown him in the sea!'

Early in May, four weeks out and becalmed far south near the Azores, Captain Desjardins decided to put ashore for water and fresh food. At eight o'clock in the morning of the 6th[2] the look-out cried 'Land ho!', and François-René ran down to the cabin to interrupt the matin-singers. It was his duty to remind them, said he, that Pope Somebody (he had forgotten the name and number) had issued a bull declaring that these islands formed part of Europe, and excommunicating anyone who dared to place them in Africa. They all saw he was only teasing, but no one ventured to dispute his facts.[3]

They anchored towards noon in forty-five fathoms, a mile off the little island of Graciosa, beautiful as its name. These low green hills with rounded tops, which had once been active volcanoes, had the agreeable curves of Grecian vases, he thought. Their slopes were terraced with cornfields and vineyards between walls of black and white lava-blocks, their ridges crowned with groups of rotating windmills; he breathed the scent of flowering wheat. There was no harbour, for the whole island had erupted vertically from the ocean bed; that was why Captain Desjardins had brought to so far from shore, on such a deep rocky bottom, and doubted whether he would ever see his anchor again. The sea-swell beat against sombre lava cliffs, festooned with silver lace of spray that sparkled in the sun. The red-tiled roofs of Santa Cruz, the Franciscan monastery on a hillock above, the whole island with its silhouette of green arcs and craggy promontories, swam mirrored in upside-down replica in the emerald sea. Over all, seven thousand feet above and fifty miles away, the tremendous cone of the island of Pico soared from a dome of white clouds.

They lowered the long-boat. François-René and Tulloch, claiming they would be useful as interpreters, were allowed to join the shore-party under the second officer François Lalande. Soon they saw signs of movement on shore. A lighter manned by apprehensive monks rowed out to hail them in Portuguese, Italian, English and French. When they responded in all these languages that they were Frenchmen, when it was observed that they had human faces, all exploded with joy. No one on Graciosa had ever seen a tricolour flag, the monks explained; they might have been Barbary pirates, come to carry the whole island to the slave-markets of Algiers![4] As it was, they were most welcome. Then they transferred into the lighter, rather than risk smashing the long-boat; even so, they had a tricky landing through the surf. François-René never forgot the strange sensation of setting foot for the first time on foreign earth.

The senior monk was particularly delighted to see them. He was an ex-sailor from Jersey, sole survivor of a shipwreck on Graciosa long ago, with brains enough to see that the monastic state was the best on the island (where half the population were monks and the rest worked for a living), and even to pick up enough Portuguese and Latin to join it. Overjoyed to hear Tulloch speaking English, he guffawed and cursed like a true British sailor. He would see personally to their entertainment, ne promised, Goddam; but first they must call on the Governor. Four alguazils armed with rusty pikes escorted them to His Excellency, who gave audience in an ancient green frock-coat which had once been trimmed with gold galloons. François-René had dressed for shore in his skyblue uniform as lieutenant of Navarre, good as new, and was not displeased to find himself taken for the leader of the deputation. Yes, they were very welcome, and might buy what provisions they wished. The jolly monks led them up hill to their monastery, whose bell-tower is still the chief landmark of Santa Cruz. Second officer Lalande left them, having made arrangements of his own with a certain Dona Lh—.

They set off on a tour of the island, through vineyards and villages of sunbrowned men and lively olive-skinned girls who carried bouquets of lilac. Here and there they passed a bubbling spring, with its figtree and oratory with frescoed porch, and ogived windows framing vistas of the sea. François-René remembered a moment of poetic beauty, when a flock of dark blue birds settled on one of these figtrees, so that it seemed suddenly to have grown purple fruit and azure leaves.[5] He thought of the fabled Carthaginian statue on the island of Corvo, a bronze man riding a bronze horse, with his hand pointing mysteriously westward over the ocean. He would bring Chactas to the Azores, make him land at Corvo instead of Graciosa, and see the statue. 'A seamew on his helmet uttered languorous cries; seashells clung to flanks and mane of his steed, and if one laid ear close to its dilated nostrils one caught, as it seemed, the breath of unintelligible murmurings.'[6]

François-René could not resist showing off again when they returned to the monastery, first by displaying his ability to read Spanish in the library, next by finding fault with the Hebrew pointing on a cherished image of the Sacred Heart. Then Tulloch sat down at the organ, although nobody asked him to play, and performed a few bars of Pleyel's latest. François-René took their polite astonishment for monkish ignorance, and felt entitled to despise them. He in turn was surprised to find they were well aware of the events in France, and had heard of plans for reform in their own monasteries. They had a splendid supper, served, he says, 'by very pretty damsels as cupbearers', with torrents of the famous Fayal wine, so that 'by one in the morning we were all falling over in our chairs'. At six the sailor declared with an incoherent Goddam that it was time to say mass. So they all trooped to the parish church, where he raced through the job in five minutes, and on the way back allowed devout passers-by to kiss his sleeve, much to the amusement of our callow young hero. At noon the Rabelaisian friars saw them on board with the provisions, swore eternal friendship, took charge of their letters for Europe, and presented an enormous bill, which had to be paid. A stiff southeaster had blown up overnight, and Captain Desjardins lost his anchor as he had feared. They sped away north and west. François-René told the Sulpicians his tale of monastic laxity with relish. They pretended not to believe him.

He avoided them again, and climbed each morning to the crow's nest, where he sat ensconced and seeing all, just, he thought, as in his willowtree at Combourg long ago. Memories of Paris came to trouble his daydreams, until the immensity around him drove away all other thoughts. It was even vaster than it seemed, until a glimpse along the trough of some valley in the swell, a wavecrest rising like a distant coast, a squadron of porpoises leaping along the horizon, gave him a fixed point to measure its scale.

At dusk he descended, supped on a ship's biscuit, a lump of sugar and a lemon, and lay wrapped in his cloak on deck. Sometimes Francis joined him again. The officer on watch and a sailor or two stood near, silently smoking their pipes; everyone else was asleep below. The multitudinous seas gleamed with the reflection of innumerable stars. They talked all night. 'Our conversations were perhaps not altogether unworthy of the sublime spectacle before our eyes, and we uttered thoughts of a kind one would be ashamed to proclaim in society, but would only be too happy to be able to capture in writing.' At such moments François-René seemed to have found the male counterpart whom even the most exclusive lover of women may need and seek in early youth. Even five years later, when the impression had faded into a mere memory, he could still write: 'I have found few men whose heart was more in harmony with mine than Tulloch's.' Francis, it appeared, was another, more intellectual Gesril, or rather another François-René for whom he in turn could be a Gesril, an initiator into the joys of liberation and danger.

It was among the conditions of their passage that, instead of sailing direct for Baltimore, the ship should first call on M. Cannevas's business at the French codfishing base on the island of Saint-Pierre (after which the *Saint-Pierre* was named) off the south coast of Newfoundland. In two weeks, with the southeaster still behind them, they made their northing to the colder seas of the Grand Banks, where in late spring the arctic pack drifts far down into the forties. One morning François-René saw ice-floes prowling near through a pale mist, and found his crow's nest occupied by another. A bellowing issued from the barrel aloft, an awful head peered from the rim, a gigantic form clad in sheepskins clambered down the rigging, seized a pail of water, and deluged every novice he could catch. It was Father Tropic; for the same ritual of sea-baptism prevailed on the Banks as on the Equator, and the presiding sprite was still called Father Tropic. The victims fled down the hatches and up the masts, but none escaped. The spectators, at least, enjoyed the fun, and Father Tropic disappeared below loaded with tips.

Towards noon on 23 May they moored at the quayside of Saint-Pierre. The coast loomed like a black hump through the fog; they heard voices on land, but could not see the town. M. Nagot was so exhausted by seasickness that he had to be carried ashore. The local priest, M. Allain, hurried up and led the Sulpicians to his presbytery. François-René preferred to take a private lodging elsewhere. He waited there 'for a breeze to sweep the mist away, and show me the place I was living in and the faces of my hosts in this land of shadows'.

The little island, hardly five miles long, had been allotted to France after the Seven Years' War in derisory compensation for the loss of Canada, and evacuated again in the War of American Independence. But the town of Saint-Pierre had already regained its population of fifteen hundred residents, together with nine thousand codfishers in three hundred ships who came from France every spring. When the breeze arrived François-René saw the busy quayside, with the church, the houses of the governor, priest, and harbourmaster, the long single street stretching along the pebbled beach, the mournful barren hills inland, and the stark firclad coast of Newfoundland fifteen miles east.

The lonely governor, M. d'Ansseville, was only too delighted to receive a visiting gentleman, and had François-René to dinner several times. When they rose from table he led his guest with modest pride to his vegetable garden in the dry moat of the fort, a moment which Chateaubriand remembered in one of the supreme passages of *Mémoires d'Outre-Tombe*. 'A delicate sweet scent of heliotrope was exhaled from a little bed of beans in flower, and wafted to us not by a breeze of our own country but by a wild Newfoundland wind, without kinship to the exiled plant, without sympathy for memory or delight. In this perfume that beauty had never breathed, nor purified in her breast, nor scattered in her footsteps, in this fragrance estranged from its natural daydawn and cultivation and world, lay all the melancholies of regret and absence and youth.' Then they climbed the lookout hill, where the new tricolour flag flapped over their heads. M. d'Ansseville enquired after the Revolution, with which he did his best to keep in step, though his heart was given to the losing side. François-René in turn asked after the Northwest Passage; but no, this warden of the arctic frontier had never set eyes on an Eskimo, and as for Canada—'Our partridges fly in from there,' he said. The poor man's eyes brimmed with tears as they gazed homeward over the sea; so did François-René's.

One morning he walked eastward to nearby Cap-à-l'Aigle, to see the sun rising over France. He sat on a granite ledge, dangling his legs over the cliff, near a cascade of melting snow-water that leapt over the brink into the waves far below. A fishermaid climbed the slope behind him, barelegged in the dew, stooping from time to time to fill her basket with the aromatic leaves that the islanders called 'wild tea'.[7] She wore the cradle-shaped local hat of plaited rushes, over masses of black hair tied in a silk kerchief, with a posy of pink heather in the white cambric blouse which moulded her bosom. She saw him, and sat by him unafraid, swinging her legs beside his over the sea, watching the risen sun. But François-René was the first who took courage to speak.

'What are you gathering there?' he asked, 'the season for bilberries and cranberries is over.' She raised her big dark eyes, proud and timid, and replied: 'I'm picking tea.' 'Do you take it to your father and mother?' 'My father has gone fishing with Guillaumy.' 'Will your father come back soon?' 'Oh, no! The captain is taking the ship to Genoa with Guillaumy.' 'But Guillaumy will come back?' 'Oh, yes, next season, when the fishers return. He's bringing me a striped silk bodice, a muslin frock, and a jet necklace.' 'So then you'll be dressed for wind, and mountain, and sea. Would you like me to send you a bodice, a frock and a necklace?' 'Oh, no!' cried she, seizing her basket not a moment too soon, and hurried down a steep path by a coppice of spruce, scaring a covey of egrets as soft and white as herself. He heard her strong young voice singing a mission hymn:

> *'Though my ardour burns immortal*
> *Yet my love's for God alone.'*

She reached her skiff, hoisted sail and scudded away, like Fortune in the emblem, and as Fortune always did, he reflected, she was leaving him behind. A quarter-century later, in 1814, when he was a famous states-man, he was to receive a letter from a Mlle Dupont, 'who had the honour of meeting you on the island of Saint-Pierre, and would like to be granted a moment's audience with Your Excellency'. Could this be Guillaumy's betrothed, still unmarried?—and if so, had the Newfound-land winters shrivelled her, or had she kept the fragrance of the governor's beanflowers? In any case, he was far too busy to see her.

Sometimes Francis played truant to walk with him. They explored the bare granite hills of the interior, where nothing grew but mosses and lichens, or a few sub-arctic thickets of dwarf firs, willow, birch, no taller than themselves. In the valleys were torrents, peatbogs, multi-tudes of solitary little lakes. One clear day they sat on the northernmost cliff opposite the seagirt rock-tower of the Grand Colombier, the Big Dovecote, white and screaming with a hundred thousand nesting sea-birds. But mostly they roamed lost and happy in the mist that hurtled past in the windgusts, listening to the roar of invisible waves. Some-times they collected botanical specimens for M. de Malesherbes, and sometimes they played at Ossian. Both adored Macpherson's mock-Celtic prose-poems, half forgery, half innovating masterwork, which read in youth left indelible marks upon the style and vision of all the great romantics of France and England, and of none more than Chateau-briand himself. Nothing could be more Ossianic than the savage gloom of this landscape, and besides, Francis was Scottish. So, as they followed a rust-red brooklet over a moor of dead woolly moss, Francis made believe to be the Bard of Cona himself, and chanted the lamentations of Fingal's son to wild melodies of his own improvisation. François-René was not behind with his own contribution. His friends Fontanes and Flins had published Ossianic verses in the *Almanach des Muses*, and as for himself, he shyly admitted, all literary Paris had admired his *'Fairest of lovers I enthralled thy heart'*, in which the ghost of a slain warrior addressed his beloved from the grave. So they spent an enthusiastic afternoon raising four huge stones as an imaginary tomb for this doubly imaginary hero.[8] Such was the absurd, boyish acme of their friendship.

But it was not so simple as that for Francis. Rogations, the three days of ceremonial prayers and processions leading to Ascension Day, began that year on Monday, 30 May, and the Sulpicians took the opportunity to celebrate in style. François-René, disillusioned and hurt, saw his false friend joining the ranks with alacrity, carrying banners and chanting hymns. All the islanders, and the visiting fishermen more numerous still, flocked to M. Nagot's Ascension Day sermon on 2 June. He and his band, M. Nagot announced, were going to convert the whole of America, in accordance with the wishes of God and the Pope.

From this time François-René became aware of a curious expression of mental reservation in the frank, sympathetic eyes of his friend, and foresaw that his other self, his namesake Francis, would give him the slip. Had he known it, the priests felt exactly the same. In fact that amenable, evasive youth found himself in the difficult position of liking François-René and the Sulpicians genuinely and equally, but not enough to go the whole way with either. He was perfectly willing to sing Ossian with the one or hymns with the others, but felt no more vocation for discovering the Northwest Passage than for priestly celibacy and the conversion of the United States.

However, François-René soon managed to regain prestige with everyone. Captain Desjardins denied liability for replacement of the lost anchor, on the outrageous plea that the passengers who had chartered the ship must pay for damage incurred in their own service. François-René as spokesman for the defendants took the common-sense line that, since it was Desjardins who had dropped the anchor, it was up to him to take care where he dropped it. A jury of six sea-captains found against their colleague. Even Mondésir was impressed for once: 'it would have been difficult to have made a better choice,' he admitted, 'he is indisputably a man of talent in words and action.' Desjardins stayed behind on M. Cannevas's business, and a spare captain, Pierre Douville, took over the *Saint-Pierre* for the voyage to Baltimore. They sailed on 8 June. François-René entrusted his letter for Tulloch's mother to M. d'Ansseville, who promised to see it forwarded by the next boat.[9] There seemed so little prospect that its contents would still be true, that François-René almost hoped she would never receive it.

They were two months out from Saint-Malo, but still twelve hundred miles and another month from their destination. Storms and calms made this last third of their journey as protracted as the first. However, François-René was in no hurry to be parted from the ocean and Tulloch, nor from another, whom he had hoped to meet on the voyage, and who now came. In those last dawns and nights he felt the presence of the Sylphide—'source of my inspirations, of my despair, of my life!'—'throbbing behind the veil of the universe that hid her from my eyes'. Venus was evening star that summer, and as he gazed the planet's rays seemed to enmesh him like a woman's hair, like the tresses of the phantom at Combourg.

One evening in mid-June, as he sat reading in the captain's cabin, he heard the bell for vespers and went aft. M. Nagot stood by the wheel with open prayerbook, officers and passengers faced him at the stern, looking westward. The Breton sailors below on the main deck, tarpaulin hats in hand, intoned in their hoarse voices the hymn to Our Lady of Help in Need, which he had heard as a child in the cathedral of Saint-Malo, and was to hear again before the year was out:

> '*All my trust I lay,*
> *Virgin, in thy aid . . .*'

The *Saint-Pierre* lay becalmed, all sail furled, but rocked still in idle swell from their final storm. The westering sun glowed alternately on either side of the rigging, swinging visibly from one horizon to another, like the pendulum of time and eternity. The full moon rose in the east;[10] far northward, on the fringe of the retiring tempest, the iridescent crystal pillar of a waterspout held up the arch of the sky. Sun, moon and spout marked out the edges of the world in a tremendous triangle. Once again, as much as was allowable for a philosophic deist or perhaps a little more, he felt the immanent presence of divine majesty in nature. And yet, 'it was not God alone Whom I contemplated on the waves in the magnificence of His works. I saw an unknown woman and the miracles of her smile; the beauties of that sky seemed breathed from her lips, and I would have given eternity for one of her caresses'.

A few days later he came near to doing so. Impatient of scorching heat and giddy rolling, he stripped and dived from the bowsprit into the sea. M. Nagot ordered the neophytes below, but several other passengers followed his example. He swam carefree and far from these, until looking back he saw the ship receding in the current, the sailors dropping a cable to haul up his companions, and others firing shots at inquisitive sharks. It was a nasty moment, worse than when he nearly drowned at Dinan, for in the Rance there were no sharks, ready to bite off one's legs. He swam with all his strength, without gaining. He saw his friend the boatswain working might and main to launch a boat from improvised davits. But he would not be in time! Suddenly a languid, providential breeze sprang up, the *Saint-Pierre* put about and reached him. But his fellow-swimmers had not yet been hoisted, and he was last on the rope. At every lurch of the ship they rose high in air, like fish on a line, then plunged as deep beneath the waves, with François-René undermost, and all the rest floundering on top of him. After some minutes of this grim farce, when he felt himself losing consciousness and knew that one more ducking would be the end, he was hauled at last on deck, half-dead. 'If I had drowned, what a good riddance for myself and everyone!' Mondésir, ever helpful, read him a lecture on recklessness, and once again François-René could only find a lame reply. 'Ah, well, now I know what it's like,' he said.

Those warm star-sown nights saw the Indian summer of his friendship with Francis. As the ship tacked against a soft westerly breeze, which seemed to bring land-scents of America from a hundred miles away, he wrote a poem on the scene, and Francis set it to his own tune. 'I have kept this precious fragment,' he wrote in England five years after (it is long lost now), 'and when I happen to repeat it in my present situation, it calls up in me emotions which few people would understand.'

On 2 July the captain said to François-René, pointing: 'There's America!'; and far away he saw with beating heart not land, but the outline of a grove of maples rising from a low invisible shore. A pilot came aboard, they entered Chesapeake Bay, and towards evening he went ashore with Father Delavau to get provisions.

They saw a farmhouse in the distance, the first in America, and walked towards it through perfumed groves of balsam-pine and Virginia cedar. Mocking-birds and scarlet cardinal-thrushes sang in the branches. They passed meadows of browsing cows, where striped squirrels[11] were frisking up and down the railings. Negroes laboured in tobacco-fields, others were sawing timber. A black girl of fourteen, 'half-naked and beautiful as a daughter of Night', opened the farmyard gate to them, and graciously accepted the gift of François-René's silk handkerchief.

He collected his tumultuous thoughts. He stood now in the new, unprecedented Republic, which announced the doom of the old society, and a transformation of the mind of man. Here was the Revolution which his own countrymen had crossed the ocean to win, and then brought back with them to France. Not very far away, on the spot where William Penn had bought a few acres of forest from the Indians, rose the flourishing city of Philadelphia, where he hoped in a few days to be talking to President Washington. Further west, beyond this narrow fringe of civilisation, he would find the savage nature to which he meant to expose his virgin Muse, the wilderness he had come to explore. Yet how strange, he thought, lovely as she was, to be welcomed to the land of liberty by a slave.

Father Delavau was no less stirred by his own reception. As he stood bargaining in broken English with the first farmer in America, up came the second, a tall and venerable colonial from the neighbouring plantation, eager to enlarge his experience. 'That gentleman, I don't doubt, is a minister of the Catholic faith,' he remarked to Risdell, and explained that he possessed a wellstocked library, in which he read books of divinity every day. He had no use for Methodists or Anabaptists, but would certainly choose the Catholic religion if he ever decided to change his own; after all, said he, it was the oldest. M. Delavau, for whom every stranger was a convert, just as for Don Quixote every windmill was a giant and for François-René every black girl a nymph, promised to keep in touch with him by post. They made their way back to the *Saint-Pierre*, loaded with baskets of maize-cakes, eggs, chickens, and demijohns of fresh milk.

At last, after three days at anchor awaiting a wind, and four more cruising two hundred miles up the glassy calm waters of Chesapeake Bay, they saw before them as if at the head of a lake the redbrick Georgian houses of Baltimore, the shipthronged wharves, the wooded hill of Fell's Point where building had just begun. François-René spent the night on board, and stepped ashore with the others at nine in the morning on Sunday, 10 July 1791. The New World was all before him, where to choose.

Francis did not even say goodbye. There was no look of regret or sensibility on his handsome features. The bishop's vicar Father Sewall (for Mgr. Carroll himself was away on a visit to Philadelphia) carried the Sulpician party off to the episcopal residence. By eleven o'clock priests and acolytes were all at mass in the cathedral. François-René took his baggage to Grout's Tavern, booked his seat in tomorrow's coach for Philadelphia, and made a final attempt to speak to his lost friend; but no, he was told, Francis could not see him. Did they ever meet again? Why, yes, thirty-one years later, but that was not the same thing at all. He settled accounts with Captain Douville, treated him to a farewell dinner, took a brief sleep, and then, at the unearthly hour of four a.m., he was off to Philadelphia in the morning.

A FALL AT NIAGARA

THE American stage coach in the 1790s was lightly built, fast, but not comfortable. The passengers sat on three backless benches, three to a bench, and one more beside the driver. A fixed roof provided shade or shelter, but the sides were open except in rain, when leather blinds could be buttoned down. Four horses, changed twice or thrice daily at stops for meals, trotted them at six to nine miles an hour for between sixty and a hundred miles a day. In the long daylight of summer one expected to start early and go far, especially on the crack trunk route which extended all the way from Boston in Massachusetts, via New York, Philadelphia, Baltimore and Richmond, to Charleston in South Carolina. The distance from Baltimore to Philadelphia was ninety-eight miles, the fare a guinea, and the early coach arrived at dinner time in the afternoon of the following day.

François-René found the country flat and treeless, but was pleased to see swallows skimming over village ponds, just as at Combourg. On the second day they passed farmers going to market, public conveyances, gentlemen's carriages, and cantered into the dignified but (as he thought) monotonous capital city of Philadelphia, laid out in a square mesh of broad treelined streets of redbrick houses, running due north to south, east to west. He missed the Catholic spires and domes of Europe, and blamed the Protestant heresy for this absence of 'any monument pyramiding over the mass of walls and roofs'.[1]

They alighted at the Indian Queen, in Fourth Street at the corner of Market Street. François-René spent the night in this famous inn, and moved next morning to a lodging-house favoured by his countrymen. Two years later Philadelphia would be crammed with uneasily variegated Frenchmen, royalists in flight from the guillotine, Girondist and Jacobin revolutionaries under their plenipotentiary minister Genêt, and fugitives from the horrors of negro uprisings in the West Indies. Even now, glad as he was of a last opportunity to speak his own language, François-René found himself odd man out. His fellow-lodgers were creole merchants on business from San Domingo, where he himself had expected only last year to collect the elusive fortune owed to his dead father, or disappointed émigrés who had sought exile from France with ideas which he could not share. Some were relics of the fiasco of Gallipolis, who had retreated after one frozen winter on the Ohio amid rumours of an imminent Indian war, or changed their minds before

going there at all. Others were absolute monarchists for whom even the
fall of the Bastille and the National Assembly's first enlightened re-
forms had made their country unendurable. Strange, he thought, with
the reverse of his feelings on seeing the slavegirl a week before, that the
land of liberty should provide sanctuary for men escaping from liberty!

However, when he surveyed this capital of the country of freedom,
he was virtuously shocked to find the same contrasts of wealth and
poverty, the luxurious carriages, frivolous conversation, ballrooms and
theatres and gambling dens, which he had left in Paris. Full of his
favourite Raynal's eulogy of the Philadelphia Quakers, those paragons
of honesty, simplicity and pacifism, with their broad black hats and
their insistence on the immorality of buttons, he asked to be shown one
of the saintly descendants of William Penn. His request was greeted
with hilarity. 'If you want to be swindled,' they said, 'you have only to
go into a Quaker's shop; if you wish to see the utmost of human
duplicity, then observe two of the brethren making a bargain.' François-
René on hearing these idle words enjoyed the same unearned sense of
superiority as when he judged the monks of Graciosa, but mingled with
real disappointment. Clearly, if he still expected to witness an innocent
society, he must pin his hopes on the noble savage. However, he
thoroughly approved of the Quaker maidens with their demure pale
faces, grey gowns, and little uniform hats.

His acquaintances no doubt showed him the other sights of Philadelphia. If so, he can hardly have missed a visit to Peale's Museum, on
the corner of Third and Lombard Street, with its collection of Indian
scalps, tomahawks and belts of wampum, stuffed American birds, mam-
mals and reptiles, gigantic mastodon bones from Kentucky, and even,
bottled in alcohol, two of the three known specimens (Yale, of course,
owned the other) of the two-headed serpent. He had read of this remarkable *lusus naturae* in Carver, seeing was believing, and he must not
be unduly blamed for mentioning the two-headed serpent, as 'very
rare', in his *Voyage en Amérique*. An indispensable Philadelphia excursion was to the botanical garden of William Bartram, nine miles up the
Schuylkill river, where the great naturalist still dwelt in the old stone
house (which exists to this day) built by his father John, and cultivated
the exotic plants of the Florida everglades which he had brought home
from his journeys. François-René no doubt bought Bartram's celebrated *Travels*, which were published in Philadelphia in this very year,
and were soon to influence Coleridge and Wordsworth and himself so
profoundly. On the way back one stopped for refreshment at another
garden, Gray's Tavern, four miles out of town, where oranges and
lemons (at that time of year in fruit and flower simultaneously), lianas
and palms grew in a mighty glasshouse, and for half-a-dollar one enjoyed the finest tea, coffee and syllabubs in Pennsylvania. He would

never see the Deep South, or rather, he would only glimpse it from afar; but its vegetation and fauna were already before him in the hot-houses and museum of Philadelphia, and its poetic reality forever accessible in Bartram's extraordinary book.

He sought advice on his journey, and found little encouragement. The disillusioned settlers of Gallipolis had nearly starved that winter, a particularly severe one, when ice had prevented the flatboats from floating down the Ohio with provisions. The Indians, it was true, had not much troubled them, because they liked Frenchmen; but they were determined to keep white men from their hunting grounds west of the Ohio; they had been raiding river boats and lonely homesteads for two years past, and now a fullscale war was brewing. General Saint-Clair was already at Fort Washington (on the site of newly-founded Cincin-nati) mustering an army of 2,000 regulars and Kentucky militiamen. The West was barred by the Redskins, the North by the British, Mon-sieur de Combourg ought to have set out in spring, he could do nothing alone, he was too inexperienced, they told him.

He found the Americans talking of Mackenzie's great journey in the summer of 1789, of which, as we have seen, he had probably heard before leaving Paris. Mackenzie had canoed along the mysterious river flowing westward out of the Great Slave Lake, which Peter Pond had mapped debouching, over 'falls said to be the largest in the known world', into Cook's Inlet and the Pacific. But its westerly way, Mackenzie found, was in fact barred by a tremendous range of icy mountains, the river turned abruptly north, and carried him to the Arctic Ocean, which Mackenzie was thus the second white man to see, six hundred miles west of Hearne's Coppermine River. François-René felt strongly tempted to make straight for the Arctic; but his scruples prevented him from altering the project he had agreed with M. de Malesherbes, for exploring the West Coast first.

All concurred that, if he was quite determined to persist in the impos-sible, he would do best to proceed to Albany, where civilisation came nearest to the frontier settlements and to friendly Indians, and he could obtain guides and information. One sympathiser even gave him a letter of introduction to Mr. Swift, a furtrader in that town. This fitted in with his own plans, for Carver had taken the same route on his way to Niagara, and the Great Lakes, and the sources of the Four Rivers. So he announced that he would set out for Niagara by way of Albany. Once there, he would see how much further he could expect to go. But in the face of so much good advice he began to understand that the alternative second-best plan which he had already envisaged in Paris might now prove inevitable: he would perhaps have to resign himself to a mere reconnaissance, and postpone his great discoveries for a second, longer journey. He wrote to M. de Malesherbes to tell him so.

Meanwhile he resolved if need be to travel in quest, not of the North-west Passage, but of the landscapes and people of his book. 'I promised to poetry whatever might be lost to science, and in fact, if I did not find in America what I was looking for, the polar world, I found a new Muse.'

He was impatient to leave, but first he must see President Washington and deliver his letter of introduction. This, as it happened, was not so easy, though not quite for the reason which he remembered thirty-one years later, when he first recorded in detail the circumstances of their meeting. 'When I arrived in Philadelphia General Washington was absent; I was obliged to wait for a week.' In fact, until only a week before, Washington had indeed been out of town, on the last long journey of his life. On 21 March 1791 he had set out on a semi-official pilgrimage through the southern states—Virginia, North and South Carolina, and Georgia—of the new republic. When he returned on 6 July, after travelling two thousand miles, south to Savannah and northward home through the back country, all the churchbells in Philadelphia rang. François-René would certainly have learned of this absence on reaching Baltimore, or even a week earlier, when he landed at the Chesapeake plantation, and have been impressed by the risk of disturbance to his plans. No wonder, then, that he mistakenly recalled, so long after, Washington's journey as the cause of delay, instead of the real reason. In fact the President, immediately after his return, was con-fined to bed by a recurrence of the carbuncle on his left buttock which had made the physicians despair of his life at New York two years before. He lay on his right side in pain and fever, struggled up out of sense of duty when Jefferson called to present a Spanish diplomat on 19 July (probably the very day of François-René's departure), was lanced on the 27th, but was obliged to close his door to ordinary visitors and neglect his correspondence until his recovery early in August.

So François-René was compelled by etiquette and necessity to post-pone delivery of his letter until the day before he left. It was presum-ably on or about Monday, 18 July, his seventh day in Philadelphia, that he called at 190 High Street, noticing with ideological approval that the President of the United States lived like any other citizen in a modest two-storied redbrick house, with only one window to the left of the marble-pedimented streetdoor and two to the right on each floor. No sentry stood guard outside, and when he rang no sublime footman answered the door, but a pleasant young girl, one of Mrs Washington's maids.[2] He was informed, as he must already have known, that the President was too unwell to receive visitors, and left his letter with the message that he was leaving early next morning for Niagara. 'I have had the pleasure to receive your letter of the 22nd of March,' wrote Washington to La Rouërie on 5 September,[3] 'Being indisposed on the day when Monsieur de Combourg called to deliver your letter I did not see him, and I understood that he set off to Niagara the next day.'

So it is quite certain that François-René did not see Washington in that July. Why then, when he summoned up remembrance of things past to write his narrative long after, did it seem that the pretty maid showed him in, and that Washington granted him a private interview, and even had him to dinner next day? Chateaubriandists have rashly concluded, some with virtuous satisfaction and some with virtuous regret, that the interview and dinner which he describes so vividly never happened. On the contrary there can be no doubt that they did occur, but on another occasion.

François-René was again present in Philadelphia for several weeks before he sailed home on 10 December; the President was then in residence, fully recovered, and receiving visitors as usual. The laws of etiquette concerning letters of introduction were strict and binding on all parties, immeasurably so in the given situation, when the recipient was a head of state, the sender a Breton hero and a family friend, and the bearer a punctilious young gentleman who admired them both. Not to have called again at the first opportunity would have been an unthinkable discourtesy to both Washington and La Rouërie, and a pointless flouting of his own desires. For next to the wilderness and the Indians, both of which by then he had already seen to his heart's content, there was nothing in America that François-René longed more keenly to encounter than President Washington. Since, then, he was able, morally obliged, and desirous to do so, affirms that he did and describes it most convincingly, and there is not the least evidence to the contrary, we can be quite sure that he did meet Washington, not indeed in July but in late November or early December, but otherwise exactly as he tells it, and as we shall read towards the end of the next chapter but one.

Next morning at the Indian Queen he took the 4 a.m. coach to New York, then the fastest on the continent, for it completed the journey of ninety-one miles in the evening of the same day. He found New York, already recovered from the destructive British occupation of 1776–83, a 'gay, populous, commercial' city. Perhaps he was not alone. Twenty years later people who had been in Philadelphia at that time remembered seeing him 'with his travelling companion'.[4] Possibly he had joined forces with a returning Bostonian, or a Philadelphian or fellow-Frenchman with business in Boston. If so, it would help to explain his next rather unexpected detour, though his own reason is enough, and just like him: 'I went on pilgrimage to Boston to salute the first battleground of American liberty'. The journey of 230 miles, via New Haven and Hartford, took as little as three and a half days in Levi Pease's mailcoach.[5] He deplored at Boston, as he had at Philadelphia and New York, the puritanical absence of 'pyramiding' edifices, but found a historic

grandeur in the quayside of the Tea Party whence the American Revolution, and therefore the French also, had sprung. He made the day's
excursion to Lexington, eleven miles northeast on the way to Concord,
where on 19 April 1775 the American insurgents first fired on British
troops. He expressed some of his feelings in *Essai sur les Révolutions*.
'I halted in silence, like a traveller at Thermopylae, to contemplate the
grave of those warriors of two worlds who were first to die, in obedience
to their country's laws. As I trod this philosophic ground, which told
me with mute eloquence how empires fall and rise, I confessed my
insignificance before the ways of Providence, and bowed my head in
the dust.' Or perhaps, if the suspicion is not unworthy, he was merely
taken to Bunker Hill, a favourite after-dinner stroll for Bostonians, was
told that this was the first battlefield of the Revolution, and thought he
had been to Lexington.

He could have been back in New York within eight days, towards
28 July. He wrote again to Malesherbes, repeating that he had found
little encouragement for his coming journey, and booked his passage
to Albany. On the waterfront a new face greeted him of an old acquaintance, as a young Breton sailor passed by. 'Are you from Saint-Malo?'
he exclaimed, 'I'm Francillon, can't you recognise me? Don't you
remember Francillon, whom you gave such a hiding one day on the
Sillon?' 'Wait a moment, now I have it,' replied this friendly enemy
from the days of Gesril, 'it was in our famous battle of stones, when I
had to come to blows with you to make you give over.' 'Just so,' said
François-René, amused and delighted, 'and I see you would still get the
better of me today!' 'And he took off his hat,' affirmed the bibulous
ancient mariner who told the tale fifty years later to a Saint-Malo visitor,
no doubt with some slight exaggeration, 'and he thanked Heaven for
showing him a face from his own country, and said he couldn't let me
go without pressing me to accept a little something, so that I could
drink with my friends to the success of his great voyage of discovery in
the polar seas.'

Albany was 145 miles up the Hudson River, New York's busy water-
way to Canada and the West. The famous Albany sloops skimmed up
on the morning tide, continued through the brief summer night, and
arrived with fair winds towards evening next day. François-René took
the packet, fastest of all, whose Captain Hatchway claimed that no other
boat on the river could keep up with him.[6]

They glided before a cool following breeze on the brimming tide.
Towards evening François-René joined a group of American army
officers and a bevy of ladies in the stern for a collation of fruit and milk.
The women sat on the bench round the tiller, the men on the deck at
their feet, conversing vivaciously until all turned silent at the sublimity
of the Palisades, where the river flows between precipices five hundred

feet high. 'That's where Major André was executed,' said someone,
when they drew near the steep path from the western bank up to
Tappan, where the gallant British spy had been hanged eleven years
before. 'More unfortunate than criminal,' General Washington had
called him, though he sternly ignored the young man's last request to
be honourably shot instead. A pretty Quaker girl was begged to give
them *Major André's Complaint*, and she obliged in a timidly voluptuous
voice, fading in midstream, resonant as they neared the cliff, and here and
there raising an echo as if André's ghost responded from the mountains.

Ah   Delia   see the   fatal hour,   Farewell my soul's de-

light But how shall wretched Damon live   thus   banish'd from thy   sight?

Each verse ended with the refrain: '*But who can tell if thou, my dear, wilt
e'er remember me?*' François-René noticed tears in the eyes of the American
officers, and shed a few himself. Far above meanwhile, between pink
and white clouds, they saw lonely cabins hanging over abysses, crests of
crag, peaks shaggy with pine. They turned the westward bend into the
Tappan Sea, all gold, where blue-doves cooed in the woods, mocking-
birds sang, and in secluded framehouses whole families leaned attentive,
over verandahs twined with red-trumpeted bignonia, to watch them
pass. A black squirrel fell into the water, and was rescued half drowned
by the fair Quaker, who declared she would keep it for a pet.

Mr. Swift of Albany, furtrader, turned out to be a practical man.
After listening patiently to François-René's plans, he objected that a
journey of such vast extent could not be undertaken alone, without
experience, preparation, official support, and letters of recommendation
to the British, American, and Spanish posts through which he would be
obliged to pass. He would infallibly die of cold and hunger in the
regions of thick-ribbed ice, supposing he were lucky enough to reach
them across the endless wilderness. No, he would do much better to
learn Iroquois, Sioux, and Eskimo, and spend four or five years living
with backwoodsmen and Hudson Bay Company agents. Then, after
obtaining the aid of the French government, he could 'proceed to his
hazardous mission'.

François-René felt much put out, though he could not dispute the
justice of these counsels. Hiding his annoyance, he asked Mr. Swift to

7

find a guide and horses to take him to Niagara and Pittsburgh. From Pittsburgh he could descend the Ohio, collect useful information, perhaps even persevere in his original intentions. 'I still had the first plan of my journey in mind,' he remarks. So Mr. Swift put him in the way of hiring a huge Dutchman, who spoke several Indian dialects, and of buying two horses, one for each. Then they rode out of Albany to Schenectady, and the Mohawk Valley, and the Iroquois Trail.

The way from Albany to Niagara led for three hundred miles through the ancient lands of the Six Nations, first by road along the settled farmland valley of the Mohawk River, then through the Finger Lake country to the Genesee, then in forest and brush to Niagara. This Iroquois Trail had been frequented from time immemorial, first by long-vanished Hurons and Algonquins, then by the Iroquois confederacy of Mohawks, Oneidas, Onondagas, Cayugas, Senecas, and Tuscaroras, and from the seventeenth century onwards by French, Dutch, British, and New England traders, soldiers, and settlers. In the Revolutionary War only Oneidas and Tuscaroras had supported the colonials. It was one of the most inglorious features of that often nasty conflict that the other tribes, with British encouragement, pay, and arms, had massacred, scalped, burned and looted along the peaceful Mohawk valley, until General Sullivan's punitive expedition in 1779 broke the Iroquois power for ever. Most of the Iroquois had then withdrawn on British invitation to Canada, or to the tract south of Lake Erie and north of the Ohio. The rest signed away their lands to the United States at the treaty of Fort Stanwix in 1788, and since dwelt inoffensively in separate reservations, where their descendants survive to this day. Now immigrants were pouring into the rich empty Genesee country, thousands every year, transporting their chattels in the flat-bottomed barges called bateaux on the Mohawk, or in heavy New England oxwagons. The Iroquois Trail had never been so busy as in the summer when François-René travelled it.

The fertile valley lands of the Mohawk had been occupied by farmers since early in the century, and the road was good for a hundred miles, with a farmstead every mile and a rising township every ten. But even here, in the great leap forward of the United States after the war, new settlers were still crowding in to fill the gaps. So it was doubtless on the Mohawk—and not, as he thought he remembered later, in the Genesee country, which would not achieve this stage until a decade later—that he was surprised to see new churchspires rising from primeval forest, and to be given hospitality, within sight of an Iroquois wigwam, in an elegant farmhouse complete with mahogany furniture, carpets, mirrors, and piano. The daylabourers plodded home with axe or hoe, all supped together, and then the host's golden-ringleted daughters sang an aria of Cimarosa, or the duet from Paisiello's *Pandolfetto*.

At last, when they left the Mohawk a little beyond recently founded Utica, he had his first sight of unfelled virgin forest, the wilderness he had come so far to see, the longed-for symbol of a freedom which does not exist in this world. Beside himself with joy, he ran from tree to tree, repeating: 'No more roads, no more towns, no monarchy, no republic, no presidents, no kings, no human beings!', testing the reality of his liberation by a multitude of gratuitous actions, until his guide, greatly vexed, thought him not quite right in the head. Soon they saw their first Red Indians, a young man walking in front of a horse on which rode a girl in her tribal finery. The Dutchman greeted them with good day.

As they neared Oneida Castle, where five hundred remaining Oneidas lived in a palisaded village, they almost collided with a lean-to shack, from which issued strange sounds. A score of halfnaked red-skins, men and women, in full paint and feathers, with slit ears and rings in noses, were capering away to the strains of *Madelon Friquet*

Je suis   Madelon Friquet,   Et   je   me   ris   et   je   me   moque

played by a little French fiddler with frizzed and powdered hair, apple-green frockcoat and muslin sleeves. His name was Monsieur Violet, he explained, at the first pause in the dance; he had been a scullion in the Comte de Rochambeau's mess during the late war, had stayed behind to instruct the Americans in the fine arts, and was now doing very nicely as dancing-master to the Iroquois, who paid his fees in beaver-pelts and bear-hams. 'These gentleman savages,' he boasted, for so out of professional etiquette he insisted on referring to his pupils, 'and these lady savagesses, are so light on their feet!' François-René could not but concede that he had never seen such capers in all his born days. Then Monsieur Violet, tuning his fiddle, shouted in Iroquois: 'Set to your partners!', and the gentlemen and lady savages fell again to leaping and bounding, like a pack of devils. François-René was hard put to it not to burst out laughing, but as a disciple of Rousseau he felt deeply humiliated.[7]

At Oneida Castle, as a preparation for sleeping out and for colder days to come, he bought from the Indians two bearskins, one for a bed, one for a wrap. He now sported the complete backwoodsman's outfit of red flannel cap with earflaps, belt, bandoleer and hunting-horn, let his beard grow long and his hair float over his bare neck. Thus dressed for the part, looking like the last but one of the Mohicans ('a mixture of savage, hunter, and missionary,' he says complacently), he joined next day one of the hunting jamborees which, as other narratives show, the

half-tame Indians of those parts put on for travellers in the 1790s. They
set off before dawn, a party of thirty white and red, in canoes up Oneida
Creek, which a few miles downstream flowed into Lake Oneida. Some
walked alongside on the bank, men with the dogs, women carrying the
provisions. A carcajou had been sighted, a real but then already un-
common beast of which the Indians told absurd fables that François-
René had read and believed in Charlevoix and Carver.[8] They found no
carcajou, but bagged a few lynxes and some muskrats, and then enjoyed
a supper of new-caught fish and duck prepared by the squaws, round a
smoking fire that kept the mosquitoes off, but stung his eyes until he
had to lie face downward.

After a short day's journey to the Onondaga country the Dutchman
decided to François-René's delight that it was time to sleep out. They
chose a site, which can be found on the map to this day, on the little
peninsula formed by the limpid green river as it rushed from Onondaga
Lake to join the Seneca and Oneida rivers at Three Rivers Point. They
built an *ajoupa* (the very word seemed bliss) of two forked stakes, a
transverse pole, and a roof of birch bark, with bearskin mattress and
saddle for pillow. They tied bells round the horses' necks and set them
free to feed. Would they not get lost, he enquired. No, explained the
Dutchman, they were too clever to stray beyond sight of the camp fire.

It was still only four o'clock when François-René wandered off with
his gun, dutifully botanising for M. de Malesherbes, but disappointed
to find nothing more exciting than the common *plantago virginica*, and
'a kind of rhododendron' which mirrored its vivid pink blossom in
the blue lake. Even birds seemed scarce. A pair of white sparrows
(*passer nivalis*, he thought) fluttered amorously before him, and an
osprey[9] with its harsh cry led him uphill to a rocky verge overlooking
a little valley, with a tumbledown shack on the opposite slope, and a
gaunt cow grazing in the meadow bottom. He sat on the edge, watching, and heard voices. Three white men appeared, leading six fat kine
to pasture, and drove the thin one away with blows of their cudgels
and shouts of heartless laughter. An Indian woman emerged from the
hut and called to the starveling, which ran to her with outstretched
neck and gentle moo. The white ruffians shook their fists at her in
menace, and left their own cattle in possession.

Still full of Rousseau, François-René felt sure that sympathy would
heal all. He ran to the hut, summoned his best Iroquois, and announced:
'Siegoh! I have come!' The woman said nothing, instead of returning
his greeting with the correct: 'You have come!'; but when he began to
caress the cow, her yellow mournful suspicious features showed surprise and softening, and she too laid her hand on the creature's head.
'She's very thin,' remarked François-René in English, having run out of
Iroquois. 'She eats very little,' replied the woman haltingly, in the same

language. 'They drove her away roughly,' he continued. 'We're used to that, both of us.' 'So the meadow doesn't belong to you?' 'It was my husband's, he is dead. I have no children, and the palefaces bring their cattle to my meadow.' She said a good deal more, which he did not understand, but interpreted optimistically as wishes for his prosperity. 'If these did not reach the ear of heaven, the fault lies not with her who prayed, but with the shortcomings of him for whom the prayer was offered.' He would have liked to give her something, but had nothing; to appeal to the law, but there was no law here.

Next morning they paid their respects to Kahiktoton, chief sachem of the Onondagas, in his nearby village, where the youths and maidens surrounded them joyously, shouting in their own language, with a few words of French and English. The Old Gentleman, as white folk called him, received them affably, and made them sit on his own mat, while the young warriors took François-René's gun to pieces and re-assembled it with alarming dexterity. Kahiktoton's ears were slit, his face striped with ceremonial paint; he wore his hair in a topknot, a pearl in his nose, bore scalping-knife and tomahawk, dangled a belt of wampum in his hands, had fought at Quebec, spoke English, and understood French. He knew all about his oppressed countrywoman, and had approached the American land-commissioners on her behalf more than once, but could get no justice; in earlier days, he added ominously, his people would have seen to the matter themselves. He liked the French, he graciously affirmed, although his tribe had always fought them, but not the land-hungry Americans. 'They will not leave the Red Man enough earth to cover his bones.'[10]

Monsieur Violet, he learned, perhaps from the Old Gentleman himself, was not his only compatriot in these savage parts. A certain Philippe Le Cocq, after fighting like Kahiktoton at Quebec, had retired to the land of the Six Nations, married an Indian wife, gone native, and now lived near by. François-René found him sharpening stakes at his cabin door, and engaged in an interview on best Rousseauish principles. The old man received him coldly, without interrupting his work, until, finding himself addressed in French, he started and shed a huge tear. 'Philippe, are you happy?' 'Happy? Yes, ever since I became a savage.' 'And would you not like to resume your old life, and return to your own country?' 'Yes, if I were not so old, I should like to see France again.' 'But not to stay there?' Philippe shook his head. 'And what made you decide to become a savage, as you call it?' 'I don't know. Instinct!', replied the sage, perhaps feeling that if Rousseau was what the young gentleman was after, then Rousseau he should have.[11]

The way led onward past the northern outflows of Cayuga, Seneca, and Canandaigua Lakes, sometimes marked only by felled trees used as bridges over streams or as corduroy tracks through bogs. Here and there they passed a clearing, a cornfield, a log cabin neatly new, another half finished with sky for roof, and at each day's journey's end an inn with signpost hung from a bough, crowded with hunters, Indians, and immigrants. When they stopped at one such caravanseray François-René retired early to make sure of his place, and was surprised to find an immense circular bed, arranged for sleepers to lie like spokes in a wheel, with their feet to the central post. Dubiously, but taking courage as no one was there, he inserted himself in this contraption and dozed off, when suddenly he felt something sliding against his body, and started wide awake. It was the leg, innocent of all ill intent, of his gigantic Dutchman. 'In all my life I have never felt a greater horror!' He leapt up, cursing, sallied forth to sleep in his bearskin under the chaste moon, and announced next morning that in future he would sleep out.

They reached the Genesee River at cabins which a few years after became New Hartford, the modern Avon, N.Y., and found a party of Indians and settlers waiting at the inn and ferry kept by Mrs Berry and her trader husband Gilbert. They crossed together and camped on the far side near the Seneca village of Canawagus, in a meadow bedizened with flowers and butterflies. A rattlesnake slithered among their bivouacs, and an Indian with a reed pipe walked up to it, signing that he would give them a display. The angry serpent reared upon its convolutions, lowering its flat head with glittering eyes and flickering forked tongue, emitting a sinister clatter from the shadowy mist of its vibrating tail. The man began to tootle on his pipe; the ecstatic monster, fainting in coils, ceased its rattle, disposed itself on the ground in concentric circles of prismatic azure, green, white and gold, and followed the man between the astonished and gratified ranks of spectators, parting the grass with its head, halting when he paused, hurrying when he hurried, till it had left their bounds. 'Shall I kill it?' enquired the charmer. 'No, spare it!' they cried as one.

Within a day or two of full moon, which in August 1791 fell on the 11th, they camped in an oak grove by Tonawanda Creek, which flows into Niagara River opposite Grand Island, a few miles above the Falls. An Indian family of three warriors, two women and two babies was there before them, but readily agreed to François-René's invitation, transmitted by the Dutchman, to join forces. Soon all sat together crosslegged by the campfire, roasting their corncobs. The Indians contributed bearcub hams, in exchange for which François-René treated them to a bottle of brandy—Frenchman's milk,[12] their favourite beverage! The older warriors grew hilarious, but their companion youth stared at him in silence, with haughty face striped black, red, blue. François-René could not but admire this savage Gesril, attributing his sullen mood to patriotic resentment, though it was perhaps due rather to impotent desire for his goods and scalp. The animated conversation of broken Iroquois and sign-language (François-René was getting quite good at it) gradually lapsed, the squaws laid their drowsing babes on skins, all slumbered, except himself.

He could not sleep a wink. Leaning on his elbow he scrutinised his hosts, breathing heavily in drunken stupor, in the red light of the fire. Here he was, dwelling at last in the wilderness with noble savages as a friend. How Rousseau or old Malesherbes would have envied him. Perhaps the scowling youth might even have become a particular friend, given time? 'Virtuous young man,' he meditated, 'how touching to me is thy sleep! Thou, who seem'st so sensible to the sorrows of thy people, thou art too great, too superior, to mistrust the stranger! What a lesson for us Europeans! Those savages whom we pursued with fire and flame, to whom our avarice left not even a spadeful of earth to cover their dead in all this universe, once their vast patrimony; these same savages, welcoming their enemy beneath their hospitable huts, sharing with him their humble repast, their bed unvisited by remorse, and reposing at his side in the deep sleep of the just!—their virtues are as far above our conventional virtues as the soul of these children of nature is above the soul of civilised man!' Thus thinking (he was right about their freedom from remorse, at least), he wandered out into that celebrated moonlight night, so supremely romantic and so supremely real, which he was to describe again and again in his works, which would win him fame and revolutionise French literature. For although many had entertained preposterous illusions about the noble savage, no one had ever seen moonlight before.

He sat on a gnarled tree-root by the stream. The moon rose slowly above the treetops, preceded by a cool eastern breeze which seemed her own fragrant breath. She paused beyond jagged peaks of cloud, like a chain of distant snowy mountains, then wandered through white flocks grazing on azure plains, seastrands with parallel undulations that seemed formed by the flux and reflux of ripples, masses of tactile cotton-wool, whose elasticity and softness he could feel in his fingertips. Swathes of blue light pierced the deepest glooms of the forest, the stream glowed in a ribbon of shot silk sprinkled with diamonds and striped with black bands, the vast savannah on the further bank was a lawn spread with sheets of moonbeams, a motionless sea on which floated shadowy islands of birchtrees. All was soundless until, as he listened to the silence, he heard the lapse of a summer leaf, branches quivering in a gust, the padding of invisible beasts, the hooting of an owl, and beneath all these a remote solemn bellowing, the roar of Niagara nine miles away prolonged from wilderness to wilderness to expire in this solitary forest. He felt an inexpressible rapture, an extraordinary terror, as though God were about to reveal to him the secret of the universe. He was aware as never before of his own identity, yet his very existence had left his body and was dissolving into the melancholy grandeur about him. The act of losing consciousness brought him to; he pulled himself together, returned to camp, lay down among the Indians, and fell into profound sleep.

When he awoke next morning the Dutchman had already saddled their horses. The warriors stood waiting, while the squaws packed their burdens of furs, maize, and smoked bear-meat. He distributed a few always acceptable gifts from his portmanteau, gunpowder, bullets, a box of vermilion. They parted with expressions of friendship and regret, each ritually touching his forehead and breast. Even the sulky youth cordially gripped François-René's outstretched hand, such is the power of sympathy, or of vermilion. The men uttered their marching shout, set off north by the mosses on the treetrunks; the women plodded behind, loaded with all the luggage, each with her papoose strapped to her back; and as they receded he saw the babes turn their heads to watch him, smiling farewell. Then he set off west, proudly using his compass.

They were halted by a patrol of Indians armed with bows and arrows, a wild police. Niagara Falls and the Niagara Tract, a strip along the river extending four miles inside the American frontier, were still held by the British. Before they could proceed they must obtain a pass from the commanding officer at Fort Niagara. The Dutchman went to get it, and François-René stayed behind in Tonawanda village.

He sat writing on his knee, notes on yesterday's moonlight, a third letter from America to M. de Malesherbes, while the warriors lounged, the women worked, and children played around him. 'I wrote from Philadelphia and New York to my illustrious and venerable master,' he began, and repeated his complaint of finding no encouragement from the Americans, and his foreboding that his journey would henceforth be abortive, or no more than 'a reconnaissance in the wilderness'. He now intended instead to train himself 'to Indian ways and to privations of all kinds, to become a backwoodsman before being the Christopher Columbus of Polar America'. Even so, he confessed, 'I am delighted with what I see, and if the explorer repines, the poet finds reason for self-congratulation.'[13] For the moonlight, and his direct contact with Indians, had made his journey come true for the first time; indeed, these few days mark in all his life that point of mystery at which a man begins to know who he is, and what is the world around him. 'An unknown Muse came to me in those nights,' he says, 'I took down some of her tones, and registered them in my book, as a workaday musician would put on paper the notes dictated to him by some great master of harmonies.'

The mothers rose from time to time, to tend their babies hanging in netted cradles from the branches of a copperbeech. Weaning, he observed, was late; a strapping boy of seven ran up to suckle his parent, and then returned to his game. M. de Malesherbes, when he was *directeur de la librairie* in 1762, had helped to see *Émile*, Rousseau's didactic novel on education by instinct, through the press; well, he would give him a sample of a Red Indian *Émile*. 'Regard me as an infant Jean-Jacques,' François-René wrote, 'I can only tell you about Iroquois urchins.' The children, he noticed, leapt, ran, played at ball in silence without quarrelling; 'there is something in their manner as serious as happiness, as noble as independence.' In that matrilinear society a child would respect its mother because she was sacred, its grandfather because he was old, but fathers were nothing. 'Boys,' cried one of the warriors beside him, 'go in and sleep, the sun will eat your heads.' 'You are right,' they answered, and went on playing. However, 'if the savage child obeys no one, no one obeys him, and that is the whole secret of his gaiety, or rather, of his rationality.' Could these admirable principles be applied to the upbringing of civilised youth? No, he argued, in his effort to compete with Rousseau almost anticipating Freud, 'because we should have to get rid of our vices, whereas we find it easier to repress them in the hearts of our children, and inhibit their outward display.'

The Dutchman returned with the British pass, signed by Colonel Gordon. Chateaubriand kept it as a souvenir for at least thirty years, though it does not seem to have survived into modern times. It would be interesting to know the date upon it, which if our present calculations are correct may have been about 12 August 1791. He felt, as a Frenchman, a qualm in his heart at the thought that until his father's time the Niagara frontier had belonged to France.

Colonel Andrew Gordon of the 26th Cameronians, commander of the Upper Posts of Oswego, Fort Niagara, Fort Erie, Detroit and Michillimackinac, was in a position of peculiar delicacy that summer. The British, in defiance of the peace treaty of 1783, still retained possession of the lake and river forts on the American side of the new boundary, ostensibly as security for American pre-war debts, but really in order to keep their monopoly of the northwest fur trade and the commerce of the Lakes. They encouraged the friendship of the Indians, their ferocious allies in the late war, by annual gifts to the chiefs, and supplies of arms and ammunition which could be used either for the necessity of hunting or for the luxury of shooting Americans. They had given land in Canada to the dispossessed majority of the Six Nations who preferred not to remain in New York State, where they had taken so many scalps. Now there were villages of Senecas on Buffalo Creek, of Tuscaroras near the mouth of Tonawanda Creek and three miles below the Falls near Lewistown, and the Mohawks under their educated and ruthless chief Thayandenaga, better known as Captain Joseph Brant, enjoyed a reservation at Grand River on the north shore of Lake

Erie. The British maintained an attitude of virtuous neutrality in the coming Indian war, but were convinced, quite unjustly, that the hidden object of General Saint-Clair's mobilisation on the Ohio was the seizure of Detroit, Niagara, and Oswego. 'We are at peace with the United States and wish to remain so,' Gordon was instructed by Lord Dorchester, Governor of Canada; but the risk of war required 'constant vigilance and readiness to meet such an event'. So, in the summer of François-René's visit, when the Niagara frontier was a potential trouble-spot where the stability of the North American continent and the peace of the world might be endangered, Colonel Gordon looked to his defences, strengthened his garrisons, alerted his little navy on the Lakes, and pampered his Indian chiefs more paternally than ever. He kept special watch for suspicious travellers, spies, and foreigners over-friendly towards his loyal savages. He might well have turned François-René and his Dutchman away as undesirable aliens, remembering the embarrassment he had suffered only three months before from the arrival of an American agent accompanied by a mysterious Frenchman.[14] However, the Dutchman managed to convince him that François-René, although French, was not a serious security risk.

Next morning François-René and the Dutchman rode out of Tonawanda village. They soon caught sight, from six miles away, of the column of spray that towers from the clashing torrents at the centre of the Horseshoe Fall. As they entered the final wood François-René felt his heart beating with mingled joy and terror at the imminence of what was then, as he truly says, 'one of the sublimest spectacles offered by nature to man'. Dismounting, they led their horses by the bridles along narrow tracks through the undergrowth, until suddenly the Dutchman seized his arm and pulled him back. He stood at the brink of arrowy waters, hurtling past soundless and foamless, ending downstream in the sky. Still he pressed forward, and still the Dutchman tugged him back; the river seemed to draw him, he fought an involuntary urge to leap in and be lost.

A moment later the same death visited him in another image. His horse, startled by the rattle of a snake in the bushes,[15] reared and shied on the very edge of the Fall. He had wound its reins round his wrist for a better grip, and could not get free; the terrified animal lost hold with its forefeet, slid down the bank, and all seemed over until, with a violent effort of its hindquarters, it recoiled and curvetted back into safety. But even this peril was not enough. He must challenge death once more, just as at Combourg long ago he had tempted his father's gun to kill him not twice, but three times.

Forty yards past the Fall an Indian ladder of twisted creepers led down an almost vertical cliff to the lower basin nearly two hundred feet below. This precarious descent was used by fishing or scavenging

Indians, or by an occasional reckless tourist eager to view the Falls from below; but as a rule it was in worse repair than a similar ladder on the Canadian side, and sensible travellers either brought their own rope, or decided not to risk their lives. François-René found it broken; but despite the Dutchman's remonstrances he started down, clinging to roots and branches, and kept his head though the waters roared and boiled below him. Forty feet from the bottom, swinging by his right hand from the last tree-root, he found no foothold on the naked rock-face; he hung there for two dreadful minutes, feeling his grip weaken, until his numbed fingers opened and he fell. He found himself lying on a ledge within a few inches of the verge, thought he had taken no great harm, and blessed his good luck; but soon, as the cold spray soaked him through, he realised that he had not been let off so lightly. An unbearable pain shot through his left arm; it was broken above the elbow.[16]

He saw the Dutchman's face craning anxiously over the edge far above, and gestured to explain his plight. The man disappeared, and returned with some Indians, who hauled him to the top with ropes of plaited birchbark, and carried him to their village. It was only a simple fracture; they bandaged his arm in two splints and a sling, and in twelve days he was fit to travel again.

Meanwhile, like other travellers in the Niagara villages, he was invited in return for the usual gifts to watch a display of ancestral song and dance. The star was a pretty little girl of fourteen, whom later, when he made her a subsidiary heroine of his Indian epic, he called Mila, a name borrowed from La Hontan's word-list, in which it is said to mean 'give'. She gave everything she had got, to the accompaniment of an orchestra consisting (if its composition was the same as Weld heard in a similar display at Buffalo village) of a drum and two gourds filled with dried peas. First she sang 'something very agreeable', and then he asked her through his interpreter to dance. With an air of ingenuous cunning she mimicked a prisoner tortured and burned at the stake, sang his death-song in a shrill voice like a bird's, fell on her back with slim legs tight closed, mouth open, eyes shut, and died. Then she sprang to life, swam across a river, canoed down rapids, climbed a mountain, and with a mother's brave distress defended her baby (a bunch of scarlet bignonias) from an ambush of enemy warriors. The spectators shouted applause, and François-René, prevented by his broken arm from clapping both hands, slapped his thigh like Olympian Zeus in Homer. He gazed fascinated at the interplay of colours between a blue glass bead hung from her nostrils, and her white teeth, her red lips. The madcap stood motionless before him, delighted with his approval. Then she began, to his appreciative embarrassment, a dance of voluptuous enticement, pausing after each movement to ask: 'Did you like that?' François-René shook his head, she danced again, and

repeated her question. 'He doesn't understand!' explained the Dutchman. She ran up, threw one arm round the neck of this uncomprehend-
ing paleface, and yelled in his ear at the top of her voice. François-René
only laughed. Blushing, or seeming to blush, Mila took his hand,
caressed it with her lips, and bit it with all her might. He snatched it
back, and the savage child in turn went into peals of mirth.

He lingered now, mending his arm, at one of the focal points of the
continent, where trails from Hudson Bay and New Orleans, the
Saskatchewan River and Philadelphia, met from a thousand miles away
and diverged again. He saw passing bands of white men or red, some
travelling westward like himself from New York State or New England
or Lower Canada, others eastward bound from the further Lakes or
from the regions south of Erie. Some of these were fur traders, bringing
last winter's catch from beyond Michillimackinac on the long way to
Quebec; others were outlying tribesmen of the Six Nations from the
Alleghany River or the Erie shore, refugees from American hostility
and the contempt of the western Indians at their uneasy neutrality, come
to seek British protection and the society of their Iroquois fellows. The
tribe of the little dancing girl was among these transients.

What was he next to do? Now that he had reluctantly all but abandoned his transcontinental expedition, constrained by the unanimous
warnings of the Philadelphians and Mr. Swift of Albany, by his own
glimpse of the realities of American travel, by news of war, and by
signs that his journey money might not last for ever, he felt all the more
determined to persist in his 'reconnaissance in the wilderness'. Evidently he must return to civilisation by the close of the year, rather than
winter out in the wilds. But in the three remaining months before the
snows of December he could expect to go far. Why should he not join
one of the groups he now saw stepping westward?

The tribe of the little dancer had moved on. The Dutchman refused
to go further than Niagara, as was his right, for his contract as guide
ended there, and he felt no temptation to risk his scalp with this reckless, arm-breaking youth in the war zone; so François-René paid the
good man off, and saw him setting out homeward for Albany. Then
among the passing bands of travellers he found just what he wanted, a
party of settlers on their way home to their families in Saint-Louis.[17]
Although they would not be likely to indulge his dream of first
'recognising the source of the Mississippi', and although he might not
even have time to accompany them all the way to Saint-Louis, this was
the very town from which he had once hoped to strike due west 'and
reach the waters of the South Sea a little above the Gulf of California'.

He rode off with them, probably on or about 25 August, with his
left arm serviceable though still sore, on the Lake Shore Trail along the
south bank of Erie.

14

OHIO MOUTH

AFTER leaving Niagara François-René might be supposed to have vanished into fairyland, like Carlyle's Frederick the Great after the Battle of Mollwitz. His commentators agree that he cannot have gone where he says he went, even though they are unable to decide where he *does* say he went, or to find evidence that he went anywhere else. Rather than track him past Niagara they would like to take him straight back to Philadelphia. As they have wandered for many years in the wilderness where he spent only a few months, and are lost there still, perhaps it is they, not he, who have been led astray by wanton sprites.

Our task, however, is to explore his vagaries, not theirs. It must be admitted that at this point his itinerary becomes vague, inexplicit, dreamlike, as he turns from the truth of factual realism to the truth of poetic beauty. He sometimes borrows his landscapes from literary sources, so that it is not immediately clear whether he is describing his own travels or quoting Bartram's, or Carver's, or Imlay's. Nonetheless, let us do what has never been done before: let us follow his narrative, attentively and without prejudice, relate it to the circumstances of that period and to the experiences of contemporary travellers, and see whether a clear and credible route can be elicited, and whether he could have accomplished it within the limited time at his disposal. He has, although he is quite unaware of this, or of any need to hasten lest his future commentators should accuse him of lying, three and a half months or about 107 days in which to complete the remainder of his journey; for he was destined to sail for Europe from Philadelphia on 10 December 1791.

At present he is riding by Erie along the Lake Shore Trail, an immemorial highway for red men and traders which led for three hundred miles, all the way to Detroit, mostly on the firm sand of the beach. The route was clear and flat and easy, except if Erie rose high in a gale, whereat one took hurriedly to the clifftop of eroded glacial clay or risked drowning—or if a rivermouth in spate had to be forded by a detour a few hundred yards inland, or even (as old hands knew) by wading one's horse out into the shallow lake. On their left, a few miles south, rose the long low ridge of the watershed, once the old lake shore, or the terminal moraine left by the icesheets of the last glaciation. From the hither slope of this divide the waters flowed to Erie, and thence to the Saint Lawrence and the North Atlantic, in a succession of short, unimpressive rivers—Catteraugus, Conneaut, Ashtabula, Grand, Chagrin, Cuyahoga, Sandusky, Maumee. On the further side the streams joined the Alleghany, or, more to the west, the Ohio, and so emerged down the Mississippi into the Gulf of Mexico, twelve hundred miles away. Perhaps Carver's fable of the Four Rivers was not so far wrong. François-René remembered ever after 'the solitudes of Erie', 'the maples of Erie', beneath which, sitting crosslegged in the doorway of his hut, he saw at last the happy savage whom he sought, 'nature's favourite, who feels much and thinks little, whose only mental processes are his bodily needs, who reaches the results of philosophy as a child does, in the hour between play and sleep'. When this primeval sage emerged from revery to gaze at the sky, François-René in his doctrinaire way interpreted this as 'a look of tender gratitude, as if he looked for some unknown power that takes pity on a poor savage', rather than as a thwarted desire for the palefaces' firewater, horses, and scalps.

Always on their right spread dangerous blue Erie, sometimes glassy smooth, oftener racing with white horses, indistinguishable from the endless ocean (for its northern shore was fifty miles out of sight) except by the taste of its then pure waters, shallowest and stormiest of all the Great Lakes. Here, parallel with the land trail, stretched a much-travelled waterway to the Far West. The British maintained a small navy of four warships on Erie and Huron, to protect their merchant shipping that plied between Buffalo and Michillimackinac; though Colonel Gordon, alarmed by the affair of Colonel Proctor, had warned its captains not to give passage to 'persons unknown, especially in numbers' during the present emergency. The Indians too, as in ages past, still sped in their birchbark canoes from end to end, bringing in furs to Buffalo or returning with trade goods, pursuing their mysterious diplomatic activities in this time of coming war, migrating seasonally with whole clans, travelling when in haste vast distances, a hundred miles a day. François-René saw one such flotilla passing in file, a grim sachem erect at foremost prow and rearmost stern, the plumed heads of the paddling warriors, the dogs straining out on their forepaws, howling, till all vanished in the spindrift of a squall. Who held the key to that savage parade?

One night, when they lodged in a lonely cabin, an extraordinary sound in the nearby waters roused him from sleep. He hurried out, expecting to find a tempest brewing; but the lake lay tranquil, mirroring the crescent new moon as it westered low, while an Indian canoe glided silently past. It was only 'the tide', he decided, deeply impressed, or was so informed by his companions, perhaps mistakenly, but not absurdly.[1]

On the sixth day of their journey his companions quarrelled as to choice of route, and split into three bands. François-René decided to join the group making for Pittsburgh in order to descend the Ohio, 'the one whose peregrination seemed to me to conform most nearly to the plan of my journey'.[2]

Easy portages to the Ohio basin existed at several points on the lake shore, or on the upper waters of rivers flowing into Erie. They had already passed two, the first by Lake Chatauqua and Conewango Creek, and another at Presqu'Ile (the modern Erie) via Fort-aux-Boeufs and French Creek, both leading by a short land haul to streams running into the Alleghany River and so to the Ohio. Others lay ahead, where the Sandusky River gave access to the Scioto and Great Miami, or at the site of modern Toledo, near the end of the lake, where the Maumee River led to the Wabash and the Illinois. All these portages had been frequented since the beginning of the century by white traders and immigrants, and by the Indians since ages past.

The two dissident groups no doubt chose the more westerly routes, although these led for hundreds of miles through the seat of war in the country of the Miamis and Shawnees. Perhaps, as non-belligerent Frenchmen travelling from the British-held western end of the lake to the Spanish-held town of Saint-Louis, they felt confident of safe passage through the Western Indians (with whom they may well already have been on friendly terms), or perhaps they simply had business in Sandusky or Detroit. François-René's group preferred to break off at the present point, somewhere between Presqu'Ile and Sandusky, and make for the upper Ohio. Perhaps in their assessment of the Indian situation they had decided, correctly as we shall see later, that the Ohio route was now safe, or perhaps they chose the great Ohio as more easily navigable than lesser rivers in this dry season, or perhaps they simply had business in Pittsburgh.

Where did François-René leave the shore of Erie, and how did he thence reach Pittsburgh? If this interesting problem has never yet been solved, the fault lies partly with the apparent geographical vagueness of his narrative, but mostly with the negligence of his critics, who have forborne even to mention, still more to discuss it. So let us discuss it now.

He found himself six days' journey from Buffalo, at a place then nameless, but thirty years later, when he tried to remember it, the site of a thriving town and the entrance of a famous new canal. He guessed wildly and mistakenly, but left enough clues for its identification. Then he continues his narrative in the form of an impressionistic and perhaps partly imaginary diary; but this also turns out to contain a sufficiency of verifiable facts which he could only know from experience.

They canoed inland, he says, up a river flowing through a deep wooded valley, until at a fork far upstream they took the southeastern branch, disembarked when this stream became too shallow, and climbed the watershed in search of the river on the further side which would carry them to their destination. After losing their way on the summit plateau they met friendly Indians, who offered to guide them and carry their canoe and baggage over the portage. Here François-René's diary breaks off; but his journey was evidently successful, for we next find him in Pittsburgh.

There is one place along the Erie shore, and one only, which fits and confirms his narrative exactly. At 190 miles from Buffalo, a journey which then took just six days on horseback,[3] is the mouth of the Cuyahoga, which provided the only portage route by river from Lake Erie to Pittsburgh. Here the city of Cleveland was founded five years later, in 1796, and the Cleveland–Ohio canal was constructed in 1827–32. The Cuyahoga led, through country which closely fits François-René's description—a deep valley, a southeastern branch, a summit portage—to the West Branch of the Mahoning, an affluent of the Big Beaver, which joins the Ohio thirty miles below Pittsburgh.

Cuyahoga mouth was closed by a sand bar, forming a natural harbour where canoes put in or were built or cached, and larger vessels on occasion loaded or unloaded goods. The French had maintained a trading station there from the 1740s, the British in the War of Independence made it a base to threaten Pittsburgh, and Jefferson and Washington had long understood its importance as the future site of a great harbour, city, and canal, as the key to the river route and the still more frequented land trail between Detroit and Pittsburgh, and as a crucial link in their plan for a water-way from the Potomac to the Great Lakes. In theory the whole region east of the Cuyahoga already belonged to the United States, by the boundary agreement with England in 1784, the Treaty of Fort McIntosh with the Western Indians in 1785, the resolution of Congress in 1786 declaring the portage routes as common highways, and its incorporation as Washington County by Governor Saint-Clair in 1788. In fact the permanent occupation of the area had to await the solution of the Indian problem by Wayne's victory of Fallen Timbers in 1794, and the long-awaited British evacuation of the Lake forts after Jay's Treaty in 1796. But meanwhile the Cuyahoga way was travelled with canoe or packhorse train by all traders plying between Pittsburgh and Detroit.

At this rivermouth where supply had encountered demand for so many years François-René's party had no difficulty in obtaining a canoe, either from the Indians who visited this neutral district every summer for hunting, or from the white agent, Mr. Neal of Duncan & Wilson of Pittsburgh, who kept a log-cabin store near the strand, or from the Americans who, as the missionary Zeisberger says, were building boats there at that very time;[4] or, most probably, they had left a canoe of their own there on their way out. Their canoe was no doubt the usual trader's craft of birch bark stretched over a cedar frame, with a small sail, paddles and poles, up to twenty feet long and five in beam, large enough to carry ten men and two tons of goods, light enough to be carried across country by five men at walking pace. They perhaps disposed of their horses among the two groups who were riding further, presumably without loss, for horses and saddles were a still more valuable commodity on the frontier than in the towns of the Eastern States.

They ascended the deep wooded gorge of the Cuyahoga due south for thirty miles until, at the site of the modern city of Akron, it bent at right angles eastward. Here they passed on their right the Little Cuyahoga, which flows from Summit (the modern Springfield) Lake eight miles south, whence a short portage led to the headwaters of the Tuscarawa, and then down the Muskingum to the Ohio at Marietta, too far below Pittsburgh for them. Five miles further upstream their course was interrupted by a portage at Cuyahoga Falls, where the river in a series of rapids and cascades descends a height of 200 feet in two miles. François-René's journal begins next afternoon when, he says, 'the sky is pure above my head, the wave limpid beneath my canoe, which flies before a gentle breeze.' Flowering grasses, festoons of blue and white convolvulus and scarlet bignonia, hung from the shale and sandstone cliffs to his left; to the right the scene changed from vast prairies to solitary valleys, bare hills, a cypress forest with sombre portals, a maple-copse with sunlight glancing through the greengold lace of its foliage. Still glided the stream.[5]

'Primitive liberty, I regain thee at last!' cried François-René, in a renewal of consciousness of selfhood inspired by contact with lonely nature, so altruistically beautiful whether or not there is anyone to see. 'Here I am, as the All-Powerful created me, I, sovereign of nature, borne in triumph on the waters, while the dwellers in the flood swim beside me, the tribes of the air sing my hymns, the beasts of the earth do me obeisance, the forests bow their crests as I pass!' But this moment of vision was not exempt from the vanity of philosophic dogmatism. 'On whose brow,' he enquired, 'is the seal of immortal origin set, on social man's, or on mine? Go, shut yourselves in your cities, obey your petty laws; cut one another's throats for a word, or to please your masters; doubt God's existence, or worship him in superstitious forms, while I go roaming through my solitudes. Not a pulse of my heart shall be constrained, not a thought of my mind be fettered; I shall be as free as nature; I shall recognise no King but Him Who kindled the flame of the suns, and with one stroke of His hand set all the worlds rolling.'

Ten miles above the falls, two past the modern university town of Kent, the river forked. The main stream of the Cuyahoga looped back northeast to its springs in the high ground near Lake Erie. They took the southeastern branch, now known as Breakneck Creek, and camped for the night where a tributary brook formed a headland shaded by a clump of tulip-trees. While the others gathered firewood and built their *ajoupa*, our hero took his gun and started, less than a hundred paces away, a covey of wild turkeys, then so conveniently abundant in the woodlands of Ohio and Kentucky, slate-grey, bronze-sheened, succulent, as they fed on sorbs and bracken fronds. He made his bag and the survivors, gobbling their dawn-cry in their treetop roosts, roused the travellers next morning in time for an early start, before the heat of the day.

Again they hoisted their sail, but soon the breeze dropped, the sky grew cloudy and the stream shallow. At noon, probably at the point, some five miles up and a little east of Muddy Lake, where the watershed is narrowest, they beached their canoe, shouldered their provisions and bearskin mattresses, and set off to find the next river, up the forest slope through the dappled halflight, till the endless succession of oaks and hickories gave him, he says, 'the idea of infinity'. Once or twice he glimpsed daylight ahead, but found only a glade of fallen pines, or the melancholy clearing of an Indian cemetery: 'is there any sanctuary where I would more gladly sleep for ever?'

Reclining on his bearskin bed that night he watched the canopy of leaves bloodred in their firelight, the nearer trunks like pillars of crimson granite, the further like a waiting circle of grey ghosts. He blew his horn (so it did come in useful after all), and listened to the echoes dying, dying. The fire dimmed, a tree fell roaring far away, one of his comrades groaned in sleep ('You suffer, therefore you exist,' he reflected), the wind hurried over the treetops and all the forest murmured like waves on a seashore. He heard, as he sank into slumber, the bullfrogs bellowing in a nearby marsh.

Next morning they splashed through one of the expanses of peat-bog, traversed by a packhorse track reinforced by withies laid from tussock to tussock, which were then characteristic of the portage way and of the land trail that here coincided with it. So far François-René's diary narrative has given a factual account of their portage journey, describing the Cuyahoga country with an accuracy which could only come from personal experience. In the next episode, however, his purpose momentarily changes; his story, without ceasing to be true, becomes composite in place and time, with the evident intention of conveying a generalised and poetic impression of travel in America. They climbed a slippery, heather-clad mountain-side for five hours, he says, from one in the afternoon till six, in search of a view of their river; they looked at last from the summit, beside a hurtling waterfall, over a green sea of forest islanded with rocks far below; and after camping for a second night, they spent all the third day returning empty-handed to their canoe. His ascent of the mountain rings true, and may well be a memory of his crossing of the Cumberlands, two months and fifteen hundred miles later;[6] but it does not belong to the portage country, where the watershed was lowlying and gentle in contours, and no more than two hours' walk across. But the forest and the corduroy-tracked marshland which precede this interpolation are authentic and in their right place, and so are the incidents of the 'third' day (though we may prefer to regard this as really the second) of their quest for the new river.

On the way back, as they breakfasted in a cloud of mosquitoes under an aged willow wreathed with climbing gourds, their Indian guides, ears to ground, announced that another party was approaching from two hours' march away. Sure enough, up came an Indian family with the ritual cry of welcome, which the travellers thankfully returned, and capped this traditional boast. 'We,' they affirmed, 'have heard you for two days. We knew you were palefaces, because your steps are heavy and your path is not straight.' The next river, they said, was only five miles away, and they offered (no doubt they were in the district to await customers, like the Tuscaroras of the Niagara portage) to help to carry the canoe and baggage. The squaws cooked, and all enjoyed, a supper of François-René's turkey with salmon trout from the stream. And so the diary breaks off.

Five miles? Perhaps the Indians meant that, in this dry season of late summer, the nearest navigable point was thus far. In point of fact Breakneck Creek and Mahoning West Branch here run parallel, the former from the south and the latter from the north, no more than three miles apart.[7] The watershed between was no mountain but a low plateau of forested knolls and shallow peat-bog valleys, nowhere rising more than 150 feet above the two streams. So they retraced their steps and made the portage, a morning's stroll for those with no burden, along the short path which can be seen both in old and in present-day maps, in the appropriately named Portage County, where the modern highway along the old track, a mile south of the modern Ravenna, is still called Summit Road. They reached Mahoning West Branch near the point where it turns due east, and its valley is now submerged beneath West Branch Reservoir, six miles long. Somewhere here the stream became deep enough to float their canoe, and they hurried down its moving waters towards the Ohio, sixty miles away.

They floated by half-deserted Indian villages in a country that the white man still hesitated to occupy. They passed Mahoning Old Town, now Newton Falls, twelve miles downstream where West and East Branch meet; then Salt Springs, the modern Weathersfield, where a mixed team of white men and Indians boiled the brine for salt that was traded all the way to New Orleans; then Kiskuskies, at the fork where the Shenango joins the Mahoning to form the Big Beaver; and at last, under the steep bluff crowned with the stockade of Fort McIntosh, they emerged into the broad Ohio, five hundred yards wide. Pittsburgh lay thirty miles upstream, no more than a normal day's journey, for the Ohio was easy to mount by keeping to the slack eddying water near the bank, and with help from sail or pole. For their journey of about 170 miles from Cuyahoga mouth we may reasonably assign seven days: two up the Cuyahoga, two on the portage, two down the Mahoning–Big Beaver, and one to Pittsburgh. If so, then François-René landed in Pittsburgh on or about 7 September 1791.

'An irregular, poorly built place,' Colonel John May from Connecticut called it in 1788, 'of about 150 houses, mostly built of logs.' 'I believe there are two dogs to a man in this place,' he adds, and refers not unfairly to these fourfooted natives, who had kept him awake with their barking, as 'sons of bitches'. Pittsburgh, founded in 1765 round the ramparts and ravelins of the old French Fort Duquesne, renamed Fort Pitt by the victorious British, was still a small, ramshackle frontier town, already smoke-palled with house-fires fuelled from the famous hill of coal at the mouth of the Monongahela opposite. The people were merchants, tavern-keepers, boatbuilders, riverboat men, and transients. The trade and immigration routes of the continent, from Detroit, Saint-Louis, New York, Philadelphia, New Orleans, converged and radiated here. Philadelphia, whence François-René in his desire to see Indian country and Niagara and wilderness had come round about, lay only ten days' ride east, 295 miles, across the Alleghenies. If he had chosen to return direct from Pittsburgh, he could have caught his boat with twelve weeks to spare. But he says he went down the Ohio with his Saint-Louis companions, and we have found no reason to disbelieve him.

He does not reveal in what kind of boat, whether pirogue, keelboat, flatboat, or barge. Certainly they must have left their bark canoe, for these frail vessels were used on the powerful Ohio only by Indians or for local journeys.[8] A pirogue was a dug-out of sycamore, cypress or pine, often built from two logs each hollowed to serve as a side with planks joining the two halves, steered with a stern-oar and propelled by poles, oars, or sails; a large pirogue might be fifty feet long and five in beam, and carry up to thirty men and forty tons of freight, yet draw hardly two feet of water. A keelboat was designed with keel and prow for the special needs of two-way traffic, to descend to all points as far as New Orleans with whisky, tobacco, furs, salt or flour, and then toil home against the current, poled by six men a side at thirty miles a day in the slack water by the bank, with a fiddler to cheer them and an hourly breather, carrying a return freight of sugar and fancy goods—a tough but wellpaid life, with a hundred per cent profit to the owner. Simplest of all was the flatboat, a fifty by twelve feet oblong square-ended roofed box of oak boards, which drifted down with heavy cargo or immigrants with their goods and livestock, and was sold as timber at its destination, being incapable of return upstream; so that the forts at Marietta and Cincinnati, the stores and elegant villas of Louisville, were built mostly of dismantled flatboats. Fastest of all, but used mainly by the army for high-ranking officers with a picked team of soldier oarsmen, was the barge.[9]

The immigrant traffic down the Ohio, as even old hands admitted, was 'immense', 'almost incredible'. The settlers came over the mountains from Philadelphia, or from New England and New York by the Genesee Trail and Lake Erie like François-René (except that they usually preferred the shorter portage route by Presqu'Ile, French Creek and the Allegheny River). Then they took passage downstream at Pittsburgh, mostly bound for Kentucky, where the population had risen from 30,000 to 100,000 in the seven years since the peace. Accurate statistics were kept on General Harmar's orders by the duty officer at his headquarters, Fort Harmar at the mouth of the Muskingum opposite Marietta. In the year ending June 1789 eight hundred boats containing twenty thousand people with their horses, cattle and goods had passed Fort Harmar. In the summer of 1791, when Pittsburgh was the base for the mustering and supply of Saint-Clair's army, the river was busier than ever. Certainly François-René's party can have had no difficulty in finding an immediate passage.

From Pittsburgh to the junction of Ohio and Mississippi was a voyage of 980 miles, passing (to name only towns which then already existed) by Wheeling (91 miles), Marietta (172 miles), Gallipolis (264 miles), Limestone, the modern Maysville (392 miles), Cincinnati (449 miles), and Louisville (581 miles). The journey down the moving highway of the river was effortless and surprisingly fast, for one's boat drifted, even if unpropelled by sail or oar, with the speed of the Ohio itself, five or even six miles an hour when the river was full, two or three when the water was low, for up to twenty-four hours a day.[10] 'Our passage down the Ohio is too delightful to be described by me,' wrote Colonel May, whose flatboat in May 1788 made the ninety-one miles to Wheeling in seventeen hours and reached Marietta the following day: 'we are passing one lovely island after another . . . Without wind or waves we, insensibly almost, make more than five miles an hour.'

May's experience was in no way exceptional. John Pope, travelling only a few months before François-René, reached Limestone in five days in November 1790, and in March 1791 floated 440 miles from Louisville to New Madrid on the Mississippi in seven days. Thomas Dean in 1817, in an oared boat manned partly by friendly Indians, arrived in Pittsburgh from Buffalo in six days by the Lake Chatauqua portage, travelled 112 miles downstream in one day, reached Cincinnati in five days, and Louisville in three more. These not unusual times, however, were far surpassed by the army barges. In May 1788 Saint-Clair's subordinates General Harmar and Major Ebenezer Denny sped 160 miles from Franklin on the Allegheny River to Pittsburgh in fifteen hours on the twelve-oar barge *Congress*. The same rapid Harmar reached Marietta from Pittsburgh in two days, Louisville from Marietta in four, and Delaware Old Town 180 miles below Louisville in two. George Rogers Clark in 1778, in his famous dash from Louisville to capture Kaskaskia on the upper Mississippi, arrived at Fort Massac, 350 miles below Louisville and only 40 above Ohio mouth, in two days. These times, if put together, give a possible record trip of eight days from Pittsburgh to the Mississippi. Even the unaided flatboats, riding on a full river, sometimes took as little as ten days. But an ordinary flatboat passage was generally reckoned as ten days to Louisville and five more to Ohio mouth.

There is no need to claim an ususually speedy passage for François-René. Perhaps his journey took even a little longer than usual, for he travelled in a season when the river was often low. On the other hand, he may have been lucky, for at any time in the year a sudden freshet (known on the Ohio as a 'tide') might be sent down by rain in the upper basins of the Allegheny and Monongahela, and the river would run fast and deep again. Moreover the yearly autumn rise at the beginning of October was no more than three weeks away, and may have come early that year, for available evidence suggests that the river in September 1791 was not unduly shallow.[11] Perhaps we may reasonably allow him, erring if at all on the generous side, about eighteen days for his voyage down the Ohio.

But he tells us little of his river-journey, perhaps because he neglected to take notes, or perhaps because any such notes were among the materials which he left behind him in France next year, and so lost for ever. Instead he presents, in *Voyage en Amérique*, a disquisition on the antiquities, topography, and natural history of the Ohio, magnificently re-orchestrated from sources which remain partly unidentified. This procedure may be regretted by the biographer, but can hardly be blamed by the critic, so aesthetically satisfying is the consequent mingling of factual precision with a sense of melancholy desolation.

François-René's Ohio is a river of solitude, without mention of the new townships of the 1780s, perhaps because his literary sources preceded the news of their foundation. As he floated through the wilderness he preferred to ignore these puny outposts of the present, and contemplated instead the enigmatic monuments of a vanished past. All the way down the river he saw, as no doubt he expected from his previous reading and from conversations with the cultivated gentlemen of

Philadelphia, the already celebrated earthworks of a lost civilisation. The conical burial tumuli, sacrificial pyramids, and fortified enclosures of the Mound Builders rose everywhere from the bluffs at river-mouths. One of the largest of these complexes covered the promontory at the mouth of the Muskingum, on the site of the newly-founded Marietta. The settlers showed him the spot where Manasseh Cutler, just three years ago, had counted tree-rings, observed a second-generation oak, and correctly deduced from these up-to-date dendrochronological methods that the mounds were built long before the arrival of Columbus.[12]

He returned alone after nightfall, when the waning moon shone over the silent graves and primeval forests. Vague thoughts passed through him, of men and women he had left and would perhaps see again, of the lost people of these wastes who would never return. Was not every man, he meditated, like himself at this moment on that sepulchral cone, 'poised in the present between past and future, as on a rock between two abysses? Behind him, before him, all is darkness. He discerns, at most, only the few wraiths who rise from one gulf or the other, swim for an instant at the surface, and sink to the depths once more.' 'Even I,' he wrote with boastful modesty in *La Génie du Christianisme*, 'solitary lover of nature, guileless confessor of the Divinity, have sat on these ruins. Traveller without renown, I have conversed with these relics as obscure as myself.'

The gay, misused Frenchmen of Gallipolis, ninety miles further downstream, had another such prehistoric mound of their own, which they planted out as a pleasure-garden, with a pretty little summer-house on the top. Their land, they were distressed to find, did not legally belong to them although they had paid for it; but no one wished to eject them, and the defaulting Scioto Company had the decency, before going bankrupt, to provide homes for their arrival and food, in the form of boatloads of flour from Pittsburgh and resident white hunters to shoot game, for their first winter. Already the multitudinous traffickers of the Ohio, merchants, immigrants, and military, made Gallipolis a regular port of call. Their neatly whitewashed log cabins, in four rows of twenty, each with a clubhouse at the end, their twice-weekly dances, their flourishing gardens of watermelon, salads, tobacco, cotton, the 'perfect' hams made from their pigs, their 'excellent bread and good venison', were admired by all. Even their luxury craftsmen, so unjustly ridiculed, did a roaring trade in home-made watches, compasses, sundials, barometers, thermometers, 'the finest ever seen', or took orders for carved mantelpieces, twelve or twenty-two guineas apiece, from General Putnam at Marietta or 'a Spanish gentleman in New Orleans'. So their lot was not so miserable, nor they themselves so feckless, as their later historians have represented. One of their dignitaries, the young Vicomte Hippolyte de Malartie, was serving as

volunteer aide to Saint-Clair, who next year gave them a garrison of
fifty regulars for protection against the Indians. François-René knew
very well about the Gallopolitans, but passed them by as guardedly in
his writings as on the river itself, for he did not wish them to spoil his
image of an unpeopled Ohio. Perhaps his party called there for eggs and
milk, or perhaps they floated past in the night. He says only: 'This
region is beginning, in 1791, to be populated by colonies belonging to
Pennsylvania, Virginia, and North Carolina, and by certain of my unfortunate countrymen fleeing before the first storms of the Revolution.'[13]

His sole allusion to the Indian war is still more oblique. The red
men's raids on Ohio boats had persisted since the peace and increased
since 1788; a notoriously dangerous spot was opposite the mouth of
the Scioto, where warriors in canoes lurked in ambush while their
lookouts gazed upstream for victims from a high rock on the Kentucky
shore. But business was business, and this peril did not deter traffic on
the river, as contemporary narratives and statistics amply show.
Curiously enough, however, at the very period of François-René's
passage, on the eve of outright war, the Ohio was safe for the first time
in many years. The stream was swept clear by military traffic, while the
savage warriors had evacuated the river district at the end of last winter,
and now massed far inland, on the headwaters of the Wabash and
Miami, to protect their towns, crops, and women and children.

Even Saint-Clair and his army were suddenly invisible. The General
had sent out three costly and ineffectual expeditions in preparation for
his own campaign, the first under Harmar in October 1790, along his
own future route up the Miami, and the second and third, under Scott
in May and Wilkinson in August 1791, to intimidate the Shawnees on
the Wabash from joining the Miami tribes. Early in September, just
before François-René passed by, he moved his troops from Cincinnati
to their advance base at the newly built Fort Hamilton on the Great
Miami. Saint-Clair was old and ill, quite brave, always busy and first up
in the mornings, but not very good at war. The season was already too
late, but still he must wait for Mr. Knox the war minister, and Mr.
Knox's friends the fraudulent contractors, to send him his last men and
supplies. What men!—levies 'purchased from prisons, wheelbarrows
and brothels at two dollars a month will never answer for fighting
Indians!' What supplies!—tents and clothing 'truly infamous', powder
'extremely weak', packsaddles 'large enough for elephants', shoes that
lasted 'not more than four days', axes that 'bend up like dumplings'.
But President Washington sent weekly exhortations, enjoining him 'by
every principle that is sacred, to stimulate your exertions in the highest
degree, and to move as rapidly as the lateness of the season will permit'.
Saint-Clair obeyed, with death in his soul. François-René doubtless
heard of all this, but saw nothing. He kept his vision of the noble

savage unimpaired, stuck to his philosophic conviction that every
Indian would be your friend if treated with kindness, and wrote truly
enough: 'Whenever I found myself exposed to danger in America, the
peril came always from the place I was in and from my own imprudence'
—as in his fall at Niagara—'but almost never from the natives.'

So his passage by this fringe of war remained quite unscathed, half
unaware, almost unmentioned. But he retained impressions which were
to enhance the quality of personal experience in his Indian epic and to
transform its central theme. Already, like his future hero René, he had
been welcomed as a brother by a noble savage (the vermilion-accepting,
hand-shaking youth on Tonawanda Creek); he had lived like René in
an Indian village, been healed by their medicine-men, sat with the
smoking warriors on the laughing green, and virtuously resisted the
caresses of a dancing maiden. Now he saw, or all but saw, a war of
liberation very like the one in *Les Natchez*, an almost ideological conflict between the heartless civilisation which, as a philosopher, he rejected, and the noble savage with whom he identified himself. In his
epic he transmuted a local rebellion on the Lower Mississippi into a
universal confederation of all the American tribes to free their continent
from the white man. The conflict of 1791 was recognised as similarly
universal, not only by the philosophic mind of François-René, but by
the Indians themselves and by the American government. Everywhere
along the vast half-circle from Canada to Georgia the tribes were in
ferment, encouraged and armed by the British in the north, the Spanish
in south and west, while Washington's envoys in this very summer,
Colonel Proctor to the Six Nations at Buffalo, Governor Blount in
Tennessee among the Cherokees, John Pope among the Creeks in
Alabama, were endeavouring to calm them with gifts and good advice.
Contingents of young bloods from tribes far away, Cherokees from
Tennessee, Chippewas and Ottawas of Upper Canada beyond Detroit,
Mohawks from Niagara, had joined Little Turtle and his Miamis, Blue
Jacket and his Shawnees, to await Saint-Clair's assault. When François-
René mustered in the grand council of his epic spokesmen from all
these, together even with Eskimos from Labrador and Sioux from the
Great Plains, he only exaggerated a little.

So he floated by Cincinnati and the adjacent Fort Washington,
whence Saint-Clair had ridden to join his army at Fort Hamilton only
a few days before, on 15 September, and passed the spot where, as he
wrote grandly borrowing from Imlay, 'at the confluence of the Kentucky and Ohio the landscape deploys an extraordinary magnificence'.[14]
Imlay also supplied his description of the Falls at Louisville, and the
hills of Silver Creek, 'ever rising heavenward as they recede, till their
summit struck with light takes the colour of the sky and vanishes
away'. The Falls were not very formidable; the river descended twenty

feet in two miles over harmless rapids which downstream traffic rode unhindered. Louisville, the last white man's town till New Madrid 440 miles below, had a hundred houses, some of two stories with verandahs, containing ladies who carried parasols, and gentlemen who played billiards, wore silk stockings on Sundays, and danced with the ladies. Land trails set off southward to Nashville on the Cumberland, west to Vincennes and Saint-Louis, east to the Kentucky towns of Danville and Lexington, and thence over the Alleghanies at Cumberland Gap to Richmond or Philadelphia, 830 miles away. François-René could have regained civilisation within five weeks, for the journey to Philadelphia took no longer, but preferred to remain with his companions on the delightful Ohio. They in turn could have reached Saint-Louis in a fortnight, either overland or by ascending the Wabash from its mouth 230 miles further downstream; but they kept to the Ohio, perhaps mistrusting the temper, even towards Frenchmen, of the Shawnees now on the warpath.

Below the Wabash came other meetings of ways, the sites of future towns,[15] then still without permanent habitation, but frequented by transient merchants, migrants, military, and friendly Indians. At the mouths of the Cumberland and Tennessee Rivers eastbound travellers paused before leaving the Ohio by land-trail or river for Nashville or Muscle Shoals, and met incoming traders or migrants bound from Virginia or the Carolinas, for New Orleans or the Illinois. Next, on the west bank ten miles below Tennessee mouth, one found the ghostly ramparts of Fort Massac, abandoned by the French in 1763, not yet reoccupied by the American army (as it was in 1795), but still the frequented starting-point of the land trail to Kaskaskia and Saint-Louis. But his companions probably completed their homeward way by water, proceeding thirty-five miles further down to Ohio mouth and turning north up the Mississippi.

Here at Ohio mouth was the furthest point of François-René's journey. He noticed at their confluence—where now stands the city of Cairo, and the mile-wide rivers are spanned by tremendous roadbridges —how the transparent Ohio and turbid Mississippi forebore at first to mingle, 'like a bridal pair of enemy blood, reluctant to unite their destinies in the bed of wedlock'. Saint-Louis, his comrades' destination and the proper base of departure for his expedition to the Pacific, was only a week or 170 miles upstream. But his present advisers gave him no more encouragement than their predecessors. 'I recognised on the edge of the Natchez country the same impossibilities as those announced to me by Mr. Swift of Albany, and realised how much I lacked for the assault of the Rocky Mountains.'[16] Then again, he 'felt rather tempted to descend to New Orleans', or even to the delta—'but what would have been the object of visiting the Mississippi mouths, when my intended way lay northward?' he asked, and added an even stronger reason: 'I needed to draw nearer to the United States, my resources were beginning to give out.' Honour was satisfied, he had pressed his reconnaissance as far as possible before winter, and besides, he remarks, 'I was so delighted with my wanderings that I had almost stopped thinking of the Pole. The poet had overcome the traveller; I roved for the sake of roving, with dreams my only goal.'

The town of Natchez itself, then Spanish but thronged with French, English and American settlers, was 650 miles further down the Mississippi, a journey of from ten to fourteen days. He had read in Raynal, and again in Du Pratz and Dumont, the old unhappy story of the massacre of his countrymen by the Natchez Indians sixty-two years before, the extermination of their tribe by the avenging French, and the flight of the few survivors to the Chicassaws, whose country he now glimpsed only a mile away on the southwest bank of the Mississippi. Perhaps it was at this moment that he resolved to make the Natchez, and the arrival among them of a young French exile, like himself, the theme of his epic. Only an unjust shortage of money and time prevented him from setting foot in their town, which lay so near and yet so far down the great river; but he saw it in imagination, and saw with the eyes of the flesh the land of their banishment.[17]

Indeed, he had 'reached the Natchez country' not only in this historical sense, but also, as his own words specify, in terms of the political situation at that very time. 'When I touched upon the Natchez country (*quand je touchais aux Natchez*) in 1791, nothing as yet was settled in that region: Spain was in nominal possession of Louisiana but was nowhere in effective control.' In fact, the tenuous fringe of Spanish Louisiana along the west bank of the Mississippi from Natchez to New Madrid and up to Saint-Louis was administered from Natchez by the governor Don Gayoso.[18] So François-René at Ohio Mouth could reasonably claim to have 'touched upon' the region of which the town of Natchez was then the political and administrative centre. Lest he should give the impression of having gone still further, he added a disclaimer: 'I have described only the upper Mississippi, which I saw in passing'. His imprecise terms suggest a regret that he had not penetrated a little further into the southland of his epic, perhaps even a willingness to allow an unwary reader to suppose that he had done so. But he has defined closely enough the furthest limit and the turning-point of his journey. He has reached Ohio mouth, caught a passing glimpse of the Mississippi and the Louisiana shore, and re-entered the Ohio, homeward bound. In the next episode of his narrative, sure enough, he is back on the Ohio.

THE TWO FLORIDIANS

HE travelled now through the closing days of September, the pleasant Moon of Big Chestnuts, when in Kentucky (as Imlay remembered) 'it was the climate of paradise'. In those last reaches the majestic river floated clear and smooth, a mile wide, a moving lake, through lush flatlands which belonged already to the south. Magnolia, tulip-tree, papaw and liquidambar flourished in the woodlands, green parrakeets with yellow breasts flocked in their branches, alligators (though only small ones) and turtles loitered past bison herding to drink in the shallows, jolly bears held noisy bathing parties or clambered conspicuously in the topmost boughs, devouring wild grapes. But even his real experience of this exotic setting seemed not quite adequate to the inner truth of the adventure of the Two Floridians, when he came to write it thirty years after.

In the manuscript materials of his *Voyage en Amérique* he found, at this point, a patchwork description of the Deep South, a composite landscape of river, lake, island and savannah, which he had compiled and translated long ago[1] from Bartram's *Travels*, together with a few hints from Charlevoix, linking the extracts with comments, descriptions and meditations of his own. Here ready to hand—in a text which already half belonged to him, since he had felt and assimilated its beauty, and transposed its Anglo-American music into his native language and the sonorities of his own prose—was the atmosphere he required, of light, heat, colour, of poetry and strangeness, surprise and bliss, for the episode of the Two Floridians in his Memoirs.

Bartram had registered his observations a thousand miles away, among the everglades of Florida and the horse-breeding savannahs of Alabama and Georgia. Bartram's finest pictures were too tropical for the Ohio, even here, so far south and near the borders of Tennessee and Louisiana. So Chateaubriand scrupulously omitted the roaring alligators, the golden Bartram's minnows, the *agave vivipara*, and other such marvels which belonged solely to the Floridas. But he felt entitled to retain sights which were common to Bartram and to his own experience on the Ohio—such as magnolias and liquidambars, a turtle, a prehistoric mound—together with scenes and meditations which were all his own work, a fishing expedition to an island, and a sunset followed by night thoughts.

Even the island in its river-lake was to be found both in Bartram and on the Ohio. In Bartram this is Drayton's Island in Lake George on the Saint John's River in Florida. On the Ohio we may confidently identify it with the island at the mouth of the Tennessee River (Island 97, counting downstream from Pittsburgh, in Cramer's *Navigator*), a favourite rendezvous for river-men, and facetiously known as Barataria, after Sancho Panza's kingdom in *Don Quixote*. Then again, as other travellers of that time remarked, the Ohio with its smooth serpentine reaches a mile wide was very like a succession of lakes. Perhaps we may also consent to believe in the band of traders, arriving from the east to attend an Indian horse-fair, with whom François-René now takes up after parting with his friends from Saint-Louis. True, he blends even these with similar traffickers encountered by Bartram far away in Florida at Cuscowilla or on the Alachua savannah. But certainly both time and place were suitable for such a meeting. The demands of Saint-Clair's cavalry and baggage-trains in that summer had denuded all Kentucky of horses; and there is contemporary evidence of horse-traders in the vicinity.[2]

Thus boldly, not to say high-handedly, but without intent to deceive, Chateaubriand refashioned from his own composite translation of Bartram, confining himself mostly to details which were common to Bartram's experience and his own, the partly imaginary setting for his true encounter with the Two Floridians.

They hoisted sail on their pirogue before a cool morning breeze, and landed on the island in the Ohio. At first François-René—or his youthful ghost as summoned by his older self long after—wandered botanising through the motley landscape of his Bartram pastiche. At one moment he crossed a meadow flowering with yellow *senecio jacobea*, pink-plumed hibiscus, and crimson-tufted *lobelia cardinalis*, and mused upon an Indian mound; all these had been remarked by Bartram on Drayton's Island in Florida, but were perhaps also to be found on or near Island 97 in the Ohio. Next he feigned to notice the new evening primrose (*oenothera pyramidalis*) which Bartram had discovered in its sole habitat, the Mobile delta in Alabama; then he encountered a brook garlanded with Venus's flytraps seen by Bartram in Brunswick County, North Carolina, round which murmured a 'multitude of ephemera' (mayflies) from St. John's River, Florida, accompanied by humming-birds from St. Simon's Island, Georgia, and butterflies from Mosquito River, Florida. Yet his reflections in real life, as he observed for old Malesherbes not these plants and creatures but those that were actually there, were his own and not Bartram's. For the first time, at this turning-point of his journey, the memory of France struck him less with passing nostalgia than with a sense of duty neglected. 'How futile, after all, are my studies!' he cried. 'Can it be that the Revolution, whose weight I felt when it drove me into the wilderness, inspires in me no more serious thought? Am I not devoting to flowers, butterflies and descriptions the very hours of my country's ruin?'

At this instant another reality broke in upon his dream. Round a bend in the river glided a flotilla of canoes, some sped by paddles and some by sails, bearing Indians and halfbreeds—the notorious *Bois-brûlés*, so called from the charred complexion of their faces—from the Creek country and the Floridas. As they disembarked he was taken aback by the elegant gaiety of these southerners, so different from the grim pride of the Iroquois he had seen in the north. The men were imposingly tall, and so, contrary to their reputation for being the tiniest in all America, were their womenfolk; but these ladies, it was explained to him, happened not to be pure Siminoles but the offspring of native squaws and Spanish traders. One pair whom he particularly noticed might have been creole beauties from San Domingo, were it not for a yellow hue and delicate mien which reminded him of the Hindu maidens he had seen long ago by the Ganges in visions with the Sylphide. Their oval faces, their umbered skin that seemed to glow from beneath a wisp of orange smoke, their hair so soft and dark, their long eyes screened by satin eyelids slowly opening, the double seduction of Indian femininity and Spanish, everything about them brought a sense of indefinable mystery. They were cousins, he was told, the daughters by Siminole women of two brothers from Castille.

His trader companions turned to business, for these were the horse-selling Indians they had come to meet. They decided to move camp to the mainland, a plain thronged with horses and half-wild cattle, where flocks of cranes, turkeys and pelicans striped the green distance of the savannah with white, black, pink. But even these hard traffickers, he found, were agitated by passions, 'not of rank, education or prejudice, but of nature, untrammelled and unimpaired, proceeding directly to their goal, witnessed only by a fallen tree in an untrodden forest, a valley that could never be rediscovered, a river without name'. He learned sad tales of Indian maids abandoned by white lovers in Pensacola; he heard and noted down a famous ballad of Tabamica the 'painted girl', a chief's daughter who infatuated an honest trader and brought him to ruin by giving his goods to her Siminole relatives.

Next day, when the others went hunting, he stayed behind with the women and children. Neither he nor the two Floridians understood a word of one another's speech, but he won their confidence by bringing water for their cup, twigs for their fire, moss for their bed. They wore short frocks and voluminous slashed sleeves in Spanish fashion, but their jackets and mantles were Indian, and their bare legs were cross-gartered with lace of birch bark. They festooned themselves with glass necklaces, plaited their hair with rushes and nosegays, hung pendants of purple seedgrains in their ears, tethered a pretty green parrakeet like an emerald to their shoulders, rubbed their breasts and arms with the juice of *apoya* or galingale, and chewed in their blue-white teeth beads of resin from the liquidambar or sweetgum tree. So they dwelt in a perfumed atmosphere that emanated from themselves, a mingled sweetness in which he identified scents of angelica, citron, vanilla. Shyly emboldened, he helped to deck their hair, and they in gentle alarm let him have his way; witches themselves, they supposed he must be binding them with a spell. Their characters, he began to understand, were not quite alike. The elder was proud, the younger sad. The proud one seemed half Christian, for she kept saying her prayers. The other sang in a velvet voice, uttering at the end of each refrain a startling cry. They fell into animated conversation, in which he seemed to detect a tone of jealousy; then the sad one dissolved into tears, and all was silence. It was high time, he thought, to suggest a fishing party.

They crossed to the island by pirogue. In the heat of the afternoon he bathed, wearing blue cotton trousers for decency and a broad-brimmed hat of rice-straw for protection against the sun, in a grotto formed by the gnarled roots of a swamp-cypress. The cousins came to watch him swim and then, wrapping themselves with equal modesty in ample gowns of mulberry cloth, plunged in beside him. Only their dark heads appeared above the water, like the heads of two Naiads; swans oared round them; 'it was enough to drive one mad'.

A friendly turtle emerged on the bank; they adorned it with sweet pea, clematis, and fresh grass. The proud one sat on its back, while the sad one gave it hickory milk from a tube of cane.

From behind a screen of catalpas and tulip-trees, through a grove of oaks trailing white skeins of Spanish moss, the sun cast lengthening pillars and creeping arabesques of shadow on the lawns, then darted a red ray through the foliage, like a carbuncle set in sombre green. Ruined towers and promontories of cloud toppled apart to reveal opening furnace mouths, growing heaps of glowing embers, flowing streams of lava. The sky became a sea of diamonds and sapphires, in which the sun, half submerged, seemed to dissolve. In the south a wan moon poised above the distant hills of the Tennessee valley.[3]

The cousins had vanished. He sat against a magnolia tree, in darkness outlined by frozen light. Fireflies shone in the branches, and then, as they entered the moonbeams, were extinguished. He heard the rise and fall of ripples, the splash of leaping trout, the cry of a water-hen, and tried in vain to remember what had happened to him, or who he was. He became a growing plant in the living nature round him. His sleep floated on a vague ocean of infinite hope.

He rose long afterwards from this oblivion to find himself between two women. Their heads rested on his shoulders; perhaps they were really asleep, or perhaps they were only pretending. A passing breeze showered pink magnolia petals. The sad one began to sing again; her languorous melody seemed to percolate along his blood, to be on the point of entering his heart and soul, of provoking who could tell what reckless and irremediable passion!—when suddenly a man's harsh shout replied. The Floridians started and sprang to their feet; a *Bois-brûlé* was calling them from the mainland; dawn was in the sky.

They returned in silence to the opposite bank. Thirty years after François-René still remembered the sad one's shamefaced smile when the paddle resisted her weary arms.

The traders raised camp at noon to attend the horse-market. Stallions and mares of all ages and colours, colts and fillies, bulls, cows and heifers fled and galloped round them. In the confusion he found himself parted from the Creeks. Far away, by the edge of a wood, he descried a dense group of men and horses, and with them the two cousins! Vigorous hands lifted them in the air and planted them on the cruppers of two mares, which a halfbreed and a Siminole bestrode bareback. The savage squadron reared, leaped, kicked, whinnied, with clashing bloody hooves and flying manes, then hurtled away in an eddying cloud of devouring flies. His Floridians disappeared, like the daughter of Ceres ravished by the dark god of the underworld.

He enquired of the guides, and was informed that the *Bois-brûlé*, lover of one of the girls, being jealous of the paleface, had resolved to remove them both from his attentions with the aid of the Siminole, the other cousin's brother. The guides, with no deference to his feelings, referred to them unceremoniously as 'painted girls', that is, common strumpets. Most humiliating of all, his successful rival the halfbreed was a thin, hideous, sootfaced fellow who looked exactly like a mosquito. The wilderness seemed empty indeed after this misadventure; the Sylphide, magnanimously hastening to console her faithless lover, found herself for once ill received; and he determined to make for civilisation with all speed. But he took with him on his homeward way the images of the Two Floridians, restoring to them the chastity which they had never possessed in reality, but would keep for ever in the world of imagination. Of the proud one he made the unattainable virgin Atala, of the sad one the virtuous wife Céluta.

He gives his return route with unusual precision, but with lamentable carelessness he (or a secretary) inserted it in the wrong place, between his arrival at Ohio mouth and the adventure (still on the Ohio) of the Two Floridians.[4] His commentators have been baffled by the discrepancy, but have not seen this simple and certain explanation, nor even understood that this was and must have been his way back. 'We took our course,' he says, 'towards the regions then known by the general name of the Floridas, where nowadays the States of Alabama, Georgia, South Carolina and Tennessee are extended. We followed more or less

5 Tour du Chat,
Combourg Castle

Combourg Castle, 'silence, darkness,
and face of stone'

Signatures of Chateaubriand, as a boy aged eleven and thirteen,
at the marriage contracts and wedding of (above) his sisters
Bénigne and Marie-Anne, 8 and 11 January 1780, and of
(below) his sister Julie, 20 and 23 April 1782

Arrival at Combourg in *Mémoires d' Outre-Tombe*, from
the autograph MS of an early version

6 Heads of Foulon (right, with hay in his mouth) and Bertier,
23 July 1789, as sketched on the spot by Girodet

The storming of the Bastille, 14 July 1789

the trails now linked by the great highroad that leads from Natchez to Nashville via Jackson and Florence, and re-enters Virginia via Knoxville and Salem.' This in fact was already, from Nashville onwards, the normal route from the lower Ohio to the eastern seaboard in the 1790s. Its daily stages and travel-times can be verified, and his veracity checked and proved, from various contemporary narratives, none of which were published in his lifetime. Such, then, was his long way to Philadelphia, some 960 miles to the east and north, though he tells us little more about it. For a young gentleman traveller in reduced circumstances, retreating from an unsuccessful effort to discover the Northwest Passage, crestfallen after his loss of the Two Floridians, it may have seemed an unmemorable anticlimax when compared with Niagara and the Ohio.

The trail from Tennessee mouth immediately left the Tennessee valley, which here bent far to the southeast, and followed the nearby Cumberland River eastward past the still nameless huts of Eddyville and Clarksville to the thriving town of Nashville—a distance of 120 miles for which six days would be ample time. Nashville, founded in 1779 on the site of the old French buffalo-hunters' rendezvous known as French Lick, was the market town and political capital of the five thousand pioneers, scattered for eighty miles along the river, who formed the Cumberland Settlement. Mr. Lardner Clark in his store sold everything needed by the frontiersman, from guns and ironmongery to lady's dresses in the latest Philadelphia fashion and unlimited cheap whisky. Here also was the junction where the Wilderness Trail to the east was met from the north by the Kentucky paths from Danville (120 miles) and Louisville (170 miles), and from the south by the Natchez Trace, along which river-men who preferred to avoid the hard pull upstream returned with packhorse trains from Natchez on the Lower Mississippi, a journey of 500 miles in three weeks through friendly Chicassaw country.

Perhaps it was on the way to Nashville that François-René met a fellow-countryman, an aged, white-bearded missionary, walking with open book and staff in hand, on his homeward path to his little flock of French settlers and Indian converts in the Illinois.[5] They travelled together for a few days, exchanging quotations from Virgil and Homer, discussing the Revolution in the tranquillity of the wilderness. The old priest was always first up in the morning, reading his breviary; when he told the story of his life, a hard one, François-René 'had never seen a smile of such serenity'. So, as luck would have it, soon after meeting the Indian maid who became Atala, he encountered a model for Father Aubry.

The way from Nashville to Knoxville was known as the Wilderness Trail *par excellence*, for in the intervening desolation no town or village

yet existed; however, by making short twenty-mile stints at the beginning, and hurrying over the Cumberland Mountains, travellers usually
found a lodging in some backwoodsman's cabin or lonely gentleman's
plantation, and need spend only a night or two in the open. Perhaps it
was here in the Cumberlands that François-René saw the scene which
he interpolated in his journal of the Cuyahoga portage, when he
reached a mountain-top by an eastward-falling cascade, and looked
over a green sea of forest islanded with rocks, far below. Past the
mountains one came to the military station and ferry at Southwest
Point, where the Clinch and Holston Rivers joined to form the
Tennessee, only two days from Knoxville. The whole distance of some
190 miles from Nashville to Knoxville was covered in eight or ten
days.

The Wilderness Trail was perilously exposed to Cherokee and Creek
raiders, though traders and immigrants thronged it undeterred. In this
summer and autumn, however, by an accident of history (as on the
Ohio but for different reasons) the danger was briefly lifted. The Creek
chief McGillivray (the educated son of a Scotch trader and a half-
French Creek princess) had made a pact with Mr. Knox at New York
in June 1790 in return for lavish subsidies, including the pay and uniform of a brigadier-general in the American army. Only three months
before François-René passed by, on 2 July 1791, the Cherokees had
buried the hatchet and ratified the Treaty of Holston with Governor
Blount at White's Fort; and their chief Bloody Fellow (a wellearned
name) was about to visit Washington in Philadelphia to ask for more.
So in the closing months of 1791 the Tennessee country as well as the
Ohio was unwontedly safe, and he could still truthfully say that danger
had come to him 'almost never from the natives'.

Knoxville itself had been officially founded only a fortnight or so
before his arrival, at the site of White's Fort on a bluff by the north bank
of the Holston River, by Governor Blount on 3 October 1791. Except
for the garrison blockhouse the town, tactfully named after Mr. Knox
the Secretary for War, consisted only of a few log cabins and vacant
lots. But John Chisholm had already opened his celebrated 'house of
entertainment', Chisholm's Tavern; Governor Blount's new frame-
house on Barbary Hill was being built as fast as might be (he moved in
on 5 January 1792); and the first issue of the *Knoxville Gazette* would
soon appear, on 5 November, though for the first few months it had to
be printed on the nearest available press at Rogersville, sixty miles
northeast on the way to Abingdon, Virginia.

After Knoxville the trail became almost a road, and the wilderness
began to be tamed by wayside cabins, taverns, farms, mills and hamlets.
Abingdon lay on the headwaters of the Holston, a five days' journey of
130 miles away, founded in 1778 on the site named Wolf Hills by

Dan'l Boone and already a prosperous township, boasting the rival hotels of Mr. James Armstrong and Mrs. May Macdonald. François-René's way now turned northeast, along the broad fertile valley between the two easternmost ranges of the Allaghenies: on his right the Blue Ridge, to the left the Kittatinnies or Endless Mountains. This was the Great Valley Road, also known in colonial times as the Great Trading Path, earlier still, when the Cherokees used it to raid the Shawnees (before the Shawnees migrated from Virginia to Illinois), as the Warriors' Path, and nowadays as U.S. Highway 11. He had now travelled 440 miles in about three weeks since leaving the Ohio towards the end of September, and had reached the last long stage of his return. He began the journey of 520 miles from Abingdon to Philadelphia, as we may suppose, towards 22 October 1791.

Somewhere in these beginnings of civilisation, soon before or soon after Abingdon, he noticed one evening a homestead by a rivulet, farmhouse beneath one of its gables, watermill at the other. He asked for bed and board, and was kindly welcomed by the good wife, who took him up a wooden ladder to his room, just above the axle of the water-wheel. He leaned from the little window, framed in ivy and the rainbow bellflowers of cobaea, and gazed at the millstream, bordered by dense willows, alders, sassafras, Carolina poplars. The mossgreen wheel revolved in the gloom below, trailing long ribbons of water; trout jumped high from the eddies, wagtails flew from bank to bank, and blue kingfishers darted by, not very different from those he had known at Combourg. What bliss it would be, he thought, to sit there dreaming at the feet of the sad one (supposing she had not proved faithless), with his head on her knees, listening to the falling cascade, the turning wheel, the grinding millstone, breathing the scents of cool water and new-ground barley-meal!

Night fell. He climbed down to the living-room, lit only by an autumnal fire of maize-cobs and bean-husks, and the gleam of the master's guns stacked horizontal in their racks on the wall. A tame squirrel leaped to and fro from the back of a huge dog to the shelf of a spinning-wheel. The family cat, knowing a friend when it saw one, took possession of his lap to watch the sport. The miller's wife hung a big stewpot over the fire, and set him King Alfred-like to watch the potatoes cooking for his supper. The flames made a crown of golden rays round the bottom of the cauldron, and illuminated an old newspaper which lay on the floor between his knees; he bent idly down to read and saw, while the pot boiled over unheeded, the words 'Flight of the King'. Louis XVI had fled with the Queen and royal children on 20 June; they were captured next day at Varennes, thirty miles from the frontier, so near and yet so far, and brought back to captivity in Paris.[6] Royalist officers were emigrating to join the flag of the Princes.[7]

So, while François-René wandered in an enchanted world outside time, history had continued. Suddenly as he sat in the quiet millhouse the clash of weapons and the roar of crowds sounded in his ears. He had thought of wintering in Philadelphia and renewing his journey westward in the spring; but now he felt in heart and brain the metamorphosis of a conversion. As a subject, a soldier, a nobleman, he must join his comrades and fight for his King. 'Return to France,' he said to himself aloud.

He tried thirty years later to remember the location of this momentous stage in his journey and his life. It was after his mountain crossing, and somewhere beyond a frontier post with an Indian name, of which the outlandish syllables still echoed in his mind. He plunged and wrote: 'We recrossed the Blue Mountains and approached the European settlements towards Chillicothe'. His words have provided a notorious crux, which we must now attempt to solve.

The Blue Mountains or Blue Ridge proper formed the easternmost of the parallel ranges of the Alleghanies; in fact he was still travelling inside them, and would only emerge at Harper's Ferry, where the Potomac cuts through the mountain barrier 360 miles northeast of Abingdon. But here and elsewhere he consistently used the name Blue Mountains in its old and then still current sense, as a synonym for the entire system of the Allaghenies.[8] He had 'crossed' these for the first time in the Albany sloop with the fair Quaker, where the Hudson River cuts through the gorges of the Palisades and the Highlands. He now felt he had crossed them again, having just passed the Cumberlands between Nashville and Knoxville in the only actual ascent and descent of a mountain range in all his journey. Hence 'we recrossed the Blue Mountains' refers, legitimately enough, to his passage of the Cumberlands and his arrival at Southwest Point.

Chillicothe may seem a harder nut to crack. Chillicothe was then a Shawnee town northwest of the Ohio, in impenetrably hostile Indian country on the upper waters of the Scioto River, past the mouth of which he had floated five weeks before. The modern town near the same site was not founded until 1796, two years after Wayne's victory of Fallen Timbers had opened the district to settlers for the first time. In 1791 no white men's homesteads existed within a hundred miles; the nearest were on the Ohio at Marietta, Gallipolis, Limestone, and Cincinnati. Chillicothe lay far west of the Blue Mountains, and 400 miles from the Knoxville–Abingdon region which he had now reached, a journey of 800 miles or six weeks there and back, via Cumberland Gap and Lexington, Kentucky. He had no reason to make this preposterous detour; he could not have accomplished it in the time available, or even escaped with his scalp, nor would he have found 'European settlements' anywhere in the neighbourhood. Most of his commentators have agreed that the one rash word 'Chillicothe' convicts him of lying; others have tried to argue that he really went there, which is no less absurd. Yet the dilemma is easily solved. He neither went to Chillicothe nor lied! The 'European settlements' he means, as is evident from the context, are those of East Tennessee and Southwest Virginia, which he encountered on descending from the Cumberlands. He tried to recall the name of the place which marked the frontier, and misremembered; but his guess is not so far out.

Halfway between Southwest Point and Knoxville he had passed a town which then marked the boundary between Indian country and American civilisation, and had almost the same name and sound as Chillicothe. His fellow-travellers no doubt remarked to him: 'Now we're out of the wilderness, yonder's Tellico!' Tellico, otherwise Tellico Blockhouse, half Cherokee town and half trading-post, with a fort and American army garrison, lay on the Little Tennessee River only twelve miles south of his route. The very word (allowing for the difference between the Cherokee and Shawnee languages) was the same as Chillicothe, and signified 'council-place' or 'chief town'. So Chillicothe is a mere slip of memory, and we may interpret the second clause of his sentence as meaning: 'we approached the European settlements in the region of Tellico'.

He does not say how far past Tellico was his millhouse. Watermills, where the settlers' grain was ground for a fee, and often also made into whisky, began even before Knoxville and became frequent after Abingdon. But it would not be surprising if François-René's lodging was the old-established mill and distillery of Robert Craig, on the upper Holston twelve miles northeast of Abingdon, where the Moravian missionaries Steiner and Schweinitz spent a night on their way to Nashville in November 1799.

Thirty miles after Abingdon, where a few cabins already marked the site of the modern Marion, he passed the sources of the Holston, and the waters ceased at last to flow into the Tennessee River, the Mississippi, and the Gulf of Mexico. Now, for two hundred miles, the Great Valley had no lengthwise stream of its own; instead, by a curious trick of geological time, powerful rivers had cut waterworn gorges through the mountain ridges on either side, and flowed across the valley's width, each with its busy ferry where it met the road. He passed the huts where leadmining Evansham (the modern Wytheville) was founded a few months later in 1792, and crossed Ingles Ferry, where the New River ran transversely west into Kentucky, piercing every range, until it became the Great Kanawha and joined the Ohio above Gallipolis. Next he came to the Roanoke and the James, which ran eastward through the Blue Ridge across southern Virginia to the Atlantic. Where the Valley Road crossed the Roanoke lay Salem, the town he chose to

name in his itinerary as representative of the whole Valley Road. On the
south and north branches of the James he passed through Fincastle and
Lexington, Virginia, already old towns in this new country, for they
were founded in the 1770s. Then at last the Valley possessed the stream
for which it seemed made, Shenandoah, the rolling river, with another
chain of still older little towns along its banks, Staunton, Newmarket,
Woodstock, Winchester, Charleston, until it joined the Potomac at
Harper's Ferry.

Between Fincastle and Lexington the road passed within two miles
of the scene which was then, next only to Niagara, the most celebrated
wonder of the New World. Tourists came all the way from Philadelphia
to visit it, and passing travellers invariably turned aside from their
route,[9] as François-René must certainly have done. Here was the
Natural Bridge, where a span of waterworn rock 90 feet long and 80
broad, shaggy with firs, linked the vertical banks of Cedar Creek (a
tributary of the James) 215 feet below. The land belonged since 1775
to Foreign Secretary Jefferson, who had installed a log cabin for visitors, with negro slaves as caretakers. François-René had brought with
him thus far, like Chactas fleeing with Atala in his Indian epic, the
memory of his proud Floridian, side by side with that of the aged missionary. So he included the Natural Bridge in the landscape where the
natural lovers meet Father Aubry, and Atala dies to keep her vow of
chastity.[10] This symbolic tunnel in the mountains of the heart—this
mystic frontier, barrier, entry, causeway, between romantic love and
renunciation, divine wrath and forgiveness—existed also in himself,
and he would cross and recross it many times.

At Harper's Ferry one crossed to the north bank of the Potomac,
where for three miles the road kept a narrow footing between the violent river and the 1,200-foot precipices of the mountain. 'The passage
of the Potomac through the Blue Ridge,' Jefferson had written, 'is,
perhaps, one of the most stupendous scenes in nature'. Possibly it was
here, when François-René finally left the Blue Mountains, at the furthest
point north where he actually set foot on their course, that he saw, or
persuaded himself that he had seen, a remarkable phenomenon: 'as
many as thirteen generations of oaks, evidently sprung in succession
from the same ground'—from which as a philosopher he felt entitled to
deduce the antiquity of the world and the unreliability of the Book of
Genesis.[11]

His road now ran through the autumnal stubblefields and leafless
orchards of Maryland, via Fredericktown and York, to Lancaster in
Pennsylvania, and at last, 165 miles from Harper's Ferry, ended full
circle where it had begun, in Philadelphia. The journey of 520 miles
from Abingdon, judging by the journey-times of other contemporary
travellers, had taken him about three weeks, or a little less.[12] Hence he

probably arrived at Philadelphia towards the middle of the second week of November, or, let us say, on or about 11 November 1791, four weeks before his sailing on 10 December.

Since leaving Philadelphia towards 19 July he had travelled some 3,360 miles in about 116 days, an achievement less extraordinary than it may seem. Nearly half this distance, 1,675 miles, was then covered at high speed by coach or river, at rates normally exceeding fifty, or even approaching a hundred miles in each day. On these sections, by analogy with the journey-times of other travellers, he can have taken no more than 28 days. We have set aside 19 days for sojourns at New York, Boston, Albany, Niagara, Pittsburgh, and Tennessee Mouth. Thus 69 days are available for the remaining 1,685 miles, which he covered on horseback or by canoe. This moderate overall average of 24 miles a day recalls what President Washington called 'my usual travelling gait of five miles an hour', and serves as an encouraging confirmation of the calculations which we have drawn not from theory, but from the actual normal times of contemporary wayfarers on each section of the route followed by François-René.

FRANÇOIS-RENÉ'S JOURNEY

The table shows land distances as the approximate true road or track mileages at the time, derived from contemporary sources checked against Tanner's *American Traveller*, and hence generally greater than direct, 'as the crow flies', or modern road distances. Distances on the Ohio are true midstream mileages, and hence smaller than contemporary estimates from dead-reckoning, which exaggerated the distance from Pittsburgh to Ohio Mouth by as much as 150 miles. Journey times are estimated at the normal contemporary average for each section of the route. The table of days and dates allows for 19 non-travelling days (figures preceded by + sign), made up of 5 for sightseeing and other business in New York, Boston, Albany, and Pittsburgh, 12 for convalescence at Niagara, and 2 for the adventure of the Floridians at Tennessee Mouth.

From	To	Miles	Days	Approximate Date
Philadelphia—New York (coach)		90	1 (+1)	19–20 July
New York—Boston—New York (coach)		460	7 (+2)	21–29 July
New York—Albany (sloop)		145	2 (+1)	30 July–1 August
Albany—Niagara (horseback)		300	12	2–13 August
(Convalescence at Niagara)		—	(+12)	14–25 August
Niagara—Cuyahoga Mouth (horseback)		210	7	26 August–1 September
Cuyahoga Mouth—Pittsburgh (canoe)		170	6 (+1)	2–8 September
Pittsburgh—Ohio Mouth (river boat)		980	18	9–26 September
Ohio Mouth—Tennessee Mouth (pirogue)		45	2	27–28 September
(Adventure of Two Floridians)		—	(+2)	29–30 September
Tennessee Mouth—Nashville (horseback)		120	6	1–6 October
Nashville—Knoxville (horseback)		190	10	7–16 October
Knoxville—Abingdon (horseback)		130	5	17–21 October
Abingdon—Philadelphia (horseback)		520	21	22 October–11 November
		3,360	97 (+19)	

Even so, in our scrupulous desire not to exaggerate his speed, we have made him travel more slowly than need be; for we have assigned to each section of his route only the *average* time of other travellers. François-René, however, was impelled on the outward half of his journey by determination to go as far west as possible before winter, on the return half by the need to reach Philadelphia before his money gave out, and by his resolve to fight for his King. This energetic wayfarer, whose rapidity astonished all observers on other journeys in later years, probably equalled here and there the fastest rather than the more leisurely of his contemporaries.[13] If so, let us give him back any days he has saved, to use for rest, sightseeing, involuntary delays, or any other incidents, in addition to the 19 days which we have already allowed him for such contingencies. All in all it appears that an arrival date no later than 11 November is not merely a possibility, but in all likelihood is the actual truth. But even if (though there is no reason to suppose it) he reached Philadelphia a week, or two, or as much as three weeks later, he would still have three weeks, or two, or one, in which to see President Washington and catch his ship on 10 December. And conversely if (as some have maintained, though we shall find good argument against it) he sailed earlier than the reported date, he would have time to do so.

So we have established for the first time, disentangling the obscurities and errors of his narrative, the route which he claims to have taken and has endeavoured to describe. We have gone a long way round, as did François-René himself, to find that he made exactly the journey he says he made.

At Philadelphia François-René was dismayed to find that his expected remittance from France had not arrived. This, he says (forgetting his career as a stocking-seller last year), 'was the beginning of the pecuniary embarrassments in which I have been plunged for the rest of my life'. How could he get home? Renewing contact with French acquaintances he found that several of his countrymen were about to return to France, 'for various reasons', on a ship bound for Le Havre. Some, no doubt, had decided like himself to join the royalist army, or hoped to save their property from confiscation by putting in an appearance before the impending laws against émigrés came into force; others may have been disillusioned settlers from Gallipolis, or refugees from the negro rebellion which had raged since August in San Domingo. He persuaded the captain of their ship to give him a passage on credit.

One piece of unfinished business in Philadelphia still remained. He knocked again on the door of the little redbrick house at 190 High Street, next to the hairdresser's; again the young maid said quietly: 'Walk in, sir,' and strove her best to pronounce the name 'Monsieur de Combourg'. But she led him this time by a long narrow corridor to a parlour, where a few minutes later a tall, elderly man entered. François-René had seen him already, not without disappointment, dashing past in carriage and four, with armorial bearings, mettlesome bays, and grooms in creamwhite livery trimmed with scarlet—how different from the new Cincinnatus he had imagined, who ought rather to have been driving a team of oxen, with steady hand to the plough! Now, however, he recognised the ancient Roman of his republican dreams, as President Washington produced the letter of introduction which he had delivered four months before, and exclaimed with pleasure, pointing to the signature: 'Colonel Armand!'

They sat down. François-René, in halting English remembered from his naval education at Rennes and Brest, described his journey and explained its thwarted purpose, the crossing of the continent, the exploration of the Pacific coast, the discovery of the Northwest Passage. He had failed, he confessed, but was determined to return and try again, as soon as the King was saved! Washington listened, commenting only in monosyllables of French or English, with visible and growing amazement. The contrast between La Rouërie's version of the young visitor's intentions—'to satisfy his soul by seeing the extraordinary man and thoses respectable citizens'—and this attempt to conquer all America was striking indeed. 'But it is less difficult to find the North-west Passage,' exclaimed François-René with some heat, 'than to create a nation, as you have done!' 'Well, well, young man,' cried the President, disarmed; he shook François-René's hand, and invited him to dinner next day.

Washington, recovered from the month's illness which had prevented their meeting in July, but still showing signs of the strain upon his health,[14] had left Philadelphia for a much-needed holiday at his country home of Mount Vernon on 15 September, and returned on 21 October to deliver his annual message to Congress on the 25th. He resumed his normal Philadelphia routine of state dinners, levees and audiences, which he regarded as part of his Presidential duty and, in his own staid way, rather enjoyed. He said little but listened much, with the aloof dignity which some mistook for pride or stupidity, keeping his finger on the pulse of his young country, impressing foreigners with its prestige, weighing the effect which every change in the outside world might have on its future power or its still precarious unity, punctilious in his courtesy to all. It was more than ever incumbent upon him to receive this well-connected young Frenchman, whom he had been obliged to turn away four months before.

The President had many reasons for finding François-René a more than usually interesting visitor. Here was a protégé of none other than the Marquis de la Rouërie, Washington's favourite among his French war-comrades, next only to Lafayette whom he regarded as a son.

Colonel Armand! This young Monsieur de Combourg could give news of him, of the schemes to tame the Revolution in France at which La Rouërie had only hinted in his letter. The President's own views as a constitutional republican were not very different from François-René's as a constitutional monarchist. He, too, had welcomed the Revolution, so long as it seemed to imply only a peaceful liberalisation of the French monarchy and a movement towards universal brotherhood, under the virtuous guidance of his dear Lafayette. He, too, had been horrified by the news of the flight to Varennes and the capture of the King and Queen;[15] for he still cherished a sincere gratitude to King Louis and his nobles, without whose aid in battle he might never have freed his country from King George.

But Monsieur de Combourg was quite as remarkable to the President for his family connections as for his acquaintance with Colonel Armand. The great Malesherbes, a wellwisher of the United States, a friend of Washington's friends Jefferson and Gouverneur Morris and a polite benefactor of Washington himself,[16] was Monsieur de Combourg's relative by marriage, his patron, and the planner of his journey to America. Through Malesherbes he had family links with M. de Montmorin the Foreign Minister, and with another valued war-friend, M. de la Luzerne, both of whom as it happened were fresh in Washington's mind; for on 5 September he had given a dinner of welcome to Montmorin's new ambassador, M. Ternant, and on 10 September he had written to La Luzerne, tactfully wishing France 'tranquillity again restored' under 'a goverment respectfully energetic'.

The President, however, was still more deeply impressed by his guest's extraordinary travels than by the importance of their mutual acquaintances. There was no point in his journey which did not hold personal memories or present preoccupations for Washington. This fortunate young man had seen Niagara, which Washington had longed to visit in 1784 but refrained, rather than disgrace his country by applying for a British passport. Long ago in 1753, as a loyal officer of King George, young Captain Washington had crossed the mountains to confront the encroaching French at Fort Le Boeuf on the Presqu'Ile portage, which Monsieur de Combourg had passed on his way along the Erie shore. Monsieur de Combourg had made the Cuyahoga portage, which Washington and Jefferson were so eager to develop as part of their projected water-route from the Potomac to Detroit. He had seen Pittsburgh and the upper Ohio, where Washington had fought the French in the 1750s, and was now a landowner; the President had made a tour of inspection there in 1784, at his first opportunity after the war.[17] In his voyage down the Ohio he had passed within a few miles of Saint-Clair's expedition, which formed the ruling theme of the President's recent message to Congress on 25 October and of his present anxieties. In fact throughout his journey, by the Great Lakes, the Ohio, and Tennessee, Monsieur de Combourg had followed the vast wilderness frontier where in that year the United States defiantly paused in the face of hostile Indians, and the encircling enemy powers of England and Spain. 'Well, well, young man!' the President cried.

Such, then, was the surprisingly rich nexus of memories, thoughts, and personal relationships, which underlay the meeting of the great Washington and the obscure François-René.

Every Thursday in Congress time, at four in the afternoon, the President held a state, or as he called it 'publick' dinner. The guests were Congress members, government officials, prominent citizens or distinguished visitors. The great table was adorned with glass lustres, porcelain figures, and a huge china centrepiece known as the Pagoda, which came from France. The fish and joints were prepared by the negro slave cook, Uncle Hercules, the cakes and desserts, including the newfangled 'iced cream', by the steward 'Black Sam' Fraunces, who also stood in the background keeping an eye on the service, in resplendent wig. The wine was madeira, circulated in ice-packed decanters. The usual atmosphere was (in the words of the disgruntled Senator Maclay) 'a cloudy gloom of settled seriousness', for democracy would have been imperilled if Washington had said anything spontaneous, or shown marked attention to anyone. But the President strove his best to cheer any noticeably embarrassed guest by helping him to a slice of pudding, or raising his glass: 'Health, sir!'—'Thank you, sir!' Then they took coffee in Mrs. Washington's drawingroom.

François-René was not intimidated. 'Man's face will never daunt me,' he wrote of it long after. But the grave simplicity of this 'soldier citizen, liberator of a world' impressed him in retrospect more enduringly than the sound and fury of Napoleon, with whom he compared him, Plutarch-fashion, when both were dead. 'I am happy that his gaze fell on me! It has warmed me for the rest of my life: there is a virtue in the eyes of a great man.'

The conversation that evening was more animated than usual, for it turned on the French Revolution. He made the acquaintance of Washington's French-speaking secretary Tobias Lear, who lived in as a member of the family, and was to befriend him unexpectedly at Tunis in 1807. Washington, as he always did when Frenchmen were present, proudly produced one of the many keys of the Bastille, later transferred to Mount Vernon where it is shown to this day. The President had found it an infallible test of a guest's politics, and was quite inured to seeing it scorned by aristocrats. For François-René this overrated souvenir was no symbol of the liberal and liberating revolution he had once hoped for, but rather of frenzied mobs, and Foulon's mangled head, and a captive king. If the President had seen, as *he* had, the conquerors of the Bastille wallowing in the gutters of Paris, he boldly intimated, he would attach less importance to this relic.

On the eve of his departure François-René no doubt learned the appalling news which reached Philadelphia on 8 December and appeared in the newspapers next day. General Saint-Clair's expedition against the western Indians, weakened by detachments and desertions to 1,400 men from its original 2,000, had been destroyed on 4 November, a hundred miles out from Cincinnati, on a headstream of the Wabash. Little Turtle's Miamis and Shawnees, armed with British rifles, had attacked before dawn, scattered the advance guard of raw Kentucky militia, surrounded the main body, and proceeded to exterminate them by withering crossfire from cover of the trees. The cannons fired, ineffectually, till all the gunners had fallen. Brave old Saint-Clair stood his ground for three hours, then broke out of the encirclement and strove to organise an orderly retreat; but his men fled in panic, flinging away their guns, far ahead of their general. Eight hundred dead were left behind in the bloody glade of the killing-ground to be stripped and scalped. When he read Saint-Clair's despatch the President burst into one of his rare but terrifying fits of rage, as well he might. 'I warned him to beware of surprise!' he cried; and yet, he too was responsible, for he had also besought Saint-Clair 'to seek the enemy and endeavour by all possible means to strike them with great severity'. This was the greatest defeat ever suffered by the United States army in all its Indian wars. The Ohio traffickers and frontier immigrants, after remaining unmolested for one summer season in 1791—as though Providence had decreed that François-René should pass by unscathed, but in reality because the Indians had retired to mass up country— were harried again, though little deterred, for three years, until Mad Anthony Wayne's Victory of Fallen Timbers on 20 August 1794 secured the Old Northwest. François-René was doubly impressed. Clearly, the noble savage had fought the tyrannical forces of white civilisation with sublime heroism; and yet, this red man of nature was himself the most relentless and cunning of destroyers. Both these contradictory truths must be embodied in his future epic.

So he caught his boat on Saturday, 10 December 1791. Perhaps she was the brig *Molly*, captain Bernard Reser, bound for Le Havre, or perhaps some other vessel.[18] They cast cable and began the long passage down the estuary of the Delaware, a hundred miles from Philadelphia to the open sea. François-René returned without the secret of the Northwest Passage, but with the invisible company of two Indian maids, Atala and Céluta, and the revelation of a New World of the imagination. He was crestfallen with failure, dazed with the burden of new experience, but nonetheless happy, like Ulysses, to have made a good voyage.

PART FOUR

The Wilderness of Exile

16

CÉLESTE

A STRONG westerly seized them at the mouth of the Delaware, and drove them across the Atlantic. How changed was this wintry sea from the languorous blue doldrums of last summer! They ran bare-masted, pursued by seething breakers, under a haggard sky. The sadness of the darkling ocean overcame him; he had made his first step in life, and now returned a failure; he felt a heaviness in his heart that seemed to presage some enormous misfortune. Sometimes he scanned the waves, as if they would tell him his destiny. Sometimes he wrote, ignoring their menace but harassed by their motion, arranging his travel notes or adding to the drafts of his Indian tale which he had begun, left arm in sling, under the wigwams of Tonawanda.

As they neared Europe the gale blew higher, but now with a demented uniformity that spread an ominous illusion of calm in wan sky and leaden sea. The captain was uneasy; without sight of sun or star he had run by dead reckoning; he climbed the shrouds, surveyed the horizon with his spyglass, posted lookouts on bowsprit and foretop. The sea shortened and turned colour: signs of land, but what land?

> 'See Belle-Isle,
> There's your isle,'

thought François-René, remembering the old Breton proverb,

> 'See Groix,
> There's your joy,
> See Ushant,
> Your death's at hand!'

For two nights he had paced the bridge, listening to baying waves and booming cordage, watching the great rollers deluging over and off the foredeck. At dusk on New Year's Eve he went weary below, climbed into his creaking hammock, hearing the ship's joints dislocate with every blow. He was awakened by running feet above, the thud of falling rope, sailors disputing about the lie of land, a frightened shout to the captain down the hatchway. He leaped to the floor just as a wave burst through the after-quarters, flooding the captain's cabin, rolling tables and bedding, seachests and shotguns promiscuous. When he reached the deck, already half-drowned, a sight of apocalyptic sublimity greeted him.

The ship had failed to put about, and now cowered helpless to the hurricane. Mountainous breakers sparkled with spray and then, as the depth changed, heaved a glassy surface marbled with black, greenish and coppery stains. A waxing moon with blunted horns[1] shone fitfully through the cloudwrack, showing a line of jagged coast to either side. Through the mingled howling of wind and abyss he heard the hiss of reefs, the roar of distant surf, and from down below in the hold a sound more bloodcurdling than any, as of a vase slowly filling with water. The binnacle light was out, the wheel abandoned, and the rudder turned hoarsely on itself. Maps lay open on a chicken-coop under a lantern. The passengers clung to bulwarks and rigging, each clutching his dearest possessions. They had entered the Channel unawares, and were now driving between the crude north coast of Alderney and the rock islets of the Casquets and Burhou, along the narrow gut called the Swinge. Shipwreck seemed inevitable.

A Breton sailor began to sing François-René's childhood hymn for those in peril on the sea, while his American Protestant comrades joined in as best they could. So also did François-René, about to drown almost within view of the cathedral of Saint-Malo where he had learned it, almost under the eyes of the mother who had stood beside him then. *'Lady, Thy Son is my King!'*

A stalwart New Yorker strode forward and gripped the vacant helm in his horny paws. Thirty years after François-René could see this hero still, in canvas shirt and trousers, barefooted, with lank drenched hair, peering back over his shoulder for the wave that would save or destroy them. Here it towered, swelling from shore to shore, and ahead of it great white gulls, calmly gliding, like birds of death. The ship touched and grounded, on the verge of capsizing; the enormous wave overtook her, their saviour swung the wheel, she righted and crossed the bar. All huzzaed to high heaven, and the French with François-René shouted also: *'Vive le Roi!'*, a prayer not to be granted.

They were not quite out of danger, for they could not clear the Cherbourg peninsula, until at last the ebbtide carried them round Cape La Hague into the open Channel. They put in at Le Havre next day, 2 January 1792, with broken masts, boats carried away, shattered quarter-deck, shipping water at every roll. The whole population thronged the quayside to see them. François-René noticed that just as he had felt no alarm when all but wrecked, so he felt no joy at being saved.

But he could not leave Le Havre until his passage was paid to the ship-owner, M. Longuesmares. He wrote to Jean-Baptiste in Paris, explaining the patriotic necessity for his return, describing his miraculous escape from shipwreck, and requesting the necessary loan. Jean-Baptiste, however, was in no mood to be his brother's keeper, and provokingly replied that he had forwarded the letter to their mother.[2]

Mme de Chateaubriand, more tenderhearted than Jean-Baptiste, promptly sent her surety for 1,200 livres to pay his release. Lucile was staying with her, she reported, and Uncle Antoine de Bédée was in town with his family. Clearly he would find a warmer welcome in Saint-Malo than in Paris. He took his way west through Normandy, passing burned and deserted countryhouses, whose owners had already joined the Princes at Coblentz, spurred on by the mocking gift of a spindle if they hesitated, leaving their wives to take refuge in the nearest town. He arrived at 479 Rue des Grands-Degrés towards 16 January, to find that his family had prepared a little surprise. They were delighted to see him, although (as they pointed out) he could hardly have returned at a more awkward time. They approved his decision to emigrate and fight; but an émigré required money, of which they had none to spare and he less than none, and also an indissoluble partner to protect his property in his absence. So it was his plain duty to get married to an heiress immediately, and Lucile had found just the wife for him.

Mlle Céleste Buisson de la Vigne, aged just eighteen, who lived nearby in the Rue de Coëtquen opposite the Porte de Dinan with her wealthy grandfather, was supposed to have five or six hundred thousand livres. This was the same pretty child with the big nose and long yellow hair, whom he had noticed three years ago striding along the Sillon, her gown and scarf billowing in the wind, while he rode his horse along the fringe of the sea. While he was away she had taken a fancy to Lucile, and Lucile to her. She was slim, dainty, white-skinned, tiny as ever, only five foot one, and still wore her fair ringletted hair down, like a schoolgirl. After all, why not? 'Go ahead,' said he.

Céleste was the ward of her grandfather, Jacques Buisson, for her father Alexis-Jacques, director in the India Company, and her mother Céleste, née Rapion de la Placelière, were long dead. The old gentleman was ex-governor of Lorient, decorated with the cross of Saint Louis, ennobled by the King in 1776; in youth he had fought pirates on the coast of Malabar, saved his captain from the krisses of four opium-crazed Malays running amuck in Pondicherry, and gone corsairing against the English. A marriage into hereditary nobility, even with an impecunious younger son in time of Revolution, would be one step up, thought the oldfashioned M. Buisson.

However, the romance of these babes in the wood did not lack wicked uncles, or rather great-uncles. Michel Bossinot de Vauvert and Denis Bossinot de Pomphily, Céleste's senior relatives on her grandmother's side, were convinced Revolutionaries, like most of their colleagues on the Saint-Malo municipal council; so they could not publicly approve her marriage to an aristocrat, still less a ceremony to be performed (as Mme de Chateaubriand insisted) by a refractory priest.

Even so, the real cause of dissent sprang not from class, politics, or religion, but from property. Céleste was an orphan, an heiress, a minor, and a gentlewoman; hence by the Custom of Brittany her estate must be administered until she came of age—just as François-René's was by Jean-Baptiste—by her senior male relatives, first her grandfather and after him (their turn would surely come soon, for he was nearly eighty) the Bossinots. So the ensuing family brawl was fought not so much over the match, which was quite satisfactory and past preventing, as over the rights of the great-uncles.

All Buissons except the bride herself were ostentatiously absent from the wedding on 21 February 1792. The non-juring priest was Father Julien Biffard, chaplain of the Ursuline Convent, who performed the ceremony in Mme de Chateaubriand's yellow drawingroom. The witnesses included François-René's trustee M. Gesbert, the family lawyer M. Amy, Mme de Chateaubriand herself, Marianne, who had come up all the way from Fougères, and Lucile.

The Bossinots struck back immediately. Their greatniece was under age, they had not given their consent, and the marriage was invalid by the law of 14 September 1791, as it had not been registered by a constitutional priest. By threatening to have old Buisson's authority set aside on the ground of alleged dotage, they frightened him into bringing proceedings in his own name for abduction against François-René, his mother, and his two sisters. These in turn appointed M. Amy on 2 March to plead their defence. Céleste was put away in the nunnery of La Victoire, under the safe keeping of Pierre's daughter Sœur des Séraphins; and Lucile insisted on joining her in imprisonment, not for the last time. A credible tradition tells how François-René used to wait on the ramparts beneath the iron-barred window of their cell, and exchange a few words with his wife and sister at moments when there were no passers-by.

Soon, behind the screen of this legal byplay, the families and their lawyers reached a compromise. First, a proper marriage contract must be agreed (it had indeed been extraordinarily high-handed of the Chateaubriands to arrange the wedding without one), and then the young couple must be married again before a constitutional priest.

The contract was ratified in old Buisson's stately drawingroom on 17 March. By its terms a Buisson family council was nominated, consisting of the grandfather, the great-uncles, Céleste's uncle François from Lorient, and three male cousins who had been raked up from somewhere; all these were present and signed. The bride's fortune was to be tied and administered by 'two of her closest relatives' until she came of age, that is, by the Custom of Brittany, when she was twenty-five, in 1799! Such conditions were normal and correct in a marriage of minors.[3] No Breton family could be expected to give its young folk

premature disposal of their prospective capital, and François-René himself remained similarly tied under the guardianship of Jean-Baptiste.
But the great-uncles now had their will; they would enjoy seven years'
perquisites as trustees, and would doubtless interpret their rights and
duties more strictly than the softhearted grandfather. Still more vexing
was the revelation of the true state of Céleste's finances. Instead of 'five
or six hundred thousand' she had only 134,000 livres, invested mostly
in church or state loans bearing interest payable in the rapidly depreciat-
ing government *assignats*, which were already 30 per cent below par.
Her income was declarable as 5,194 livres in theory, but was worth only
3,750 in fact, and still dwindling. The Chateaubriands, doing their best
to compete, could not exaggerate François-René's assets to more than
60,000, most of which had a merely notional existence.[4] The lawyers
constituted a marriage portion of 10,000 livres for the young couple to
set up home, 5,000 to be contributed by each. Then the seven victorious
Buissons signed, followed by Mme de Chateaubriand, Uncle Bédée and
his daughter Flore de Blossac, and M. Amy.

A last disagreeable pill remained, to legalise the genuine marriage by
submitting to a mock one. Banns were called next day, with a special
dispensation for waiving second and third banns, and on 19 March
François-René and Céleste were remarried by the constitutional priest
M. Duhamel. No one could have been a more democratic cleric, for he
had been elected curé of Saint-Malo last June by unanimous vote of all
republican citizens; he was obliging too, for he intimated that he would
forget to make trouble about the previous marriage performed by his
refractory colleague, if the Chateaubriands would pay him extra.[5] They
did so, but this time it was their turn to stay away from the wedding,
except for the bridegroom.[6] On 28 March grandfather Buisson formally
withdrew legal proceedings against his son-in-law, and the incident was
closed.

Where did they spend their honeymoon? Not in Mme de Chateaubriand's little house, where Lucile occupied the only spare bedroom,
but perhaps in old Buisson's pleasant Manoir des Chênes at Paramé.
Towards the beginning of May they said goodbye to Mme de Chateaubriand (whom François-René, as it turned out, was never to see again),
and moved with Lucile to Marianne's Hôtel de Marigny at Fougères.

They visited Bois-Février, and found M. de Langan had already
emigrated to join the army of the Princes, much against the wishes of
Armand de la Rouërie, who had other plans for his friends. François-
René delighted Mlle Émilie de Langan with tales of his adventures.
'He went to New England,' she wrote in her memoirs, supposing that
to be another name for the United States, 'returned full of reminiscences,
and told us lots of interesting things in his usual clever way'—but of
those interesting things, unfortunately, she tells us not one.

Émilie, aged seventeen, now had an exciting hobby. She was La Rouërie's secretary, and helped to write the mysterious letters with which Thérèse de Moëlien galloped across the countryside, white-plumed, wearing on her bosom for token the Order of Cincinnatus which President Washington had bestowed upon the Marquis. Last May, when François-René was in mid-Atlantic on his voyage to America, La Rouërie had sailed from Saint-Malo in his turn to visit the Comte d'Artois in Germany, with Thérèse to keep him company, and passports for London to conceal his tracks. He found the Prince on 5 June 1791 at Ulm, on his way from Turin to Coblentz, ready as ever to promise anything to anyone, charmed to see an old acquaintance whose path he had crossed long ago in Paris in many an actress's dressingroom. Artois listened with delight to La Rouërie's plan for a Breton counter-revolution, timed to coincide with his own coming invasion of France, agreed in return to restore the Estates of Brittany immediately after victory, and gave him a signed commission to raise recruits. Since then the Marquis had enlisted noble and bourgeois adherents and organised cells in every town and parish from Cancale to Brest. Even money was not scarce, for his agents found many gentlemen only too happy to contribute a year's revenue in exchange for a certificate guaranteeing immunity for their homes in the coming troubles. His château was full of guns, 'for protection against brigands', as the Marquis airily explained to local authorities. François-René's schoolfriend Limoëlan had joined the plot, as had many friends of Mme de Chateaubriand at Saint-Malo.

The Marquis doubtless sounded François-René himself when he called, as etiquette demanded, to report on his interview with Washington. The Prince's commission declared that 'the services a gentleman would render by joining the league of zeal and loyalty were more important than any he could give by leaving France', and recommended that 'any gentleman who had not yet left home should refrain from taking the course of emigration'. But François-René had come back to fight, not to conspire; this was a movement for country squires, not for soldiers; he must go to Paris to consult his brother and wise Malesherbes. Here was a parting of ways, the moment of his irrevocable farewell to Brittany, where as fate would have it he was never to live again.

So, towards mid-May, off they flew, François-René, his new little wife, and his favourite sisters Julie and Lucile, almost with the same gaiety of birds in the wilderness as in the spring of 1789. Julie had found an apartment for all four in the Cul-de-sac Férou, in the second-best town-house of their friendly acquaintance the Marquise de Villette, Voltaire's niece. On one side the Petit Hôtel de Villette overlooked the Luxembourg Gardens; on the other was the seminary of Saint-Sulpice,

with its superior M. Émery, Mme de Villette's cousin, who had sent
out M. Nagot and his Sulpician ark to Baltimore last year. François-
René must have had much to tell M. Émery; perhaps he kept back how
he had almost un-converted Francis Tulloch, but then, perhaps the
sagacious M. Émery was fully informed on that subject already. However, this good shepherd had wolves for neighbours, and to save his
flock had invited the wolves into his sheepfold. The dread Mucius
Scaevola section from the Luxembourg, Maratists all, had taken headquarters in the seminary, complete with meeting-hall for their pande-
monium, court of 'justice', guardroom for their private army, and
bedrooms for their womenfolk in cells once the refuge of innocent boy
novices. In recompense M. Émery was officially declared a good citizen,
the seminary remained unmolested ('provided you don't call yourselves
seminarists'), and in the chapel Christ's body could still be housed and
mass be said daily.

François-René hurried to see his literary friends. During his absence
he had moved a little further right, while they, almost unaware of
motion, had hurtled along the torrent of history, pleased with their own
consistency, and proud of their ability to keep up with the times. The
Revolution had become an inexhaustible source of odes for Lebrun,
jobs for Ginguené, epigrams for Chamfort, lectures for Laharpe.
Laharpe's literature course at the Lycée in the Rue Saint-Honoré had
never been more fashionable or more unliterary;[7] the audience cheered
when he clapped the red revolutionary nightcap on his wig and cried:
'This bonnet goes right through my head, it sets my brain on fire!'
Chamfort's modulated voice had taken a doctrinaire stridency. His new
patrons the Jacobins were about to murder his old patrons the aristocracy, who had feasted him twenty years long for declaring them unfit
to live; yet Chamfort seemed none the happier. 'Fraternity or Death,'
he scoffed, when he saw those words scrawled on a wall, 'that means:
"Be my brother, or I'll kill you!" It's the fraternity of Cain and Abel!'
Whose throat did Chamfort really want to see cut? Could it be his own?
The city-dwelling Ginguené was editing a revolutionary newspaper for
simple countryfolk, the *Feuille villageoise*, but was thought to know a
great deal about the horrors brewing nearer home.

Fontanes and Flins, he found, were lying low, compromised as they
were by having edited the constitutional monarchist newspapers *Le
Modérateur* and the *Journal* of the Société des Amis de la Constitution
Monarchique (a predecessor of the Club of 1789, whose banquet
François-René had attended two years before). Fontanes, extricating
himself from the embraces of the literary lady Mme du Fresnoy, had
retreated to Lyons to woo the heiress discovered for him by his great
friend Joubert. Little Flins had scored a tremendous hit in 1790 with
his patriotic comedy *Le Réveil d'Épiménide*, and its pop-song:

'Our brave defenders' glory
No foreign foes can rob,
But I detest the fury
Of a sanguinary mob!'

None sang that ditty now, least of all its author, who had vanished into a quiet bureaucratic sinecure in the Mint.

In compensation for these disappointments François-René managed to meet Bernardin de Saint-Pierre at last, only to find his favourite author's character sadly inferior to his prose style. Bernardin had just become director of the Jardin des Plantes, where he inaugurated the menagerie by commandeering the King's private zoo from Versailles, and was about to marry his publisher's daughter Mlle Didot, thirty years his junior (their children, of course, would be named Paul and Virginie); but no matter how he prospered, Bernardin could never cease complaining of neglect and persecution, and begging for more money. François-René was also introduced to the aged Abbé Barthélemy, whose *Voyage du jeune Anacharsis*, a many-volumed tale of travels in ancient Greece, had been the best-seller of 1789. 'He describes the drawingroom of an Athenian lady rather too much as if it was Mme de Choiseul's at Chanteloup,'[8] thought François-René; but the idea of a journey in time through the classical world continued to kindle his imagination and guide his studies, and became the ruling theme of *Les Martyrs*.

He called on old Malesherbes, who in the summer of his protégé's voyage to America had spent his last happy days on earth, visiting his émigrée daughter Montboissier at Lausanne, and making pilgrimages to the lake-isle of Saint-Pierre and other haunts of Jean-Jacques Rousseau, his friend of long ago. At Lausanne he met the great Gibbon, whom he gratified with a memorandum on the position of princes in the social hierarchy of France—a subject baffling to foreigners, and at that time devoid of importance, except to an eminent historian, or an old man in love with the past. Now Malesherbes was deeply perturbed about the safety of the King, and had begun for the first time in his life to attend the Sunday levées at court. 'I can't bear dressing,' he grumbled, 'especially this damned sword that trips me up on the stairs; still, it's my biggest pleasure of the week to see that good man looking well. I never go and speak to him, but I don't mind, it's enough to set eyes on him, and I think he's glad to know I'm there.'

Malesherbes greeted François-René with his old enthusiasm, heard the story of his travels, and discussed his plans for a second attempt on the Northwest Passage next year, when the Revolution would surely be over. 'I had only to make, first of all, another little journey, this time to Germany. I would hurry off to the army of the Princes, rush back to

Paris, spit the Revolution on my sword, all in two or three months.
Then I would hoist sail, return to the New World, leaving behind me a
revolution the fewer and a marriage the more.' So François-René wrote
ironically afterwards, but thought in all seriousness then.

He had filled a whole notebook with his detailed plans. Wiser for
the advice of Mr. Swift of Albany and his own experience, he now saw
that he had failed for want of time, equipment, transport, and companions. So his new scheme called for a journey of five or six, perhaps
even nine years, with a party of three hired white men and three
Indians from the Six Nations, a horse for each, like those that had served
him so well from Albany to Niagara, and two huge covered wagons
each pulled by four yokes of oxen, setting out from New York.[9] Once
again he meant to solve the Indian problem by kindness, which so far
had served him well enough. 'Rather than cost the simple denizens of
the wilderness a single tear, I would renounce my journey,' he declared;
'I resolved that the Man with the Long Beard'—for so the Iroquois had
been pleased to call him in his hirsute days at Niagara—'should be
remembered for many a day as a friend and benefactor of all mankind!'[10]

Malesherbes listened with sparkling eyes, with a look of youthful
ardour on his ancient face, as though he himself were about to confront
the perils of which he was hearing. He promised to present François-
René's plans to the Government, if the surviving remnant of powerless
and despairing ex-ministers could still be so called. As it happened,
Malesherbes was then in particularly close touch with the two who
would be most likely to take interest in a project affecting France's lost
territories in the New World.[11] He listened no less appreciatively to
François-René reading the first fragments of the future *Atala*, and was
reminded again of his lost Jean-Jacques, inventor of the noble savage
whom this young relative had seen, or believed he had seen, with his
own eyes.

Lastly François-René required his opinion on emigration, rather
expecting him to disapprove of it, especially in a member of the family;
for Malesherbes had always deplored the departure of his daughter
Montboissier and her husband in 1789, and their efforts to persuade
himself, the Rosanbos and Aline to join them.[12] But no. 'How can one
hesitate,' replied Malesherbes, 'between the cause of the victims, and
the cause of their executioners? Anything would be better than the
present state of affairs. As for your own particular case, no man who
bears a sword can be excused from joining the brothers of an oppressed
and captive King. You were quite right to come back from America,
and I'm urging your brother to go with you.' How could it be right,
François-René objected, to fight on the side of a foreign invader against
one's own country? But Malesherbes was ready with historical prece-
dents, Guelfs and Ghibellines, English barons and Magna Carta, and

in their own time the rebellious Americans asking French aid to fight King George. 'I myself, Malesherbes,' he cried, 'did I not welcome Benjamin Franklin in 1776, and was Franklin a traitor?' Finally he invoked the principles of natural law. 'Any government that transgresses the fundamental laws of society ceases to exist, and restores man to a state of nature. He is then entitled to defend himself as best he can, and may take all appropriate means to overthrow tyranny.' So Malesherbes appealed, in favour of the monarchy against the Jacobins, to the same persuasive but reversible gospel according to Jean-Jacques which the Jacobins cited to overthrow the monarchy!

François-René was impressed, but unconvinced, although he was determined to go in any case. 'My zeal surpassed my faith, I felt the emigration movement was stupid and crazy; my lack of enthusiasm for absolute monarchy left me with no illusions on the course I was taking.' He was joining the Princes not because he believed in their cause, but because it would be dishonourable to do otherwise.

Oddly enough, it was Jean-Baptiste who needed persuading, though not for any lack of courage or conscience. For a head of family to emigrate, leaving his wife and babes in hideous danger, exposing present and future generations to confiscation and ruin, was no light matter.[13] Besides, he belonged to a club of *enragés*, as the diehard monarchists were called, and one school of thought among these maintained that one's first duty was to stick by the King in Paris. At first, trying in his usual muddled manner to have it both ways. Jean-Baptiste had asked Malesherbes to use his influence with M. de Molleville to find him a diplomatic post abroad. But Molleville, who had no reason to like Breton nobles, replied there was nothing doing; then he resigned from office,[14] France was at war with half Europe, and unemployed diplomats were more numerous than vacancies. Jean-Baptiste surrendered at last; he would emigrate with his younger brother. However, he was no more eager than before to supply that difficult young man with money.

François-René was still penniless. Céleste's guardians were in no hurry to produce her marriage portion, nor the State to pay interest on her stocks. Clearly it was someone's duty to lend him the means to emigrate. Lucile obliged, by pledging her own security for a loan of 10,000 livres from a distant but providential cousin, a Mme du Rocher du Quengo, of the family of their paternal great-grandfather's wife.

On 16 June 1792, as François-René was returning from the notary's with his pocket-book bulging with inflated *assignats*, whom should he meet in the Rue de Richelieu but his old comrade Achard, now like himself an absentee from the regiment of Navarre? The Palais-Royal was conveniently near. Why should they not have a quiet talk, suggested the gallant Count, and escorted him to a gambling hell. François-René, led by the same desire for self-destruction which had caused him to challenge death from his father's gun in the woods of Combourg and to fall at Niagara, began to play and lose, to play and lose again. He had never gambled before, and never did so after; it produced in him a kind of intoxication, but a dolorous one, and he knew that if the passion mastered him it would overturn his brain. He stopped, in time to save his reason, but not his money. Only fifteen hundred of the ten thousand was left. Dazed with shame and horror he fell into the first cab, drove to Saint-Sulpice, left his pocket-book on the seat, and rushed upstairs to his family. 'Where's the money?' 'I left it in a cab.'

He ran back over the Pont-Neuf, suppressing an impulse to throw himself in the river. The ostlers at the Palais-Royal told him the number of the cab, the police gave him the address of the stables, far away in the Faubourg Saint-Denis. He went there and waited hour after hour in the yard, seeing cab after cab drive in, but not his own. It came at two in the morning. The man remembered him, and his next three fares: a citizen who alighted at the Jacobin Club (no use asking *him!*); a young female for 13, rue de Cléry ('No, Monsieur, I never saw anything in the cab!'); and a priest in the Recollect monastery in the Rue Saint-Martin. 'That must be Father So-and-So,' cried the porter, and led them through abandoned corridors to a cell where the last remaining monk, in dusty civilian frock-coat, sat scrupulously compiling an inventory of his foundation's treasures for confiscation. 'Are you the Chevalier de Chateaubriand?' he asked, 'I found your name and address in your wallet. I was going to bring it you after I finished my work. Here it is.'

Three days later, with the resilience of youth, he made a brief excursion to Rousseau's Ermitage at Montmorency, meaning to say farewell to the memory of that beloved writer, and to the solitude and peace which he, too, had sought in vain. Others were making the same sentimental journey. As he strolled in the park next morning he recognised two familiar faces, but only understood afterwards the full irony of their presence on that day. One was Barère, soon to be Robespierre's jackal and betrayer, the other Maret, later Napoleon's secretary of state and Duc de Bassano; the day on which they had prudently preferred communion with the ghosts of Jean-Jacques and Julie to the perils of Paris was 20 June 1792, when the mob invaded the Tuileries palace. The King, with his usual stolid presence of mind, put a red bonnet on his royal head, drank a glass of sour wine with them, and suffered no harm; but the Jacobins had now proved that His Majesty was in their power to arrest or depose whenever they might choose. If François-René was still to have a King to save, he must emigrate very soon. Jean-Baptiste brought his great mind to bear: they would leave early in the morning of 15 July, when all good patriots would be sleeping off the effects of the third annual feast of Liberty and Brotherhood.

In those last weeks, while Paris waited for some atrocious and irreparable catastrophe, François-René roamed the streets again, and saw 'a nation marching drunk over abysses and bypaths to its destiny'. He attended the Legislative Assembly. For a moment he could not think why he recognised none of the faces there; but of course, the now defunct Constituent Assembly had suicidally enacted that none of its members should be eligible for re-election, and besides, Mirabeau was dead. Near their lodgings was the meeting-place of the Maratists in the church of the Cordeliers, stripped now of all its sacred movables, a flayed skeleton of stone. Thrice he descended into that inferno, heard the goblin Marat, the snubnosed Danton, and observed bloodloving Fouché, 'in the circle of attentive wild beasts below the rostrum, like a hyena with clothes on'. The orators drew their metaphors from slaughter, sex, and excretion, called one another blackguard, thief, or catamite, amid howls and hisses from their attendant ghouls. Little owls flew screeching in through the shattered stained-glass of the rosewindows; the audience took potshots at them with their guns, like René-Auguste at Combourg; the birds fluttered down, quivering, mangled, and prophetic, into the congress of demons.

Early in July strange figures appeared in the streets, ragged, sunburnt, with looks of abject villainy and crime, the advance guard of Danton's hirelings, the men of Marseilles. The faces of passers-by, he remarked, were either frightened or ferocious. Some slipped by, hugging the house-fronts, others prowled alert in quest of prey. He saw timorous eyes, downcast and averted, then grim eyes that fixed and probed his own. He went to the theatre, and found that all the plays in that bloody season were about innocent shepherds and virginal shepherdesses, babbling brooks, woolly sheep, green meadows, and the golden age.

He said goodbye to Malesherbes at the Rosanbos' one morning. 'I shall never get used to the Court!' exclaimed the old man, and turned the conversation as usual to Rousseau. How wild he had been, how passionate, how like François-René, who perhaps, he suggested, was destined to a similar greatness. Then he remembered that poor Jean-Jacques had gone mad, or the hostile world had crushed him, it was difficult to tell which. 'I'm wrong to talk to you about these things,' said he, repenting, 'I ought rather to urge you to curb the ardour of soul which did our friend so much harm. I was like you once, injustice revolted me; I did what good I could, without counting on men's gratitude. You're young, you'll see a great deal, whereas I have very little longer to live.' To François-René the pang in his heart as they parted seemed a presentiment that he would never see M. de Malesherbes again.

What of Céleste, from whom he was now to be separated, perhaps only for a few months, perhaps for much longer? He tells us little (perhaps he knew no more), she and others nothing at all; it is only many years later that we can know her, from her letters and memoirs, her actions and reactions, the remarks of friends and strangers. In that distant future she would be amusing and crossgrained, generous and demanding, lively and illtempered, brave and timid, innocuously malicious, never contented, rather fascinating and rather queer. She would write witty complaining letters in excellent eighteenth-century prose; she would admire her husband, but not to the extent of reading his books. No doubt such characteristics were already budding in her at the age of eighteen. Probably even then, as later, their relationship was one of respect and affection, but not of love. They had not married to please themselves, but to oblige Lucile and Mme de Chateaubriand. He had undertaken 'the gravest action of my life'—or so it seemed when he tried thirty years after to recapture his feelings as a newmade husband—because 'to avoid an hour's bickering I would resign myself to a century of slavery'. 'All the future delights I had imagined for myself were to be buried in the conjugal bed with a young woman whom I did not know, to whom I would not bring happiness, from whom it was my duty to part almost immediately; I was to expose myself to the risk of begetting a new life, I who considered life the most fatal of gifts.' This danger, at least, although doubtless he incurred it often enough in those five months, was never to be realised. 'Mme de Chateaubriand is better than I,' he concluded, 'I owe a tender and eternal gratitude to my wife, whose attachment has been as touching as it was profound and sincere. She has made my life more serious, more noble, more honourable, by always inspiring in me respect for my duties, if not always the strength to carry them out.' So, then, they were to part, with regret and with anxiety for one another's safety, but not with the anguish of love.

Jean-Baptiste obtained false passports for Lille, declaring that he and François-René were patriotic wine-merchants, on a mission to procure supplies for the thirsty army of the frontier. Furthermore both were gallant members of the National Guard, as anyone could see at a glance from the uniforms in which they were disguised. Jean-Baptiste, foreseeing that he might yet be obliged to return for his family's sake even with the Revolution still unvanquished, took out on 7 July a certificate of continued residence with the Rosanbos at 28, rue de Bondy, a document which provides our only surviving description of his appearance.[15] His faithful manservant Louis Poullain was to accompany them under his own name, with instructions to pretend he did not know them; Louis was supposed to be visiting his family in Flanders, although in fact he was a Breton from Lamballe.

Secured by these ingenious precautions, they arranged a farewell

party on 14 July in the Tivoli gardens at Clichy, otherwise known as
Boutin's Folly, with the Rosanbos, Aline, Julie, Lucile, and Céleste.
Tivoli was the pleasure-park of the financier Boutin, whose daughter
was the mother-in-law of Malesherbes's daughter Mme de Montboissier.[16] The grounds contained a miniature stream worked by a
pump, complete with a pair of mountains each fourteen feet high and
several Greek temples.[17] In this agreeable spot the family said goodbye,
showing no signs of sadness; all believed, or made belief, that their
journey would be no more than a brief pleasure-trip. François-René
took Lucile aside. 'I'm putting my wife in your hands,' he said, 'you
must promise never to part from her.' Lucile vowed, and kept her vow.
On the way home they passed groups of returning revellers, with the
slogan 'Pétion or death' scrawled in chalk on their hats.

At six in the morning they took their seats in the Lille diligence next
to the driver, while Louis Poullain joined the common herd inside. At
supper that evening the poor simple man was shocked to find himself
eating at table with his masters, instead of waiting upon them. Still
more perturbed when the conversation turned on the necessity of hanging all aristocrats from street-lamps, he drowned his dismay in drink.
In times of stress Saint-Louis (as the family called him) was given to
walking in his sleep. With open glaring eyes, in total trance, he would
undress Jean-Baptiste and put him to bed, repeating 'Yes, yes, I know!'
in answer to all remonstrances; only if one threw a bucket of cold
water in his face would he come to.

Towards midnight they heard the other passengers shouting:
'Driver, stop the coach!' The door opened, the angry voices cried: 'Get
down, citizen, this is too much, get down, you pig! He's a brigand, out,
out!' Looking down they saw Saint-Louis falling to the ground, picking
himself up, gazing about with vacant eyes, and running hatless in the
direction of Paris, still fast asleep. They could not rescue the hapless
fellow without betraying their mission, so kept quiet. Next morning at
breakfast the passengers talked of nothing else. 'He was dreaming out
loud, he wasn't right in the head, he said such peculiar things! He must
have been a conspirator, or perhaps the law was after him because he'd
murdered someone!' Meanwhile the ladies cooled their blushes with
their green, Constitution-coloured fans. Saint-Louis, arrested at the first
village police-station, explained that he was the Comte de Chateaubriand's manservant, and lived in Paris at 28, rue de Bondy in the
President de Rosanbo's house. The Paris authorities took note of Jean-
Baptiste's unexplained absence, so soon after his certificate of presence.

At Lille they made contact with the royalist agent who would escort
them across the frontier. They left just before the closing of the city
gates, waited in a secluded house for nightfall, and set off at ten o'clock
through ripening cornfields. Each carried nothing but a little walking-

cane; just so, thought François-René, he had sauntered through the
forests of America behind his Dutchman. Patrols were out on both
sides. They glimpsed here and there a solitary horseman, silhouetted
gigantic, musket in hand; they heard the trot of hooves in sunken lanes,
and François-René, putting his ear to the ground in remembrance of a
trick learned from the Iroquois, caught the regular tramp of infantry on
the march. Sometimes they walked on tiptoe, sometimes they ran. After
three hours, from behind a hedge in a coppice loud with belated nightingales, a squadron of Uhlans pounced upon them with sabres raised.
'Halt! Who goes there?' 'Officers joining the Princes,' they cried, and
were marched off to Tournai for identification. In the light of dawn
these fierce allies detected the national guard uniforms beneath their
overcoats, and insulted the republican colours of blue, white and red
which in a few years Frenchmen would carry to victory all over
Europe.

At Tournai François-René, still guarded by one soldier, was allowed
to view the cathedral, while his brother visited the Austrian commander to explain that they were not spies. Jean-Baptiste returned with
passes for Brussels, where they found the modish chivalry of the High
Emigration, staff officers to a man, all in bright new uniforms, surrounded by the most elegant ladies of former Parisian society, who had
come to share and console their exile. 'They're making love in anticipation of glory,' thought François-René, 'just the opposite of the knights
of old.' This top brass looked on disdainfully at small provincial gentry
trudging past on their way to battle. François-René was better pleased
to see that his humble luggage in advance had been safely smuggled
across the frontier and arrived before him. It consisted of his uniform
as sub-lieutenant of Navarre, some clean shirts, and those of his papers
from which he could not bear to part, such as his American notebooks
and his sketches for *Atala*.

Jean-Baptiste very decently took him to dine in the best company,
with the Baron de Breteuil, the King's chief agent with foreign powers.
Breteuil could claim to be the first of all émigrés, for he had served just
three years before in the 'ministry of a hundred hours', which began
with the dismissal of Necker and ended with the fall of the Bastille. If
M. de Breteuil had not then fled so promptly, François-René might have
seen his head brandished on a pike along with Foulon's, instead of
dining with him now. Also present were his host's beautiful grand-
daughter Mme de Montmorency, a martyred bevy of exiled bishops
resplendent in shot silk and gold crucifixes, and a clever-faced man who
held forth like an oracle, as if confident that no one would dare interrupt
his monologue. François-René did not shine in that august company.
His face was still bronzed with the sun of America and the wind of
ocean, his hair was unfrizzed and unpowdered, and he wore the insignia

of an obscure sub-lieutenant. But Rivarol (for that was he) was disconcerted by his silent gaze. He whispered to Breteuil to ask who he was,
and then enquired of Jean-Baptiste: 'Where does your brother the
Chevalier come from?' Perhaps the great man intended no harm, but
the question was loaded with innuendo; for in the absurd hierarchy of
the émigrés the first to arrive were first in prestige, while late comers
were considered deficient in honour and courage. Everyone listened as
François-René answered: 'From Niagara.' 'From the waterfall!' cried
Rivarol, 'and where is Monsieur going?' 'Where there's fighting to be
done,' retorted François-René. Rivarol, for once, could find no reply.
All rose from table, and François-René, collecting his haversack from
behind the door, set off alone for Coblentz. Jean-Baptiste stayed for a
while in Brussels. As a retired cavalry-officer with good connections he
had found a cushy post as aide-de-camp to his wife's great-uncle, the
aged Comte de Montboissier.[18]

François-René travelled by way of Liège, Aix-la-Chapelle and
Cologne, where he took a river-boat up the storied Rhine to a suddenly
empty Coblentz. The army of the Princes had already departed; they
had marched for Bingen on 19 July to be reviewed there on the 22nd by
their ally and overlord the King of Prussia, and had left again for
Trèves on 1 August.

So François-René set out on foot for Trèves, and half-way there
came upon the whole Prussian army, halted on the road for a breather.
Working his way up the column he found the guns and Guard at the
head, with a square of giant grenadiers, veterans and former bedfellows of Frederick the Great. Inside the square stood the tall King of
Prussia with his commander-in-chief the Duke of Brunswick; they
recognised François-René's white uniform trimmed with blue, sent for
him, and took off their royal hats, with the overwhelming politeness of
majesty on its best behaviour. They asked his name, regiment, and
where he expected to join the Princes; and François-René, touched
with loyal emotion, declared: 'I learned of my King's misfortune in
America, and returned to shed my blood in his service.' The bystanding
officers and generals made gestures of approval, and King Frederick
William II observed gravely: 'Sir, I recognise as always the honourable
sentiments of the French nobility.' Then he doffed his hat again, and
stood bare-headed at attention until François-René had vanished
through the grenadiers.

No such welcome awaited him when he reached his comrades in their
quarters at Trèves. 'You ought to have been here three years ago,' they
said, 'you're one of those people who wait to see how things will turn
out before they make up their minds. You've arrived when victory is
certain; we've no use for you!' However, by great good fortune Armand
de Chateaubriand, his cousin and playmate of long ago, turned out to

be there, took him under his wing, and assembled the Bretons to hear his case. 'I have come all the way from America to have the honour of serving with my comrades,' declared François-René, 'the campaign has opened, true enough, but it hasn't begun. I'm still in time for the first shot to be fired. I'll withdraw if no one will have me, but not before I am given satisfaction for an insult that I have not deserved!' Now the gallant Bretons were won over, everyone invited him to join his own unit, and his only trouble was the embarrassment of choice.

In a conference at Mainz on 21 July, much to the disgust of the Princes, Austria and Prussia had enforced the partition of the émigré forces into three corps, each subordinate to an Allied commander. The Prince de Condé's division (5,000 men) would operate under Prince d'Esterhazy and his Austrians to the south in the Breisgau; the Prince de Bourbon's (4,000 men) under the Austrian Clerfayt on the northern wing; and Monsieur with Artois would lead the Army of the Princes proper under the King of Prussia and Brunswick in the centre. This was the command in which François-René now found himself; it was the largest, a hundred thousand strong, being intended for the main thrust towards Paris through the Argonne, and consisted of 42,000 Prussians, 36,000 Austrians, 10,000 Hessians, and some 12,000 émigrés, half cavalry, half infantry. The émigré infantry included thirty-seven companies of officers from the old pre-revolutionary regiments, marching as private soldiers. François-René learned that he could enroll, if he pleased, in the Company of Navarre, still commanded by the Marquis de Mortemart, and was strongly tempted to join his messmate La Martinière, even if he should turn out to be as deep in love and gooseberry liqueur as ever. But there were also seventeen companies of provincial gentlemen, these too serving as rankers, including seven from Brittany. His home province won the day. He enlisted in the seventh Breton company, under a native of his beloved Plancoët, M. de Gouyon-Miniac.

17

THE FOREST OF ARDEN

FRANÇOIS-RENÉ'S company, luckier than some, had tents, and even muskets, though these were Prussian rejects, appallingly heavy, and mostly in no condition to be fired. All through the campaign he carried on his aching shoulder a gun with a trigger that would not pull. So his ammunition-pouch was an equally useless encumbrance; he tried to stuff his manuscripts in with the cartridges, but his teasing comrades made snatches at the loose leaves protruding from the flap. At Trèves he sat in the ruins of the Roman amphitheatre, spread out the pages on the green turf, and re-read or revised his description of moonlight at Tonawanda, or an episode from *Atala*.

The King of Prussia reviewed them again on 11 August, and marched with Brunswick next day for the long road through the Argonne passes, that would lead to the cannon of Valmy, but not to Paris. At Montfort in Luxembourg on 16 August news arrived of the storming of the Tuileries on the 10th, the massacre of the Swiss guard, the imprisonment of the dethroned King. Here the émigrés, again to their disgust, were detailed to join a task force of 20,000 Austrians under Prince von Hohenlohe, with the mission of capturing the frontier fortress town of Thionville, and guarding the left flank against Kellermann at Metz to the south. This was a sideshow, though an essential one; they were not to be allowed to take part in the coming battle for the road to Paris. They marched along the left bank of the Moselle from Grevenmacher to Stadt-Bredimus near Remich, where they lingered for ten days, while the Prussian advance-guard went ahead to occupy the villages round Thionville.

On the march they sang the appropriate royalist ditty 'Oh Richard, ô mon Roi', the aria of the faithful minstrel Blondel to the captive Richard Coeur-de-Lion in Grétry's opera.

Oh Ri -chard ô mon Roi, l'uni -vers t'ab -an -donne

The torrential rains of that fatally wet autumn had begun. François-René recognised the bereaved father of his young comrade Boishue, whom he had seen slain three years ago at Rennes, on the day of swords in the streets, 27 January 1789. The old gentleman was splashing bare-

7   Chateaubriand's portrait by Girodet, 1809

8 Washington's house, 190 High Street, Philadelphia

Chateaubriand's fall at
Niagara, August 1791

Burial of Atala beneath the Natural
Bridge, from Gustave Doré

foot through the mud, alone and woebegone, with his shoes slung from his bayonet to save wear. This was a motley army. François-René heard country squires jargoning in all the dialects from Brittany to Languedoc, from Picardy to Gascony. Fathers and boys, uncles and nephews, brothers and cousins had joined up together. He saw venerable gentle-folk, sternfaced and greyheaded, trudging staff in hand, leaning on the arms of sons.

His own iron strength was giving way, not to mere hardship, but to the deeper malaise which told him he was on the wrong road, and there was no right road! He found the sixty pounds of his haversack killing; it contained, besides his shirts, cape, messtin and waterbottle, his manu-scripts and his pocket Homer. One morning, when he awoke from sleeping in a hayloft, he found himself robbed by marauding Prussians, and thanked Heaven for its crowning mercy. The good thieves had taken the heavy shirts and left his papers, thus saving both his life and his future glory. On the other hand, he now had only two shirts, the one he had on him, and one that his cousin Armand lent him. Every day he had to wash yesterday's shirt, handkerchiefs, breeches, and a turban of birch cloth, a souvenir gift from the two Floridians. As he crouched head down over a friendly brook, soaping his laundry, giddi-ness seized him, and an insufferable pain in his chest; he sat down in the cresses, and watched the peaceful water rippling by, as though there were no war.

At the end of each day's march they pitched their tents, first beating the canvas to keep the rain out, and led their donkeys to the nearest village in search of provisions. They paid scrupulously, unlike the Prussians, who were inclined to loot, rape, and burn. When François-René absentmindedly took two pears from a château orchard, he was very properly punished with extra picket-duty. They slept ten to a tent, and took turns to find bread, meat, firewood, bedstraw, or to cook. François-René received the most gratifying compliments on his stews, especially when he made them with milk and cabbage in the mode of Brittany. 'I made *wonderful* stews,' he recalled with simple pride. Besides, no one could withstand like him the smoke of wet green wood, which he had learned not to mind in the land of the Iroquois.

They left Stadt-Bredimus at last on 29 August, two days behind Hohenlohe. The sky was black with storm; dark woods loured on the horizon ahead. 'Those woods are in France!' he heard someone say, and felt a stab of anguish and a presentiment of future ill. They crossed the frontier between Rodemacher and Roussy-le-Village, and next day arrived at their posts outside Thionville.

Thionville, defiantly bursting with 6,000 inhabitants and a garrison of 5,000 commanded by Baron Wimpffen, lay on the west bank of the Moselle in a narrow plain, hemmed in by hills on which the besiegers

9

now took up their positions. Hohenlohe pitched camp four miles southward at Richemont, near the junction of Moselle and Orne, on the highroad to Metz. To his left on the high ground west of Thionville
Marshal Wallis and Prince von Waldeck at Quentrange served as link
with the Princes and the émigré cavalry stationed at Hettange to the
north. East of the town the swift Moselle separated besieged from
besiegers, except where a roofed wooden bridge, with stone piers and
ingeniously fortified outworks, crossed to the right bank under the
wooded slopes of Haute-Yutz. François-René found himself encamped
in front of Hettange with the royalist infantry and light cavalry under
Marshal de Castries, in support of the émigrés' exiguous siege artillery
of two four-pounders and one antique cohorn grenade-mortar.

They pitched their tents on the reverse slope of the hill in neat streets
(the Bretons occupied the two forward lines, with Navarre next below
to the rear), and dug a trench along the front, where they stacked their
muskets. Thionville was out of sight; but if you strolled a few hundred
yards to the crest, you could look down over the vineyards on the deep
valley, the suburban village of La Grange, and the swarming fortress
town crammed within its eleven bastions bristling with cannon.
Through a spyglass one also discerned a wooden horse on the ramparts,
with a bundle of hay in its mouth, and slung from its neck a placard
that said:

> *'When this horse begins to eat,*
> *Thionville will own defeat.'*

They fell to digging a turf emplacement and a communication trench
for their guns. Picks and shovels were on issue, but not wheelbarrows,
so they carried the dirt in their coats. While François-René drudged on
this fatigue-duty, his cousin Armand distinguished himself in a raid on
the village of La Grange. They shot their way from house to house,
and occupied all they could capture. The fourteen-year-old Duc de
Berry, Artois's son and heir, came to get his first baptism of fire, and
remarked gracefully: 'I wish I were a Breton, they always get the closest
look at the enemy.'

François-René's turn came soon, when he was on guard duty at the
battery with a hundred Bretons and a picket of cavalry. The first bomb-
shell from their cohorn mortar had fallen hopelessly short of the ramparts, to the sound of distant jeers from the garrison; but on 2 September
their battery was reinforced by Austrian artillery newly arrived from
Remich, the spyglass showed activity on the walls, and at dusk troops
were seen filing through a postern gate along the covered way to La
Grange. Next day at dawn five hundred republican infantry retook the
village and wheeled up the vineyard to assault their battery on the flank.
The cavalry picket charged bravely, but could do nothing among the

vines, and were hurled back. François-René and his hundred, exposed
and outnumbered, advanced at marching pace with bayonets at the
ready, for their muskets were not worth firing. The enemy melted away,
very luckily: 'if they'd kept on, they'd have smashed us,' decided
François-René. Even so, the Bretons had several wounded and one
killed. The dead man was the young Chevalier de la Baronnais, one of
the twenty-two sons of an impoverished and philoprogenitive gentleman at Dinard opposite Saint-Malo. Everyone knew the story of how
M. de la Baronnais had Marshal d'Aubeterre to dinner, when he came
to open the Estates of Brittany in 1775. 'You shouldn't have invited so
many people,' scolded the Marshal amiably, when he saw the table laid
for twenty-five, but: 'Your Excellency,' replied the proud father, 'I
haven't asked anyone but my children.' A bullet ricochetting from
François-René's musket-barrel had burst through the Chevalier's head,
his brains splashed François-René's face, and there he lay, 'a noble and
useless victim in a lost cause'.

Monsieur and Artois sent trumpeters on the 4th and 5th to summon
Wimpffen to surrender, but received dusty answers. Hohenlohe decided to bombard, not with the orthodox intention of breaching the
walls for an assault, but rather to scare the civilians into coercing the
governor to capitulate, a stratagem which had served the Prussians very
well at Longwy on 23 August and Verdun on 2 September.[1] The main
cannonade under Prince von Waldeck would begin at midnight on
5 September from the chapel of St. Anne below Quentrange to the
northwest, and be followed by a dawn attack. At the same time a
detachment of émigrés with their own guns reinforced by two companies of Austrian artillery would mount a subsidiary bombardment
and a feint assault on the far side of the Moselle, southeast of the town,
under Marshal de Castries.

François-René marched at dusk on the 4th, with five Breton companies, Picardy, Navarre, and a regiment of peasant volunteers, escorted
by cavalry including Jean-Baptiste's battalion. They crossed the Moselle
six miles upstream at Königsmacher, where Austrian engineers had
built a bridge of copperplated pontoons, and at dawn proceeded south
in column. François-René, with his mixed feelings towards his brother,
was not displeased to join in ironic cries of 'Forward, the aides-de-
camp!' when action was imminent.

At nine in the morning a carabineer officer galloped up, sabre in hand,
his wounded horse snorting foam and blood. A detachment from
Kellermann at Metz was attacking their left flank. François-René heard
cries from farmboy volunteers struck by caseshot, and with profound
pity saw several fall dead. Before his column could turn to confront the
enemy two bullets hit his haversack, but thanks to the manuscript of
Atala did him no harm. Drums beat the charge, he advanced close

enough to see through the smoke the dreadful faces of men resolved to kill him or be killed, when suddenly the Austrian field-guns fired, the foe gave way and fled pursued by the cavalry.

Near François-René marched Armand de Chateaubriand, who had enlisted with the émigrés long before him. Last autumn in Saint-Malo Armand had met royalist friends who urged him to join them in Jersey; when his father Pierre forbade him[2] he seemed to submit; but next day in their country home at Val Guildo he put on his hunting-jacket, went out with his dog and gun, and was seen no more. After writing to his family from Jersey on 7 October 1791 Armand made his way to Coblentz, where a deaf and dumb German girl named Libba fell enamoured of him, and still followed him everywhere. That day, during the long halt after the skirmish, François-René came upon poor Libba sitting in the bloodstained grass that reddened her gown. With elbows on knees, hands in her straying yellow hair supporting her head, she was staring at the dead boys, now speechless and unhearing like herself, and weeping. Deaf Libba had never heard Armand's voice, nor the loud sighs she heaved whenever she saw her lover, and she would not hear the wailing of the baby she was already fated to bear him.

At last they resumed marching, reached their station opposite the bridge gate of Thionville at dusk, and set up the guns behind hasty screens of sandbags, uncomfortably close to the walls; but so far no one had noticed them. Punctually at midnight Waldeck sent up a signal rocket at the opposite side of the town, and began firing. They joined in, taking the besieged by surprise for a moment; but soon the garrison brought up a double battery, which pierced their breastworks and disabled two of their guns. François-René was taken with the beauty of the spectacle. Each flash from the guns lit the whole heaven of low cloud, firepot flares showed the parapets of the town thronged with dark gunners, and incendiary bombs traced intersecting parabolas of light. Between the explosions one heard the tattoo of drums, bursts of military music, and outposts crying—in French on both sides, as François-René observed with regret—'Sentries, on guard!'

He fell into exhausted sleep between the wheels of the gun-carriages, and was roused by a violent blow on his right thigh; a shell had burst near, and a splinter had struck him. For the moment he felt no pain, and only knew he was wounded from the wet flow of his blood. It seemed little more than a graze; he staunched it with his handkerchief, and found he could limp well enough.

At four in the morning, when torrential rain put out two or three small blazes in the town, the Austrians ceased fire; they had lost three dead and ten wounded, and the enemy, with three gunners killed, remained undaunted. When the intrepid Waldeck advanced to the walls ahead of his men, hoping for a surrender, a sixteen-pounder cannonball took off his left arm.[3] In the dawn light François-René heard the trill of larks replacing the last echoes of musket-fire, and saw the enemy cannon yawning mute in the embrasures. Their war had brought nothing about. Castries withdrew the infantry to his temporary headquarters in the château of Distroff, three miles east, and posted the cavalry in the neighbouring villages, Valmestroff, Illange, and Kuntzig. All rested that day and the next, hoping for a renewed attack on the 8th; but instead to their astonishment they were recalled, and marched back to base camp.

Orders had arrived from the Duke of Brunswick on 7 September for Hohenlohe to join him immediately with most of his Austrian army, and all the émigré cavalry. The Prussians had begun their main advance through the defiles of the Argonne, 'the Thermopylae of France', as Dumouriez called it; soon Dumouriez would be obliged to accept battle, and would surely be beaten; so Brunswick needed the émigré cavalry on his right flank, ready to pursue the fugitive enemy over the plains of dusty Champagne. At this news the cavalry were delighted, but the infantry, especially the Bretons, were indignant to the verge of mutiny. This was a plot to leave them stranded at Thionville, while the rest took Paris! They refused to remain, unless 'at least one Prince' would stay with them. Artois couldn't spare a prince, but with his usual charm visited their camp in person, induced them to accept old Marshal Broglie instead, and promised to persuade Brunswick to send for them as soon as possible. So on 11 September the horsemen trotted away in drenching rain, reached Verdun on the 13th, and proceeded to Vouziers and Buzancy on the eve of Valmy. Wallis was left to continue the siege of Thionville with only 8,000 Austrians and 5,000 émigré infantry.

Quieter days followed. François-René hobbled on his wounded leg to the market behind their camp, where sausages were fried, pancakes tossed, and casks of white Moselle wine broached at cart-tails. One could buy aniseed cakes, barley loaves, eggs plain or painted red, and green apples. Village maids on wooden stools milked cows straight into one's cup, while comrades queued for their turn. Meanwhile strange bridals were pledged and consummated behind the curtains of covered wagons.

At night they gathered round the spigot of a wine-tun tilted on a cart, took shelter from the drizzling rain under a canvas awning, and listened to the tales of a Breton captain whom they nicknamed Dinarzade, partly no doubt because he came from Dinard, but also after Schehera-zade's sister. Dinarzade was short in body and long in leg, sad-moustached, hollow-voiced, and never seen to smile; he paused in his narrative only to drink from the neck of his bottle, light his pipe, or gobble a sausage. He told the story of the Green Knight—'When the wind wafted his red hair back on his helmet, it looked like a wreath of oakum round a green turban!'—how he wound his horn outside the castle of the Lady of Big Battalions, and was so kindly received by her that he even thought of marrying. The Lady was tall, thin, exhausting in her demands, but quite fascinating, except that when she smiled her nose seemed so short, and her teeth so long, that one hardly knew which way to look. Still, the Knight loved her, and she evidently loved him, so he made his offer; but first, said he, she must explain a number of odd things, and tell her name. Here the outer circle of listening canteenwomen edged closer, as Dinarzade drew his huge sword from its coffee-coloured scabbard and thrust it in the ground between his knees. 'Gentlemen,' he roared, 'the Lady of Big Battalions was Death! Death! Death!' He burst through the circle, chasing the girls before him, still shouting 'Death', while all dissolved in mirth and tumult. Then they made their way back to camp, hearing the guns of Thionville thud louder and nearer.

The besiegers were not left quite in peace. Wimpffen kept up his annoying and successful raids on provision-trains. The garrison fired every evening after supper, every morning after their breakfast mug of brandy, and whenever they saw a white-scarved noble straying incautiously near. They gave prizes for hits, paid forfeits for misses, and danced round the guns with their sweethearts every Sunday. One afternoon François-René saw a bomb falling in the middle of a circle of naval officers at dinner. Their messcan was blown to smithereens, the jolly mariners tumbled backwards, and all shouted with one voice the traditional cry: 'Fire to starboard, fire to larboard, fire in my wig!' As he passed through the woods of Quentrange on a visit to the Austrian camp he heard the burst of a shell, followed by a curious commotion in the undergrowth. A gigantic fat man was wriggling face downwards, unable to rise. François-René tugged at his pigtail, and collapsed with unfeeling laughter as the face turned round with frightened eyes. It was his cousin Annibal Moreau, quite unscathed, and three times larger than when they last met outside Mme de Chastenay's bedroom. François-René helped him to his feet, a task of formidable difficulty; 'it really needs a crane,' he thought. Cousin Moreau was wearing a chaplet for luck; he had a post in the commissariat department, he explained, and was on his way to propose a deal in beef to the Austrians.

The wet weather persisted. François-René woke with his head outside the tent-flap in the rain, and rose to stroll along the lines with a distant cousin and schoolfriend from Dinan days, Ferron de la Sigonnière. The lamplights along the streets of tents reminded them of the dimlit corridor outside their dormitory. They talked of old times and of the future, and agreed that the Princes were blind to hope that foreign invaders would restore their brother's crown. Seized by a fit of prophecy, François-René foretold that the King would die on the scaffold, and their expedition against Thionville would be one of the most damning charges against him. So it was to be.

The siege lingered on. The village of La Grange changed hands again several times, and twice François-René was present at these skirmishes; the patriots shouted insults at the émigrés, calling them 'enemies of liberty, aristocrats, satellites of Capet!', and they shouted back: 'Brigands, executioners, traitors, revolutionaries!' Sometimes he looked on at a formal duel, with both sides gathered impartially round to see fair play. On patrol in the vineyard one day he saw an elderly gentleman beating the bushes with the stock of his musket, hoping to start a patriot as on his own estate in peacetime he would have started a hare. A surprise attack on Thionville was arranged for 15 September at the prompting of the spy Godchaux, but was prudently called off; so was a bombardment on the 17th, after two redhot cannonballs had been fired into the town without causing damage.

Perhaps Artois had remembered a promise for once. Suddenly they received marching orders for Étain,[4] left on 20 September still in appalling weather, and arrived on the 23rd. The Bretons were detached to Verdun next day, where the Prussian commander refused them quarters; so they billeted in the suburbs, rested, made foraging raids on the unwilling peasants, and waited for the great advance on Paris. When François-René visited the town he found it still hung with faded garlands presented to the King of Prussia three weeks before by royalist maidens, fourteen of whom were guillotined later for their kindness.

The news worsened. Brunswick had attacked at Valmy on 20 September, his advancing infantry baulked under steady cannon-fire, the inevitable rain began to pour, and he called off the action. Goethe, who was present, prophesied: 'A new epoch of world history begins today'; and indeed, the tremendous succession of events which would end only at Waterloo, twenty-three years later, had been set in motion that day under the windmill of Valmy. Artois and his white-scarved cavalry had trotted south towards the sound of guns, too late; the firing died away, the sun set, and the long chalk-blanched road stretched ever before them. At a council of war on 24 September they pleaded to be allowed to renew the attack, even alone. But Brunswick had resolved on retreat; his men were starving, sick or dying with the 'Prussian malady', dysentery. His over-long lines of communication had been blocked by the rain. 'You will bear witness that I have been defeated by the elements,' he told Goethe. Direst of all for the émigrés was the news of the mass murders of nobles and priests in the prisons of Paris on 2 September.[5] Céleste, Julie, and Lucile in the Cul-de-sac Férou lived only a few streets away from the bloodiest massacres at Les Carmes and the Abbaye. 'My wife and sisters are in greater danger than I,' thought

François-René. How, and when, would he learn whether they were safe or dead?

Orders to advance, which they had already ceased to expect, never came; instead, on 30 September they were told to join the general retreat to Longuyon and the frontier. He marched in pain, leaning on a crutch, with his thigh swollen from the angry inflammation of his unhealed wound. Others beside himself were unable to keep up with the ranks, for the Prussian dysentery had spread to the émigrés; his company gradually dispersed, as he lagged in the rear with Ferron and another friend, who refused to leave him. They passed abandoned guncarriages, cannon sunk in the mud, overturned waggons, vivandières trudging with their children on their backs, Prussian soldiers dying or dead in the ditches. One day as they crossed a ploughed field he sank in the white clay up to his knees, and death seemed more desirable than life. 'Leave me,' said he, 'I'd rather die'; but Ferron and the other hauled him out, despite his protests, and helped him on. Then dysentery took him, like so many others, with fever, unquenchable thirst, diarrhoea of blood and mucus from his ravaged colon, and exhaustion. But his comrades stuck by him, they struggled on, and towards 14 October reached the frontier near Longwy, a week ahead of the victorious enemy. Five miles further they caught up with the Breton companies in camp at Musson, where on 16 October his captain M. de Gouyon-Miniac awarded him 'a very honourable certificate of leave'.[6]

The lost army of the émigrés was mustering for the last time at Arlon in Luxembourg, only to lay down arms and disperse. As they neared the town François-René passed a motionless line of army waggons, with horses, some stiffly standing, others collapsed with noses in the mud, all dead between the shafts. 'What do you mean to do?' asked Ferron, who had a rendezvous at Luxembourg. François-René pondered. Just before he left Paris word had come that Uncle Bédée was planning to escape with his family from Saint-Malo to Jersey. 'If I can get to Ostende,' he replied, 'I shall take a boat to Jersey and find my uncle Bédée; once there, I shall be able to join the royalists in Brittany.'

At Arlon a third malady attacked him. After twenty-four hours of vomiting and fever his face and body were covered with recurrent eruptions of red pustules. He naturally supposed he had smallpox, as did all who saw him; but from his symptoms it seems more likely to have been a typical case of chicken-pox, aggravated by his wound and by weakness from dysentery and hardship.[7] But go he must, and in these atrocious conditions he set out alone, towards 20 October. Ferron lent him six silver pieces of three francs each, and said goodbye.

Outside Arlon a peasant took him five miles[8] in his cart for three sous, and set him down on a pile of stones. He hopped a few paces on his crutch to a roadside spring, washed the bandages of his wound, and found himself much relieved by the emergence of his rash. He slept supperless in a barn, but the farmwife refused payment, and brought him a bowl of coffee and milk and a hunk of black bread next morning. Delicious! He set off gaily, although now and then he staggered and fell, and was soon overtaken by a group of his comrades, who were not quite so ill as he and insisted on carrying his haversack. In five days, taking relays of lifts on village carts, they made forty miles through Attert, Flamizoul, and Bellevue to the forested uplands of Haute Fagne in the heart of the Ardennes. Here, where the old imperial road forked right to Liège, left to Namur, his friends departed; no doubt, like many of the émigrés, they were bound for Liège, where the prince-bishop had offered hospitality for the winter. He pressed on alone, feeling none the better. His pustules had turned white, then dried and scabbed, but his fever persisted.

He stumbled six miles in six hours, and at nightfall came upon a gipsy family camping at the wayside with two nannygoats and a donkey. When he let himself drop by their hearth these singular beings hastened to aid him. Then a young woman in rags, darkskinned and mocking, came singing and dancing, hopping and twirling, holding her baby slantwise to her left breast as if it was the hurdygurdy to which she sang. She squatted on her heels beside him, scrutinised his face intently in the firelight, took his powerless hand and demanded 'one little penny' to tell his fortune. His fortune! Was it worth even this modest sum, he wondered, as he gave her a coin. But first she tended him—'No nurse could be more skilful, or more kind, or more poverty-stricken,' he thought—then he lapsed into oblivion. When he came to the wanderers were gone, and his Sibyl of the Ardennes had taken the secret of his future with her; but she had left an apple by his pillow to refresh his sick mouth. He munched it, and watched the pink light of dawn, and the dew of late October glistening on the bushes. 'Dawn and I are old friends, though we're both young,' he thought, light-headed, 'she's very beautiful, and I'm hideous; her rosy face is a sign of good health, better health than mine; this morning her tears are all for me.'

The road led ever deeper into the trees. He sang Cazotte's ballad, how 'Sir Enguerrand rode home from Spain'—

> 'And found in Arden forest on a rock
> A castle full of ghosts . . .'

Were the figures he now saw real, or emblems of another world? Pedlars passed, poor vagrants carrying all their earthly goods on their backs, like himself with his haversack. A woodcutter wearing kneepads of felt eyed him, as though mistaking him for a dead bough fit for lopping, then strode among the trees, axe on shoulder. Jackdaws, skylarks, yellow-hammers trotted along the road before him, or perched

motionless on the roughstone wall, while a kestrel glided in circles
above. He heard the trumpet of a swineherd calling his sows and pig-
lets to the acorn-wood. He rested in a shepherd's caravan, where no one
was at home but an effusive kitten, who welcomed him with all manner
of charming caresses. Far away stood the wizard shepherd in a clearing,
with his dogs sitting round the grazing sheep. So this was the forest of
Arden, he mused, remembering his Shakespeare and his Boiardo, the
magic wood in which anything might happen.

He paused for breath in a deer-covert, where fawns gazed shyly, and
a troop of huntsmen filed by on the further side. A translucent spring
gushed at his feet; this, certainly, must be the very fountain in whose
depths the paladin Roland, lost in Arden, saw a palace of crystal,
thronged with knights and ladies, and went down to join the revels of
the water-nymphs. Roland had left his horse Gold-Bridle tethered at
the edge. If only that horse were still there; or better still, if Rosalind
and the exiled Duke would come to his aid!

As he continued his way through Arden his thoughts floated outside
his body in a wordless imprecision that was not without charm. The
Sylphide and other phantoms of his youth gathered round him, in
barely perceptible shadows, to bid farewell. In an unfathomable distance, high in air, he saw his father and mother, his family and friends,
mingled with other shapes whom he did not know. Memory left him.
As he sat against a milestone, multitudinous faces smiled towards him
from doorways of remote cottages, in blue smoke curling from chimneys, in treetops, in the level sheaves of sunrays stretched in a mesh of
gold over the heather; the Muses, he concluded, had come to attend the
death of a poet. At last he could walk no more; his malady was sinking
into his body, concentrating for a new outbreak, he felt stifled and
exceedingly ill.

Towards sunset he lay down on his back, pillowed by the haversack
still containing *Atala*, his crutch beside him. He greeted with all the
kindness of his fading mind the setting sun, the same that had shone on
the heaths of his boyhood. 'He'll rise again tomorrow, glorious as
ever,' he thought, 'but I shall not.' The last sounds he heard as he lost
consciousness were the rustle of a falling leaf, and the piping of a
bullfinch.

Two hours later a train of wagons passed. The driver of one leaped
down to cut a switch of birch, stumbled over his body in the darkness,
and pushed it with his foot, taking it for a corpse. François-René gave
signs of life, the man called his mates, who voted for taking pity, and
hoisted him into a cart. He owed his life to another's death, for this was
the funeral convoy of the Prince de Ligne's men, carrying home to
burial at Beloeil the body of their Austrian master's beloved son and
heir, shot in battle at La Croix-aux-Bois in the Argonne on 14 Septem-

ber.⁹ Soon the jolting wheels brought him to; he found he could speak, and stammered to his rescuers: 'I am a soldier from the army of the Princes, and if you will take me as far as Brussels I will pay you for your trouble.' 'Agreed, comrade!' they answered, 'but thou must get down at Namur, for we aren't allowed to take passengers. We'll pick thee up again on the other side of the town.' He begged for a drink, and they gave him a draught of spirits which brought on a new eruption of rash and eased the oppression of his chest.

They set him down outside Namur at ten in the morning of the second day. The guard on the gate handed him a slice of issue bread, and the Austrian corporal produced a blue glass mug of peppered brandy. '*Teufel!*' swore the good fellow in a rage when François-René showed polite hesitation, 'thou must take it!' As he staggered through Namur, leaning against the housefronts, the goodwives emerged from their shops, calling to one another in Brabant patois. One took his arm and helped him along; when he tried to thank her, she answered: 'No, no, soldier!' They brought him bread, fruit, milk, a bowl of broth, and wrapped a shawl round his shoulders. 'He's wounded,' cried one, and 'He has the smallpox,' exclaimed others, and dragged the children away. 'Now, now, young man, you can't walk, you'll die, you must come to the hospital.' When he refused they escorted him to the further gate, relaying one another from door to door, helped him to clamber into the wagon, and made the driver vow to take special care of him. The Prince de Ligne's men put him down on the outskirts of Brussels, and declined to accept his last piece of silver.

There was no room at any inn. François-René's matted hair hung over his pockmarked and villainously bearded face; he wore a twist of hay on his festering thigh, and the woollen wrap of the women of Namur knotted round his neck over his tattered uniform. All took one look, cried: 'Go your ways!' and slammed the door. He entered a coffeehouse, and was thrown out. He was about to try once more at the hotel where he had stayed with his brother, when Jean-Baptiste in person alighted from a carriage with the Baron de Montboissier, looking spruce as ever but utterly aghast. François-René saw his brother's dismayed features through a curious haze, an aura of death which emanated not only from himself, as he thought at the time, but also, as he decided later, from the doomed Jean-Baptiste. Without knowing it, they were never to meet again.

As usual, but for the last time, Jean-Baptiste did right by his younger brother. He found him a room on the premises of an unfastidious wig-maker, summoned a doctor for his disease and a surgeon for his wound, approved his plan of making for Jersey, and gave him twenty-five louis. Jean-Baptiste had received letters from Paris. Malesherbes wished him to return to France, in the hope of evading the new law of 23 October

condemning émigrés to confiscation of property and banishment for
life; so, having done his duty to his King, Jean-Baptiste was now about
to do the still more dangerous duty to his family. He was able to give a
detailed account of the horrors of 2 September, which François-René
so far knew only from the vague reports that had reached the army a
month earlier. M. de Montmorin had been thrust through with bayonets,
impaled on a pike, and hacked to pieces. M. Émery and his seminary
had been left alone. Julie, Lucile, and Céleste were safe, thank heaven,
for Mme Ginguené, who was in the know, had warned them of coming
trouble and given them shelter in her own home; a kind and cousinly
deed, but what an ill light this inside knowledge shed on the company
cultivated by her literary husband! One could hear the screams of
the victims being chased and cut down in the garden of Les Carmes. The
authorities had relaxed passport restrictions on 8 September, and the
three girls had escaped to Fougères, arriving on the 12th. Lucile had
shown her usual clairvoyance. A few days before the massacres she
pointed to a mirror on the wall and cried out: 'I've just seen Death
come into the room!'

The doctor was amazed by the erratic behaviour of François-René's
smallpox, which defied all the rules by subsiding and reappearing,
reaching none of the correct crises, and above all by not killing him
(these, of course, are the very features which nowadays would suggest
a diagnosis of chicken-pox). The surgeon, after all but refusing to touch
him for fear of contagion, treated his wound with quinine plasters.
More than this first aid François-René would not take; though far from
cured he insisted on leaving. Odious Brussels was filling up once more
with the domesticated heroes who had made the retreat from Verdun
in their private carriages; besides, destiny pressed him on. So his stay
in Brussels lasted little more than a week. He had arrived towards
30 October, some ten days out from Arlon, and left Brussels a few days
before Jean-Baptiste, who later re-entered France with a passport pur-
porting to come from the French embassy in London and dated
11 November. Quite unexpectedly, they had departed just in time to
escape falling prisoners to their own invading countrymen. Dumouriez
had routed the Austrians at Jemmapes near Mons on 6 November, and
the last Austrians and émigrés fled only a few hours before the republican French entered Brussels on the 15th.

François-René made an easy trip to Ostende, by canal-barge, and
there found other Breton comrades who shared his purpose. They
chartered a half-decked smack, and slept in the hold on pebbles that
served as ballast. He could no longer withstand the violence of his old
friend, the wintry sea; his last strength left him, he could not speak, nor
take any sustenance but a few drops of water and squeezed lemon.
Heavy weather forced them to put in at Guernsey, where an émigré

priest said prayers for the dying over him, just in case. The captain, not wishing to have a corpse on board, had him carried to the quayside and propped against a wall in the November sunshine; there he sat, gazing vacantly over the sea to the coast of Alderney, where eleven months before he had confronted death in a different form.

The wife of an English pilot passed by, saw him with pity, and called her husband, who with the help of friendly sailors bore him to their cottage. Even in his extremity François-René could not help feeling all the more gratitude for her sympathy, and the more shame for his own repulsive state, because she was fair-haired and beautiful. She put him in a decent bed with white sheets, nursed him with every care, clasped his burning swollen hands in hers, which were slender and cool, and almost wept when he left next morning.

They landed at the western end of Jersey. A comrade of his own age, Joseph du Tilleul from Fougères, whom he had already encountered there in happier times, crossed the island to Saint-Helier to inform Uncle Bédée, who sent him back next morning with a carriage. As they drove through the inland valleys François-René, though almost dying, tried to express his rapture in the scenery of the leafless woodlands, but could talk nothing but nonsense, for he was now delirious.

Bédée and his family had arrived at Saint-Helier during the last week in July, and lodged in the Rue des Trois Pigeons (the modern Hill Street) at the house of a prominent citizen, Thomas Anley Esquire.[10] The jolly uncle and crosspatch aunt, their son the Chevalier Marie-Annibal, and the three girls Flore (Mme de Blossac), Claudine, and his old sweetheart Caroline, all took turns at nursing by his bedside. His supposed smallpox had ended, but left him with a persistent respiratory ailment of which, together with exhaustion and exposure, he again all but died. Bédée wrote immediately to his sister Apolline, Mme de Chateaubriand, one of whose pathetic replies survives, dated 8 December from Saint-Malo, distracted, devoted, and wrapped in riddles to deceive the revolutionaries. She sends 782 livres in assignats, also '12 golden apples and a yellow rennet apple' (doubtless louis d'or) 'to pay the board and bed-linen of the child who has smallpox'; also ten new shirts, six second-hand, with handkerchiefs, cravats, stockings, gloves, a coat, and trousers. She has written to Céleste for a winter coat and 'all the best her charity can do'. As for 'your friend Jean', he has 'sent satisfactory reports from his teachers, but his family don't know what to do with him now he's leaving school; he's heartbroken to know you are in such difficulties, but the boy is so young that *he can do nothing at all for you*' (a guarded reference to Jean-Baptiste's return from emigration and his inability to exert influence on Bédée's behalf). Lastly Bédée must 'see that the invalid writes to answer his relatives' questions, but tell him not to mention his family, and that he will have to forget his sisters and brothers'. This letter of 8 December is evidently not her first since hearing of François-René's arrival, and shows that he must have reached Jersey before the end of November.

For some weeks he lay between life and death. Dr. Delattre, a Breton émigré from Saint-Servan next to Saint-Malo, forbade him to talk about anything serious, especially politics. But Tom Anley's house was uncomfortably crowded, and as soon as he was fit to be moved the Bédées found him a pleasant lodging at Captain Renouf's, in the new street of sea-edge cottages on the sand-dunes called Les Mielles, in the neighbourhood of the modern Parade Place. His windows came down to floor-level, and he could watch the sea as he lay in bed.

One day towards the end of January Uncle Bédée came in, unwontedly serious and dressed in full mourning. François-René trembled, fearing news of a death in the family; but no, explained Bédée, the King had been guillotined on the 21st. François-René was shocked but not surprised; he had foreseen this calamity ever since his moment of decision in the Virginia millhouse. Malesherbes had spoken for the defence at the King's trial, to no avail, but to the admiration of all Europe, including even the *Gazette de Jersey*. This, then, was the melancholy fulfilment of his lifelong ambition, to do his royal master a service that even *he* would be obliged to notice. Malesherbes was well aware of the price he would pay for this reward. One of the accusers reprimanded him for using the forbidden terms 'Sire' and 'Your Majesty' when addressing the prisoner Capet. 'What makes you so bold?' 'Contempt for you,' replied Malesherbes, 'and contempt for my life.' But he knew also with anguish that he risked involving his entire family in his own doom; and in fact from that time the implacable eyes of the Jacobins were directed upon all his kin, young and old, male and female, including even the Chateaubriands, not because such insignificant creatures were dangerous, but because they were relatives of Malesherbes.

Ordinarily, however, the Bédées were merry as ever, even though François-René recalled an example of their joviality which is unlikely to amuse modern doglovers. A huge hound named Azor, a lineal descendant of the grim beast who had couched in her lap at Monchoix long ago, had consented to emigrate with aunt Bédée. But Azor bit everybody and was afflicted with mange, so the girls took it upon themselves to have him secretly hanged. Mme de Bédée consoled herself for his mysterious disappearance: Azor, she decided, had been abducted by English officers, bewitched by his beauty and pedigree, and was now feasted and pampered in one of the stateliest homes of King George's realm. But they had little present cause for mirth, and laughed most over memories of the old days and Monchoix. Bédée in exile, with his lands sequestrated and his very clothes and favourite gold-knobbed walking-cane impounded at Saint-Malo,[11] could no longer support his family. His son the Chevalier left for London, 'to live on poverty and hope'; Caroline had to teach French (a language she hardly knew, if one judged by her spelling) at a girls' boarding-school; and François-René determined to leave Jersey rather than be a burden on his kind uncle.

First he must get well. He appreciated the exquisite local honey, the richness of the cream, the dark yellow butter in which he detected a fragrance of violets. In May he was strong enough to walk out at last, and explored the delightful island—'covered with cows and country-houses'—in the mild sea air of spring.

He consulted the Prince de Bouillon, the acknowledged leader of the three thousand émigrés on Jersey. Ought he to join the royalists in Brittany, he asked, as he had intended at Brussels? Alas, La Rouërie was no more! The Marquis had timed his insurrection for September last year, but was obliged by news of Valmy to postpone it till the spring; then he died of a stroke, caused by frantic despair on hearing of the execution of the King, in his hiding-place at the château of La Guyomarais between Plancoët and Lamballe, on 30 January 1793. One of the conspirators—none other than young Chèvetel, son of the physician who had attended François-René after the year of the Sylphide at Combourg—was a government spy in the pay of Danton, and seized this opportunity to betray them. The authorities dug up La Rouërie's body[12] in March, and arrested such of his friends as they could lay hands on. They were taken to Paris,[13] the merciless Fouquier-Tinville was prosecutor, and on 18 June twelve were guillotined, including Thérèse de Moëlien. The beauty of Thérèse, which had overwhelmed François-René as a boy at Julie's wedding eleven years before, roused the callous admiration of spectators at the scaffold.[14] Meanwhile, however, La Rouërie's movement was far from broken, and had already begun to merge into the risings of the Chouans in Brittany and the Vendeans south of the Loire. But the Prince dissuaded the thin and fevered François-René from joining the outlaws in Brittany. 'You're in no state to live in caves and forests,' said he, and advised him to move to England and wait for an opportunity to take regular service, in the émigré corps which was forming there since Great Britain declared war against republican France on 1 February. Thus the last of several chances to engage in the Breton counter-revolution passed François-René by. Bouillon recruited Armand de Chateaubriand instead; and for the next sixteen years Armand plied as secret agent between Jersey and Brittany—a dreadful trade!

Thirty louis arrived from his family by a smuggling boat from Saint-Malo, and he booked a passage to Southampton on the *Jersey Packet*. So did many other émigrés on the overcrowded island, some to enlist, others to seek their livelihood, and some to remove their families after the invasion scare of 23 April, when a French fleet hove in sight, but turned out to be only a munitions convoy bound for Cherbourg. On 10 May, by order of the new commandant Colonel Craig, all resident émigrés were instructed to register. Some could not remember the exact date of their arrival, and François-René, supported by two witnesses, gave what was perhaps the day of his removal to Captain Renouf's, 20 January 1793.[15]

He sailed about 15 May. In the throng of fellow-émigrés on the boat he made the acquaintance of François Hingant de la Thiemblay, a native of Dinan aged thirty-two, who happened to be an ex-colleague of Jean-Baptiste and cousin Bédée in the extinct Parlement of Rennes, and found him cultivated and amusing. Then he went below, and saw through the open door of Captain Antoine's cabin a young man in French naval lieutenant's uniform, who sat playing chess, and looked up idly without knowing him. True, François-René's face was altered by time and illness; but he recognised Gesril immediately. They told one another of their travels. Since their last meeting on the quayside at Brest, ten years before, Gesril had served in the Indian Ocean, received his lieutenancy on 9 October 1789, and joined the army of the Princes in 1791. He too had fought at Thionville, in the cavalry regiment of naval officers which had camped just to the right of François-René's infantry; but somehow their paths had never crossed either there or on Jersey, where Gesril had landed a few days before him on 11 November. Having told their stories they embraced, on the waves of the same sea where long ago they had played the dangerous games of children, but now in everlasting farewell.

NOTES

CHAPTER 1   THIS PITILESS STORM

1 Mme de Plouër was the daughter of Louis, Marquis de Contades (1704–1793), Marshal of France, and his wife, *née* Nicole Magon de la Lande, who belonged to the same wealthy Saint-Malo family as the Chateaubriands' new landlord.

2 The siege occurred in the War of Succession between the rival claimants for the dukedom of Brittany, Jean de Montfort supported by the English, and Charles de Blois supported by the French. Charles attempted to recapture La Roche Derrien, near Tréguier, from the Englishman Thomas de Dagworth, but was taken prisoner during a night attack on 20 June 1347, in which Geoffroy VIII was slain.

3 The livre was a value-measure equivalent to the franc.

4 The first wife of Christophe de Chateaubriand, Protestant and second murderer, was a Sévigné. Plélo was the nephew of Jeanne de Bréhan, wife of Mme de Sévigné's spendthrift son Charles.

5 The Parlement of Rennes, a body of a hundred or so noble magistrates sitting all the year round, except for the three months of summer vacation, not only constituted a high court of justice subject only to the Parlement of Paris, but had the duty of registering the Estates' edicts for taxes, and the right, if it saw fit, of rejecting these and remonstrating to the King.

6 The Estates, as provided by the 1532 Act of Union between France and the Duchy of Brittany, consisted of the three Estates or orders of the nobility, the clergy, and the Third Estate or deputies of the towns. Their chief task, besides the local affairs of Brittany, was to discuss and vote or protest against the taxes and subsidies demanded by the King. They met every two years after harvest-time at Rennes, Nantes, Dinan, or Saint-Brieuc.

7 The Abbé de Chateaubriand de Bellestre was a descendant of Jacques de Chateaubriand, younger brother of Christophe II, grandson of Briand the murderer.

8 In fact Clémenceau's prisoner was not La Chalotais, but the lesser accused Bouquerel, whom Des Fourneaux himself had delivered into his custody. The purse belonged to Bouquerel; Clémenceau had tried to hand it to Des Fourneaux for safe keeping, and on his refusal conscientiously deposited it with the registrar of Rennes. As for the poison, it existed only in Des Fourneaux's fantasies of persecution. 'Milk is the best antidote for poison,' he used to say, and would add, slapping his pockets, 'I always carry a bottle of it with me!'

9 M. René-Claude de Montbourcher, president of the court of justice of the Parlement of Rennes, contributed 40,000 livres of the purchase price, receiving in return the barony of Aubigné which formed the southeast portion of the property.

CHAPTER 2   THE RAMPARTS OF SAINT-MALO

1 The street and hamlet took their name from the medieval priory of Saint-Maur-du-Bas-Plancoët (a dependency of the Benedictine abbey of Saint-Jacut at the mouth of the Arguenon), at the foot of the hill near the river, not from the Dominican convent founded in 1647; but Chateaubriand by a confusion of memory believed that Saint-Nazareth was a Benedictine abbey. The hamlet then counted as part of the parish of Corseul, four miles to the southeast, and has belonged to Plancoët only since 1841.

2 La Villeneuve's real name was Claude-Modeste-Thérèse Leux. In 1771 she was aged thirty-two, and unmarried.

3 'I don't know what a *"tête d'achôcre"* is, but I am sure it must be frightful,' wrote Chateaubriand. *Achôcre* is a word still current in the patois of the Cotentin peninsula in Normandy, and means a dunderhead.

4 Stanislas, or Pierre-Stanislas, was born on 23 February 1767, Armand on 15 March 1768.

5 The lordship of Le Plessis-Bertrand (the boundary between which and the domain of the bishopric of Saint-Malo was marked by a calvary half-way along the Sillon) was founded by Bertrand III du Guesclin in 1237, whose grand-daughter Tiphaine married Bertrand de Chateaubriand de Beaufort. Their son Briand V inherited the lordship on the death of his cousin Tiphaine, a niece of the earlier Tiphaine. Through this alliance the Chateaubriands of Beaufort were kinsmen of the great Constable Du Guesclin (1320–80), the hero of Brittany, who nearly drove the English from France in the first half of the Hundred Years War. A different Le Plessis (a small estate acquired in 1592 by Gilles de Chateaubriand, son of Briand the murderer) was still used as a courtesy title by René-Auguste's brother Pierre de Chateaubriand du Plessis, and before him by René-Auguste until his purchase of Combourg.

6 Jean-Baptiste, however, was rarely at home. He was already at school in Saint-Brieuc, aged twelve, when the three-year-old François-René returned from Plancoët in 1771. In 1774 he was fifteen, studying in the college at Rennes for a legal career in Parlement, and as wellbehaved as ever.

7 '*Des fouetteurs de lièvres*', meaning ne'erdowells.

8 Joseph de Chateaubriand du Parc, after a promising career during fourteen years as codfisher, slaver and corsair under René-Auguste's orders, had lost heart and abandoned the sea when he returned from captivity in England in 1760, although he continued to take shares in René-Auguste's ventures. The account of this disappointing uncle in *Mémoires d'Outre-Tombe* shows no knowledge of his energetic beginnings, and applies only to his last twelve years of premature retirement, when he buried himself in a Paris library, engaged in historical research of which no relic seems to have survived, and wrote home once a year to his solitary mother at Guitté. Chateaubriand is also mistaken in supposing that Joseph existed on his meagre heritage of 416 livres a year, for his earnings in trade, his prize-money from corsairing and his later investments must have made him wealthy. However, it is evident that this youngest brother was thought to have let the family down. Joseph returned to Guitté seriously ill, and was nursed by his aged mother at the nearby watering-place of Dinan, where he died on 12 August 1772, only forty-four years old.

9 René-Auguste's distant cousin, Abbé Charles-Hilaire de Chateaubriand de Bellestre, had dutifully resigned his rights as eldest brother (just as had

René-Auguste's own elder brother Abbé François) to enable his youngest brother Louis de Chateaubriand de Vaurenier to make a rich marriage. But Louis's wife had been forced by his misconduct to obtain a judicial separation, and the prodigal brother, now aged sixty, his inheritance squandered, living in taverns and brothels on a small pension from his wife, on begging and blackmailing letters to his relatives, and on the sale of his very clothes for drink, had become a public scandal. René-Auguste, at the earnest request of the entire family, had been obliged to write in his best prose a petition to the King for a *lettre de cachet*, and to obtain the signatures of Pierre and even of the half-estranged elder branch, the Chateaubriands of La Guérande. The astonished minister at Versailles, the Duc de la Vrillière, expressed natural doubt: 'Can his conduct at the age of sixty be really so depraved as to justify his punishment by the loss of his liberty?', he enquired of his officials in Brittany; but the report came back that Louis de Chateaubriand, 'though sixty, retains the vigour of youth and makes full use of it', and that not only family honour but public order demanded that he should be put away. The *lettre de cachet* was duly issued in the summer of 1774, and the elderly scapegrace was imprisoned in the gaol of Saint-Méen at Rennes.

10 Gesril was born on 23 February 1767.
11 In fact Mlle du Boisteilleul had merely adapted a well-known satirical ditty of her youth on the amours of the Duc de Richelieu with the Regent's daughter, and substituted the name of Trémigon. 'How many things in this world,' wrote Chateaubriand, 'end like the love-affair of my great-aunt, with Tirra-lirra!'
12 On 11 May 1745, when the English captain Lord Charles Hay politely cried: 'Gentlemen of the French Guard, fire first!' The King and the Dauphin watched the battle from a neighbouring hill.
13 'The first time in my life that I was decently dressed,' he wrote resentfully; but many years later his neighbours in the Rue des Juifs, the Gilberts, remembered him in Saint-Malo at the age of five or six as 'wearing on feast-days a blue bonnet with white plumes'.
14 Until early in the twentieth century a set of child's clothing which might have been François-René's was still to be seen, brown with age and preserved under glass, near the Virgin's statue at Notre-Dame de Nazareth.
15 Less the 40,000 for which he had sold the dependent barony of Aubigné and the 15,000 for which he had undertaken the Combourg lawsuits.

CHAPTER 3 COMBOURG CASTLE

1 The name was originally *Combour*, meaning valley on the borderland (from *cumba* = valley or coomb, and *ora*), and the final *g*, giving a false etymology from *bourg* = castle, was not added until the sixteenth century.
2 In fact Combourg came to Maclovie de Coëtquen, Duchesse de Duras (1724–1802) only in 1746. Her father Malo de Coëtquen died in 1727, a few months after the death of Jules-Malo, his son and heir by a previous marriage. Jules-Malo's own son died young, bequeathing the seigneury to his sister Augustine, who died in 1746, leaving her aunt Maclovie, now sole survivor of the family, to inherit Combourg.
3 'He recovered the domain of Combourg, desiring to return to the lands through which his forebears had passed . . . Several branches of my family had possessed Combourg by marriages with the Coëtquens . . . The Maréchal de Duras, who held Combourg from his wife Maclovie de

Coëtquen, whose mother was a Chateaubriand, made an arrangement with my father'. In fact Mme de Duras's mother was Marie Loquet de Granville, of a wealthy Saint-Malo family, who married Malo de Coëtquen in 1723 when he was governor of Saint-Malo.

4 For example, Jehan de Tinténiac, victor in the celebrated Combat of the Thirty in 1351 and husband of Jeanne de Dol, Lady of Combourg, was the son of Eustachie, daughter of Geoffroy VI Baron of Chateaubriand. Brian de Chateaubriand de Beaufort joined forces with Raoul de Coëtquen in 1379 in support of Jean IV, Duke of Brittany, in his war with Charles V of France. His grandson Briand was ward of Raoul de Coëtquen in 1409, and in 1423 made a feudal accord with Geoffroy de Malestroit, lord of Combourg. Briand's son Bertrand de Chateaubriand did homage for the seigneury of Beaufort to the Lord of Combourg in 1466. Catherine, sister of François de Chateaubriand de Beaufort (great-grandson of Bertrand and father of Briand the murderer), married Jean de Coëtquen in 1547.

5 When the castle was restored in the 1870s by Jean-Baptiste's grandson Comte Geoffroy de Chateaubriand (1828–89) the four towers were given new names which they keep to this day. The north tower with the clock was called Tour du More, or Moor's Tower, after the famous lines in Chateaubriand's poem on the home of his boyhood:

> ... *cette tant vieille tour*
> *Du Maure*
> *Où l'airain sonnait le retour*
> *Du jour.*

The west tower was named Tour du Croisé (Crusader's Tower), after Baron Geoffroy IV who had attended Saint-Louis in the Seventh Crusade; the east tower was called Tour Sibylle, after their daughter Sibylle de Chateaubriand (1876–1962) and her thirteenth-century namesake, the faithful wife of Baron Geoffroy; and the south tower was named Tour du Chat, Cat's Tower, after a mummified cat which was discovered there during the restorations, and is still exhibited to visitors in the present library in the Tour du Croisé.

6 René-Auguste formally regained possession of it, after his son's schooldays were over, on 9 July 1784.

7 M. Petit married Marie-Anne de la Bliardière on 18 November 1780. René-Auguste, Julie and Lucile signed the register.

8 Néel de Lavigne, a visiting friend of David de la Bliardière, remembered being ordered out of Mme de Chateaubriand's drawingroom when their games became too noisy. 'Go for a walk, young gentlemen, I beseech you, and take my stupid beast of a son with you!'

9 Lauzun, who became posthumously famous for his scandalous memoirs published in 1821, was then a court roué and favourite of Marie-Antoinette; he fought the English in America in 1780–3, later served the Revolution, and was guillotined in 1793 for winning battles, unlike other generals who were guillotined for losing them.

10 Lucretius, *De rerum natura* (i, 1): *Mother of Romans, joy of gods and men* ...

11 Tibullus (I, i, 45–6): *How sweet to hear the raging winds in bed*
   And clasp my lady fondly in my arms!

12 Massillon, *Carême*, sermons xvii and xxxvii respectively.

13 This abbey, which still survives as the old-age home of Dol, was founded in 1076, became a seminary of the Eudists (an order instituted by St. Jean

Eudes in 1643 for training to the priesthood and improvement of preach-
ing) in 1697, and was rebuilt in the 1770s. It had known gayer times in the
seventeenth century, before the coming of the Eudists, when, as it was
said, 'various young ladies of the neighbourhood can remember having
danced in the priory as freely as one could do in some profane place'.

14 Not a quotation from Virgil, as Chateaubriand thought later (although
Virgil does say: *Macte nova virtute, puer, Aeneid* ix, 641), nor from Statius,
as his editors affirm (though Statius does say: *Macte animo, juvenis, Thebaid*
vii, 280), nor apparently from any Roman author, but merely one of the
traditional *Gradus ad Parnassum* tags available in the concoction of school
Latin verses.

15 Abbé Leprince moved to a living at Saint-Simon-sur-Rille in Normandy
in December 1781, but died in the following summer.

16 After the death in battle of the last baron, Geoffroy VIII, in 1347, the
barony of Chateaubriand had passed through the female line into the
house of Montfort-Laval, and thence in 1539 to that of Montmorency,
and to Condé-Bourbon in 1689.

17 Despite the Abbé's claim the Chateaubriands of Bellestre (who sprang
from Jacques, younger brother of Christophe II, eldest son of Gilles,
eldest son of Briand the murderer) were in fact slightly junior, as if it
mattered, both to the Chateaubriands of La Guérande (who derived from
Michel, eldest son of Jean, eldest son of Christophe II) and to the
Chateaubriands of Combourg (whose ancestor was René-Amaury,
Michel's younger brother). Abbé Charles-Hilaire, born in 1708 and now
seventy-two, was famous for his long battle with the cathedral chapter of
Rennes, who asserted special rights over the church of Saint-Étienne at
Rennes, where he became rector in 1748, including that of celebrating
high mass there on certain days and, worst of all, of pocketing half the
chief annual collection on St. Stephen's Day. His finest hour was on St.
Stephen's Day, 26 December 1761, when he boldly took his own mass
and collection before the canons arrived; but the case was taken to the
Parlement, who declared against him in 1763. He resigned in 1767,
returned to Rennes as rector of All Saints in 1770, retired in 1776 to
become rector of Val-aux-Bretons near Pleine-Fougères (ten miles east of
Dol), and died there in 1782. When he visited François-René in the
winter of 1780–1 he was perhaps on his way home after his victory with
the Estates at Rennes.

18 The Abbé Leprince died in 1782 (see note 15 above). Abbé Égault became in
1783 chaplain and master of the village school at his birthplace, Saint-
René in the parish of Saint-André-des-Eaux ten miles south of Dinan,
and lived till 1821, leaving an unpublished poem on the art of making
acrostics. Abbé Portier died at Dol on 13 January 1791. Of his schoolfellows at Dol Chateaubriand mentions only Le Gobbien. Two others are
known by name: Joseph Sébillot, a nephew of Abbé Égault, who claimed
to have been still better at Greek than his classmate Chateaubriand, and
Chesnel, who addressed him as *tu* (a form then used even by schoolboys
only with particular friends), and remembered him writing his name
above a fireplace at school.

19 In *Génie du Christianisme*, I, i, ch. 8, Chateaubriand approves the prudence
of the Church in timing the sacrament of confirmation 'at the moment
when the heart is about to blaze with the fires of its passions, and God
becomes the immense Genius who suddenly torments the adolescent and
pervades the faculties of his restless and growing soul'.

20 For example, in the certificate of his tonsure on 16 December 1788, and the register of his marriage on 21 February 1792.
21 Until the Restoration, when he signed as Vicomte de Chateaubriand.

CHAPTER 4 RENNES AND BREST

1 Mont Thabor, just beyond the northeast corner of the city walls, was then acrimoniously shared by the Bishop of Rennes and the Benedictine Abbey of Saint-Melaine, although the townsfolk were already admitted.
2 The present Lycée of Rennes was built on the same site and to a similar ground-plan during the nineteenth century. None of the original buildings survives except the chapel, which became the parish church of Toussaints in 1803, the old church (where Chateaubriand's distant uncle had been rector in 1770–6) having burned down in 1793.
3 Chateaubriand remembers the Abbé Germer in a passage of his Memoirs written at Venice in September 1833, in which he compares the fresh water supply of Venice, brought in barges over the salt lagoon from the mainland, to 'Naiads swimming across the Hellespont', and adds in ironical self-congratulation for this learned simile: 'My teacher of rhetoric, the Abbé Germer, must be well pleased with me this morning on the dark shores, among the *pallentes umbras Erebi*, the pallid ghosts of Hades'. The Latin is spoken by Dido in his favourite Book Four of the *Aeneid* (line 29).
4 Chateaubriand mentions only these three masters in this order, and was no doubt instructed by all three in succession. He probably spent the autumn of 1781 on probation in the second class at Rennes, and was then allowed to take rhetoric with 'physics' during a calendar year rather than a school year, in view of his need to take the naval examination at Brest in the spring of 1783, and hence to leave Rennes at the end of 1782. Gesril, who was eighteen months his senior and left Rennes for Brest at the end of 1781, had apparently done likewise. In any case there is no need to doubt, as some have, that he took rhetoric at all; not only because he was a pupil of the Abbé Germer ('my teacher of rhetoric'), but also because he had already taken his second class at Dol, and because at a period when higher education (for church, law, army, navy and other professions) began at fifteen or earlier, it was normal to commence rhetoric at about thirteen, instead of about sixteen as nowadays.
5 A decree of 2 August 1779 forbade in the public exercises 'any thesis or verbal expression contrary to religion or moral purity', and complained of 'licentious or even irreligious remarks made by young people who, knowing nothing because they have never learned anything thoroughly, and blinded by dangerous reading, have shown proof of ignorance, wrongheadedness, and an already corrupted heart'. Another of 27 January 1782 prescribed a written examination in religious subjects for the end of each school year.
6 Mme de Chateaubriand's mother, Bénigne de Bédée, was daughter and grand-daughter of a Farcy. Her father Benjamin de Ravenel du Boisteilleul had married Catherine de Farcy in 1685, and his father Jean had married Judith de Farcy in 1650.
7 Bezout died on 27 September 1783. Stanislas joined the merchant navy instead, went slaving like his father before him, on a ship that sailed from Saint-Malo on 15 March 1785, and died two months later off the coast of East Africa, on his first voyage, aged only eighteen.

CHAPTER 5   SISTER AND SYLPHIDE

1 Jacques-Charles-Louis de Malfilâtre (1732–67), of whom a contemporary wrote the celebrated line: '*La faim mit au tombeau Malfilâtre ignoré*'.

2 Renée de Chateaubriand, last of the Chateaubriands of Beaufort, had sold the seigneury in 1666 to a certain Marille de Forsanz, who resold it to Claude de Goyon in 1675. The ruined castle of Beaufort may still be seen, six miles southwest of Dol on the edge of the marshlands, which it was built to command under the overlordship of the first Counts of Combourg.

3 The title alludes to Bernardin de Saint-Pierre's *Études de la nature*, published in 1784, which he may well have read in the year of its first appearance.

4 '*Forêt silencieuse*', he says in his Memoirs, was written 'at this time', and '*Nuit d'automne*' was published in the *Mercure de France*, 3 July 1802, as 'lines by a young man aged sixteen'.

5 These included, two or three years later and perhaps even already—besides the French and Latin classics he had read at school, contemporary poets such as La Harpe, Delille, Fontanes, Parny, and the seventeenth-century bucolic poet Segrais—the great pre-romantics Rousseau and Bernardin de Saint-Pierre, and the recent French translations of Goethe's *Werther*, Gessner's idylls, Macpherson's *Ossian*, Gray's *Elegy*, and Thomson's *Seasons*.

6 Perhaps Mme Gesbert ('very pretty') rather than Mme de Trémaudan ('extremely beautiful'), as the former, whose marriage he had attended at Bécherel in 1782, was still in her early twenties, whereas the latter, who married in 1769, the year after he was born, was about ten years older and the mother of five children; but not, as has been suggested, Thérèse de Moëlien, who never married and did not live near Combourg.

7 Rousseau, explaining in his *Confessions* (Book XI, first published posthumously in 1788) that his *La Nouvelle Héloise* was not a *roman à clef*, says: 'It is undeniable that I wrote this novel in the most burning esctasies, but people were mistaken in supposing that these ecstasies required real objects to produce them: the degree to which I was capable of inflaming myself for imaginary beings was far from being understood. Were it not for a few memories of my youth, and Mme d'Houdetot, the loves I felt and described would have been experienced only with Sylphides.'

8 Either the passage-grave at Chevrot, two miles northeast on the road to Saint-Léger, or the standing-stones on the heath of Saint-Mahé two miles northwest on the way to Lanhélin.

9 Said by local tradition to be the *Indien*, captain Jean Bazin, owner M. Maison-Neuve.

10 M. Magon de Boisgarein had sold it in 1780 to M. Dupuy-Fromy, who let it soon afterwards to the innkeeper M. Chenu. To this day it remains part of the premises of the neighbouring Hôtel de France et de Chateaubriand.

11 A *maître des requêtes* was a magistrate appointed to report on petitions to the King's council.

CHAPTER 6   ROYAL HUNT

1 The Rue du Mail still exists, running from the Place des Petits-Pères, near the northeast corner of the Palais Royal, into the Rue de Montmartre. Mme Récamier was to live at no. 12 ten years later, during the Directory.

2 Mme de Sévigné cultivated Auguste-Robert de Pommereul, a prominent official in the government of Brittany under Louis XIV. 'He is the politest and wittiest of legal gentlemen, a great friend of mine, and treated here like a god,' she wrote to her daughter Mme de Grignan on 11 December 1675.

3 The identity of Chateaubriand's Mme de Chastenay remains unascertained but she was no doubt some aunt or older cousin of Victorine de Chastenay (1771–1855), then still a young girl, who met him long after, and wrote witty Memoirs published in 1896.

4 Mutual donation of property at the time of marriage was a quite usual form, especially when, as in the case of M. and Mme de Chateaubriand, the assets of the couple were approximately equal. It occurs also in Lucile's marriage-contract in 1796. Mutual donation served to protect the survivor after the death of one of the parties, together with any children when these were under age, from claims by the family of the deceased, and to give a widow bargaining power to procure an adequate dower. Even the disputation over the right to apply seals, quaint as it seems, was not a mere empty form, as right to seal went far to establish right to administration of the property.

5 Because no military gentleman below the rank of cavalry-captain could be presented to the King, it followed conversely, by the logic of etiquette, that anyone who *was* presented became *ipso facto* a captain of cavalry.

6 Françoise de Chateaubriand was a Foix, Lautrec's sister, and her husband was one of the Lavals to whom the barony of Chateaubriand had passed through the female line in 1347. Brantôme tells how, when the King cast her aside and demanded the return of the jewels he had given her, she had them melted down and sent him the gold, keeping in her heart, as she said, the words of love that were engraved upon them. According to legend her wronged husband imprisoned her in a black-draped room at Chateaubriant, and then murdered her by opening her veins; but in fact she died a natural death many years after.

7 At that time the children of noble families came of age at twenty-five. Lucile was twenty-two, François-René only eighteen.

8 The fact that a loaf of sugar and a pound of candles were found locked in René-Auguste's study cupboard does not mean that no one else was allowed any, but that the old man prudently kept a private store of sweetness and light for his 5 a.m. coffee, rather than send to the kitchen. The value of François-René's bed is the same as his pampered brother's (200 livres), and surpassed only by his mother's (500) or Uncle Antoine de Bédée's (320). It is true that no fire-irons are listed for his room, but then, none are mentioned for his father, Lucile, or M. de Bédée, who must certainly have had bedroom fires; so it is absurd to argue that he was not allowed one.

CHAPTER 7 SWORDS IN THE STREETS

1 Mgr des Laurents died on 15 October 1785, having collapsed by the Calvary halfway along the Sillon on his way home from official business in Paris, and his last words were: 'Oh my dear Saint-Malo, I see you for the last time!'

2 It was estimated that of an annual ten and a half million livres of taxes paid by Brittany the nobility contributed only 125,000.

3 'The hearth-tax was to the French Revolution what the stamp-tax was to the American Revolution,' wrote Chateaubriand.

4 The Champ Montmorin was laid out in the southeast part of Rennes by the foreign minister M. de Montmorin in 1785 when he was commandant of Brittany, and still survives as the Champ de Mars.

5 Among the councillors deputed to soothe the rioters was Lucile's former wooer, M. de Malfilâtre.

6 The brave and illfated Victor Moreau, François-René's former school-fellow, then aged twenty-six, was in his seventh year as a law-student, but had always attended the Café de l'Union more assiduously than the law-school. He had run away from home at the age of seventeen to join the army, but his father had insisted on buying him out. The Parlement, when he led his comrades to victory in the street fighting of the previous May, had complacently called him 'Parlement's General', and a general indeed he was destined to become; but now he had committed his forces to the support of the Third Estate.

CHAPTER 8   LOVE AMONG THE RUINS

1 *L'écueil blanchit sous un horizon pur . . .* (iii, 1.6)
Le vieux soleil glace de pourpre et d'or
Le vert changeant des mers étincelantes . . . (viii, 1.16–17)

2 *. . . des îles de bonheur . . . des mondes enchantés,*
Baignés des eaux d'une mer inconnue . . . (viii, 20–24)

3 Thérèse de la Lande de Calan (1735–1822) took refuge at Nice after the events of 14 July 1789, leaving her business affairs to be handled by Jean-Baptiste. One of her husband's ancestors had married a Chateaubriand of Beaufort in 1543, and others had since been godparents to various Bédées. Her mother was a Bégaignon as was Mme de Chateaubriand's maternal grandmother, and the position of her uncle François-Jacques (1707–95) as Grand Treasurer of the Knights of Malta may have suggested Jean-Baptiste's plan to have François-René made a member of the Order.

4 Nos. iv (*Le soir, dans une vallée*), v (*Nuit de printemps*) vii (*Le Printemps, l'été et l'hiver*), ix (*L'Amour de la campagne*).

5 The little waterfall which forms the outflow of the millpond of Choiseul near Fleurigné, the home-village of Bois-Février, is still called Chateaubriand's cascade.

6 Marguerite de Loaisel de Villedeneu had died on 20 May 1783, aged seventy-two, and her sister not long after.

7 M. Réveillon was rumoured to have said that the people could live on 15 sous a day, whereas in fact he had sympathetically declared: 'I have to give my men 40 sous a day now, and they don't live as well as they did on 15 in my young days.'

8 The Cahier of Combourg contained complaints against church tithes, which had nothing to do with the Castle, but none against feudal dues. Once again, there is no sign of special resentment against the late Count or his family.

9 It was the Bishop of Chartres, speaking out of turn, who renounced the preservation of game. 'His Grace has taken my shooting,' murmured the Duc du Châtelet, 'now I'll take something of his', and he proposed and carried the abolition of tithes. One agitated nobleman passed a note to the president: 'Suspend the sitting, they've all gone crazy.' 'Each freely gave what did not belong to him,' reported another.

10 The town hall and tax offices of Rouen were sacked on the night of 3 August 1789 by a mob led by an actor sent from Paris for the purpose, the celebrated Harlequin François Bordier, who found he had played one trick too many. The regiment of Navarre dispersed the rioters and saw him safely hanged on the 21st. But all was not well even with Navarre, for fifty soldiers joined the insurrection, tried to persuade their comrades to join them, and had to be dismissed with ignominy.

11 It was not M. Gelée's fault. He had dressed these last clients under duresse from the mob, went raving mad with shock, and cut his throat a week later.

12 This wellmeaning hero, as Rivarol said, 'slept against his King', for Lafayette was in bed at the time. Mme de Villette, an advanced Vol-tairean liberal, had the extreme courage to go to law against her brother's murderers, but of course nothing was done to bring them to justice.

13 The word was then in the air. 'This humane nation will turn into a horde of cannibals, and end as a vile gang of slaves,' wrote a deputy on 5 August; and Lally-Tollendal in October called the Assembly 'a den of anthropophagi'.

14 Only Parny and Flins were absent from the 1790 *Almanach des Muses*, and even they appeared in the preceding and following numbers.

CHAPTER 9 THE STOCKING-SELLER

1 The house still survives as 4, rue des Jeûneurs, near the corner of the Rue de Cléry. It was a fashionable address, for Necker himself had his mansion near by in the same street, on the corner of the Rue de Mulhouse.

2 'Under twenty-five' meaning under age for a nobleman, like François-René himself.

3 This polite formula, *Je n'ai besoin de rien pour le moment*, clearly means no more than this, and not (as generally interpreted) that his financial difficulties were over.

4 Having done more than any man to overthrow the King and raise anarchy, Mirabeau had now decided that France could only be saved from the populace if he himself became His Majesty's sole adviser, at a suitable price. He wrote to Lafayette on 28 April 1790 proposing co-operation in return for the payment of his colossal debts and the embassy at Con-stantinople, 'where I discern at the present moment the lever of an entirely unprecedented influence!' 'They're buying me, but I'm not selling myself,' he told his friends, in evident allusion to the epigram of his rival Rivarol, the Mirabeau of the Right, who said: 'I've sold myself, but they aren't paying me.'

5 The date is not necessarily that of writing, for it is not in François-René's hand, but added after receipt by La Morandais. The two remaining letters in his stocking-selling correspondence are equally doubtfully dated 21 September and 'October' in yet another hand.

6 Saint-Cloud, where the captive King was graciously permitted by the Assembly to reside during the summer and early autumn of 1790, was a particularly suitable rendezvous for royalists. Either Panat or François-René was mistaken in the matter of Rivarol's presence, for 'This was the unique occasion on which I saw him in my life,' says the latter of his meeting with Rivarol at Brussels in 1792. However, each was giving his recollection of this period thirty years after.

7 Perhaps François-René really said Worms, where the Prince de Condé

was already beginning to collect émigré officers, though few had taken the plunge yet, or Turin, where the King's brother Artois was doing likewise. But he cannot have said Coblentz, where the muster of a royalist army did not begin until Artois's arrival there in June 1791.

CHAPTER 10   HYPERBOREAN STRANDS

1 A slip of memory, or a misprint which he never corrected, for the true date is 1729.
2 The offer was first made in September 1788, when his unpopular cousin Lamoignon was dismissed from this key post at the fall of Loménie's government, and repeated a year later after the fall of the Bastille.
3 A presentation copy to Malesherbes from the author of *Voyages dans l'Amérique septentrionale* by the Marquis de Chastellux (1786) survives to this day.
4 'Laugh often, little cousin, forget politics,' wrote La Luzerne's daughter Alexandrine on this occasion to Jean-Baptiste's wife Aline, 'or this bitch of a Revolution will be the death of us all.'
5 Or, as Chateaubriand put it more explicitly in *Voyage en Amérique* (1826), 'doubt still remained on the possible existence of a passage between the 40th and 60th degrees of north latitude'.
6 'If no discovery'—that is, of De Fuca's Sea of the West or De Fonte's transcontinental strait—'had changed my direction, I would have advanced to the mouth of Cook's great River, and thence to that of the Coppermine River in 72° north', he wrote in *Essai sur les Révolutions*, but in other versions: 'I decided to identify Bering Strait, and return eastward along the shores of the Polar Sea.'
7 Or rather, since Cook, from Icy Cape some 200 miles northeast of Bering Strait, where Cook was turned back by the Arctic pack-ice.
8 In fact the mouth of the Coppermine River was over 200 miles further south, at 67° 47', Hearne having miscalculated from dead-reckoning.
9 A group of Breton merchants at Lorient (where René-Auguste had business associates, and François-René's future wife was born) agreed to send Ledyard to Nootka for sea-otter furs; but their application to the King in February 1785 for a commission for a voyage of discovery with powers to claim any new lands for France, to sail in August, was not granted, no doubt because it would have clashed with La Pérouse's expedition which set out in the same month.
10 Jones, who was in Paris to collect prize-money from his captures of English ships in the late war, planned to send Ledyard with two ships at the end of 1785, found he could not afford the expense, but kept Ledyard alive with small loans until Jefferson took over.
11 Jefferson's accounts show gifts to Ledyard totalling 846 livres in 1786. 'My friend, my brother, my Father—I know not by what title to address you,' wrote Ledyard in pathetic gratitude from London.
12 However, as Jefferson's letter to Ezra Stiles of 1 September 1786 records, Ledyard had already promised Jefferson two years before to cross the American continent from east to west, as a last resort if his other hopes of reaching Nootka by sea or through Siberia should fail.
13 He could have read the news of Mackenzie's first expedition even before he left Paris, in a brief note in *The Gentleman's Magazine* for November 1790: 'Mr. M'Kendrie [*sic*] has penetrated from Montreal to the Ocean about 69° N.'

CHAPTER 11 SULPICIAN ARK

1 Victor was a Broglie name, but the usual assumption that the Troubadour was a Broglie seems impossible. The old Marshal, then in exile (aged seventy-two) and his son (aged thirty-four) were too old and busy to fit, and the grandson, who was to marry Mme de Staël's daughter Albertine, was a schoolboy of fifteen.

2 At the end of 1790 Mme du Belloy was twenty-one, Mme de Beaumont twenty-two (just three weeks older than himself), Mme de Custine twenty, Natalie de Noailles sixteen, and Mlle Bernard, the future Mme Récamier, a child of thirteen.

3 Christian de Chateaubriand, born 21 April 1791.

4 This literary lady was editress of *The Lyrical and Entertaining Courier, or Dressing-Table Pastime* (*Courier lyrique et amusant, ou passetemps des toilettes*), and wrote love elegies in the *Almanach des Muses* to the coy Elmandre, who was none other than Fontanes himself; whereas he, meanwhile, addressed his amorous verses not solely to her, but also to Mlle des Garcins of the Comédie Française. Fontanes was sowing his last wild oats before settling down. Through his friend Joubert he had been in negotiation since 1788 with the Baron de Juis, the guardian of a wealthy heiress, Mlle Cathelin, who became Mme Fontanes in 1792.

5 Mayor Gesbert invited the Supreme Being to 'deign to extend His favour to the pact of federation which a nation that is entirely devoted to Him is about to contract under His auspices'. A mass with Te Deum was celebrated at a special altar erected in the courtyard of Combourg Castle.

6 Mme de Bédée had moved in 1787 from her Maison Notre-Dame (which was to be confiscated from the Dominicans in 1791 for the use of the local constitutional priest), and had recently moved again to the Maison Lôrre. The precise position of her last two homes is unknown, but both were in the Rue de l'Abbaye.

7 However, it could have been in December 1788, when he visited Saint-Malo for his tonsure, for the exact year of La Villeneuve's death is unknown.

8 He was entitled to use the family seigneury as a surname. Many Breton gentlemen did so, for example Limoëlan, whose name was Picot, or La Rouërie himself, whose name was Tuffin. It was also normal to travel slightly incognito, under a byname which foreigners would find easier to pronounce. La Rouërie had been known in America as Colonel Armand. By 'State of Brittany' La Rouërie meant the Estates, which François-René was privileged to attend, and had attended, as a nobleman.

9 Probably this was Father Chédeville, who alone of his clerical colleagues had sworn the constitutional oath on 6 February, and was also a member of the municipal council.

CHAPTER 12 DISCOVERY OF AMERICA

1 *Psalm* xxvii, 3.

2 Father Nagot, in a letter from Baltimore of 26 July 1791, said they arrived at Graciosa on 3 May, perhaps rightly. However, he may have guessed wrongly from memory, whereas Chateaubriand, although writing five years later (*Essai sur les Révolutions*, II, liv), seems to have used notes written on the spot, and the later date would suit the delays of their voyage.

3 Perhaps François-René was thinking of Alexander VI's bull in 1493,

which gave Portugal the Azores and all ocean lands east of a demarcation line in mid-Atlantic, and Spain all to the west.

4 Their fear was far from absurd. Graciosa had a long memory for the Barbarine raids of the late seventeenth century, when the Azores were returned from Spain (who held them from 1580 to 1640) to the weaker control of Portugal, and the Moslem corsairs were in their heyday. The danger seemed renewed since 1785, when Spain made a hundred years' truce with Algiers, and Portugal took over the task of blocking the Straits of Gibraltar. The corsairs slipped through to raid Atlantic shipping in this very summer of 1791 and again in 1793, though they never again visited the Azores.

5 The dark blue birds were no doubt bee-eaters, settling in the branches as is their gregarious habit to wait for passing insects, although François-René took them for *sarcelles* (teal).

6 The legend of this equestrian figure began with the transference to Corvo of a tale, reported by the twelfth-century Arab geographer El-Edrisi, of red-coloured statues on the Canary Isles, which Alexander the Great had set up to warn seamen not to venture further west. It was later rationalised by the existence of natural lava formations at the western extremity of Corvo. The alleged find of Carthaginian coins on Corvo in 1749 was equally fictitious, though believed by Chateaubriand and still often repeated. In fact, no authentic remains of human visitors before the late medieval period have been found on any of the Azores islands.

7 This was *Gaultheria recumbens*, a member of the Ericaceae family, also variously known as wintergreen, partridge-berry, red, mountain, New-foundland, or Labrador tea.

8 Fontanes's poem was '*Le Chant du Barde*', a lament of Ossian for his father Fingal (*Almanach des Muses*, 1783, pp. 227–30). Flins continued the theme with '*Chant d'une jeune fille d'Écosse*' (*Almanach des Muses*, 1784, pp. 169–70), in which an Ossianic maiden mourns the death of her lover slain in battle. He was, she says, 'fairest of warriors' (*le plus beau des guerriers*), and she longs, in lines which must have held a special appeal for François-René,

> '*To join my mother and the Sylphs I knew*
> *In the cloud-palace of the dead for ever*'
> (*A des Sylphes connus me joindre pour jamais*
> *Et retrouver ma mère au palais des nuages*).

François-René no doubt read these poems of Fontanes and Flins, and Le Tourneur's French translation of Macpherson's *Ossian* (1767), in boyhood at Combourg. His own poem, which did not achieve publication in the *Almanach des Muses* and remains lost except for his citation of its opening line (*Il plaisait à ton cœur le plus beau des amants*), was evidently a response to Flins's, addressed by the ghost of the slain warrior to the bereaved maid.

9 Perhaps the letter was detained on the way, or never sent. The visiting codfishers of 1791 brought the Revolution with them, and left a Jacobin club behind them in the autumn. In February 1792, after riots in which a woman was killed, D'Ansseville at the request of the island assembly restored order by deporting the ringleaders, who were given a heroes' welcome in France as victims of aristocratic despotism. D'Ansseville resigned, Abbé Allain, rather than take the oath of allegiance to the Republic, left for Canada with the most faithful of his flock, and further troubles were resolved by the deportation of the entire population by the British in 1793. Saint-Pierre remained under British occupation, except

for a brief interval in 1802 after the Peace of Amiens, until 1816, since when it has continued French to this day.

10 The moon was full on 16 June 1791.

11 This was Fisher's chipmunk (*Tamias striatus fisheri*), then known as the 'ground squirrel' or 'little striped squirrel'.

CHAPTER 13   A FALL AT NIAGARA

1 However, Christ Church Philadelphia, completed in 1744 with its 200 foot steeple, was monumental even by European standards.

2 She was probably Mary Wilson, who joined Washington's household in the spring of 1791, for the other chief housemaid at this time, Katy Jacobus, was the elderly wife of Washington's elderly coachman.

3 Washington's delay of seven weeks in replying to La Rouërie was due not only to his illness, but to his custom of polishing off his French correspondents in a batch after waiting until he had a suitable messenger to take them to Europe in person. He wrote to Lafayette and La Luzerne at the same time as to La Rouërie. His full letter to La Rouërie does not survive, but only the précis here quoted, which was written by a secretary in Washington's letter-book. The actual letter would no doubt have included Washington's promise to see Monsieur de Combourg after his return to Philadelphia, as he surely did in the following November or December.

4 'When very young he visited this country, and was introduced to General Washington,' wrote the knowledgeable reviewer of the American translation of *Les Martyrs* in the Cambridge, Mass. *General Repository and Review* for January 1813. 'We have seen persons here that remember to have conversed with him and his travelling companion at Philadelphia'.

5 At Worcester, on the road from Hartford to Boston, Chateaubriand must have passed within a few miles of Milford, where the great Peter Pond was then living in retirement. It is conceivable that he visited Pond to ask for advice on the Far Northwest, as did the French naturalist André Michaux only ten months later, when he too was planning a transcontinental one-man expedition. 'Peter Pound [*sic*]', Michaux noted in his diary, 'is a traveller who has lived in the interior for nineteen years, and has journeyed to the West as far as Rainy Lake, Lake of the Woods, Lake Winnipeg, Lake Manitoba. He says one has to be at Montreal by the end of April to join the Canadian traders when they set out.'

6 The record passage from New York to Albany was sixteen hours, the average about thirty-six, though three or four days might be needed against a strong north wind. A usual fare was two dollars, with excellent meals on board at a dollar a day. There were numerous sailings daily; in that year, 1791, the *Albany Gazette* reported forty arrivals on a single day in April, and eleven sloops on 6 June.

7 Other similar French dancing-masters were at large in upper New York State at this time, such as M. Robardet, who left Albany to teach President Washington's step-children in that very year, 1791, or M. Dulompré, who advertised his dancing-school at Albany in 1784, 'at the most moderate terms of one guinea entrance and one guinea a quarter'. Or perhaps M. Violet was the 'little French Canadian who lives always with this family', whom Patrick Campbell met near by only a few months later, on 25 March 1792, in the Indian tavern at Oneida Castle.

8 In Indian and trappers' folklore the carcajou was supposed to hang from

trees by its tail (in fact its tail is long, busy and curved, but not prehensile), to hunt in friendly alliance with foxes (foxes do in fact follow it to its caches of meat), and to kill deer and caribou by lying in wait for them in trees, dropping on them, and biting their throats (a confusion with the raccoon or kinkajou, a member of the bear family, or with the larger felines such as the lynx or cougar). These fables were seriously reported in standard literature, not only in Charlevoix and Carver, from whom Cheateaubriand copied them in good faith, but in many others whom he did not read. In reality the carcajou, quickhatch, glutton, wolverine, Labrador badger, or black devil is the largest of the weasel family, a foot high at the shoulder, three feet long, weighing up to thirty pounds, with black head and limbs and reddish brown belly. It is now found only in the Canadian northwest and arctic, but was then still extant in upper New York State and the Lakes region, though becoming scarcer. Its fine-haired fur was specially valued for hood linings, as it does not ice up with freezing breath, and was priced by French fur traders in the top class of fur with bearskins, otter and raccoon at five francs, above beaver and red fox at three francs. The carcajou feeds on small animals and carrion, is a great robber of traps and caches, and is notoriously wily and hard to catch. It was a special attraction in the recreational hunting parties organised for travellers by the local Indians. 'My savages said they wanted to make my joy complete,' says La Hontan, 'meaning that they tacitly promised to find me some carcajous.'

9 Chateaubriand comes rather well out of this display of natural history, for which he probably relied on notes taken for Malesherbes at the time. Both the 'white dwarf plantain' and the *rhododendron maximum roseum* or 'big laurel' are typical of this region, as is the osprey, or fish hawk as Americans call it. His *passer nivalis* was no doubt not the true snow bird— which is a common winter visitor to these parts but migrates far north in summer to breed, and is mostly grey and black in plumage, being named from its season rather than its hue—but the 'chipping sparrow' (*fringilla socialis*), a summer visitor, mostly white, and at that time popularly confused with the snow bird, which was mistakenly supposed to change colour and stay the summer.

10 An interesting sidelight is thrown on Chateaubriand's narrative by the diary of Elkanah Watson, merchant and canal-promoter (1758–1842), who visited the district only a few weeks later. Kahiktoton (as he is spelt in the Fort Stanwix treaty of 1788), or Kiadote as Watson calls him, was indeed in touch with the American land-commissioners at this time. 'In the evening,' wrote Watson on 14 September 1791, 'we pitched our tent at Mr. Moses De Witt's camp at the Three River Point, who is locating the military lands (destined as gratuities for the troops of the New-York line in the late war) with a company of surveyors.' Next morning he was visited by 'old Kiadote, king of the Onondaga Indians, with several warriors and the queen, who brought us some excellent fresh salmon and eels in a basket slung to her back, for which we gave them in exchange rum and biscuits. Kiadote possesses a sensible, sedate face—the name means a tree with thorns and fruit upon it.'

11 The incident is again extraordinarily confirmed by Elkanah Watson, who wrote on 13 September 1791: 'Near the west end of the lake (Oneida) are two small islands, in one of which resides a respectable Frenchman who came from France a few years since, and has voluntarily sequestered himself from the world, and taken up his solitary abode upon this island, with

no society but his dogs, guns, and library, yet he appears happy and content.' Either this was Le Cocq himself, or someone not unlike him. Chateaubriand told the story in *Essai sur les Révolutions*, adding in a manuscript note in the so-called 'confidential copy' that he found Le Cocq 'near the mouth of the Morohawe [*sic*] on Lake Ontario'. The Mohawk, of course, flows into the Hudson River a little north of Albany, and at this point some 150 miles further west he was near its source, not its mouth. But this absurd error, caused by geographical vagueness of memory, is not difficult to disentangle. The river route to the west left the Upper Mohawk by a short portage at Fort Stanwix to Wood Creek, proceeding across Oneida Lake to the Oneida River, Three Rivers Point, Oswego River, and Lake Ontario at Fort Oswego. Both Three Rivers Point and Lake Oneida's western end were within a few miles of François-René's camp at the outlet of Onondaga Lake, and no doubt he met Le Cocq somewhere in this neighbourhood.

12 Or, in the words of a chief to Isaac Weld in the same district: 'a little of that precious water you possess, to wash our eyes with'!

13 This remarkable passage, first published in 1928 but never appreciated as evidence, corroborates the truth of Chateaubriand's own affirmations, that he had concerted his plans of exploration with Malesherbes before leaving Paris, and left with the intention of discovering the Northwest Passage, and disproves the notion of his critics that he invented these projects retrospectively after his return. It further shows that he had set out with literary plans, and had confided these to Malesherbes; and it confirms his claim to have worked on them during his journey as far as Niagara.

14 Colonel Thomas Proctor and a French Captain H. G. Houdin had reached Niagara early in May 1791 as unofficial envoys from Knox the American Secretary for War, with tactless messages for the Iroquois Indians under British protection. They asked Gordon for passage along Lake Erie to Sandusky in a British frigate, which he indignantly refused, much to his superior's approval; 'the application has to me an appearance of insult,' wrote Dorchester. Next they proceeded to Buffalo village, where they invited the Seneca chiefs to attend a council at Fort Washington (Cincinnati) on the Ohio, and to persuade the Western Indians to keep the peace. The envoys were received with derision, for by an unfortunate crossing of wires the Senecas had just received an entirely incompatible appeal from Saint-Clair to join the war on his side against their Indian brothers. François-René's Dutchman was no doubt one of the several such interpreters active in upper New York State and mentioned in the Niagara archives of this year, such as Hendrick Wemple, or N. Rosencrantz, and it would not be surprising if their employer Mr. Smith, merchant, of Schenectady and Canandasago, were the same as Chateaubriand's 'Mr. Swift of Albany'.

15 An incident confirmed by mentions of the remarkable prevalence of rattlesnakes at Niagara by many travellers of this and the next decade.

16 Or below the elbow? In *Essai sur les Révolutions* (written in 1796) and in the corresponding passage of *Mémoires d'Outre-Tombe* (written in 1822 and many times revised) he says *au-dessus du coude*, whereas *Voyage en Amérique* (published in 1827) reads *au-dessous*, probably a mere misprint which remained inadvertently uncorrected.

17 Saint-Louis, founded by Frenchmen in 1764 as a furtrading centre, was still the only white man's settlement (except the smaller Sainte Genevieve some sixty miles further downstream) on the west bank of the Upper

Mississippi, where it lay twenty miles below the outfall of the Missouri. In 1791, under its Spanish governor, it had about 600 white inhabitants, nearly all French, including a number of wealthy merchants. These had kept their culture and morale more successfully than the depressed remnants in the Illinois settlements at Cahokia and Kaskaskia on the east bank lower down, or at Vincennes on the Wabash. It would not be surprising if Chateaubriand's companions were connected with the most powerful of the Saint-Louis merchants, the celebrated François Vigo, who traded with Pittsburgh and the Eastern States by the same river routes which they were about to follow. Until the end of the War of Independence (in which he gave indispensable help in supplies and credits to the great George Rogers Clark, the conqueror of Illinois) Vigo resided at Saint-Louis, with which he still maintained connections; but in 1783 he transferred his headquarters to Vincennes. In the summer of 1791, together with his usual business, Vigo was aiding Saint-Clair's mobilisation and transport of supplies on the Ohio.

CHAPTER 14   OHIO MOUTH

1 Chateaubriand's harmless anecdote has been unjustly doubted. It is true that the Great Lakes are exempt from any perceptible lunar tides; but they are subject to variations of ebb and flow, some sudden, some seasonal or in periods of years, which at that time were loosely given the name of tides, and were discussed as a scientific problem or described as a curiosity in the narratives of many travellers. The south shore of shallow Erie was notoriously liable to flooding. François-René was no doubt on the lookout for some surprising phenomenon, and made do in good faith with a chance gurgle of the waves on a calm night.

2 Chateaubriand's critics have been unable to reconcile this remark with his ultimate aim to reach the Arctic and discover the Northwest Passage, forgetting that he had planned first to cross the continent and reach the Pacific coast in about 40° N. The Ohio route to Saint-Louis was the quickest, easiest, and safest, and was in fact chosen by Lewis and Clark in the first successful transcontinental expedition fifteen years later.

3 The American geographer John Melish made the trip in the six days 21–23 and 25–27 October 1811, without hurrying, and in a worse season, with trails and rivers flooded after the autumn rains.

4 The Moravian missionary David Zeisberger had resided on the Cuyahoga with his band of Christian Indians in 1786–7, and continued to record news of the district in his diary. Neal's store was stocked in the summer of 1786 by six trips of a train of ninety packhorses and ten men under James Hillman, who recollected that the overland packhorse trail left the upper Mahoning River at Salt Springs (the modern Weathersfield), crossed the divide near the modern Ravenna (where it coincided for a few miles with the portage trail over which river travellers—including, as we shall see, François-René—carried their canoes from the Cuyahoga to the Mahoning headwaters), and joined the Cuyahoga at the mouth of Breakneck Creek, near the modern Kent.

5 These landscapes in Chateaubriand's 'Journal sans date', and those that immediately follow, are characteristic of unchanged parts of the district to this day, are described as primeval in the Ohio Geological Survey of the 1870s, and are not found in any contemporary account published in Chateaubriand's lifetime. So he must have seen them himself.

6 This likelihood is strengthened by the fact that the diary-narrative is immediately followed in *Voyage en Amérique* by, as he says, 'a detached page which transports us to the midst of the Appalachians'.

7 So it would hardly be possible even for less experienced travellers than François-René's companions, or even without the Indian guides they brought with them, either to miss the crossing or to take more than an hour or two to walk it. The actual purpose of their reconnaissance (which he must have misunderstood, or forgotten, or altered for literary reasons) was surely to find the nearest place deep enough for their canoe, and to make contact with the Indian carriers who, as they rightly expected, would be somewhere near waiting for clients.

8 But they may have taken their canoe with them, or had the use of another, for canoes or small pirogues were often towed or lashed alongside to accompany flatboats and other larger vessels, for use in visits ashore and similar conveniences.

9 'Barge' in this context meant a long, narrow, swift rowing-boat, as used by naval officers on a man-of-war, not a flatbottomed cargo-boat for sailing or towing (though the latter was also in use on the Ohio). There is no reason why François-René and his companions should not have been allowed a passage on such an army barge as far as Cincinnati, where Saint-Clair was then completing his mobilisation, but there is no positive evidence to suggest it.

10 It was usual to travel through the night, with a night watch consisting of a lookout forward, a steersman on the stern oar, and two men on the sweeps. May did so, travelling thirty-three miles in six hours by moonlight on the first night, and continuing in a storm of thunder and lightning throughout the second.

11 The despatches of Saint-Clair and his officers complain of low water in 1791, but not in September, when their belated supplies seem to have arrived without further hitch. The same source mentions a 'favourable rise in the river' in mid-September of the previous year. The daily weather reports in the *Columbian Magazine* of Philadelphia record rainy weather throughout the first half of September 1791.

12 Cutler, the learned land-promoter, inspected the site on 6 September 1788, counting up to 400 annual rings in selected trees sawn down for the purpose, and took particular note of a white oak 'with 289 circles, four feet in diameter' growing amid 'traces of three ancient stumps, from six to eight feet in diameter'. These details were recorded in Cutler's minute kept at Marietta and first published in the centenary year 1888. Evidently Chateaubriand learned of them orally on the spot, and did indeed 'sit on these ruins'.

13 The strictly contemporary applicability of this remark to the year 1791 has not been noticed. Until the admission to the Union of Kentucky next year, in 1792, Tennessee in 1796, and Ohio in 1803, the boundaries of Virginia and North Carolina were considered to run uninterruptedly west as far as the Ohio and Mississippi Rivers. The state of Pennsylvania, of course, extends as far as Pittsburgh on the Ohio to this day. West Virginia, with its western boundary on the Ohio at Wheeling, was not separated from Virginia until 1861.

14 'Everything here assumes a dignity and splendour I have never seen in any other part of the world,' remarked Imlay of the country near Limestone, 130 miles upstream from the Kentucky mouth.

15 Paducah at Tennessee Mouth, Metropolis, Ill., at the site of Fort Massac,

Cairo at Ohio Mouth. Smithland at the mouth of the Cumberland never thrived.

16 A slight anachronism, for until three or four years later the existence of the Rockies remained unknown, and the standard geographies, such as Morse, continued to affirm that the Alleghenies were the highest mountains on the continent. Towards 1794 the northern ranges seen and crossed by Mackenzie began to be marked on maps, followed by the tremendous coastal peaks observed by Vancouver, and these were correctly surmised to continue southwards to the Cordilleras of Spanish California; but the vast breadth of the parallel chains of the Rockies within the United States remained unrealised until the return of Lewis and Clark's expedition in 1806.

17 The five last speakers of the Natchez language lingered on at the Chicassaw reservation in Oklahoma as late as 1911.

18 John Pope, whom Gayoso had 'regaled with delicious nuts and excellent wines' at Natchez only six months before, found him 'of majestic deportment, softened by manners the most engaging and polite'. Gayoso regularly patrolled his domain in his galley *Vigilant*, and sometimes encamped, for a Pisgah view of American territory or a conference with American dissidents, on that very bank opposite Ohio Mouth, where Michaux met him on 16 December 1795.

CHAPTER 15   THE TWO FLORIDIANS

1 Probably no later than 1792, when still under the first impact of Bartram's book, as most of the extracts are taken from its first few chapters. Chateaubriand no doubt reworked these in England towards the later 1790s for possible inclusion in the lost second part of *Essai sur les Révolutions*, or in *La Génie du Christianisme*. The compilation formed part of the manuscripts which he left behind in London on his return to France in 1800, and regained in 1816. He adapted it in the manner here described when writing the American episodes of his Memoirs in London in 1822, and in 1827 published the unadapted form which he had recovered in 1816 in *Voyage en Amérique*.

2 The American surveyor Andrew Ellicott met near Ohio Mouth in 1796 'Mr. Philip Nolan, so well known for his athletic exertions and dexterity in taking wild horses'. Nolan (*c.* 1770–1800) began his career as a smuggler of Spanish horses from Louisiana to Kentucky in this very year, 1791. No doubt he had other rivals and predecessors.

3 This southerly moon seen at sunset would doubtless be the waxing young moon of about 30 September. The moon was full on 12 October 1791.

4 A very easy accident, for in later life Chateaubriand wrote, revised, and inserted on loose leaves, delegating to his secretaries and amanuenses the task of putting these in the correct order and making a fair copy. In this way various passages were omitted from the final text, or like this one interpolated out of sequence, without his intention or knowledge.

5 The priest, after a river-journey up the Mississippi from New Orleans to New Madrid, was paying a duty call at Nashville before proceeding home, for otherwise their ways would not have coincided. During the first years of postwar slump the French settlers in the Illinois had been left to their own devices; the Governor Saint-Clair had visited Vincennes and Kaskaskia in 1790 and taken them under the civil administration of the United States, while the newmade Bishop Carroll began to gather their

Church under his wing, and sent François-René's shipmate Father
Levadoux to Vincennes soon after his arrival. This new regime was not
welcome to the old-established French priests of Illinois, whose links
were rather with their fellow-countrymen of Saint-Louis and New
Orleans, who were then under Spanish rule. No doubt the journey of
François-René's companion was connected with this dissidence, and the
old priest himself may well have been Father Gibault of Vincennes, or
Father Saint-Pierre of Cahokia, both of whom defected to the Spanish
shortly afterwards.

6 The news of the Flight to Varennes and the King's arrest first appeared
in the New York and Philadelphia papers on 23 and 24 August 1791, just
before (according to our calculations) François-René's departure from
Niagara. Either the newspapers had not yet arrived when he reached
Pittsburgh towards 7 September, or else he missed seeing them. There-
after he would travel ahead of Philadelphia news until it met him from the
opposite direction, in the region of Knoxville or Abingdon, exactly as we
may gather from his narrative that it did. The botanist Michaux, travelling
the same route in 1795, provides an interesting parallel. As a French spy
he was keenly awaiting news of President Washington's official recognition of the French Republican envoys, an event which occurred on
25 June 1795; but a newspaper account of it first reached him when he was
botanising near Tennessee Mouth (close to the presumable meeting-place
of François-René and the Two Floridians) in the period 13–16 October.

7 Individual and spontaneous defections of officers from the frontier regiments began in the week of Varennes, and continued increasingly in July.
Mass emigration of officers from the whole French army, organised by
royalist agents and in response to the call of honour, began in August,
when Austria and Prussia in concert with the exiled Princes declared support for the King in the Declaration of Pillnitz. Perhaps François-René
learned of this from a later newspaper in the millhouse, or from his
countrymen in Philadelphia after his arrival there three or four weeks
later.

8 'The Blue Mountains, or Appalachians,' he says in *Voyage en Amérique*,
and again: 'The Alleghenies, or as they were earlier called, the Endless,
Kittatinny, or Blue Mountains'.

9 As Michaux had in July 1789, and Louis-Philippe would in April 1797.

10 'It was a natural bridge,' Chactas explains to René, 'like the one in Virginia, of which you have perhaps heard.' Chactas speaks in the person of
Chateaubriand when he says: 'Whoever has seen, as I have, Father Aubry
travelling alone through the wilderness with his staff and breviary . . .'
Father Aubry is still further identified with the old priest met on the
Cumberland (although Chactas, not having had a classical education, is
unable to exchange quotations with him), by the enthusiasm with which
he has carved 'lines of an ancient poet named Homer' on 'the old oaktrees
that served him as books'. His very name is chosen to suggest the region
of their meeting. Charles-Philippe Aubry was the last French governor of
Louisiana; he founded Fort Massac in 1757, and fought the British on the
Tennessee and Ohio, at Fort Duquesne (Pittsburgh) and Niagara.

11 Or alternatively it may have been between Marion and Wytheville, where
the passage of the subsidiary ridge forming the watershed between the
Holston and New River was then spoken of (by Michaux and other
travellers) as 'crossing the Alleghenies'. François-René imitates Manasseh
Cutler's observation at Marietta of 'traces of three ancient stumps' near a

mature living oak on an Indian mound at Marietta; he feels entitled to go ten better, and by postulating a life-span of five centuries for each to invalidate the Biblical date for the Creation.

12 Michaux took twenty-two days from Abingdon to Philadelphia in 1793, hampered by bad weather and a lame horse, but only twenty days in 1789, including a day's excursion to Natural Bridge. Louis-Philippe in 1797, again with a visit to Natural Bridge, took thirteen days from Charleston Virginia to Abingdon—the equivalent, if we add Michaux's six days in 1793 from Charleston to Philadelphia, of only nineteen days for the whole distance.

13 For example, if he travelled from Albany to Niagara in eight days, as did Édouard de Montulé in 1817, down the Ohio in fifteen days as many did on a full river, between Nashville and Knoxville in eight days like Louis-Philippe in 1797, from Knoxville to Abingdon in four days as the post-rider did in the 1790s, and between Abingdon and Charleston Virginia in thirteen days, again like Louis-Philippe, he would have saved twelve days and could have arrived in Philadelpia at the end of October.

14 'The President looks better than I expected to see him,' wrote his niece Frances Washington on 21 September 1791, 'but still there be traces in his countenance of his two last severe illnesses which I fear will never wear off'—referring to his earlier carbuncle of June–August 1789 at New York, and his pneumonia in May 1790, on both of which occasions there had been fears for his life.

15 Jefferson himself thought the President 'had never seemed more dejected' than when the news reached Philadelphia on 23 August 1791.

16 In 1783, when Washington was rehabilitating Mount Vernon after the war, Malesherbes had sent him a gift of vine-stocks from his own château, through the good offices of Barbé-Marbois, the French consul in Philadelphia. 'I always think of him when I go into my little vineyard,' wrote Washington in his letter of thanks.

17 Washington was defeated in an attempt to drive the French from Fort Duquesne, the future Pittsburgh, at Great Meadows in 1754, but was allowed to leave with the honours of war. He fought at Braddock's Defeat in 1755, and saw the final capture of Fort Duquesne in 1758. In 1774 he bought 32,000 acres of undeveloped land on Miller's run, near the Ohio a few miles below Pittsburgh, and inspected these on his horseback journey in 1784, when the beginning of the Indian troubles prevented him from visiting another holding further down the Ohio, on the Little Kanawha.

18 The brig *Molly* is announced in Philadelphia newspapers as due to sail for Le Havre on or about 26 November; but she cannot in fact have left as early as this date, for her clearance papers were not issued until 1 December. The *Molly*'s true sailing date remains unknown, and it is not permissible to argue from these circumstances that the sailing-date of 10 December given by Chateaubriand is incorrect, or even that the ship he sailed on was in fact the *Molly*. The difficult passage down the Delaware often necessitated a long wait for a favourable wind; moreover, there is no guarantee that the Philadelphia newspaper lists of European sailings were complete, or even that Le Havre was the ultimate destination (and not merely a first port of call) of François-René's ship. His Atlantic journey time of twenty-three days and arrival on 2 January 1792 are confirmed by other evidence. We may conclude that he did indeed sail on 10 December 1791, whether on the *Molly* or on another vessel. In any case, an earlier

sailing date would in no way affect the credibility of his American journey, since by our calculations he would still have three or four weeks in hand after reaching Philadelphia towards 11 November.

CHAPTER 16 CÉLESTE

1 Once again he is right about the moon, which became half-moon and lost its horns at 4.30 a.m. in the morning of 1 January 1792.

2 Fifteen years later Chateaubriand would rather have had his own letter than the money, for it would have given him material for the storm in *Les Martyrs*, book xix, which is itself modelled on the tempest which wrecks Chactas off the coast of Newfoundland in *Les Natchez*. 'I should have recovered from this letter circumstances which have doubtless escaped my memory, although my memory has rarely deceived me,' he remarks very justly in the notes to *Les Martyrs*. His critics, with their usual credulous incredulity, suppose that he invented the storms in his two epics, and later claimed to have experienced them in reality. Instead of arguing *a priori* that an actual event cannot have occurred, they would have done well to look at the newspapers, which confirm both the gale and the speed of his crossing. Newspapers in the first week of January 1792 record a tremendous gale in the Western Approaches and the Channel, a score of shipwrecks with many lives lost, harbours crowded with ships taking refuge or unable to leave, and the arrival at Falmouth on 31 December 1791 of the *Grantham* packet twenty-two days out from New York, having left on 10 December, the same day as François-René from Philadelphia.

3 M. Collas exaggerates when he calls the conditions laid down by this marriage contract 'insultingly Draconian', and 'a stinging defeat for the Chateaubriands'. He is also mistaken in saying they were 'in derogation of the Custom of Brittany', for they are in scrupulous accordance with articles 483 and 489 on the restrictions to be applied to married minors.

4 François-René's fortune consisted of the Montaigu loan of 17,191 livres, which was irrecoverable, and of one fifteenth of his father's estate (Jean-Baptiste, it will be remembered, received two thirds, and the other five children one fifth each of the residue), which was inalienable. Since the abolition of feudal dues the revenue from Combourg rents and fees had dropped from 70,000 in a good year to less than 10,000, from which François-René received or expected a tiny income of about 850 livres.

5 M. Duhamel also had a profitable sideline in the embezzlement of stamp-money received in the course of his clerical duties, left the priesthood in 1794 to get married on the proceeds, and was sentenced to twelve years in gaol when his misdeeds came to light in 1798.

6 Even the Buissons made only a token presence at the civil marriage. Céleste's grandfather showed where his real sympathies lay by staying away, and the register was signed only by Uncle François, M. de Vauvert, and their lawyers.

7 The Lycée was opened in 1786, under the patronage of Montmorin and the King's brothers Monsieur and Artois, for the education of the upper classes by the *philosophes*. The lecturers were among the most distinguished minds of the age, including Marmontel for history, Fourcroy for chemistry and natural history, and Condorcet for mathematics. Seven hundred subscribers of both sexes paid fees of four louis a session.

8 When the great Duc de Choiseul fell from power in 1770 the Abbé Barthélemy had followed his patron into retirement at the Château de

Chanteloup, where he spent twenty years writing *Anacharsis*, and was supposed to be the lover of the Duchesse. 'I found him rather jealous, rather servile, and rather lovesick,' wrote Mme du Deffand to Horace Walpole.

9 François-René's ox-wagons, though critics have derided them, were a sound idea, and even in advance of his time, for oxen were used for the first covered wagons of the transcontinental pioneers a generation later. Ox transport was normal for heavy loads in the roadless up-country of New England and New York State, where he had no doubt seen it in action.

10 Another good idea. Experienced traders knew that in order to travel and live among Indians it was important to refrain from killing them, and Lewis and Clark succeeded with the same principle, which François-René had derived ethically from Rousseau and his own heart, but practically from Mr. Swift.

11 M. de Montmorin, foreign minister until his enforced resignation in February 1792, and M. de Molleville, ex-minister for navy and colonies. Malesherbes was in consultation with these moderates, too late, in a group which also included the ex-minister for war La Tour du Pin and the constitutionalists Stanislas de Clermont-Tonnerre and Malouët, with a view to persuading the King to rally liberal monarchist support, or to make a show of force, or escape from France; but they could never decide which of these incompatible plans should be put into action, and the King refused to approve any of them.

12 In point of fact Mme de Montboissier had returned to Paris that April, like many other emigrated ladies, in the hope of saving the family property from confiscation under the recent laws, while her husband joined the army of the Princes. She fled after the September massacres to the Château de Malesherbes, and thence to London early in October 1792.

13 By the laws of 9 November 1791, 9 February and 8 April 1792, emigration was punishable by death and confiscation. Each district was ordered to send lists of absentees.

14 The reader will perhaps recall, as Molleville did most vividly, that in June 1788 when he was Intendant of Brittany the Breton populace had chased him from their province with brickbats and nooses, in peril of his life. He also had reason to remember the name of Chateaubriand, for François-René, acting on Jean-Baptiste's behalf, had signed the Breton nobility's manifesto of infamy against him. Molleville had been navy and colonies minister from October 1791 to 7 March 1792 (third in succession to La Luzerne, who had resigned in October 1790), and was now in charge of the King's secret police, with the special task of keeping an eye on the Jacobins.

15 François-René, according to the passport with which he entered England in 1793, was five feet four inches in modern English measurements, whereas Jean-Baptiste was five feet eight. Jean-Baptiste had 'dark brown hair and blue eyes, high forehead, oval face'. We may imagine him, it seems, as a taller, staider, genius-less version of his younger brother.

16 Mlle Marie-Madeleine-Charlotte Boutin had married M. de Montboissier's father Charles-Henri, who died young in 1751, and not Malesherbes himself, as Chateaubriand mistakenly remembered. However, the real Mme de Malesherbes was herself the daughter of a financier, the farmer-general Grimod de la Reynière, and he too owned a park at Clichy which was a favourite haunt of Malesherbes in youth; so the confusion was an

easy one. Malesherbes, though otherwise a blameless husband, was pre-occupied with state affairs and looking after Rousseau. The poor lady took to shooting as a solace (people called her 'the shooting chatelaine'), and on 11 January 1771 tied a ribbon to the trigger of her gun and shot herself through the heart.

17 'There is something so sociable in being able to shake hands across the river from two mountains,' wrote Horace Walpole to the Countess of Ossory, 'that nothing but so amiable a nation could have invented it.' The witty singer Sophie Arnould said the stream was 'as like a river as two drops of water'.

18 Philippe-Claude de Montboissier (1712–97), with the rank of Lieutenant-General, commanded the two light horse companies, 1,200 strong, in the army of the Princes. His nephew Baron Charles-Philippe de Montboissier, Malesherbes's son-in-law, was commandant of the third squadron of the second company.

CHAPTER 17   THE FOREST OF ARDEN

1 The surrendering commandant at Longwy, Lavergne, was guillotined by way of encouraging the others, along with his wife for good measure. Beaurepaire, his colleague at Verdun, shot himself instead. The wily Wimpffen was in secret negotiation with Artois through a Jewish en-graver at Thionville named Godchaux, but saw what was good for him and resolved to stick it out.

2 So Pierre de Chateaubriand deposed in evidence when he was imprisoned at Saint-Malo in January 1794, during the Terror, for the crime of having an émigré son. In such circumstances every parent was obliged to disown his offspring for leaving without the family's knowledge or approval. It is far more likely that Armand went with his father's blessing.

3 Waldeck's severed arm was picked up by his men next morning, quite useless. To the Princes' condolences Waldeck replied, with true eighteenth-century courtesy: 'Tell them I will use my remaining arm to put their brother back on his throne.' He did his best to keep his promise even after the execution of Louis XVI released him from it, fought the Republican French with distinction for two more years, and died at Cintra as Austrian ambassador to Portugal in 1798.

4 Wallis had departed on 17 September for Luxembourg, and was replaced on the 23rd by 8,000 Austrians brought up from Landau by General von Erbach. Wimpffen continued his harassing sorties. The Austrians finally raised the siege and evacuated on 17 October.

5 The émigré cavalry learned of the massacres on reaching Verdun on 14 September, and the infantry probably heard before leaving Thionville on the 20th.

6 François-René's leave was quite in order, even without the ground of sickness. The Austrians and Prussians had abandoned responsibility for the upkeep and winter quartering of the Army of the Princes, and Broglie had given orders as early as 7 October for indefinite leave to be granted to all who wished it.

7 Everyone who set eyes on him—including casual passers-by, the doctors who eventually treated him at Brussels and on Jersey, his Bédée relatives who nursed him and wrote to his mother that he had this disease, and the English official who recorded in his passport seven months later as a mark of identification: 'Face pitted with smallpox'—believed he had

smallpox, so he was certainly entitled to think so. His face remained permanently though unobtrusively and undisfiguringly pockmarked, as was noticed by various observers up to fifty years later. However, the following considerations may seem to point to chicken-pox: (1) chicken-pox is most prevalent in autumn and in young people up to their early twenties; (2) chicken-pox would not quite prevent him from struggling on, whereas small-pox in such unfavourable conditions would surely have incapacitated or killed him; (3) he had successive outbreaks of pustules, with intervening periods of relief; these symptoms (which surprised his doctors as differing from the smallpox with which they were familiar) are typical of chicken-pox, but would be anomalous in smallpox; (4) the pitting left by chicken-pox, when it does not disappear altogether, is less noticeable than that left by smallpox. A severe case of chicken-pox seems the more likely diagnosis, but the possibility remains that he may have had a mild and atypical attack of smallpox.

8 Chateaubriand says five leagues (fifteen miles), but in fact Attert, which he afterwards reached, is no more than six miles from Arlon. Perhaps he wrote leagues inadvertently and intended miles; or perhaps he met his next companions on the far side of Attert.

9 The Prince de Ligne (1735–1814), one of the most elegant and seemingly heartless luminaries of the eighteenth century, was inconsolable. He had just time to inter his son under an obelisk in his magnificent park at Beloeil (between Ath and Mons) before losing his estates to the invading French after the battle of Fleurus in 1794. He fled into half-ruined twilight at the imperial court of Vienna, but lived to publish twenty witty volumes and see the fall of Napoleon.

10 Thomas Anley Esquire, a captain in the town militia, was a celebrated local character. He was very tall, very thin, made a point of wearing democratic tight-fitting pantaloons, with a red cockade in his hat to display his republican leanings, but insisted on being addressed as Esquire. Once an opposing lawyer argued that a case brought by him should be dismissed, as there was no Thomas Anley Esquire in Jersey, but only a butcher's clerk who at most was entitled to be called Mr. But Tom Anley proved to the satisfaction of the court that, although it was true he was clerk to a butcher, his captaincy in the militia gave him right to the title.

11 Antoine de Bédée's personal effects, stored in his former lodgings at Saint-Malo, were seized on 3 December 1792 and sold in August 1793 at auction for 11,910 livres. His three sisters, Mme de Chateaubriand, Mme Angélique de Vauvert, and Julie Moreau, each claimed their legal ninth in the proceeds, not from greed, but in order to save anything they could for him.

12 They cut off the Marquis's ghastly head and, when his friends denied all knowledge of his death at the interrogation, threw it before them enquiring: 'Then do you recognise this?'

13 'These fine heads must be kept for Paris,' reported the officer who ordered their transfer.

14 Callous is not too harsh a word. One of these ogres wrote appreciatively of the whiteness of Thérèse de Moëlien's thighs, which he observed when her headless body was thrown on the heap of corpses.

15 Similarly his cousin Caroline de Bédée registered her arrival as 3 August, although she must have landed at least ten days before, having sailed from Saint-Malo on 21 July 1792, while Du Tilleul gave his as 1 January 1793, although he arrived in company with François-René towards the

last week of November. Christophorov's attempt to argue 20 January as the true date of Chateaubriand's arrival is of course made inadmissible by Mme de Chateaubriand's letter of 8 December 1792, which is evidently her second and not first response to a message smuggled from Jersey to Saint-Malo by Antoine de Bédée to give news of her son's arrival. François-René had known Du Tilleul at least since 1788, when they signed the Breton nobles' manifesto together on 6 May (see p. 102 above), as members of a group which also included his brother-in-law M. de Marigny and the Marquis de Langan from Bois-Février.

SELECT BIBLIOGRAPHY

This Select Bibliography lists books and articles used in the present volume and cited in the Source References. Works by Chateaubriand, miscellaneous works, and works specially relevant to Chateaubriand's American journey (chapters 10–15) are classified under separate sub-headings. Each entry is preceded by the abbreviated form used in the Source References.

I WORKS BY CHATEAUBRIAND

OC (*Garnier*)   *Oeuvres complètes.* 12 vols. Garnier Frères. 1861.

OT   *Mémoires d'outre-tombe.* ed. Maurice Levaillant & Georges Moulinier. (Bibliothèque de la Pléiade.) 2 vols. 1958.

OT (*1856*)   *Mémoires d'outre-tombe.* 6 vols. 1856.

OT (*Biré*)   *Mémoires d'outre-tombe.* ed. Edmond Biré. rev. Pierre Moreau. 6 vols. 1946–7.

OT (*Levaillant*)   *Mémoires d'outre-tombe.* ed. M. Levaillant, 4 vols. Deuxième éd. 1964.

Souv   *Souvenirs d'enfance et de jeunesse de Chateaubriand. Manuscrit de 1826.* 1874.

VR   *Oeuvres romanesques et voyages.* ed. Maurice Regard. (Bibliothèque de la Pléiade.) 2 vols. 1969.

CG   *Correspondance générale.* ed. Louis Thomas. 5 vols. 1912–24.

II MISCELLANEOUS WORKS

Albert   Albert, Maurice. *Un Homme de lettres sous l'Empire et la Restauration. Edmond Géraud.* 1893.

Argens   Argens, Olivier d'. *Mémoires pour servir à l'histoire de la guerre civile de 1793 à 1796.* 1824.

Aubrée   Aubrée, E. *Lucile et René de Chateaubriand chez leurs sœurs à Fougères.* 1929.

Balleine   Balleine, George R. *A Biographical History of Jersey.* 1948.

Banèat (IV)   Banéat, Paul. *Département d'Ille-et-Vilaine. Histoire, archéologie, monuments.* 4 vols. 1927–9.

Banéat (VR)   ———, ———. *Le Vieux Rennes.* 1911.

Bellier Dumaine   Bellier Dumaine, Charles. Histoire du collège de Dinan, in *Annales de Bretagne* XI (1895–6) 3–26, 198–222, 442–65, 672–90; XII (1896–7) 83–90, 227–37, 360–81.

Bézier   Bézier, Paul. *Inventaire des monuments mégalithiques du départment d'Ille-et-Vilaine.* 2 vols. 1883.

Bittard des Portes   Bittard des Portes, René. *Histoire de l'armée de Condé.* 1896.

Boishamon   Boishamon, Maurice de. *Les Bédée et l'ascendance maternelle de Chateaubriand.* 1936.

Boissy d'Anglas   Boissy d'Anglas, F. A. de. *Essai sur la vie, les écrits et les opinions de M. de Malesherbes.* 2 vols. 1819.

Bord   Bord, Gustave. *La Conspiration révolutionnaire de 1789.* 1909.
BSC   *Bulletin de la Société Chateaubriand.*

Cahuet   Cahuet, Albéric. *Lucile de Chateaubriand.* 1935.
Carrier   Carrier, J. *La Vérité historique sur la tonsure de Chateaubriand.* 1892.
Cazotte   Cazotte, Jacques. *Oeuvres badines et morales.* 3 vols. 1816.
Chabanon Chabanon, Michel P. G. de. *Tableau de quelques circonstances de ma vie.* 1795.
Challamel Challamel, Augustin. *Les Clubs contre-révolutionnaires.* 1895.
Champier Champier, Victor & Sandoz, G. R. *Le Palais Royal 1629–1900.* 2 vols. 1900.
Centenaire *Chateaubriand. Le livre du centenaire.* 1949.
Christophorov Christophorov, P. *Sur les pas de Chateaubriand en exil.* 1960.
Chuquet   Chuquet, Arthur. *Les Guerres de la Révolution.* 11 vols. 1886–96.
Collas (Dix ans) Collas, Georges. Dix ans au château de Combourg, 1786–96, in *Annales de Bretagne* XXXV (1922) 1–31, 268–99.
Collas (Drame) ———, ———. Un Drame d'amour en Bretagne au XVIe siècle. L'affaire Guitté de Vaucouleurs, in *Annales de Bretagne* XLI (1934) 73–103.
Collas (RA) ———, ———. *René-Auguste de Chateaubriand, comte de Combourg, 1718–86.* 1949.
Collas (Veuve) ———, ———. Veuve d'un vivant, in *Annales de Bretagne* LXV (1958) 169–200.
Collas (VD) ———, ———. *La Vieillesse douloureuse de Madame de Chateaubriand.* 2 vols. 1960, 61.
Contades Contades, G. de. *Emigrés et chouans.* 1895.
Crossard Crossard, Baron J. B. L. de. *Souvenirs militaires et historiques.* 2 vols. 1829.

Duchemin Duchemin, Marcel. *Chateaubriand. Essais de critique et d'histoire littéraire.* 1938.
Duine   Duine, F. *Histoire civil et politique de Dol jusqu'en 1789.* 1911.
Dupouy   Dupouy, Auguste. *Histoire de Bretagne.* 1932.
Durry   Durry, Marie-Jeanne. *La Vieillesse de Chateaubriand.* 2 vols. 1933.

Espinchal Espinchal, Comte J. J. d'. *Journal d'émigration.* 1912.

Funck-Brentano Funck-Brentano, Frantz. *Les lettres de cachet à Paris.* 1903.

Gastard (C) Gastard, Joseph. *Combourg, le passé, la ville et le château. Chateaubriand à Combourg.* 1929.
Gastard (J) ———, ———. *La Jeunesse de René en Bretagne.* 1933.
Giraud   Giraud, Victor. *Nouvelles études sur Chateaubriand.* 1912.
Grand-Bey *Le Grand-Bey. Hommage de la Bretagne à M. le vicomte de Chateaubriand par vingt-quatre écrivains bretons.* 1850.
Granges de Surgères Granges de Surgères, Marquis de. Lettres anecdotiques de Jean-Baptiste de Chateaubriand, 1789–90, in *Revue de la Révolution* XIV (1889) pt. 2, 1–14.
Grosclaude Grosclaude, Pierre. *Malesherbes, témoin et interprète de son temps.* 1961.
Guillotin (C) Guillotin de Corson, A. *Combour. Étude historique.* 1899.
Guillotin (PR) ———, ———. *Pouillé historique de l'archevêché de Rennes.* 6 vols. 1880–6.

Hartmann Hartmann, L. *Les Officiers de l'armée royale et de la Révolution.* 1910.

Heckmann Heckmann, Paul. *Félix de Wimpffen et le siège de Thionville.* 1926.

Hérissay Hérissay, Jacques. Un Comédien révolutionnaire, Bordier, in *Revue hebdomadaire* 12 Sept. 1912 366–93.

Herpin (AC) Herpin, Eugène. *Armand de Chateaubriand.* 1910.

Herpin (Chopin) ——, ——. Chateaubriand a l'école du Père Chopin, in *Annales de la Société historique et archéologique de l'arrondissement de Saint-Malo* 1934 57–8.

Herpin (CE) ——, ——. *La Côte d'émeraude. Saint-Malo, ses souvenirs.* 1894.

Herpin (MS) ——, ——. Chateaubriand et sa cousine Mère des Séraphins, in *Annales romantiques* IX (1912) 118–27.

Janzé Janzé, Alix de. *Les financiers d'autrefois.* 1886.

Kerviler (Ch) Kerviler, René. *Essai d'une bio-bibliographie de Chateaubriand et de sa famille.* 1896.

Kerviler (BB) ——, ——. *Répertoire de bio-bibliographie bretonne.* 17 vols. 1886–1908.

La Bigne La Bigne, Paul de. Combour et ses seigneurs, in *Revue de Bretagne* XXXIX (1908) 184–201, 273–308; XL (1908) 57–75, 130–40, 189–201, 249–56.

La Harpe La Harpe, Jean F. de. *Oeuvres.* 16 vols. 1821.

La Lande de Calan La Lande de Calan, Comte P. F. M. J. de. *Notes et souvenirs de famille, 1240–1932.* 1932.

La Motte-Rouge La Motte-Rouge, D. de. La Correspondance du Comte de Bédée, in *Bulletin et mémoires de la Société d'émulation des Côtes du Nord* LXXIX (1950) 38–78.

Lapierre Lapierre, A. *Campagne des émigrés dans l'Argonne en 1792.* 1911.

Lemasson Lemasson, Auguste. *Les Origines du pèlerinage et du sanctuaire de Notre-Dame de Nazareth près Plancoët.* 1914.

Lenôtre Lenôtre, G. *Le Marquis de la Rouërie et la conjuration bretonne.* 1899.

Le Savoureux Le Savoureux, Henri. *Chateaubriand.* 1930.

Levot Levot, Prosper J. *Biographie bretonne.* 2 vols. 1852–7.

Lievyns Lievyns, A. *Fastes de la Légion d'Honneur. Biographie de tous les décorés.* 5 vols. 1842–7.

Ligne Ligne, Prince Charles Joseph de. *Mémoires et lettres.* 1923.

Madelin Madelin, Louis. *La Révolution.* 1911.

Malouet Malouet, Pierre V. de *Mémoires.* Deuxième éd. augmentée. 1874.

Marcellus Marcellus, Comte M. L. J. A. C. de. *Chateaubriand et son temps.* 1859.

Marcillac Marcillac, P. L. A. de. *Souvenirs de l'émigration.* 1825.

Maugras Maugras, Gaston & Croze Lemercier, P. de. *Delphine de Sabran, marquise de Custine.* 1912.

Mémoire *Mémoire de la noblesse de Bretagne au Roi.* 1788.

Michelet Michelet, Jules. *La Mer.* 1861.

Minutoli Minutoli, Heinrich C. von. *Der Feldzug der Verbündeten in Frankreich im Jahre 1792.* 1847.

Molleville (F) Molleville, Antoine F. B. de. *Private Memoirs relative to the last year of Louis XVI.* ed. G. K. Fortescue. 2 vols. 1909.

Moniteur *Réimpression de l'ancien Moniteur.* 1847.

Montlosier Montlosier, Comte Francois D. de. *Souvenirs d'un émigré, 1791–1798*. 1951.

Moriolles Moriolles, Comte Alexandre N. L. C. de. *Mémoires sur l'émigration*. 1902.

Mourot Mourot, Jean. *Études sur les premières œuvres de Chateaubriand*. 1962.

Néel Néel de Lavigne, Charles. *Souvenirs*. 1850.

Neuilly Neuilly, Comte Ange-Achille de. *Dix années d'émigration*. 1865.

Ogée Ogée, Jean. *Dictionnaire historique et géographique de la Bretagne*. Nouvelle éd. 2 vols. 1843, 53.

Outland Outland, C. H. Les Origines de Chateaubriand, in *Revue de Paris* juillet 1926 166–85.

Pailleron Pailleron, Marie L. *La Vicomtesse de Chateaubriand*. 1934.

Pailleron (Beaumont) ———, ———. *Pauline de Beaumont, l'hirondelle de Chateaubriand*. 1930.

Peignot Peignot, Gabriel. *Recherches sur la vie et les ouvrages de M. de la Harpe*. 1820.

Pinasseau Pinasseau, Jean. *L'Émigration militaire. Campagne de 1792*. 2 vols. 1957, 63.

Pocquet (C) Pocquet, Barthelemy. *Le Duc d'Aiguillon et La Chalotais*. 3 vols. 1900.

Pocquet (RB) ———, ———. *Les Origines de la Révolution en Bretagne*. 2 vols. 1885.

Prampain Prampain, Édouard. *Saint-Malo historique*. 1902.

Rathery Rathery, Edme. *Le Comte de Plélo*. 1876.

Relation *Relation des évènements qui se sont passés en Bretagne rédigée par les députés du clergé et de la noblesse*. 1789.

Renan Renan, Ernest. *Oeuvres complètes*. 1947–61.

Renouard Renouard, Carl. *Geschichte des französischen Revolutionskrieg in 1792*. 1865.

Ricordel Ricordel, P. Le Collège de Rennes après le départ des Jésuites, in *Annales de Bretagne* XLIII (1936) 101–30, 391–423; XLIV (1937) 120–53.

Rougerie Rougerie, Jean. *Étude médico-psychologique sur Bernardin de Saint-Pierre*. 1938.

Salonne Salonne, Marie P. *Chateaubriand et les dames de Plancoët*. 1933.

Saulnier (LC) Saulnier, Frédéric. Lucile de Chateaubriand et M. de Caud, in *Revue historique de l'Ouest* I (1885) 11–28.

Saulnier (PB) *Le Parlement de Bretagne, 1554–1790. Répertoire alphabétique et biographique*. 1909.

Stern, A Stern, Alfred. *La Vie de Mirabeau*. 2 vols. 1895–6.

Stern, J ———, Jean. *Belle et bonne, une fervente amie de Voltaire*. 1938.

Tapié Tapié, Victor L. *Chateaubriand par lui-même*. 1965.

Teppé Teppé, Julien. *Chamfort, sa vie, son œuvre, sa pensée*. 1950.

Tieghem Tieghem, Paul van. *Ossian en France*. 2 vols. 1917.

Tocqueville Tocqueville, Comte Hervé Clérel de. *Épisodes de la Terreur*, in *Annales de la Charité* nouv. sér. XII (1867) 94–126.

Turquan Turquan, J. & Auriac, J. d'. *Monsieur le comte d'Artois*. 1928.

Vidalenc Vidalenc, Jean. *Les Emigrés francais 1798–1825.* 1963.
Villemain Villemain, François. *M. de Chateaubriand, sa vie, ses écrits, son influence littéraire er politique.* 1858.
Villeneuve Villeneuve de Laroche-Barnaud, Louis G. *Mémoires sur l'expédition de Quiberon.* 2 vols. 1819, 22.

Whitmore Whitmore, Felix. *Mr. Whitmore to the Marquis of Stacpoole in reply to his observations on Mrs. Whitmore's Memoir.* 1827.
Wilson Wilson, Aileen, *Fontanes.* 1928.

Zinkeisen Zinkeisen, Johann W. *Der Jakobiner-Klub.* 2 vols. 1852–3.

III CHATEAUBRIAND'S AMERICAN JOURNEY
(CHAPTERS 10–15)

Adams Adams, James T. *Album of American History.* 6 vols. 1944–60.
Allemagne Allemagne, d'. *Nouvelles du Scioto.* 1790.
Alvord Alvord, Clarence W. *The Illinois Country, 1673–1818.* 1920.
American Musical Miscellany. The American Musical Miscellany. 1798.
American Pioneer. The American Pioneer. A monthly periodical. 2nd. ed. 2 vols. 1842.
Armstrong Armstrong, Kate. Chateaubriand's America, in *PMLA* XXII (1907) 345–70.
Ashe Ashe, Thomas. *History of the Azores.* 1813.
Augur Augur, Helen. *Passage to Glory. John Ledyard's America.* 1946.

Baily Baily, Francis. *Journal of a Tour in unsettled parts of North America in 1796 and 1797.* 1856.
Baldensperger (1915) Baldensperger, Fernand. A propos de Chateaubriand en Amérique, in *RHLF* XXII (1915) 574.
Baldensperger (1928) ———, ———. Deux passages à restituer à une page célèbre de Chateaubriand, in *Revue de littérature comparée* 1928 134.
Baldwin Baldwin, Leland D. *The Keelboat Age on Western Waters.* 1941.
Barnby Barnby, H. G. *The Prisoners of Algiers.* 1966.
Bartram Bartram, William. *Travels through North and South Carolina.* 1791.
Bartram (N) ———, ———. *The Travels of William Bartram. Naturalists' edition.* ed. F. Harper. 1958.
Bellin (Atlas) Bellin, Jacques N. *Le Petit atlas maritime.* 5 vols. 1764.
Bellin (Remarques) ———, ———. *Remarques sur la carte de l'Amérique septentrionale.* 1755.
Belote Belote, Theodore T. *The Scioto Speculation and the French Settlement at Gallipolis.* 1907.
Bishop Bishop, Morris. Chateaubriand in New York State, in *PMLA* LXIX (1954) 876–86.
Boid Boid, Edward. *A Description of the Azores.* 1835.
Britton (Flora) Britton, Nathaniel L. *Manual of the Flora of the Northern States and Canada.* 1901.
Britton (Trees) ———, ———. *North American Trees.* 1908.
Brown, L. A. Brown, Lloyd A. *Early Maps of the Ohio Valley.* 1959.
Brown, R. H. Brown, Ralph H. *Historical Geography of the United States.* 1948.
Burpee Burpee, L. *The Search for the Western Sea.* 2 vols. 1935.

Campbell   Campbell, Patrick. *Travels to the Interior Inhabited Parts of North America in the years 1791 and 1792.* 1937.

Carré   Carré, Henri. Les Émigrés français en Amérique, 1789–93, in *Revue de Paris* 15 mai 1898 311–40.

Carver   Carver, Jonathan. *Travels through the interior parts of North America.* 1778.

Carver (FR)   ——, ——. *Voyage dans les parties intérieures de l'Amérique septentrionale.* 1784.

Charlevoix   Charlevoix, Pierre F. X. de. *Histoire et description générale de la Nouvelle France.* 3 vols. 1744.

Chastellux   Chastellux, Marquis François J. de. *Travels in North-America in 1780–2.* 2 vols. 1787.

Clark   Clark, Joshua. *Onondaga.* 2 vols. 1849.

Clark Papers   *George Rogers Clark Papers.* ed. J. A. James. 2 vols. 1912, 24.

Colbert   Colbert, Comte Édouard C. V. *Voyage dans l'intérieur des Etats-Unis et au Canada.* 1935.

Colles   Colles, Christopher. *A Survey of the Roads of the United States of America, 1789.* ed. W. W. Ristow. 1961.

Collot   Collot, Victor. *A Journey in North America.* 1826.

Columbian Magazine   *The Columbian Magazine, or Monthly miscellany.* Philadelphia, 1786–93.

Cook   Cook, James. *A Voyage to the Pacific Ocean in 1776–80.* 3 vols. 1784.

Cook (Fr)   ——, ——. *Troisième voyage de Cook.* 3 vols. 1785.

Coues   Coues, Elliott. *Fur-bearing Animals.* 1877.

Cramer   Cramer, Zadok. *The Navigator.* Sixth edition. 1808.

Crèvecoeur (Lettres)   Crèvecoeur, Michel G. de. *Lettres d'un cultivateur américain.* 3 vols. 1787.

Crèvecoeur (Voyage)   ——, ——. *Voyage dans la Haute Pennsylvanie et dans l'état de New York.* 3 vols. 1801.

Crouse   Crouse, Nellis M. *The Search for the Northwest Passage.* 1934.

Cruikshank   Cruikshank, E. A. *Records of Niagara.* 1930.

Cuming   Cuming, Fortescue. *Sketches of a Tour to the Western Country.* 1810.

Cutler   Cutler, Manasseh. *Life, Journals and Correspondence of Rev. Manasseh Cutler, LL.D.* 2 vols. 1888.

Dalrymple   Dalrymple, Alexander. *Memoir of a Map of the Lands around the North-Pole.* 1789.

Davidson   Davidson, Gordon C. *The North West Company.* 1918.

Davis   Davis, Andrew McFarland. *The Journey of Moncacht-Apé.* 1883.

Dean   Dean, Thomas. *Journal of Thomas Dean. A voyage to Indiana in 1817.* 1918.

Decatur   Decatur, Stephen, *Private Affairs of George Washington.* 1933.

Delamare   Delamare, Ernest. Florule de l'ile Miquelon, in *Annales de la Société botanique de Lyon* année XV (1887) 65–143.

Denny   Denny, Ebenezer. Military Journal, in *Historical Society of Pennsylvania Memoirs* VII (1860) 237–498.

Desgeorge   Desgeorge, Amédée. *Monseigneur Flaget, éveque de Bardstown et Louisville.* 1855.

De Voto   De Voto, Bernard. *Westward the Course of Empire.* 1953.

Diaria Britannica   *Diaria Britannica, or the British Diary. An almanack for the year 1791.* 1790.

Dixon   Dixon, George. *A Voyage round the World in 1785–88.* 1789.

Dobson   Dobson, Arthur. *Observations upon the Russian Discoveries in a Letter from a Russian sea-officer.* 1754.

Dow Dow, Charles M. *Anthology and Bibliogrophy of Niagara Falls.* 2 vols. 1921.
Dumont Dumont, G. M. *Mémoires historiques sur la Louisiane.* 2 vols. 1753.

Earle Earle, Alice M. *Stage Coach and Tavern Days.* 1901.
Eberlein Eberlein, Harold D. 190 High Street. The home of Washington and Adams, in *Historic Philadelphia, Transactions of the American Philosophical Society* new ser. XLIII pt. 1 (1953) 161–78.
Edrisi Edrisi, El. *Géographie d'Edrisi.* 2 vols. tr. A. Jaubert. 1836–40.
Ellicott Ellicott, Andrew. *The Journal of Andrew Ellicott.* 1803.
Engel Engel, S. *Extraits raisonnés des voyages faits dans les parties septentrionales de l'Asie et de l'Amérique.* 1790.

Flint Flint, Timothy. *A Condensed Geography and History of the Western States.* 2 vols. 1828.
Forman Forman, Samuel S. *Narrative of a Voyage down the Ohio and Mississippi in 1789–90.* 1888.
Freeman Freeman, Douglas S. *George Washington. A biography.* 8 vols. 1948–57.

Gipson Gipson, Lawrence H. *Lewis Evans.* 1939.
Greene Greene, Nelson. *The Story of Old Fort Plain and the Middle Mohawk Valley,* 1915.
GSO *Report of the Geological Survey of Ohio.* 1873– .

Hadfield Hadfield, Joseph. *An Englishman in America, 1785.* ed. D. R. Robertson. 1933.
Hale Hale, E. E. The Real Philip Nolan, in *Mississippi Historical Society Publications* IV (1901) 281–329.
Hanna Hanna, Charles A. *The Wilderness Trail.* 2 vols. 1911.
Hearne Hearne, Samuel. *A Journey to the Northern Ocean.* ed. J. B. Tyrrell. 1911.
Heckewelder Heckewelder, John. Narrative of John Heckewelder's Journey to the Wabash, in *Pennsylvania Magazine of Biographical History* XI (1887) 466–75; XII 34–54, 165–84.
Hennig Hennig, Richard. *Terrae incognitae.* vol. 1. 1936.
Herbermann Herbermann, Charles G. *The Sulpicians in the United States.* 1916.
Howay Howay, F. W. *The Dixon-Meares Controversy.* 1929.
Howe Howe, Henry. *Historical Collections of Ohio.* 1852.
Howe (V) ——, ——. *Historical Collections of Virginia.* 1845.
Hulbert Hulbert, Archer B. *Red-Men's Roads. The Indian thoroughfares of the Central West.* 1900.
Hutchins Hutchins, Thomas. *A Topographical Description of Virginia.* ed. F. C. Hicks. 1904.

Imlay Imlay, Gilbert. *A Topographical Description of the Western Territory of North America.* 2 vols. 1793.

Jauffret Jauffret, G. J. A. J. *Mémoires pour servir à l'histoire de la religion au XVIIIe siècle.* 2 vols. 1803.
Jefferson (Notes) Jefferson, Thomas. *Notes on the State of Virginia.* 1787.
Jefferson (Papers) ——, ——. *The Papers of Thomas Jefferson.* ed. J. P. Boyd. 1950– .

Jefferson (Writings) Jefferson, Thomas. *The Writings of Thomas Jefferson.* ed. P. L. Ford. 10 vols. 1893–9.

Johnson Johnson, Crisfield. *History of Cuyahoga County, Ohio.* 1879.

Johnston Johnston, Samuel H. F. *History of the Cameronians, 1689–1910.* 1957.

Kalm Kalm, Peter. *Peter Kalm's Travels in North America.* 2 vols. 1937.

Kegley Kegley, F. B. *Kegley's Virginia Frontier.* 1938.

Ketchum Ketchum, William. *History of Buffalo.* 2 vols. 1864.

Kirby Kirby, William. *Annals of Niagara.* 1927.

La Hontan La Hontan, L. A. de. *Nouveaux voyages dans l'Amérique septentrionale.* 1703.

Lambert Lambert, John. *Travels through Lower Canada and the United States.* 3 vols. 1810.

Lasseray Lasseray, André. *Les Français sous les treize étoiles, 1775–1783.* 2 vols. 1935.

La Vérendrye La Vérendrye, Pierre de. *Journals and Letters.* ed. L. Burpee. 1927.

Le Page du Pratz Le Page du Pratz. *Histoire de la Louisiane.* 3 vols. 1758.

Le Sage Le Sage, R. E. E. & Orneval. *Le Théatre de la foire, ou l'opéra comique.* 10 vols. 1722–34.

Lincklaen Lincklaen, John. *Travels in the years 1791 and 1792.* 1897.

Loskiel Loskiel, George H. *History of the Mission of the United Brethren among the Indians of North America.* 1794.

M'Robert M'Robert, Patrick. *A Tour through part of the northern provinces of North America.* 1935.

Martineau Martineau, Alfred. Esquisse d'une histoire de Saint-Pierre et Miquelon, in *Revue de l'histoire des colonies* année XVI (1928) 677–718.

Maude Maude, John. *Visit to the Falls of Niagara in 1800.* 1826.

May May, John. *Journal and Letters of Colonel John May relative to two journeys to the Ohio country in 1788 and '89.* 1873.

Meares Meares, John. *Voyages made in the years 1788 and 1789.* 1790.

Melish Melish, John. *Travels through the United States of America in the years 1807–11.* 1818.

Michaux Michaux, André. Portions of the Journal of André Michaux, botanist, written during his travels in the United States and Canada, 1788 to 1796. ed. C. S. Sargent, in *Proceedings of the American Philosophical Society* XXVI no. 129 (Jan.–July 1889) 1–145.

Mondésir Mondésir, Édouard de. *Souvenirs.* ed. G. Chinard. 1942.

Monette Monette, John W. *History of the Discovery and Settlement of the Valley of the Mississippi.* 2 vols. 1846.

Moore Moore, Thomas. *Memoirs, Journal and Correspondence.* 8 vols. 1853–6.

Moreau Moreau, M. C. *Les Prêtres émigrés aux États-Unis.* 1856.

Moreau de Saint-Méry Moreau de Saint-Méry, M. L. E. *Moreau de Saint-Méry's American Journey.* trs. K. & A. M. Roberts. 1947.

Morris Morris, Gouverneur. *The Diaries and Letters of Gouverneur Morris.* 2 vols. 1889.

Morse Morse, Jedidiah. *The American Geography.* Second edn. 1792.

Munford Munford, Kenneth. *John Ledyard.* 1939.

Munsell Munsell, Joel. *Annals of Albany.* 10 vols. 1850–9.

Niemcewicz Niemcewicz, J. V. *Under their Vine and Fig Tree. Travels through America in 1797–1799.* ed. M. J. E. Budka. 1965.
Notes *Notes on a Tour through the western part of the State of New York in 1829.* 1916.

Olden Time *Olden Time. A monthly publication.* Cincinnati, 1846–8.

Parker Parker, Jane. Louis Philippe in the United States, in *Century Magazine* Sept. 1901 746–57.
Perrin du Lac Perrin du Lac, F. M. *Voyage dans les deux Louisianes.* 1805.
Pope Pope, John. *A Tour through the Southern and Western Territories of the United States.* 1888.
Prowse Prowse, Daniel M. *A History of Newfoundland.* Second edn. 1896.

Ramsey Ramsey, J. G. M. *The Annals of Tennessee.* 1853.
Raynal Raynal, Guillaume T. F. *Histoire philosophique et politique des deux Indes.* 6 vols. 1770.
Rich Rich, E. E. *History of the Hudson's Bay Company.* vol. 2, 1763–1820. 1958.
Ride *A Ride to Niagara in 1809.* By T. C. 1915.
Rothrock Rothrock, Mary U. *The French Broad-Holston Country.* 1946.
RMA Records *Records of the Royal Military Academy, 1741–1892.* ed. H. S. Buchanan-Dunlop. 1895.

Saint-Clair *The St. Clair Papers.* ed. William Henry Smith. 2 vols. 1882.
Saintoyant Saintoyant, *La Colonisation française pendant la Révolution.* 2 vols. 1930.
Samuels Samuels, Edward A. *Ornithology and Oölogy of New England.* 1867.
Sargent Sargent, Winthrop. *The Life and Career of Major John André.* 1902.
Schultz Schultz, Christian. *Travels on an Inland Voyage in the years 1807 and 1808.* 2 vols. 1810.
Shea Shea, John D. G. *A History of the Catholic Church within the United States.* 4 vols. 1886–92.
Sparks Sparks, Jarel. *Travels and Adventures of John Ledyard.* Second edn. 1834.
Speed Speed, Thomas. *The Wilderness Road.* 1886.
Stevens Stevens, Wayne E. *The Northwest Fur Trade, 1763–1800.* 1928.
Summers Summers, Lewis P. *History of Southwest Virginia.* 1903.

Tanner Tanner, H. S. *The American Traveller.* Second edn. 1836.
Terrien Terrien, Jacques. *Histoire du R. P. de Clorivière.* 1892.
Thwaites Thwaites, Reuben G. *A Brief History of Rocky Mountain Exploration.* 1904.
Turner (Holland) Turner, Orsamus. *Pioneer History of the Holland Purchase.* 1850.
Turner (Phelps) ——, ——. *History of the Pioneer Settlement of Phelps and Gorham's Purchase.* 1851.

Vincent Vincent, W. T. Early Annals of the Scotch Church, Woolwich, in *Woolwich District Antiquarian Society Annual Report* XII (1908) 90–93.
Virginia *Virginia. A guide to the Old Dominion.* 1940.
Volney Volney, Comte Constantin F. de. *Tableau du climat et du sol des États-Unis d'Amérique.* 2 vols. 1803.

Wagner   Wagner, H. R. *A Cartography of the Northwest Coast of America to the year 1800.* 1937.

Wansey   Wansey, Henry. *Henry Wansey and his Journal.* ed. D. J. Jeremy. 1970.

Washington   Washington, George. *The Writings of George Washington.* ed. J. C. Fitzpatrick. 39 vols. 1931–44.

Watson   Watson, Elkanah. *Men and Times of the Revolution.* 1856.

Weld   Weld, Isaac. *Travels through the States of North America.* Second edn. 2 vols. 1799.

Wheat   Wheat, Carl I. *Mapping the Trans-Mississippi West.* 1957.

Williams, G.   Williams, Glyndwr. *The British Search for the Northwest Passage in the Eighteenth Century.* 1962.

Williams, S. C.   Williams, Samuel C. *Early Travels in the Tennessee Country.* 1928.

Winsor (M)   Winsor, Justin. *The Mississippi Valley. The struggle in America between England and France, 1679–1763.* 1895.

Winsor (W)   ———, ———. *The Westward Movement. The Colonies and the Republic west of the Alleghanies, 1763–1798.* 1899.

Winterbotham   Winterbotham, William. *An historical, geographical, commercial, and philosophical view of the American United States.* 4 vols. 1795.

Zeisberger   Zeisberger, David. *Diary of David Zeisberger.* tr. & ed. Eugene F. Bliss. 2 vols. 1885.

REFERENCES

The references for each paragraph are grouped separately, preceded by the page number and first words of the paragraph. For full titles of the books or articles cited, see Select Bibliography.

1 THIS PITILESS STORM

Page and paragraph

3 *On Sunday* . . . OT I 17–18; *Collas (RA)* 52, 136–7; *Grand-Bey* 81–3; *Le Savoureux* pl. I; *Tapié* 14;

3 *The summer* . . . *Collas (RA)* 136–8; *Grand-Bey* 83–7.

3 *François-René* . . . OT I 17–20, 1245, II 1268; *OT (Biré)* I 31; *OT (Levaillant)* I 27, 576; *Collas (RA)* 90, 131, 133, 137–8; *Grand-Bey* 81–2; *VR* I 119.

4 *Brittany* . . . OT I 41.

4 *On the* . . . OT I 41; *Michelet* 26; *Renan* II 755.

5 *The noblemen* . . . OT I 12, 1121–2.

5 *The first* . . . OT I 7–12, II 945–8, 1241; *OT (1856)* VI 320–5, 328–80; *Collas (RA)* 14; *Gastard (J)* 24–7.

6 *Meanwhile* . . . OT II 948, 953–60, 1241–3; *OT (1856)* VI 319, 385, 389; *Collas (Drame)*; *Collas (RA)* 198; *Dupouy* 121; *Gastard (C)* 40; *Gastard (J)* 27–46; *Outland* 172; *Salonne* 41.

6 *Gilles* . . . OT I 8–9, 12, II 1242–4, 1339; *OT (1856)* VI 294–303, 330–2, 372–5, 395; *Collas (RA)* 15.

7 *These* . . . OT I 11, II 945, 961–2.

7 *Jacques-François* . . . OT I 12, II 1463; *Souv* 7; *Collas (RA)* 15.

7 *Les Touches* . . . OT I 12–13; *OT (1856)* VI 294; *BSC* V (1935) 27; *Collas (RA)* 15–16; *Herpin (AC)* 7–9.

8 *The eldest* . . . OT I 12–13; *Souv* 8–9; *Collas (RA)* 25, 197; *Collas (VD)* I 302–3.

8 *When* . . . OT I 14; *Souv* 11–13.

8 *He slept* . . . OT I 14; *OT (1856)* 371; *Outland* 172; *Rathery* 11–12.

8 *Stanislas* . . . OT I 14, 121; *OT (Levaillant)* I 25; *Collas (RA)* 17–18; *Rathery* 282.

9 *Home* . . . OT I 15; *Souv* 13; *Collas (RA)* 19–20; *Gastard (J)* 66–8; *Outland* 179.

9 *It was* . . . *Collas (RA)* 23–36.

10 *His bride* . . . OT I 15–16, II 1244; *Collas (RA)* 36–9; *Salonne* 49–66, pl. iii.

10 *He stayed* . . . *Collas (RA)* 39–45; *Gastard (J)* 70–1; *Outland* 181–2.

11 *The Seven* . . . *Collas (RA)* 48–52; *Grand-Bey* 78; *Herpin (AC)* 16; *Pocquet (C)* I 75–81.

11 *After* . . . *Collas (RA)* 52–67.

11 *A first* . . . OT I 16–17; *Collas (RA)* 50–2, 90, 103.

12 *Meanwhile* . . . *Collas (RA)* 87–108.

12 *In 1766* . . . *Collas (RA)* 108, 117–23, 128–31.

12 *Meanwhile* . . . OT I 20; *Collas (RA)* 109–10, 120–1; *Dupouy* 202, 300–1, 308–11.

12 *René-Auguste* . . . OT I 163, II 1254; *Collas (RA)* 109–10, 120; *Pocquet (C)* II 183–200.

13 *The Bédées* . . . *Collas (RA)* 125–7, 134–5, 139–40; *Pocquet (C)* III 196–223, 243.

13 *It was* . . . OT (*1856*) VI 294; *Collas (RA)* 69–85; *Gastard (C)* 22.

14 *Combourg* . . . *Collas (RA)* 78; *Gastard (C)* 10, 17; *La Bigne* XL 57–8.

14 *The domains* . . . *Souv* 70; *Collas (RA)* 71–6.

14 *The personal* . . . *Collas (RA)* 69–74.

14 *For several* . . . *Collas (RA)* 77–85.

15 *Long* . . . *Collas (RA)* 113–17, 187, 204–5, 241.

15 *The contract* . . . *Collas (RA)* 115–17, 179, 187.

15 *It was* . . . *Collas (VD)* I 37.

16 *1768* . . . *Collas (RA)* 116, 128–36.

2 THE RAMPARTS OF SAINT-MALO

17 *Soon* . . . OT I 17–18; *Collas (RA)* 139.

17 *Ange-Annibal* . . . OT I 22–4, II 1203, 1407; *Souv* 49; *Boishamon* 32; *BSC* 1960, p. 10, 1962, p. 10, pl. I; *Salonne* 17–22, 96, 115, 124.

18 *François-René* . . . OT I 18; OT (*Biré*) I 41; OT (*Levaillant*) I 39; *Souv* 19–20; *BSC* 1962 p. 12; *Grand-Bey* 120, 159–62; *Lemasson*; *Annales de Bretagne* XXIX (1914) 657; *Salonne* 86, 88, 161, 168, 178.

18 *The three* . . . OT I 19–20.

18 *A servant* . . . OT I 20, II 1463; OT (*Levaillant*) I 136; *Souv* 24; *Collas (RA)* 220.

19 *His sisters* . . . OT I 20–1; *Souv* 18.

19 *The three* . . . OT 20–1; *Souv* 25–8.

19 *François-René* . . . OT I 21; *BSC* (1958) 12.

20 *La Villeneuve* . . . OT I 32–3; *Souv* 32–5; *Banéat (IV)* III 529, 574, 590.

21 *As* . . . OT I 33.

21 *At first* . . . OT I 10, 22, 28–30, II 1242, 1284, 1432; OT (*1856*) VI 292–4, 302, 368; *Souv* 27–8; *Banéat (IV)* III 530–2; *Collas (RA)* 67; *Grand-Bey* 78, 90; *Herpin (AC)* 9, 16–17; *Salonne* 57.

21 *But* . . . OT I 31; *Souv* 30–1; *Gastard (J)* 106; *Herpin (CE)* 267–8; *Prampain* 113.

22 *From* . . . OT I 19, 21, 30, II 1244; *Souv* 29–30; *Collas (RA)* 22, 34, 49, 53, 55, 94, 167, 184–6.

22 *The Chevalier's* . . . OT I 30, 34; OT (*Biré*) I 48; *Banéat (IV)* III 511; *Centenaire* 10; *Collas (RA)* 191; *Collas (VD)* I 43; *Grand-Bey* 88; *Herpin (AC)* 16.

23 *François-René* . . . OT I 1125; OT (*Levaillant*) I 46; *BSC* V (1935) 18, pl. I; *Collas (RA)* 192; *Herpin (Chopin)*.

23 *Joson* . . . OT I 34; *Souv* 37–9; *Grand-Bey* 89, 91.

24 *François-René* . . . OT I 35–7, II 1308; *Souv* 37–40.

24 *Along* . . . OT I 36–7; *Souv* 40–2; *Banéat (IV)* III 599; *Collas (VD)* I 43, 330; *Gastard (J)* 104; *Grand-Bey* 91–2; *Herpin (AC)* 18.

25 *Disgrace* . . . OT I 37; *Souv* 42–6.

25 *Mme. de Bédée* . . . OT I 16, 22–3, II 1213; OT (*Levaillant*) I 576; *BSC* (1959) 48–9; *BSC* (1962) 10; *Grand-Bey* 163; *Salonne* 43, 59, 72–6, 93, 145.

26 *Every* . . . OT I 23–4; *BSC* (1960) 17.

27 *Monchoix* . . . *Boishamon* 37–9; *BSC* (1962) 14, pl. II; *Salonne* 110.
27 *François-René's* . . . OT I 25; *Boishamon* 37; *Salonne* 107–8.
27 *René-Auguste* . . . OT I 1124; OT (*Levaillant*) I 38; *Souv* 46; *Collas* (*RA*) 193–4; *Salonne* 95.
27 *Mme.* . . . OT I 25–6, II 1408; *Souv* 51–4; *Grand-Bey* 95; *Salonne* 168.
28 *They* . . . OT I 40, 1125; *Souv* 55; *Collas* (*RA*) 196; *Grand-Bey* 92–4.
28 *There* . . . *Collas* (*RA*) 196–7.
29 *M. Magon* . . . OT I 40; *Souv* 55; *Collas* (*RA*) 196, 221; *Grand-Bey* 94–5; *Herpin* (*AC*) 18.
29 *René-Auguste* . . . OT I 15.
29 *The eight* . . . *Collas* (*RA*) 139, 144, 153–4.
29 *Slave-trading* . . . *Collas* (*RA*) 133, 146–7, 152, 160, 162, 173, 181, 184.
29 *Meanwhile* . . . *Collas* (*RA*) 121, 131, 135, 140, 147–9, 160–1, 169–72, 181–3, 188, 190, 193, 198–202, 254.
30 *René-Auguste* . . . *Collas* (*RA*) 34, 49–52, 55, 57, 59, 61, 63–4, 217, 240, 254.
30 *War* . . . *Banéat* (*IV*) III 557; *Collas* (*Dix ans*) 8; *Collas* (*RA*) 199, 202, 208, 216–18, 240.
31 *Ever* . . . OT I 38; *Collas* (*RA*) 98 ,101, 111–2, 115, 145, 149, 163–8, 180, 192–3, 202–5, 219, 223–4, 229, 231–2, 241–2, 245.
31 *Pierre* . . . OT I 12, 34; OT (*1856*) VI 396; *Collas* (*RA*) 167, 191, 207; *Herpin* (*AC*) 21–36, 342–3.
31 *René-Auguste* . . . OT I 38; *Souv* 55–6; *Collas* (*RA*) 208; *Grand-Bey* 95; *Turqueau* 65–6.
32 *At sunrise* . . . OT I 42, 1126; *Collas* (*Dix ans*) 270; *Collas* (*RA*) 209.

3 COMBOURG CASTLE

33 *As* . . . OT I 41–3; *Duine* 186; *Gastard* (*C*) 60–1; *Gastard* (*J*) 115.
33 *I have* . . . OT I 43; *Souv* 58.
33 *Half* . . . OT I 31, 43–4; *Souv* 31, 58–61; *Collas* (*RA*) 210; *Grand-Bey* 390.
34 *The castle* . . . *Banéat* (*IV*) I 444–5; *Gastard* (*C*) 7–8, 16–17; *La Bigne* XXXIX 185–6, 191–4, 290, XL 57–61.
34 *François-René* . . . OT I 19, II 1263, 1286, 1452; OT (*1856*) VI 306, 312–6, 367–9; *Collas* (*RA*) 70; *Salonne* 26.
35 *Surprised* . . . OT I 44–5; *Souv* 62.
35 *The north* . . . OT I 45; *Gastard* (*C*) 48–9, 52; *La Bigne* XL 69–75.
35 *Above* . . . OT I 44–5, 80, 82; *Souv* 60; *Collas* (*RA*) 210–13.
36 *Over* . . . OT I 44, 81; *Souv* 126; *Collas* (*Dix ans*); *Collas* (*RA*) 177, 212; *Grand-Bey* 123, 392.
36 *Far* . . . OT I 45.
37 *As* . . . OT I 46; OT (*1856*) VI 293, 370, 376; *Souv* 63; *Duine* 128–30, 179; *Gastard* (*J*) 122–5.
37 *His* . . . OT I 47–8, 67, II 1289; *Duine* 208–11.
37 *His schoolfellows* . . . OT I 48, 406.
38 *His school-holidays* . . . OT I 50–2; OT (*Biré*) I 75; OT (*Levaillant*) I 72; *Souv* 69, 73–4; *BSC* VI (1937) 13; *Collas* (*RA*) 144, 213–4, 231; *Néel* 21.
38 *One* . . . OT I 52–3; *Souv* 76.
39 *Like* . . . OT I 50; OT (*Levaillant*) I 70; *Souv* 70–1; *Collas* (*RA*) 69, 72, 112; *Gastard* (*C*) 18–19; *Gastard* (*J*) 87.
39 *But* . . . OT I 51; *Souv* 72; *Collas* (*RA*) 113, 215; *Gastard* (*C*) 19–20.
39 *In* . . . OT I 54–5; *Banéat* (*IV*) III 117; *Collas* (*RA*) 144, 218; *Duine* 180.
40 *After* . . . *Collas* (*RA*) 220–2.

40 *Saint-Malo* ... OT I 55; *Collas (RA)* 220–2.
41 *Even* ... OT I 55, 1127–8; *Collas (RA)* 219, 222.
41 *Early* ... OT I 55; *OT (Levaillant)* I 74; *Souv* 78–9; *Collas (RA)* 221–3; *Gastard (J)* 144.
41 *After* ... OT I 49, II 1369; *Souv* 68; *Aubrée* 76.
42 *Early* ... OT I 56, II 1240, 1368, 1414; *Aubrée* 30–3, 64–8, 83–4; *Collas (RA)* 224–5; *Collas (VD)* I 265; *Le Savoureux* pl. VII.
42 *His* ... OT I 56–7.
43 *In class* ... OT I 57; *VR* I 994; *Duine* 211.
44 *In* ... OT I 58–60; *Souv* 83–8; *Banéat (IV)* I 519–20; *Duine* 111, 138, 185, 213–4; *Gastard (J)* 129–30; *Guillotin (PR)* II 459, 462, III 273, 409, IV 509.
44 *The lane* ... OT I 59–60.
45 *His* ... OT I 61, II 1352.
45 *Soon* ... OT I 61–2, 1129; *Collas (RA)* 229–30.
46 *François-René* ... OT I 63–4, II 1241, 1254; *Collas (RA)* 218–9, 230; *Guillotin (PR)* IV 120, V 557–8, 655, 658.
47 *The time* ... OT I 64.
47 *On* ... OT I 65; *Souv* 95–9; *BSC* VI (1937) 133–4.
48 *A last* ... OT I 67, II 1289; *OT (Levaillant)* I 90–1, 555; *BSC* VI (1937) 133; *Collas (RA)* 231; *Duine* 208, 211–13; *Gastard (J)* 150; *Le Savoureux* pl. II.

4 RENNES AND BREST

49 *Rennes* ... OT I 68; *Ogée* II 2252–3.
49 *The college* ... OT I 68; *OT (Levaillant)* I 91, IV 681; *Banéat (VR)* 178, 221–2, 231, 286; *Gastard (J)* 150–61; *Ricordel* 101–30.
49 *The college* ... OT I 68.
50 *The collegians* ... OT I 68–9; *Souv* 102–3.
50 *Every* ... OT I 69–70; *Souv* 104–6.
50 *Gesril* ... OT I 70–1; *Souv* 106–7; *Gastard (J)* 157–61; *Ricordel* 110–13.
51 *On* ... OT I 71, II 1296; *OT (1856)* VI 338, 353–7; *Souv* 107–8; *Aubrée* 84–91; *Boishamon* 58–9; *Collas (RA)* 233; *Le Savoureux* pl. VII.
51 *Summer* ... OT I 71; *OT (1856)* VI 338, 353–4; *Collas (RA)* 235.
51 *Jean-Baptiste* ... OT I 48, 71–2, II 1213; *Souv* 109.
52 *Fifty* ... OT I 72; *Souv* 109–10; *Collas (RA)* 235.
53 *He sat* ... OT I 72; *Souv* 110–11.
53 *A different* ... OT I 72–3; *Souv* 111–12.
53 *Spring* ... OT II 961; *Collas (RA)* 235–6.
53 *On* ... OT I 73; *Souv* 110, 112; *Gastard (J)* 166.
54 *Cutters* ... OT I 73; *Kerviler (BB)* XVI 31.
54 *Others* ... OT I 74.
54 *His* ... OT I 34, 74, II 1246; *BSC* (1971) 14–16; *Centenaire* 16; *Collas (RA)* 236.
54 *François-René* ... OT I 73–4.
54 *One* ... OT I 74.

5 SISTER AND SYLPHIDE

56 *Only* ... OT I 79; *Aubrée* 72, 95; *Collas (RA)* 230–1, 235–7, 249.
56 *Lucile* ... OT I 7, 78, II 944, 1245; *OT (1856)* VI 376–7; *Souv* 6, 121–2, 145; *Cahuet* 36–8; *Collas (RA)* 233, 236; *Herpin (MS)*.

56 *As if* . . . OT I 40, 78; *Souv* 55, 121.

57 *The college* . . . OT I 78: OT (*Biré*) I 354; *Bellier Dumaine* 3–26, 198–222, 442–65; *Néel* 11.

57 *His last* . . . OT I 78; OT (*Biré*) I 354; *Souv* 121; *Bellier Dumaine* 202; *Kerviler* (BB) IV 509; *Kerviler* (Ch) 93; *Outland* 167.

57 *He stayed* . . . OT I 78; OT (*Biré*) 354–5; OT (*Levaillant*) I 105; *Souv* 121–2.

58 *Uncle* . . . OT I 25, 78; *Boishamon* 39–42; *Collas* (RA) 245; *La Motte Rouge* 40; *Salonne* 100, 105–6, 111–5.

58 *Towards* . . . OT I 78; *Souv* 121–2.

58 *A complex* . . . OT I 94, 105.

59 *René-Auguste* . . . OT I 81; *Collas* (*Dix ans*) 271–2; *Collas* (RA) 211; *Collas* (VD) I 32.

59 *At half* . . . OT I 81–2.

59 *But* . . . OT I 82–3; *Souv* 128–30.

60 *On* . . . OT (*Biré*) I 114, 121; *Souv* 130.

60 *The castle* . . . OT I 83; *Souv* 131.

60 *The spell* . . . OT I 83; OT (*Levaillant*) I 111–5; *Souv* 131–4; *Collas* (RA) 194; *Kerviler* (BB) X 22–3; *La Bigne* XL 57–8.

61 *Such* . . . OT I 84–5; *Souv* 134–6.

61 *In counterpart* . . . OT I 85; *Souv* 137–8.

62 *His father* . . . OT I 86; *Souv* 138–9.

62 *Lucile* . . . OT I 86–7; *Aubrée* 26–8; *Gastard* (J) 194, 214; *Grand-Bey* 274; *Le Savoureux* pl. III.

63 *Recently* . . . OT I 90, II 1363; *Collas* (RA) 252; *Saulnier* (LC) 13; *Saulnier* (PB) 610.

63 *Winter* . . . OC (*Garnier*) II 432–3; OT I 79, II 1200, 1242, 1306, 1311, 1376, 1414; *Souv* 123–4; *Collas* (RA) 144, 213, 249.

64 *Alone* . . . OT I 88; *Souv* 141.

64 *Of what* . . . VR I 139.

65 *Nevertheless* . . . *Souv* 145, 148.

65 *Already* . . . OC (*Garnier*) III 531; OT I 88; *Souv* 141.

66 *François-René* . . . OC (*Garnier*) III 531, 534, 537–8; OT I 88; *Souv* 141.

66 *Meanwhile* . . . OT I 89–90; *Souv* 142.

67 *Soon* . . . OT I 91.

67 *Now* . . . OT I 91–2.

67 *One* . . . OT I 52, 92; *Souv* 150–1; *Collas* (RA) 235; RHLF 1909, 54–5.

67 *Accordingly* . . . OT I 93; *Souv* 151.

68 *Now* . . . OT I 93; *Souv* 152.

68 *In* . . . OT I 93–4.

68 *The dream* . . . OT I 94; *Souv* 153.

68 *But* . . . OT I 94; *Souv* 153.

68 *I do* . . . OT I 92.

69 *He resumed* . . . OT I 94–5; *Souv* 153–4; *Banéat* (IV) 445, 449; *Bézier* 37, pl. X; *Gastard* (C) 8, 85; *Gastard* (J) 169–70, 210.

69 *The stormclouds* . . . OT I 95: *Souv* 154.

69 *On fine* . . . OT I 95; *Souv* 155.

70 *Hand* . . . OT I 95–6.

70 *In the* . . . *Collas* (RA) 66, 73, 240–1, 252–4, 263–4.

70 *Jean-Baptiste* . . . *Collas* (RA) 240, 249, 252.

71 *Autumn* . . . OT I 96; *Souv* 156.

71 *Every* . . . OT I 97; *Souv* 157.

71 *She came* . . . OT I 97–8 ;*Souv* 158–60

72 *He could* . . . OT I 99; *Souv* 160–1.
72 *The bell* . . . OT I 99; *Souv* 161.
72 *He had* . . . OT I 100; *Souv* 163.
72 *He still* . . . OT I 100; *Souv* 164.
72 *A sudden* . . . OT I 101, II 1255; *Souv* 165; *Collas (RA)* 180.
73 *François-René lay* . . . OT I 101–2; *Souv* 165–6.
73 *François-René felt* . . . OT I 102; *Souv* 166.
73 *What* . . . OT I 102; *Souv* 167; *Collas (RA)* 252; *Grand-Bey* 97.
74 *The ship* . . . OT I 103; *OT (Levaillant)* I 28; *Souv* 167–8; *Grand-Bey* 67–71.
74 *She was* . . . OT I 104; *Collas (RA)* 201, 227–9, 248, 254, 256.
74 *René-Auguste* . . . OT I 104–5; *Collas (RA)* 256, 259; *Durry* I 423.
74 *Death* . . . *Aubrée* 67–70; *Collas (RA)* 249, 257–8.
75 *Meanwhile* . . . OT I 103–4; *Souv* 168–9.
75 *Tomorrow* . . . OT I 104; *Souv* 169.
76 *M. du* . . . OT I 1138; *OT (Levaillant)* I 138; *BSC* VI (1937) 147; *Collas (RA)* 258.
76 *Even* . . . OT I 104; *Souv* 169–70; *BSC* VI (1937) 135–6, 147–8; *Collas (RA)* 234, 249, 258.
76 *François-René* . . . OT I 105; *Souv* 170.

6 ROYAL HUNT

79 *François-René* . . . OT I 109, 1137; *OT (Levaillant)* I 147; *BSC* VI (1937) 148; *Collas (RA)* 164, 259.
79 *So* . . . OT I 109–10.
79 *The landscape* . . . OT I 110.
79 *Early* . . . OT I 110; *BSC* (1957) 38.
80 *He climbed* . . . OT I 111.
80 *A distant* . . . OT I 111–12, II 1383.
80 *As they* . . . OT I 112–4; *Collas (VD)* I 51–2.
81 *Julie* . . . OT I 114.
81 *At* . . . OT I 115, II 1314, 1411; *Villemain* 24.
81 *Mme.* . . . OT I 115–6.
82 *He obeyed* . . . OT I 116.
82 *Next* . . . OT I 116–7, II 1180; *OT (Levaillant)* I 139, 154–5; *BSC* VI (1937) 147.
82 *His* . . . OT I 48, 116–7, II 1180, 1362.
82 *La Martinière* . . . OT I 117.
82 *François-René* . . . OT I 117–8.
83 *Towards* . . . OT I 118–8; *Collas (Dix ans)* 4–8; *Collas (RA)* 259–61; *Collas (VD)* 18–20; *La Bigne* XL 67.
83 *A letter* . . . OT I 38, 118 120, 122; *Collas (VD)* I 20.
84 *On 23* . . . *Collas (Dix ans)* 8–11; *Collas (RA)* 261–2; *Collas (VD)* I 20–22.
84 *François-René* . . . OT I 117; *Aubrée* 119; *Collas (VD)* I 24.
84 *Julie* . . . OT I 122, 135; *Aubrée* 83–4, 105, 120–1; *Collas (VD)* I 25.
85 *Towards* . . . OC (Garnier) I 241; OT I 122–3.
85 *François-René* . . . OT I 123.
85 *He stayed* . . . OT I 123–4.
86 *Cousin* . . . OT I 124–5.
86 *The dreadful* . . . OT I 124, 129.
86 *The King* . . . OC (Garnier) I 529; OT I 129–30.
87 *He rejoined* . . . OT I 130.

87 *But* . . . OT I 130–3.
87 *Under* . . . OT I 131–2.
87 *King* . . . OC *(Garnier)* I 529; OT I 132–3.
88 *In any* . . . OT I 122; *Collas (Dix ans)* 11–17; *Collas (RA)* 262–4; *Collas (VD)* I 30–1.
88 *The long* . . . *Collas (VD)* I 31–3, 329.
88 *The inventory* . . . *Collas (Dix ans)* 268–75, 288–99; *Collas (VD)* I 31–3.
89 *Next* . . . *Collas (RA)* 263; *Collas (VD)* I 35–6.
89 *So far* . . . *Collas (VD)* 34.
90 *It is* . . . *Collas (RA)* 262–4; *Collas (VD)* I 36–7, 329.
90 *Only* . . . OT I 135–6; *Collas (VD)* I 48.
90 *Was* . . . OT I 136, 1140–1; *OT (Levaillant)* I 177; *Aubrée* 68–9, 102–4, 115–6; *BSC* I (1930) 26–9, pl. VII; *Collas (VD)* I 48.
91 *Soon* . . . OT I 122, 135–6, 160.
91 *Although* . . . *Aubrée* 126–31; *BSC* 1962 20–1; *Collas (VD)* I 25–8, 79.
92 *M. de* . . . *Aubrée* 101–4; *Collas (VD)* I 49–51.
92 *Meanwhile* . . . OT I 77, 136; *OT (1856)* VI 292, 377; *Souv* 120; *Collas (VD)* I 52.
93 *Julie* . . . OT I 135–6.

7 SWORDS IN THE STREETS

94 *The philosopher* . . . OT I 136–7; *BSC* (1957) 38; *Collas (VD)* I 53.
94 *Among* . . . OC *(Garnier)* I 319; OT I 137–8; *OT (Biré)* I 174.
94 *Flins* . . . OC *(Garnier)* I 319; OT I 138; *Chabanon* 145; *La Harpe* XVI p. xvi.
95 *The poet* . . . OT I 139–41; *OT (Biré)* I 180.
95 *With* . . . OC *(Garnier)* I 330; OT I 140–1.
96 *But* . . . OC *(Garnier)* I 325; OT I 139.
97 *However* . . . OC *(Garnier)* I 340–1; OT I 141–2.
97 *Such* . . . OT I 142.
98 *Without* . . . OC *(Garnier)* I 248, 341.
98 *Fortunately* . . . OT I 143–5.
98 *Jean-Baptiste* . . . *Collas (VD)* I 52–3, 56–8, 66.
99 *Malesherbes* . . . OC *(Garnier)* I 522; *OT* 144–5; *Collas (VD)* I 57–8; *Tocqueville* 108.
99 *He noticed* . . . OC *(Garnier)* I 522; OT I 143–5.
99 *Malesherbe's* . . . *Boissy d'Anglas* II 110; *Grosclaude* 358–88, 559–603, 631.
100 *Even so* . . . OT I 124–8, 146; *Collas (VD)* I 62.
101 *In March* . . . OT I 13, 77; *Collas (VD)* I 65–6; *Grosclaude* 653.
101 *François-René* . . . OT I 147–55; *Collas (VD)* I 62–4; *Pocquet (RB)* I 39, 43–9.
102 *What* . . . OT I 155–6; *Collas (VD)* I 64–5; *Mémoire* 23; *Pocquet (RB)* I 55–73.
102 *Next* . . . *Collas (VD)* I 64; *Pocquet (RB)* I 74–111.
103 *Three* . . . OT I 156; *Collas (VD)* I 64–5; *Pocquet (RB)* I 111–94.
103 *On 5* . . . OT I 156; *Collas (VD)* I 76; *Pocquet (RB)* I 195–246, II 122.
104 *His* . . . OT I 161–2; *Collas (VD)* I 48, 62–3, 67–8, 330.
104 *Jean-Baptiste had left* . . . OT I 105; *Collas (VD)* I 65–6.
104 *Jean-Baptiste had not* . . . OT I 156–8.
105 *Soon* . . . OT I 9, 158–9; *OT (1856)* VI 288–9, 358–60; *OT (Biré)* I 360–1; *Banéat (IV)* III 599; *Grand-Bey* 98–9.
106 *While* . . . OT I 159–60.

106 *Very* ... OT I 162; *Collas* (*VD*) 72–5; *Pocquet* (*RB*) II 144.
106 *Soon* ... OT I 163.
107 *This* ... *Pocquet* (*RB*) II 163.
107 *Next* ... OT I 163; *Pocquet* (*RB*) II 151–62.
107 *Their* ... OT I 155; *Collas* (*VD*) I 75; *Pocquet* (*RB*) II 143, 163–212.
108 *At last* ... OT I 163–4; *Collas* (*VD*) I 76; *Pocquet* (*RB*) II 232–45;
      Relation 10.
108 *That* ... OT I 163; *Collas* (*VD*) I 76; *Pocquet* (*RB*) II 245–9.
108 *Next* ... *Pocquet* (*RB*) II 249–50.
109 *At three* ... OT I 164; *Collas* (*VD*) I 77; *Pocquet* (*RB*) II 251–4.
109 *Single* ... OT I 164–5; *Collas* (*VD*) I 77; *Pocquet* (*RB*) II 255–8.
109 *M. de* ... *Boishamon* 7, 30, 31, 52, 55; *Kerviler* (*BB*) II 445–6; *Pocquet* (*RB*)
      II 259–96.
110 *On 10* ... OT I 164; *Collas* (*VD*) I 82–4; *Pocquet* (*RB*) II 319–65.
111 *He was* ... OT I 69, 165.
111 *Now proceed* ... OT I 165.

8 LOVE AMONG THE RUINS

112 *François-René* ... OC (*Garnier*) III 535, 540–2; *CG* I 3; *Collas* (*RA*)
      253; *Grosclaude* 613–30.
112 *Sometimes* ... OT I 287; *Pailleron* 274.
112 *He thought* ... *CG* I 1–3; *Albert* 173–5; *Kerviler* (*BB*) IX 50; *Lievyns*
      V 77–8.
113 *Early* ... *CG* I 1–2.
113 *His* ... *CG* I 2–3; *Boishamon* 11, 16, 31, 52; *Collas* (*VD*) I 104; *Granges
      de Surgères*; *La Lande de Calan* 47, 268, 277, 279.
114 *The coxcomb* ... *Aubrée* 37; *BSC* 1968–9 60–4; *Le Savoureux* pl. III.
114 *Leaving* ... OT I 160; *Aubrée* 68, 132–5, 138–9 *Banéat* (*IV*) I 540;
      Collas (*VD*) I 78–9; *Kerviler* (*BB*) VIII 155.
114 *Even* ... OT I 161.
114 *Meanwhile* ... OC (*Garnier*) III 535–43; *Aubrée* 135, 145.
115 *He returned* ... *Aubrée* 104; *Collas* (*VD*) I 332; *Grand-Bey* 273–4.
115 *At* ... OT I 164–5; *Collas* (*VD*) I 67–8; *Lasseray* I 149; *Lenôtre* 34–5;
      Revue de la Révolution XIV (1889) 396.
116 *Meanwhile* ... *Boishamon* 40; *Collas* (*VD*) I 89–90; *Salonne* 115, 129.
116 *Then* ... OT I 165; *Collas* (*VD*) I 86–7; *Madelin* 44.
117 *On that* ... OT I 165–6; *Bord*; *BSC* (1957) 38; *Madelin* 61–2, 77–8.
118 *Two other* ... OT I 166–7; *BSC* I (1930) 28.
118 *Like other* ... OT I 167–8.
118 *To arms* ... OT I 168; *Bord*; *Funck Bretano* 45–6; *Madelin* 63–4.
119 *It's* ... OT I 166–71; *Madelin* 70–2.
119 *A week* ... OT I 171; *Madelin* 76; *Morris* I 137.
120 *François-René* ... OT I 145, 176, 186; *Stern, J.* 132.
120 *The Revolution* ... OC (*Garnier*) I 313; OT I 172, 186–70; *Hérissay*;
      Madelin 74, 81–8.
121 *Before* ... OT I 171–4; *Madelin* 71, 94–9; *Stern, J.* 133.
122 *The severed* ... OT I 171, 385; *Madelin* 80; *Villemain* 34–6.
122 *So* ... OT I 182–3, 187–8; *Grosclaude* 484–5.
123 *But* ... OT I 179–81.
123 *How* ... OT I 176; *Milton, Paradise Lost* ii 966–7.
124 *Amid* ... OC (*Garnier*) III 531–2, 542–3; OT I 134, 137.

9 THE STOCKING-SELLER

125 *Meanwhile* . . . *CG* I 323–9.
125 *François-René* . . . *CG* I 323–6; *Collas* (*RA*) 77, 118, 129–30, 239.
125 *Five* . . . *CG* I 327–34; *BSC* (1957) 38–9; *Collas* (*VD*) I 333–4.
126 *La Morandais* . . . *CG* I 330–2.
126 *He arrived* . . . *CG* I 326, 333.
127 *Jean-Baptiste* . . . *OT* I 77; *Collas* (*VD*) I 98–104, 110–11; *Granges de Surgères* 8; *Stern, A.* II 181–2, 196.
127 *François-René* . . . *CG* I 324, 331.
128 *Early* . . . *OT* I 186.
128 *At moments* . . . *OT* I 181–2.
128 *Soon* . . . *OT* I 145, 177; *Granges de Surgères* 6–12; *Moniteur* V 140.
129 *Jean-Baptiste* . . . *OT* I 145; *Collas* (*VD*) I 128–30; *Granges de Surgères* 6–12; *Grosclaude* 719–23.
129 *François-René* . . . *OT* I 187; *Pocquet* (*RB*) II 373, 380, 384–5, 390.
130 *His* . . . *OT* I 176–9; *OT* (*Levaillant*) I 228; *Challamel* 418, 429; *Moniteur* IV 687–8; *Stern, A.* II 192, 207; *Zinkeisen* I 307–9.
130 *The labourers* . . . *OT* I 185–6; *CG* I 335.
131 *During* . . . *Collas* (*VD*) I 108.
131 *In* . . . *Souv* 70; *Granges de Surgères* 8; *Collas* (*VD*) I 119–20, 335.
131 *François-René* . . . *CG* I 335–7; *BSC* V (1935) 74.
132 *His army* . . . *Collas* (*VD*) I 106, 118, 138, 153, 166, 333, 340; *Hartmann* 167–8, 177–8, 180, 208–11; *Moniteur* 23/9/1790.
132 *The amiable* . . . *OT* I 312; *Villemain* 35–6.

10 HYPERBOREAN STRANDS

135 *Although* . . . *OC* (*Garnier*) II 432; *OT* I 102; *Collas* (*RA*) 30–1, 48.
135 *In old* . . . *OT* I 121; *Grand-Bey* 272; *Raynal* VI 53, 114–8, 209–11, 215–20, 287–95.
136 *His thoughts* . . . *OC* (*Garnier*) I 623; *VR* I 16.
136 *In the* . . . *OC* (*Garnier*) II 464; *Charlevoix* I 511; *Raynal* VI 53.
137 *And yet* . . . *OC* (*Garnier*) I 623; *VR* I 16; *Raynal* VI 53, 114–8.
137 *Soon* . . . *VR* I 16, II 36, 701; *Marcellus* 125.
138 *But* . . . *OC* (*Garnier*) VI 451; *OT* I 145, 188, 228–9; *VR* I 16.
138 *M. de* . . . *Boissy d'Anglas* II 113–4, 153, 210, 221; *Collas* (*VD*) I 105; *Granges de Surgères* 9; *Grosclaude* 654, 687, 728.
139 *François-René's* . . . *OC* (*Garnier*) I 542, VI 541–2; *OT* I 188; *Grosclaude* 464–83, 609; *Marcellus* 44–5, 61; *Villemain* 37.
139 *At* . . . *OT* I 188.
140 *He had* . . . *CG* I 46; *BSC* II (1931) 45; *Grosclaude* 464, 478, 698–700; *L. C. Harper* (*New York*) *Cat.* 201, no. 172.
140 *For* . . . *OT* I 251–2; *VR* I 33, 863–5.
141 *How* . . . *OT* I 188, 229.
141 *What* . . . *CG* I 46; *Collas* (*VD*) I 127–8; *Grosclaude* 629; *Madelin* 142–3; *Moniteur* May 1790.
141 *At that* . . . *OT* I 183; *VR* I 667; *Allemagne*; *Almanach des Muses* (1791) 11, 224; *Belote* 9–47; *Carré*; *Howe* 180; *Winson* (*W*) 310–14, 402–7.
142 *He would* . . . *OC* (*Garnier*) I 542; *Carver* 17; *Winsor* (*W*) 101–6.
142 *The thought* . . . *VR* I 33, 659–60, 703; *Carver* (*Fr*) 23, 47; *De Voto* 245–51; *Charlevoix* III 185.

142 *Other* . . . VR I 655, 827; *Bellin (Recueil)* no. 16; *Burpee* I 46, 53, 76; *Carver (Fr)* 425–41; *Charlevoix* I, map, III xviii, 185, 396; *Crouse* 370; *Davis*; *Dumont* II 246–54; *Engel*, map; *La Vérendrye* 52–63; *Le Page du Pratz* III 88–140; *Wager* I 209; *Winsor (M)* 193–216.

143 *François-René* . . . OC (*Garnier*) I 542; VR I 666; *Burpee* I 273–7; *Morse* 17; *Thwaites*; *Winsor (M)* 206.

143 *The second* . . . VR I 639, 827; *Dobbs*; *Williams, G.* frontispiece, 142–53, 173–5, 273–82.

144 *For* . . . *Cook* I xxxiii; *Williams, G.* 194–205.

144 *Cook* . . . *Dalrymple* 6, 9, 10, 13; *Dixon* xiv, 236; *Howay*; *Meares*, map, 65; *Williams, G.* 214–21, 227, 241.

145 *Such* . . . OC (*Garnier*) I 542; OT I 228–9; VR I 666.

145 *Yet* . . . OC (*Garnier*) I 542; OT I 228; VR I 666; *Burpee* II 325–53; *Davidson* 42–4; *De Voto* 308; *Gentleman's Magazine* (March 1790) 197–9; *Wheat* 169–73; *Williams, G.* 201–2, 230–5.

145 *He stood* . . . OT I 190–1, 228; VR I 665.

145 *And yet* . . . VR I 650.

146 *Throughout* . . . OT I 145, 228; VR I 650, 664; *Burpee* I 138–64; *Cook (Fr)* I lxx–lxxvii; *Hearne*; *Rich* II 44–65; *Williams, G.* 3–7, 133–6, 172–3.

146 *By a* . . . *Rich* II 83–9.

147 *Another* . . . *Augur*; *De Voto* 279–80, 297–9, 415–6, 595–8; *Jefferson (Papers)* IX 261, 273, X 258, 260, 548; *Jefferson (Writings)* I 94, IV 298, 448, V 75; *Michaux* 89; *Munford*; *Sparks*; *Thwaites* 67–80.

148 *So* . . . OT I 228; *Jefferson (Papers)* XI 490; *Jefferson (Writings)* IV 392–3.

148 *Thus* . . . OC (*Garnier*) I 542; OT I 228; VR I 666; *Cook (Fr)* III 170–92; *Gentleman's Magazine* (March 1790) 197–9.

148 *Such* . . . OC (*Garnier*) I 543; OT I 228–9; VR I 664–5.

149 *His journey* . . . VR I 650–6; *Burpee* II 415–91; *Gentleman's Magazine* (November 1790) 1046; *Rich* II 134–8, 166–7.

150 *And so* . . . OC (*Garnier*) I 540, VI 426–7, 562; OT I 229; VR I 663, 888; *Marcellus* 43–4.

11 SULPICIAN ARK

151 *He emerged* . . . OT I 182–4.

151 *In* . . . OT I 183; *Collas (VD)* I 55.

151 *Villemain* . . . *Collas (VD)* I 130, 202; *Maugras* 70–6, 82–103; *Villemain* 34.

152 *Aline* . . . OT I 304, II 367.

152 *Up to* . . . OC (*Garnier*) I 324, 389; *Wilson* 117–23.

153 *At Fougères* . . . OT I 189; *Lasseray* II 454–61; *Lenôtre* 12–17; *Washington* XXVII 274–6, XXVIII 288, 514, XXX 437.

153 *Early* . . . OT I 105; VR I 136–7.

153 *He learned* . . . *Collas (VD)* I 111–2, 121–2, 131–3, 142.

154 *At* . . . *Collas (VD)* I 123, 133–4, 139.

154 *But* . . . OT I 189; *Collas (VD)* I 45–6, 145.

154 *His* . . . OT I 492–3; *Collas (VD)* I 145, 198–9; *Herbermann* 15–20; *Shea* I 377–9; *Stern, J.* 159.

155 *The ex* . . . *Collas (VD)* I 45–6, 144–5; *Mondésir* 25, 31; *Terrien* 225–76.

156 *The ways* . . . *Terrien* 251–565.

156 *François-René* . . . OT I 103; *Collas (RA)* 252–3, 255–7.

156 *In* . . . OT I 189; VR I 1284; *Armstrong* 351–2.

157 *Father* . . . *Terrien* 275–6.

157 *The Saint-Pierre* ... BSC V (1935) 23; *Collas* (*VD*) I 45, 98–104, 112, 114, 123, 140–1, 145–6; *Gastard* (*J*) 284; *Mondésir* 19–20.
157 *François-René* ... OT I 178, 190; *Madelin* 163.
158 *Late* ... OT I 190; BSC V (1935) 23; *Collas* (*VD*) I 146.
158 *The* ... OT I 191.

12 THE DISCOVERY OF AMERICA

159 *The wind* ... OT I 189–90, 198; *Jauffret* II 408; *Marcellus* 59; *Mondésir* 21; *Shea* I 379.
159 *M. Nagot* ... OT I 189; BSC V (1935) 24–5; *Collas* (*VD*) I 145–6; *Jauffret* II 407–8; *Mondésir* 9–13, 19–20, 25–7, 30–1.
160 *If* ... OC (*Garnier*) I 604; *Giraud* 169; *Mondésir* 20, 22.
160 *So* ... OT I 202.
160 *Their* ... OT I 199–203.
161 *The captain* ... OT I 201–2; *Wansey* 47.
161 *The ship* ... OC (*Garnier*) II 119; OT I 199.
161 *The most* ... OT I 200.
161 *The bell* ... OT I 203.
162 *In those* ... OC (*Garnier*) II 113; OT I 198, 203–4; *Wansey* 46.
162 *It was* ... OC (*Garnier*) I 603–4; OT I 204; BSC V (1935) 24–5; *Gentleman's Magazine* (Nov. 1799) 994, (Dec. 1819) 562, (July 1835) 102; *Giraud* 169–70; *Mondésir* 19; *Mourot* 196; RMA *Records* 1–32; *Scottish NQ* 3 III (1925) 14; *Vincent*; *Whitmore*.
162 *François-René* ... OC (*Garnier*) I 604; OT I 204.
163 *M. Nagot* ... *Jauffret* II 410; *Mondésir* 31.
163 *He* ... *Jauffret* II 410; *Mondésir* 20–1.
163 *Early* ... OC (*Garnier*) I 604; OT I 204; *Jauffret* II 408; *Mondésir* 22–3.
164 *They anchored* ... OC (*Garnier*) I 604–6; OT I 204–6; VR I 671; *Ashe* 286–8; *Boid* 252, 311.
164 *They lowered* ... OC (*Garnier*) I 606–7; OT I 206; VR I 671; *Barnby* 79, 102; *Boid* 254; BSC V (1935) 23; *Jauffret* II 408; *Mondésir* 23; *Wansey* 46.
164 *The senior* ... OC (*Garnier*) I 607–8; OT I 206–7; *Jauffret* II 408–9; *Mondésir* 23.
165 *They set* ... OC (*Garnier*) I 607, II 12, 100; OT I 207–8; VR I 281; *Hennig* I 109–20.
165 *François-René* ... OC (*Garnier*) I 608–9; OT I 208; *Boid* 317; *Edrisi* I 105; *Jauffret* II 409–10; *Mondésir* 23.
165 *He avoided* ... OC (*Garnier*) II 113; OT I 208–9.
166 *At dusk* ... OC (*Garnier*) I 604, II 113; OT I 204, 209.
166 *It was* ... OC (*Garnier*) I 604; OT I 209–10; BSC V (1935) 23; *Collas* (*VD*) I 145–6; *Jauffret* II 411; *Mondésir* 19.
166 *Towards* ... OC (*Garnier*) I 604; OT I 210; *Jauffret* II 411; *Mondésir* 31; *Prowse* 572.
167 *The little* ... OT I 210, 212–3; VR I 672; *Bellin* (*Atlas*) I 16–19; *Martineau* 688–94; *Prowse* 57; *Saintoyant* II 283–9.
167 *The lonely* ... OT I 210–11; *Almanach Royal* (1791) 211; *Prowse* 572.
167 *One* ... OT I 211; *Delamare* 88.
167 *What* ... OT I 212, II 624; *Michaux* 69.
168 *Sometimes* ... OC (*Garnier*) I 604–5, II 100–1, 400, III 135, 651; OT I 212–4, 414, 417; VR I 672; *Almanach des Muses* (1783) 227–30, (1784) 169–70; *Marcellus* 118; *Mondésir* 41; *Tieghem* I 360, 363, 383.

169 But ... *OC (Garnier)* I 605; *Jauffret* II 411–2; *Mondésir* 27.
169 From ... *OC (Garnier)* I 605.
169 However ... *OC (Garnier)* I 605; *OT* I 214; *BSC* (1935) 24; *Jauffret* II 411–2; *Mondésir* 23; *Saintoyant* II 286–9.
169 They ... *OT* I 215; *Diaria Britannica*.
170 One ... *OC (Garnier)* II 113–4; *OT* I 33, 215, 482, 1060; *VR* I 672; *Campbell* 15; *Diaria Britannica*.
170 A few ... *OT* I 215–6; *VR* I 672–3; *Mondésir* 21–2.
171 Those ... *OC (Garnier)* I 604.
171 On 2 ... *OT* I 216; *VR* I 673; *Jauffret* II 413–4.
171 They ... *OT* I 217; *VR* I 674–5; *Bartram* 280; *Bartram* (N) 633; *Chastellux* I 457.
171 He ... *OT* I 216; *VR* I 674.
172 Father ... *OT* I 217; *Jauffret* II 413–6.
172 At last ... *OT* I 217; *VR* I 675; *Jauffret* II 416.
172 Francis ... *OC (Garnier)* I 605; *OT* I 217–9; *VR* I 675; *Jauffret* II 416–7.

13 A FALL AT NIAGARA

173 The American ... *OT* I 219; *Crèvecoeur (Lettres)* III 459–60; *Earle* 262–3; *Lambert* III 21–2; *Perrin du Lac* 109–11; *Wansey* 63–5, 116; *Weld* I 26, II 4–5.
173 François-René ... *OT* I 219–20; *VR* I 676; *Wansey* 105.
173 They ... *OT* I 220; *VR* I 677; *Wansey* 124.
174 However ... *OC (Garnier)* I 363; *OT* I 220; *VR* I 676–7; *Raynal* VI 287–97.
174 His ... *VR* I 202, 747; *Carver* (Fr) 375–6; *Wansey* 72–3, 104–5, 112.
175 He sought ... *OT* I 229; *VR* I 677; *American Pioneer* I 182; *Belote* 55–6; *Howe* 180; *Winsor* (W) 426–8.
175 He found ... *OT* I 228–9; *Gentleman's Magazine* (March 1790) 197–9.
175 All ... *OT* I 229, 231; *VR* I 677, 683; *Carver* 17.
176 He was ... *OT* I 220; *VR* I 677; *Freeman* VI 214–5, 324; *Jefferson (Writings)* V 356, 359.
176 So François-René ... *OT* I 221; *VR* I 677–8; *Decatur* 194, 215; *Eberlein* 161–78; *Freeman* VI 324; *Jefferson (Writings)* V 356–9; *Washington* XXX 437–9, 448, XXXI 355.
177 Next ... *OC (Garnier)* I 364; *OT* I 220, 229; *VR* I 682; *Baldensperger* (*1915*) 574; *Lambert* III 78; *M'Robert* 44; *Michaux* 69; *Wansey* 57, 63–74, 90, 96, 124.
178 He could ... *VR* I 682, 1287; *Grand-Bey* 281–2.
178 Albany ... *OC (Garnier)* I 540–1, II 105; *OT* I 230, 1061; *VR* I 682; *Campbell* 237; *Lambert* II 134–42; *M'Robert* 7; *Maude* 19; *Munsell* III 147, 186, 222.
178 They glided ... *OC (Garnier)* I 540–2, II 105; *OT* I 230, 1061; *VR* I 683; *American Musical Miscellany*; *Maude* 7; *Sargent* 448–9, 464–6.
179 Mr. Swift ... *OT* I 231; *VR* I 683; *Kalm* I 342; *Munsell* III 178; *Stevens* 97, 100–1; *Turner (Phelps)* 490–1; *Watson* 267.
179 François-René ... *OC (Garnier)* 623; *OT* I 231; *VR* I 683–4.
180 The way ... *American Pioneer* II 120; *Bellin (Atlas)* I 29; *Clark* I 348, 359; *Crèvecoeur (Lettres)* III 486; *Gipson* 164; *Ketchum* II 32; *Maude* 102; *Munsell* II 209, III 149; *Turner (Holland)* 412.
180 The fertile ... *OT* I 239–40; *VR* I 691; *Greene* 165–71; *Marcellus* 59; *Watson* 269.

181 *At last* ... OC (*Garnier*) I 622; OT I 231; VR I 684; *Campbell* 217;
    Decatur 228; *Munsell* II 195; *Turner* (*Phelps*) 422.

181 *As they* ... OC (*Garnier*) I 618; OT I 232; VR I 684–5, II 1163–4,
    1741; *Campbell* 217; *Decatur* 228; *Greene* 139, 142; *Le Sage* III 172;
    Maude 37, 285; *Munsell* II 195.

181 *At Oneida* ... OT I 223; VR I 61, 96, 745, 779, 803, 1312; *Armstrong*
    356; *Campbell* 57, 71; *Charlevoix* I 20, III 129; *Colbert* 48; *Coues*
    34–58; *Glover* 186–92; *Kalm* II 522; *La Hontan* II 81; *Lincklaen* 68;
    Maude 285; *Michaux* 85; *Perrin du Lac* 167; *Weld* II 142, 150.

182 *After* ... OC (*Garnier*) I 623; OT I 234; VR I 685–6; *Clark* I 17, map;
    Colbert 48.

182 *It was* ... OT I 235; VR I 686–7; *Britton* (*Flora*) 859; *Britton* (*Trees*)
    752; *Marcellus* 84; *Samuels* 314–7, 320–1.

182 *Still* ... OT I 235–6; VR I 687–8; *M'Robert* 35.

183 *Next* ... OT I 236–8; VR I 689–91; *Clark* I 102–3, 348–62; *Lincklaen*
    66; *Watson* 299–300; *Weld* II 253, 260.

183 *Monsieur* ... OC (*Garnier*) I 619; *Mourot* 198; *Watson* 298.

183 *The way* ... OT I 239; VR I 691–2; *Lincklaen* 63–5; *Marcellus* 59.

184 *They reached* ... OC (*Garnier*) II 63; OT I 240–1; VR I 692; *Bartram*
    262–3; *Campbell* 143; *Maude* 102; *Turner* (*Holland*) 313–5; *Weld* II 294.

184 *Within* ... OC (*Garnier*) I 623–4; OT I 241; VR I 692; *Maude* 124, 133;
    Niemcewicz 251; *Ride* 26; *Turner* (*Holland*) 315, 321; *Weld* II 310,
    313, 332.

185 *He could* ... OC (*Garnier*) I 624–5; OT I 241.

185 *He sat* ... OC (*Garnier*) I 625–6, II 114–5, 222–3; OT I 241; VR I 46,
    1191.

186 *When* ... OC (*Garnier*) 626–7; OT I 242.

186 *They* ... OT I 242; VR I 692–3; *Notes* 34; *Turner* (*Holland*) 393.

186 *He sat* ... OT I 243; VR I 693–6, 1287–8; *Baldensperger* (*1928*).

186 *The mothers* ... VR I 693–6, 1287; *Weld* II 246.

187 *The Dutchman* ... OT I 242; VR I 693.

187 *Colonel* ... *Army List* (1794); *Campbell* 184; *Cruikshank* 19, 22, 41, 75,
    82–3, 90, 99, 106–7, 110, 116, 123–5; *Ketchum* II 35; *Kirby* 111;
    Johnston I 156–7; *Winsor* (*W*) 229–41, 415–26.

188 *Next* ... OT I 243–4; VR I 696.

188 *A moment* ... OC (*Garnier*) I 543; OT I 245; VR I 697; *Campbell* 153;
    Maude 150; *Weld* II 134.

188 *Forty* ... OC (*Garnier*) I 543; OT I 245; VR I 696–7; *Dow* I 40, 43, 58,
    63, 70, 77, 141–2; *Hadfield* 96–9; *Maude* 147; *Schultz* 77.

189 *He saw* ... OC (*Garnier*) I 543; OT I 246; VR I 697.

189 *Meanwhile* ... OT I 246–8, 1062–3; *Charlevoix* III 207; *La Hontan* II
    204; *Moore* I 79; *Schultz* 50; *Weld* II 228, 236, 289.

190 *He lingered* ... OT I 246, 255.

190 *The tribe* ... OC (*Garnier*) I 542; OT I 255, 1064; VR I 697, 1288.

190 *He rode* ... *Jauffret* II 423; *Winsor* (*W*) 23, 120, 171, 416, 562–3.

14 OHIO MOUTH

191 *At present* ... OC (*Garnier*) I 395; OT I 255, 268, 1064; VR I 887;
    Hulbert 11, 13, 23.

192 *Always* ... OT I 255–6; VR I 698–9; *Cruikshank* 47, 123–5; *Weld* I 195.

192 *One* ... OC (*Garnier*) VI 379–80; VR I 699–700; *Carver* 147; *Charlevoix*
    III 206; *Weld* II 75–82; *Zeisberger* I 354.

192 *On the* ... *OT* I 1064; *VR* I 1288.

193 *Easy* ... *VR* I 713; *Hutchins* 90; *Winsor (M)* 26–30.

193 *He found* ... *OT* I 1064; *VR* I 1288.

193 *They canoed* ... *VR* I 703–9.

194 *There* ... *Brown, R. H.* 224, 226; *Cramer* 43; *Gipson* 172; *Hanna* I 144, 156, 333–7, 343; *Hutchins* 91, 138; *Kegley* 206; *Melish* 463–85; *Schultz* 134.

194 *Cuyahoga* ... *Brown L. A.* 16, 45, 51; *Crèvecoeur (Lettres)* III 413; *Hulbert* 11, 13, 23; *Jefferson (Notes)* 23; *Jefferson (Papers)* I 662; *Johnson* 32–6; *Olden Tine* II 350–1; *Saint-Clair* II 79; *Washington* XXVII 477, XXVIII 167, XXIX 89, 348, 370; *Weld* II 160; *Winsor (M)* 244–5; *Winsor (W)* 128, 248, 256, 269, 310, 437, 490.

194 *At this* ... *Hanna* I 349; *Johnson* 32–6; *M'Robert* 40; *Perrin du Lac* 225; *Zeisberger* I 278–82, 289, II 205.

195 *They* ... *VR* I 703; *GSO* I 202–3, III 133–5; *Hanna* I 205.

195 *Primitive* ... *VR* I 703.

195 *Ten* ... *VR* I 704–5; *Bartram* 14; *Imlay* 491; *May* 44.

196 *Again* ... *VR* I 705–6.

196 *Reclining* ... *VR* I 455, 706–7, 1292.

196 *Next* ... *VR* I 707–9; *Hanna* II 200; *Saint-Clair* II 302–9.

197 *On* ... *VR* I 708–9.

197 *Five* ... *VR* I 708; *US Geological Survey Map*, Ravenna Quadrangle 1:24000 (1960).

197 *They* ... *OT* I 256; *Crèvecoeur (Lettres)* III 433–4; *Hanna* I 349; *May* 86, 95–7, 137; *Winsor (W)* 269, 293.

198 *An irregular* ... *VR* I 713; *Crèvecoeur (Lettres)* III 396; *May* 35, 54.

198 *He does* ... *Baldwin* 41; *Crèvecoeur (Lettres)* III 407; *May* 52, 67.

199 *The immigrant* ... *Hutchins* 90; *May* 37; *Saint-Clair* II 20, 38, 45; *Winsor (W)* 30, 178, 270, 304, 320, 372.

199 *From* ... *May* 54–7, 82; *Speed* 62.

199 *May's* ... *Cramer* 21; *Dean; Denny* 288; *Imlay* 28; *May* 46; *Pope* 18, 21–2; *Saint-Clair* II 20, 26, 45; *Speed* 56–63; *Winsor (W)* 118.

200 *There* ... *Columbian Magazine* Oct.–Dec. 1791; *Cramer* 20–1; *Saint-Clair* II 185.

200 *But* ... *OT* I 256–7; *VR* I 710–20.

200 *François-René* ... *OC (Garnier)* II 75, 558; *VR* I 710–3; *Columbian Magazine* (May 1787) 425–7; *Crèvecoeur (Voyage)* III 202; *Cutler* I 419, II 14–17, 253–4.

201 *He returned* ... *OC (Garnier)* II 74–5.

201 *The gay* ... *OT* I 183; *VR* I 717; *American Pioneer* I 43, 89, 141; *Belote* 47–59; *Collot* 80; *Heckewelder* 35–6; *Howe* 180; *Saint-Clair* II 190, 195, 206, 252, 265; *Volney* 381–93; *Winsor (W)* 174, 327, 404–7.

202 *His sole* ... *Flint* II 282; *Speed* 54; *Winsor (W)* 303–4, 417.

202 *Even* ... *OC (Garnier)* I 543; *Saint-Clair* II 243–52, 288, 290, 294; *Winsor (W)* 419–20, 424, 427.

203 *So his* ... *Monette* II 400; *Saint-Clair* II 196.

203 *So he* ... *OT* I 256; *VR* I 716, 718; *Crèvecoeur (Lettres)* III 419–33; *Forman* 32–42; *Imlay* 28, 377–8.

204 *Below* ... *Alvord* 411; *Baily* 251–2; *Collot* 191–5; *Imlay* 491.

204 *Here* ... *OT* I 257, 1065; *VR* I 720; *Forman* 45.

205 *The town* ... *Winsor (W)* 32, 372.

205 *Indeed* ... *OT* I 1065; *Adams* 71; *Forman* 47–51; *Michaux* 127; *Pope* 21–2, 29; *Winsor (W)* 309, 366.

15 THE TWO FLORIDIANS

206 *He travelled* ... OT I 257; *Collot* 185; *Imlay* 125, 491; *May* 32, 80, 83; *Michaux* 127; *Schultz* 204.

206 *In the* ... VR I 724–34.

206 *Bartram* ... VR I 724–8; *Bartram* xix, 43–4, 100, 104, 123–8, 175–7.

206 *Even* ... OT I 257–8; *Bartram* 100–1; *Clark Papers* 225; *Cramer* 81; *Ellicott* 29; *Hale.*

207 *They* ... OT I 258–9; VR I 724–7; *Bartram* xiii, xix–xx, 59, 78, 100–3, 404–5.

208 *At this* ... OT I 249, 260–1; VR I 862; *Bartram* 482–3.

208 *His* ... OT I 261; VR I 734, 844–5; *Bartram* 109–11, 186–206.

208 *Next* ... OT I 262–3; VR I 725; *Bartram* 299, 501.

209 *They* ... OT I 263, 1064; *Bartram* 87.

209 *A friendly* ... OT I 1064, II 720; *OT (Levaillant)* I 565; VR I 730.

209 *From* ... OT I 263–4; VR I 729.

209 *The cousins* ... OT I 264; VR I 730.

209 *He rose* ... OT I 264–5; *Bartram* 243, 503–6.

210 *They* ... OT I 265, 1065; *OT (Levaillant)* I 565.

210 *The traders* ... OT I 265; *Bartram* 382–4.

210 *He enquired* ... OT I 266–7.

210 *He gives* ... OT I 257–8.

211 *The trail* ... *Winsor (W)* 143, 179, 359, 411.

211 *Perhaps* ... OC *(Garnier)* II 465; *Alvord* 366–72, 403–4; *Desgeorge* 9–12; *Herbermann* 42–4; *Jauffret* II 422–6; *Mondésir* 29; *Moreau* 168–9.

211 *The way* ... VR I 709; *Baily* 411–39; *Michaux* 117; *Williams, S. C.* 436–9.

212 *The Wilderness* ... OC *(Garnier)* I 543; *Flint* II 38; *Ramsey* 356–60; *Winsor (W)* 385, 516–21.

212 *Knoxville* ... *Rothrock* 32, 397.

212 *After Knoxville* ... *Summers* 616–7, 626, 630, 667; *Williams, S. C.* 449; *Winsor (M)* 180.

213 *Somewhere* ... OT I 267; VR I 886; *Colles* 104.

213 *Night* ... OT I 268; VR I 886–7; *Hartmann* 245–70.

214 *So* ... OT I 268.

214 *He tried* ... OT I 267.

214 *The Blue* ... OC *(Garnier)* VI 414; VR I 713, 717; *Collot* 25 *Crèvecoeur (Lettres)* II 75; *Gipson,* maps 1749, 1755; *M'Robert* 7; *Winterbotham* II 399.

214 *Chillicothe* ... VR I 905, 913, 922.

215 *Halfway* ... *Michaux* 136; *Williams, S. C.* 436–8, 462–70.

215 *He does* ... *Williams, S. C.* 449.

215 *Thirty* ... *Howe (V)* 514; *Michaux* 55, 98; *Virginia* 435.

216 *Between* ... VR I 65, 68–9; *Alvord* 239–41; *Chastellux* I 87–93, 386–416; *Howe (V)* 457–60; *Jefferson (Papers)* VI 191; *Virginia* 430; *Weld* I 221, II 310–324; *Winsor (W)* 33.

216 *At Harper's* ... OC *(Garnier)* I 279; *Cutler* I 419; *Jefferson (Notes)* 27; *Michaux* 55, 99; *Volney* 83; *Weld* I 239.

216 *His road* ... *Michaux* 55, 98; *Parker.*

217 *Since* ... *Freeman* VI 18.

218 *At Philadelphia* ... OT I 279–80.

218 *One piece* ... OC *(Garnier)* I 386; OT I 220–1; *Decatur* 172; *Eberlein* 161–78; *Wansey* 100.

219 *They* . . . OT I 221.
219 *Washington* . . . *Freeman* VI 214–5, 324, 330–2.
219 *The President* . . . *Freeman* VI 327.
220 *But Monsieur* . . . *Freeman* VI 327–8; *Washington* XXVII 54–6; XXXI 355–64.
220 *The President* . . . OT I 221; *Freeman* VI 3, 12, 14–22, 33, 331–2.
221 *Every* . . . *Decatur* 51–4, 121–6, 134, 169, 174, 198–9, 214, 258, 267, 288; *Eberlein* 174.
221 *François-René* . . . OT I 221–2.
221 *The conversation* . . . OT I 221–2; *VR* II 1164; *Decatur* 128–9, 144–5.
222 *On the* . . . *Freeman* VI 329, 336–9; *Winsor (W)* 427–30.
222 *So he* . . . OT I 280; *Bishop* 878.

16 CÉLESTE

225 *A strong* . . . OT I 280.
225 *As they* . . . OT I 280.
225 *For two* . . . OT I 280–1.
226 *The ship* . . . OT I 281–2; *VR* II 661.
226 *A Breton* . . . OT I 33, 282.
226 *A stalwart* . . . OT I 282–3.
226 *They were* . . . OT I 283.
226 *But* . . . OT I 285–6; *VR* II 661–2; *Collas (VD)* I 173; *Mondésir* 41; *The Star, The Times, Woodfall's Register* 30 Dec. 1791–9 Jan. 1792.
227 *Mme* . . . *OC (Garnier)* I 488; OT I 286–7, 1155; *Collas (VD)* I 176, 195.
227 *Mlle* . . . OT I 287; *Collas (VD)* I 176, II 700; *Kerviler (BB)* VII 121; *Pailleron* 16, 274.
227 *However* . . . OT I 287–8; *Collas (VD)* I 176; *Kerviler (BB)* IV 422.
228 *All* . . . *Collas (VD)* I 178–9, 342–3; *Pailleron* 22–3, 26, 78.
228 *The Bossinots* . . . OT I 288; *Collas (VD)* I 179–81; *Grand-Bey* 103; *Pailleron* 24.
228 *Soon* . . . OT I 288; *Collas (VD)* I 179–81.
228 *The contract* . . . *Souw* 70; *Aubrée* 77; *Collas (VD)* I 181–2, 346; *Collas (Veuve)* 170–1; *Pailleron* 26–8.
229 *A last* . . . OT I 288; *Collas (VD)* I 182–3, 323; *Grand-Bey* 103–5; *Pailleron* 24, 28.
229 *Where* . . . *Collas (VD)* I 187, II 506; *Pailleron* 18, 28.
229 *They* . . . *Aubrée* 101; *Collas (VD)* I 198; *Lenôtre* 94, 96.
230 *Émilie* . . . *Aubrée* 102; *Collas (VD)* I 197, 221; *Lenôtre* 46–115.
230 *The Marquis* . . . *Collas (VD)* I 198; *Lenôtre* 94, 96.
230 *So* . . . OT I 291, 492–3; *Collas (VD)* I 198–9, 344–5; *Mondésir* 17; *Pailleron* 28.
231 *François-René* . . . OT I 291, 307; *Peignot* 98–9, 112; *Teppé* 53.
231 *Fontanes* . . . *OC (Garnier)* I 319; OT I 291–2, 307; *Wilson* 117–23.
232 *In compensation* . . . OT I 291; *Rougerie* 34–5, 43–4.
232 *He called* . . . OT I 302; *Collas (VD)* I 204, 207–8; *Grosclaude* 696–7, 727–35; *Molleville* II 116–7.
232 *Malesherbes* . . . OT I 302: *VR* I 16–17.
233 *He had* . . . *OC (Garnier)* I 542–3; OT I 231, 302; *VR* I 16–17.
233 *Malesherbes* . . . *OC (Garnier)* I 542; OT I 302; *VR* I 16–17; *CG* I 46; *Collas (VD)* I 206–8, 215–17; *Malouet* II 230–2.
233 *Lastly* . . . OT I 303; *Grosclaude* 728–34.

234 *François-René* ... OT I 302–4.

234 *Oddly* ... OT I 145, 303, 307; *Collas (VD)* I 172; *Molleville* I 5–6, II 161.

234 *François-René* ... OT I 304; *CG* I 263; II 56, III 321–3, V 241; *BSC* (1937) 35–6; *Collas (VD)* I 205, 346.

234 *On 16* ... OT I 305, II 1181; *Champier* II 136–40.

235 *He ran* ... OT I 305–6.

235 *Three* ... OT I 306–7.

236 *In those* ... OT I 293–302.

236 *Early* ... OT I 292–3.

236 *He said* ... OC *(Garnier)* I 522.

236 *What* ... OT I 287–90, 1066.

237 *Jean-Baptiste* ... OT I 307, II 1120; *Collas (Dix ans)* 276, 278; *Collas (VD)* I 208, 261–2, 346; *Duchemin* 440–5.

237 *Secured* ... OT I 308, 595, II 1120; *Grosclaude* 34–9; *Janzé* 217–28; *Pailleron* 30–1; *Pinasseau* II 152; *Walpole* 5 Aug. 1771 to Chute, 11 Aug. 1771 to Countess of Ossory.

238 *At six* ... OT I 308.

238 *Towards* ... OT I 309.

238 *At Lille* ... OT I 309–10.

239 *At Tournai* ... OT I 310–12.

239 *Jean-Baptiste* ... OT I 312–3; *Collas (VD)* I 224; *Espinchal* 283; *Neuilly* 282; *Pinasseau* II 151–2.

240 *François-René* ... OT I 313–4; *Chuquet* I 159; *Espinchal* 352, 360.

240 *So* ... OT I 314; *Chuquet* I 158–9.

240 *No such* ... OT I 315; *Argens* 21.

241 *In a* ... OT I 315–6; *Collas (VD)* I 225; *Pinasseau* I 5–19, II 157.

17 THE FOREST OF ARDEN

242 *François-René* ... OT I 316–7; *Argens* 21; *Espinchal* 367; *Vidalenc* 148.

242 *The King* ... OT I 318; *Argens* 21; *Espinchal* 366, 372, 408; *Lapierre* 22; *Minutoli* 79; *Neuilly* 49.

242 *On the* ... OT I 318–9.

243 *His own* ... OT I 317–9; *Montlosier* 111, 273.

243 *At the* ... OT I 318; *Marcellus* 86.

243 *They* ... OT I 320–1; *Argens* 21; *Chuquet* II 91, 372; *Espinchal* 408–11; *Lapierre* 24–5; *Minutoli* 119; *Renouard* I 141.

243 *Thionville* ... OT I 321; *Argens* 22; *Chuquet* III 235–7; *Espinchal* 411; *Lapierre* 26; *Minutoli* 152–3; *Renouard* I 139.

244 *They pitched* ... OT I 321; *Chuquet* III 240; *Heckmann* 143–6; *Moniteur* XIV 68; *Renouard* I 139.

244 *They fell* ... OC *(Garnier)* IX 495; OT I 321–2; *Argens* 22; *Crossard* I 6–7.

244 *François-René's* ... OT I 322–3, II 1194; *Argens* 23; *Renouard* I 141.

245 *Monsieur* ... OT I 330; *Chuquet* III 236–8; *Heckmann* 55–64; *Lapierre* 22–3, 28; *Moniteur* XIV 58; *Moriolles* 42; *Renouard* I 150.

245 *François-René* ... OT I 320, 331; *Argens* 22; *Bittard des Portes* 29–30; *Crossard* I 8–9; *Heckmann* 112; *Marcillac* 51; *Renouard* I 140–1.

245 *At nine* ... OT I 331.

246 *Near* ... OT I 332; *Collas (VD)* I 165, 341, II 374; *Herpin (AC)* 38.

246 *At last* ... OT I 323, 332; *Lapierre* 28.

246 *He fell* ... OT I 333.

247 *Orders* . . . OT I 335; *Argens* 24; *Bittard des Portes* 31; *Chuquet* I 91–2, 261–2, III 239; *Espinchal* 413–24; *Marcillac* 53; *Minutoli* 93; *Mont-losier* 113; *Renouard* I 151–2.

247 *Quieter* . . . OT I 326.

247 *At night* . . . OT I 326–8.

248 *The besiegers* . . . OT I 325, 1068; *Argens* 24; *Collas (VD)* I 165; *Moniteur* XIV 38, 68, 100, 113, 166; *Moriolles* 43.

248 *The wet* . . . OT I 329–30.

249 *The siege* . . . OT I 324–5; *Argens* 23; *Chuquet* III 240–1; *Espinchal* 432; *Moriolles* 43.

249 *Perhaps* . . . OT I 333–4; *Argens* 24–5; *Espinchal* 432–3, 449; *Heckmann* 91; *Lapierre* 129; *Moniteur* XIV 100, 113, 166, 211, 273, 327; *Renouard* I 307.

249 *The news* . . . OT I 335; *Chuquet* II 262–3.

250 *Orders* . . . OT I 335–6; *Argens* 25–6; *Crossard* I 13–14; *Espinchal* 418, 433; *Lapierre* 126–30; *Neuilly* 52.

250 *The lost* . . . OT I 336; *Argens* 27; *Contades* 89; *Espinchal* 449.

250 *At Arlon* . . . OT I 336; *Duchemin* 440, 442; *Durry* I 56.

250 *Outside* . . . OT I 337–8.

251 *He stumbled* . . . OT I 338.

251 *The road* . . . OT I 338–9; *Cazotte* III cxxxiii; *Marcellus* 92.

252 *He paused* . . . OT I 339.

252 *As he* . . . OT I 339–40.

252 *Towards* . . . OT I 340.

252 *Two hours* . . . OT I 341; *Chuquet* I 119–21; *Contades* 58; *Ligne* 1, 25, 34, 124–5; *Villeneuve* I 82.

253 *They set* . . . OT I 341–2.

253 *There* . . . OT I 342–3.

253 *As usual* . . . OT I 87, 140, 343; *Collas (VD)* I 223, 226–7, 238, 259, 262, 349–50; *Pailleron* 37; *Pailleron (Beaumont)* 47–8.

254 *The doctor* . . . OC *(Garnier)* I 242; OT I 344; *Collas (VD)* I 238, 279.

254 *François-René* . . . OT I 344–5.

255 *The wife* . . . OT I 345.

255 *They landed* . . . OT I 345; British Library MS. Add. 8039 ff. 58 recto, 62 verso; *Mémoire* 23.

255 *Bédée* . . . OT I 345; *Balleine* 14–17; *Christophorov* 24; *Collas (VD)* I 103, 111, 212–3, 238, 240–2, 346–7; *Pailleron* 34–6.

256 *For some* . . . OT I 345; *Christophorov* 24–6.

256 *One day* . . . OC *(Garnier)* VI 541; OT I 345; *Boissy d'Anglas* II 143; *Christophorov* 27–8; *Collas (VD)* I 246–56.

256 *Ordinarily* . . . OT I 348; *Boishamon* 42–4; *BSC* VI (1937) 106; *Collas (VD)* I 242–4, 273–4, 283–4.

257 *First* . . . OT I 346.

257 *He consulted* . . . OT I 101, 348; *Collas (VD)* I 209–10, 221–2, 233–4, 259–60, 265–7, 274, 276; *Lenôtre* 203–56, 361–72.

257 *Thirty* . . . OT I 348; *Christophorov* 13, 31–3, 35; *Collas (VD)* I 353.

258 *He sailed* . . . OT I 349; *Christophorov* 26, 35; *Levot* 786–7; *Kerviler (BB)* XVI 31–2.

INDEX

23 of Meaulnes
139
271 n 7
174 buttons!
289 Bartram
283 n 9

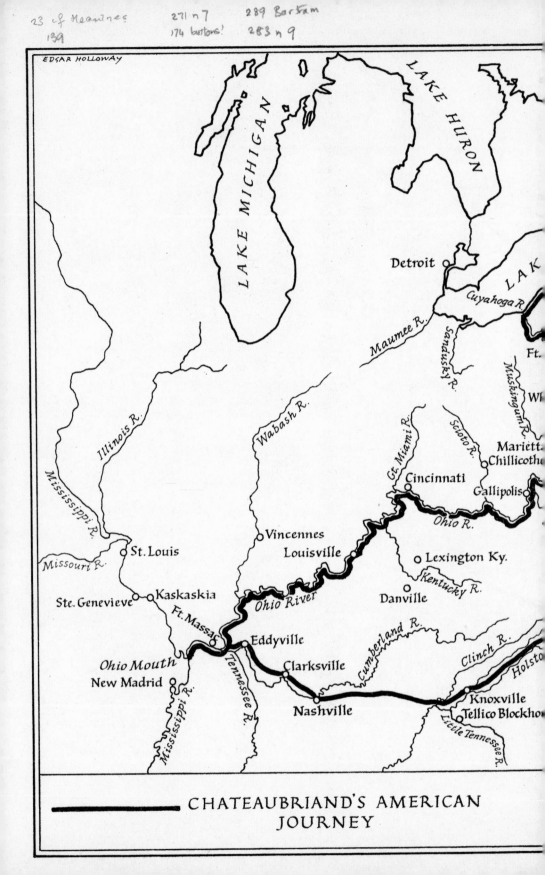

EDGAR HOLLOWAY

LAKE MICHIGAN

LAKE HURON

Detroit

LAK

Cuyahoga R.

Maumee R.

Sandusky R.

Muskingum R.

Ft.

Wh

Illinois R.

Wabash R.

Gt. Miami R.

Scioto R.

Marietta
Chillicothe

Cincinnati

Gallipolis

Ohio R.

Mississippi R.

Vincennes

Louisville

Lexington Ky.

Missouri R.

St. Louis

Kentucky R.

Ste. Genevieve

Kaskaskia

Ft. Massac

Ohio River

Danville

Ohio Mouth
New Madrid

Eddyville

Tennessee R.

Clarksville

Cumberland R.

Clinch R.

Holsto

Mississippi R.

Nashville

Knoxville
Tellico Blockho

Little Tennessee R.

CHATEAUBRIAND'S AMERICAN
JOURNEY